The Works of Walter Quin

THE WORKS OF
WALTER QUIN
an Irishman at the Stuart Courts

edited with an introduction and notes by
John Flood

FOUR COURTS PRESS

Set in 10.5 pt on 13 pt Bembo for
FOUR COURTS PRESS
7 Malpas Street, Dublin 8, Ireland
www.fourcourtspress.ie
and in North America for
FOUR COURTS PRESS
c/o ISBS, 920 N.E. 58th Avenue, Suite 300, Portland, OR 97213.

A catalogue record for this title
is available from the British Library.

ISBN 978–1–84682–504–0

Printed in England
by CPI Antony Rowe Ltd, Chippenham, Wilts.

For Frances (Norris) O'Shea
Killonerry – Tybroughney – Piltown

Contents

List of illustrations   9

List of abbreviations   10

Preface   12

Acknowledgments   13

Introduction   15

Note on the texts and apparatus   33

1 From Robert Turner's *Oratio et epistola* (1590)   41

2 From Joannes Croesselius' *Parentalia anniversaria* (1591)   44

3 *Anagrammata* (1595)   47

4 *Sertum poeticum* (1600)   63

5 Poems for the Marriage of William Alexander and Janet Erskine
   (1601)   110

6 From William Alexander's *The Tragedy of Darius* (1603)   114

7 From Alfonso Ferrabosco's *Lessons* (1609)   117

8 From Thomas Coryate's *Coryate's Crudities* (1611)   119

9 From Josuah Sylvester's *Lachrimae Lachrimarum* (1612)   124

10 *Corona virtutum* (1613)   132

11 *Elogium serenissimi regis* (1616)   139

12 *The Memory of the Most Worthy and Renowned Bernard Stuart* (1619)   146

13 From John Stradling's *Beati pacifici* (1623)   207

14 *In nuptiis principum incomparabilium* (1625)   210

15 *Recueil des reparties, rencontres et autres dits mémorables du roi Henri le grand*
   (1625)   228

16 From Thomas Herbert's *Some Years' Travels* (1638)   262

Appendix: Writings to and about Quin   264

Glossary   273

Bibliography   275

Index of titles   286

General index   290

The Literature of Early Modern Ireland series

Also in the series:

Faithful Teate, *Ter Tria*, ed. Angelina Lynch (2007)

Henry Burkhead, *Cola's Furie*, ed. Angelina Lynch and Patricia Coughlan (2009)

Richard Nugent, *Cynthia*, ed. Angelina Lynch and Anne Fogarty (2010)

William Dunkin, *The Parson's Revels*, ed. Catherine Skeen (2010)

Henry Burnell, *Landgartha*, ed. Deana Rankin (2013)

Early Irish Fiction, *c*.1680–1820

Titles in the series

[Anon.], *Vertue Rewarded; or, The Irish Princess* (1693), ed. Ian Campbell Ross and Anne Markey (2010)

Sarah Butler, *Irish Tales* (1716), ed. Ian Campbell Ross, Aileen Douglas and Anne Markey (2010)

Henry Brooke, Margaret King Moore, John Carey, *Children's Fiction, 1765–1808*, ed. Anne Markey (2011)

Thomas Amory, *The Life of John Buncle, Esq.* (1756), ed. Moyra Haslett (2011)

Elizabeth Sheridan, *The Triumph of Prudence over Passion* (1781), ed. Aileen Douglas and Ian Campbell Ross (2011)

William Chaigneau, *The History of Jack Connor* (1752), ed. Ian Campbell Ross (2013)

Charles Johnston, *The History of Arsaces, Prince of Betlis* (1774), ed. Daniel Sanjiv Roberts (2014)

Illustrations

1 Walter Quin's signature   22

2 Title page of *Sertum poeticum* (1600)   66

3 Josuah Sylvester's *Lachrimae Lachrimarum* (1612), sig. Cr   126

4 *Elogium serenissimi regis* (1616), left side   140

5 *Elogium serenissimi regis* (1616), right side   141

6 *In nuptiis principium* (1625), sig. A1v   211

7 The beginning of *Recueil* (1625), BL Royal MS 16 E XLI, fo. 25r   232

Abbreviations

[ ]	Editorial addition
Alexander and Erskine	Quin, Poems for the Marriage of William Alexander and Janet Erskine (1601)
Anagrammata	Quin, *Anagrammata in nomen Jacobi sexti [...]* (1595)
Bernard Stuart	Quin, *The Memorie of the Most Worthie and Reknowmed Bernard Stuart* (1619)
BL	British Library
col./cols	column/columns
Corona virtutum	Quin, *Corona virtutum principe dignarum, ex variis philosophorum, historicorum, oratorum, et poetarum floribus contexta, et concinnata [...]* (1613)
CSP	*Calendar of the State Papers*
ed./eds	edited by/editor/editors
EEBO	*Early English Books Online*
Elogium	Quin, *Elogium serenissimi regis [...]* (1616)
ESTC	*English Short Title Catalogue*
fl.	*floruit*, alive at the time
fo./fos	folio/folios
In nuptiis	Quin, *In nuptiis principum incomparabilium [...]* (1625)
Lachrimae Lachrimarum	Sylvester, *Lachrimae Lachrimarum or the Distillation of Teares [...]* (1612)
NA	National Archives, Kew
NLS	National Library of Scotland
NS	New Style dating
OCD	Hornblower, & Spawforth (eds), *The Oxford Classical Dictionary*. 3rd ed.
ODNB	*Oxford Dictionary of National Biography Online* (full details of individual entries are found in the bibliography)
ODNB Archive	*The Dictionary of National Biography* archived in *ODNB*.
ODR	Campbell (ed.), *Oxford Dictionary of the Renaissance*
OED	*Oxford English Dictionary Online*
r	recto (not superscripted)
r.	reigned
Recueil	Quin, *Recueil des reparties, rencontres et autres dits mémorables du roi Henri le grand* (1625)

Selected Writings	Rhodes et al. (eds), *King James VI and I: Selected Writings*
Sertum poeticum	Quin, *Sertum poeticum, in honorem Jacobi sexti [...]* (1600)
sig./sigs	signature/signatures
SP	National Archives, State Papers Collection
STC	Pollard and Redgrave (eds), *Short-Title Catalogue*. 2nd ed.
[T]	designates a translation of the preceding text
trans.	translated by/translator
USTC	Pettegree (ed.), *Universal Short Title Catalogue*
v	verso (not superscripted)

Preface

This series of editions of English-language texts from seventeenth- and eighteenth-century Ireland was begun in 2007, under the general editorship of Professor Andrew Carpenter of University College Dublin, in the belief that the study of early modern Ireland was in a new and exciting phase. With thousands of web-based images of English-language texts from early modern Ireland increasingly available to scholars and students – notably through Early English Books Online (EEBO) and Eighteenth Century Collections Online (ECCO) – the necessity for critical editions of key texts was, and remains, acute. The intervening years have confirmed the high levels of interest in early modern Ireland and the series continues to offer authoritative editions of texts, edited to the highest standards and set in context by scholars of international standing, at a time when the very need for such critical editions is increasingly little understood outside of departments of English and related disciplines.

The Literature of Early Modern Ireland series runs in tandem with the Early Irish Fiction, *c.*1680–1820 series of prose fictions, under the general editorship of Professor Aileen Douglas of Trinity College Dublin, Professor Moyra Haslett of Queen's University Belfast, and the present General Editor. The series now includes seven titles, offering works published between 1693 and 1808, with other titles under active discussion.

Ian Campbell Ross
General Editor
Dublin, August 2014

Acknowledgments

Walter Quin was effusive in his praise (it did, after all, earn him and his family two lifetimes of patronage), and if what follows is somewhat sober by comparison, I trust that it will not be thought inadequate.

It was Prof. Alasdair MacDonald, a friend and colleague of mine at the University of Groningen, who first drew my attention to the existence of Walter Quin and who suggested that I give a paper on him at a seminar that he was running on James VI and I. At the time I did not suspect that I would end up producing an edition of Quin's works, but when I eventually embarked on this project, Alasdair proved to be its chief sustainer as well as its only begetter, just as ready with pertinent historical information as he was happy to discuss translations of Latin or French.

Particular debts are owed to Dr David Butterfield (Queens' College, Cambridge), who provided me with a translation of most of Quin's Latin works and to Prof. Eiléan Ní Chuilleanáin (Trinity College Dublin), and Prof. Cormac Ó Cuilleanáin (Trinity College Dublin), who are responsible for the Italian texts in this volume. One of my visiting students, Émilie Garneau (Université Laval), was kind enough to look through my French transcriptions.

Dr Jamie Reid Baxter has been consistently helpful and enthusiastic while I have been working on Quin, and his fingerprints are to be found in many places here. Several others generously provided advice and assistance during my research, including the participants at the 'New Departures in the Literary Culture of the Reign of James VI and I' seminar held in Groningen in 2010, Bríd Flood, J.H. Gmelin (Groningen), Dr Anne Markey (Trinity College Dublin), Prof. Roger Mason (St Andrews), Dr Steven Reid (Glasgow), and David White (Somerset Herald of the College of Arms).

As always, it has been a pleasure to work with Four Courts Press who have been patient with the usual delays and whose editors, anonymous readers and staff have been helpful, efficient and encouraging in seeing this book from its inception to its finish. Prof. Ian Campbell Ross (Trinity College Dublin), the general editor of the series in which this book appears, made many very useful suggestions and corrected several errors that had escaped my notice.

This book was published with financial assistance from the Nicolaas Mulerius Foundation of the University of Groningen which I gratefully acknowledge. In applying for this I was greatly helped by Mr Gorus van Oordt in the faculty research office and by the dean of the faculty, Prof. Gerry Wakker.

This volume could not have been prepared without the resources of the British Library, the Bodleian Library, the National Archives at Kew, the national libraries of Ireland and of Scotland, and the libraries of the universities of Dublin and Groningen. Special thanks are due to Damien Burke (Irish Jesuit Archives), J.A.N. Frankhuizen (University Library, Leiden), Thomas Gordon (John Rylands Library), Dr Anette Hagan (Senior Curator of Rare Books Collections at the National Library of Scotland), and Rachel Hart (Muniments' Archivist of St Andrews).

The copy-texts in this volume have been used with the permission of the National Library of Scotland, the Master and Fellows of Balliol College, Oxford, and the Bavarian State Library. I am grateful to the Society of Antiquaries of Scotland for permission to use fos 44–7 of Hawthornden MS 2065. I also acknowledge the permission of the British Library Board to use the following: General Reference Collection C.175.d.42, Music Collections K.8.h.1, General Reference Collection C.194.a.1114, General Reference Collection 721.a.44, General Reference Collection 11626.e.54, General Reference Collection, C.28.g.8.(4), General Reference Collection C.55.g.8. The material from National Archives SP52/57 is used under the Open Government Licence v.2.0.

John Flood
Groningen, August 2014

Introduction: Walter Quin and his work

W alter Quin (d. 1640) was born in Dublin and educated in Germany and Scotland.[1] In Edinburgh, his political poetry attracted the notice of King James VI who had him appointed to the household of Henry, his eldest son. In 1603, when James ascended to the English throne as the first Stuart monarch, Quin also went to London where he continued in royal service for the rest of his life. His literary output – in poetry and prose, written variously in English, Latin, French and Italian – includes works in praise of the Stuarts, along with historical and philosophical writing. Although absent from most histories of Irish literature, including those that deal specifically with the early modern period, Quin's nationality is of some note. In his time, the corpus of printed literature by Irish authors was comparatively small, as was the corpus of Irish writing in English, a language that was not widely used outside the Pale.[2] The first printed work by an Irish-born writer was produced by Richard Stanihurst (1547–1618), whose *Harmonia, seu catena dialectica in Porphyrianus* appeared in London in 1570.[3] In 1582 Stanihurst published an English translation of four books of the *Aeneid*, verse by Sir Thomas More and some original compositions of his own in both Latin and English. He also published an English sonnet by Gerald Fitzgerald, Lord Offaly (1559–80).[4] Towards the end of the sixteenth century Richard Nugent composed *Cynthia*, an English sonnet

---

1 The principal biographical accounts of Quin are to be found in Sidney Lee, 'Quin, Walter (*c.*1575–1641)', *ODNB Archive*; Sidney Lee & J.K. McGinley, 'Quin, Walter (*c.*1575–1641)', *ODNB*; Andrew Ashbee, 'Quin, Walter. Teacher of Music, 1611–1632' in Andrew Ashbee & David Lasocki (eds), *A Biographical Dictionary of English Court Musicians, 1485–1714* (2 vols, Aldershot: Ashgate, 1998), ii, pp 936–7. I expanded these in a publication of 2013, but this account has in turn been emended and superseded by the information in the present volume: John Flood, 'Walter Quin: Virtue in a Life of Change' in David J. Parkinson (ed.), *James VI and I, Literature and Scotland: Tides of Change, 1567–1625* (Leuven: Peeters, 2013), pp 251–66.

2 Alan Bliss, 'The English Language in Early Modern Ireland' in T.W. Moody et al. (eds), *A New History of Ireland, Vol. III: Early Modern Ireland, 1534–1691* (Oxford: Oxford UP, 1991), p. 547.

3 Colm Lennon, 'Stanihurst, Richard (1547–1618)', *ODNB*.

4 Andrew Carpenter (ed.), *Verse in English from Tudor and Stuart Ireland* (Cork: Cork UP, 2003), pp 65–6.

sequence that was printed in 1604.[5] A 1602 poem by Richard Burke, the fourth earl of Clanricarde and a favourite of Elizabeth I, is 'the only surviving courtly Elizabethan love lyric by an Irishman'.[6] Quin has probably been overlooked since, given the circumstances of his life, he might also be claimed for Scotland (where he established his career) or England (where he wrote most of his work). This is appropriate for one who, chameleon-like, adapted himself readily to new situations and about whom we know enough to recognize that he was enigmatic.

THE DUBLINER

Sertum poeticum (1600), Quin's first printed volume of work, announces on its title page that it is written by a Dubliner and this is almost all that is known about his early life. Since he enters the University of Ingolstadt in 1590, his date of birth is probably *c.*1575.[7] At Ingolstadt, which was a Catholic institution, he moved in Catholic circles and so something can be reasonably inferred about his family. Furthermore, to send a son on a journey of more than a thousand miles to go to university argues the possession of some wealth, although this was not enough to have Quin recorded in the university's matriculation book as one of the students with notable kindred. During the reign of Charles I, Quin writes about a nephew, Peter Quin, who is a Dublin merchant.[8] If Quin's background was a mercantile one, then his mention of his native city may have some of the civic pride to be found in the work of his somewhat older contemporary, Stanihurst.[9]

There are many Dublin Quins at this time although none of them is called Walter. Listing all of them would seem otiose, but a narrower selection of those who were merchants may be useful.[10] Various Quins were freemen of Dublin in

5 Richard Nugent, *Cynthia*, ed. Angelina Lynch (Dublin: Four Courts Press, 2010).
6 Carpenter (ed.), *Verse in English*, pp 121–2.
7 The ages at which early modern students went to university could vary quite substantially: contemporary records from Oxford show that while some entrants were younger than 15, a similar number were older than 19. The median age of entrants was 16: Stephen Porter, 'University and Society' in Nicholas Tyacke (ed.), *The History of the University of Oxford, Vol. IV: Seventeenth-Century Oxford* (Oxford: Clarendon Press, 1997), p. 56. The Oxford statistics give a better idea of local expectations than do those of Ingolstadt. Records from Trinity College Dublin do not yield generalizable data for this period.
8 BL, Add. MS 69915, fo. 60.
9 Colm Lennon, *Richard Stanihurst the Dubliner, 1547–1618: A Biography With a Stanihurst Text On Ireland's Past* (Dublin: Irish Academic Press, 1981), p. 42.
10 A Dublin merchant, or merchants, Richard Quinn is or are recorded in 1617 and 1630: *Calendar of Inquisitions Formerly in the Office of the Chief Remembrancer of the Exchequer Prepared from the MSS of the Irish Record Commission*, ed. Margaret C. Griffith (Dublin: Stationery Office, 1991), pp 458, 465. Christopher Quin of St Michan's parish was attainted in 1642: John

the late sixteenth and early seventeenth century.[11] Quin's nephew is likely to
have been the Peter Quin who appears in the records of the Court of Claims of
1663 and who was one of the twenty-six brethren of the Staple in 1631.[12] The
Staple, which had ties to the Dublin City Assembly, played an important role in
regulating both trade and debt and in 1640 a Dublin merchant, Peter Quin, is
listed as a creditor for the amount of £600.[13] This branch of Quin's family was
evidently successful.

Why did Quin attend Ingolstadt? There were other Irish students in the university at the time, but there were not many.[14] There were also Irish staff:
Ambrose Wadding of Waterford (1583–1619) studied theology in Ingolstadt
where he became a tutor of metaphysics; Quin's contemporary, Stephen White
(c.1574–post 1646) who was born in Clonmel into a wealthy merchant family,
joined the Society of Jesus in Salamanca in 1596 and was professor of theology
at Ingolstadt between 1606–9.[15] Ingolstadt had been a Jesuit university since
1556, so it may be tempting to follow that link in respect of Quin's education;
however, in the early 1580s, 'the Jesuit mission in Ireland was practically non-
existent'.[16] Stephen White had joined the order in Salamanca, and it was from
there that he took up his Ingolstadt post. Quin went to the university to study
law, and there is no indication that he thought of ordination.[17]

D'Alton, *Illustrations, Historical and Genealogical, of King James's Irish Army List, 1689* (Dublin:
For the Subscribers, 1855), p. 333.

11 John Grenham, 'Dublin City Library and Archive, Ancient Freemen of Dublin' (Dublin City
Library & Archive, 2011), http://dublinheritage.ie/freemen/index.php, accessed 1 Mar. 2014.
The best-known merchant of the name in the late seventeenth century was Mark Quin (d.
1674), who was elected lord mayor of Dublin in 1667 and who was memorable for his wealth,
his slitting of his throat and his being the grandfather of the actor James Quin (1693–1766). A
connection between him and Walter has long been hypothesized, but there is no particular
evidence for it: see the anonymous 'An Account of James Quin', *The European Magazine and
London Review*, 21, 1 (1792), 323–5.

12 Geraldine Tallon (ed.), *Court of Claims: Submissions and Evidence, 1663* (Dublin: Irish
Manuscripts Commission, 2006), pp 105, 118; Jane Ohlmeyer & Éamonn Ó Ciardha (eds),
The Irish Statute Staple Books, 1596–1687 (Dublin: Four Courts Press, 1999), p. 348. A Nicholas
Quin was elected mayor of the Staple in 1601 and a John Quine had been one of the brethren
in 1626: ibid., pp 323, 347.

13 Ohlmeyer and Ciardha (eds), *Irish Statute Staple Books*, p. 138.

14 George Wolff (ed.), *Die Matrikel der Ludwig-Maximilians-Universitat: Ingolstadt-Landshut-
Munchen, Teil 1* (Munich: J. Lindauersche, 1937), col. 1229.

15 Terry Clavin, 'Wadding, Ambrose', *Dictionary of Irish Biography*, ed. James McGuire & James
Quinn (Cambridge UP, 2013), http://dib.cambridge.org, accessed 1 Mar. 2014; Colm
Lennon, 'White, Stephen (b.c.1574, d. in or after 1646)', *ODNB*.

16 Thomas M. McCoog, *The Society of Jesus in Ireland, Scotland, and England 1541–1588: 'Our Way
of Proceeding?'* (Leiden: Brill, 1996), p. 219.

17 There is a Dublin Quin, Thomas, son of Richard (1603–63), who was an early member of the
Jesuits. Having graduated with an MA he joined the society in 1623 and was ordained in 1628

A STUDENT AT INGOLSTADT

On the 19 June 1590 (NS) 'Gwalterus Quintius Hibernus studiosus iuris' was entered in the matriculation book for the summer semester.[18] He was a student of both civil and canon law.[19] The matriculation entries note the students who are nobles, clergy, the family of academics or students who have scholarships, but Quin is not listed in these categories; however, no fee payment is listed against his name.

The year he arrived in Ingolstadt Quin supplied some short Latin verses for *Oratio et epistola*, a memorial volume for Martin von Schaumberg, the prince-bishop of Eichstätt, which was compiled by Robert Turner, a Devonshire recusant who had been a rector of the university. The following year, Quin composed a poem for *Parentalia anniversaria*, another memorial volume for a bishop (this time, prepared by the librarian, Johann Krösel, in memory of one of the library's benefactors). Krösel's 1591 volume was the second edition of a work that had first appeared in 1590. Evidently, Quin had made enough of an impression to be included in the expanded edition.

In May 1591 Turner addressed a letter to him which is one of the few personal documents we have relating to his life (see Appendix, p. 269). Turner warns him against the seductions of the court where he was teaching, and although he does not specify which court he means, it is most likely to have been that of William V, duke of Bavaria (1548–1626), which was in Landshut, about fifty miles from Ingolstadt. William was a product of Jesuit education and he and his sons had attended university at Ingolstadt. A strict Catholic, he fought against heresy and witchcraft and spent lavishly on religious causes.[20] It is possible that as well as carrying letters from Turner to one of the Bavarian courtiers, that Quin was looking for employment and patronage in support of his studies. The university had students designated *pauperes* who were mainly the sons of burghers, farmers or tradesmen. They had lower fees and often had to look for financial help.[21] The institution had an impressive array of scholarships founded by private benefactions, so it was more socially inclusive than its roll call of noble alumni might suggest.[22]

after which he moved between the Low Countries and Dublin (where he was the superior for Leinster): Francis Finegan, 'Members of the "Third mission" of the Society of Jesus in Ireland, 1598–1773' (2013), http://www.jesuitarchives.ie/research/digital-material/, accessed 2 Feb. 2014.

18 Wolff (ed.), *Die Matrikel der Ludwig-Maximilians-Universitat*, col. 1297.

19 Johannes Croeselius, *Parentalia anniuersaria reverendissimo et illvstrissimo principi ac domino, dn. Ioanni Egolpho à Knoeringen* (2nd ed.; Ingolstadt: David Sartorius, 1591), p. 15.

20 Sigmund Ritter von Riezler, 'Wilhelm V., der Fromme, Herzog von Baiern', *Allgemeine Deutsche Biographie* (Bayerischen Staatsbibliothek, 1897), www.deutsche-biographie.de/pnd118771841.html, accessed 12 Feb. 2013.

21 Rainer A. Müller, *Universität und Adel* (Berlin: Duncker & Humblot, 1974), pp 95–7, 175–6.

22 Heinz Jürgen Real & Arno Seifert, *Die privaten Stipendienstiftungen der Universität Ingolstadt im*

Not having been very wealthy, Quin would still have found a place in the university, although it would have been a subordinate one, as there was some social stigma attached to being one of the *pauperes*.[23]

University records can form the basis of a general picture of Quin's life in Ingolstadt. About 70 per cent of the students were from Bavaria, while only 1 per cent of students came from non-Germanic states. The law faculty was the largest in the university and had one chair in canon law and four in civil law. There had been a steady growth in numbers in the decade before Quin arrived.[24] The law faculty attracted more non-Bavarians than the other faculties, especially students from Poland who were drawn by its reputation as a Catholic university. Although it was clearly Catholic, it educated Protestants as well (many of its sons of the nobility were Lutheran), and these encountered no difficulties as long as they were willing to be discreet.[25]

Quin's course of study focused on glosses on the *Codex iuris canonici* and the *Codex iuris civilis*.[26] The Ingolstadt law faculty followed an Italian model based on Aristotelian categories (it was originally from Bologna – there was a lot of traffic of students and staff with Italy) whose basics had remained the same for half a century.[27] To be eligible for the degree the statutes prescribed that students had to attend a certain number of lectures (bringing their books).[28] The study day was divided into one-hour lectures. A timetable from 1571 lists lectures on the *Codex iuris civilis* that began at 6am, with lectures on the *Institutes* and on the *Pandects* at noon and 2pm respectively.[29] Apart from lectures, there were formal disputations led by the lecturer and *consistoria practica* in which students delivered judgments on cases posed by the staff.[30] Law students also studied the history of law and, like Quin, several graduates wrote historical works.[31]

Quin's time would not have been wholly devoted to study, as can be seen from his court stay. There were two hundred days of the year on which there were no lectures, although students were expected to be continuously studying.[32] There are records of gambling, fights, 'suspicious womenfolk' and debts owed in the city.[33] That young men were not always absorbed in their studies is more understandable in the light of the fact that only a small percentage of stu-

ersten Jahrhundert ihres Bestehens (Berlin: Duncker & Humblot, 1972). Quin's name is not listed in this volume although he may, of course, appear in the archives it draws on.

23 Müller, *Universität und Adel*, p. 96.

24 Helmut Wolff, *Geschichte der Ingolstäder Juristenfakultät, 1472-1625* (Berlin: Duncker & Humblot, 1973), pp 42, 169.

25 Müller, *Universität und Adel*, pp 171–2. See those listed as 'protestanticus' in Quin's time: Wolff (ed.), *Die Matrikel der Ludwig-Maximilians-Universitat*, cols 1117, 1186, 1194.

26 Wolff, *Geschichte der Ingolstäder Juristenfakultät*, p. 32.

27 Ibid., p. 33.   28 Ibid., p. 46.   29 Ibid., p. 50.

30 Ibid., pp 56–60.   31 Ibid., pp 196, 219. 32 Ibid., p. 75.

33 Ibid., p. 179.

dents finished a degree programme – most students stayed only two years out of the seven required – and were more interested in obtaining certificates of atten-dance.[34] There is no record of Quin having completed his degree.

Although Quin was enrolled for the study of law, Turner describes Quin's 'goal' as 'literature, and God through literature'. Turner evidently regards Quin as someone with similar religious commitments to his own. The professor was a great admirer of the Jesuit martyr Edmund Campion and he instructs Quin: 'If you can purchase, or steal, or receive as a gift any collection of writing by Campion get them for me.' He tells Quin of a letter he has received from Stanihurst and it is clear that he expects his protégé to be familiar with the name of his countryman. Given the relatively small number of people in Dublin who would have had collections of books, this is hardly surprising.[35]

SCOTLAND AND JAMES VI

The next phase of Quin's education is a curious one. In the matriculation book of the University of St Andrews there is, in 1600, the signature of 'M[agister]. Walterus Quinnus' who is a member of St Mary's College and thus a postgrad-uate student of theology.[36] A poem congratulating King James VI on behalf of St Salvator's College appears in *Sertum poeticum*, so it is possible that he studied arts there before proceeding to divinity.

Between 1590 and 1597 Andrew Melville (1545–1622) was the rector of the university as well as dean of St Mary's, one of its three colleges (a post he held until 1601).[37] Melville had studied under Philip Melanchthon at Wittenberg and Theodore Beza at Geneva, and had been on the Continent during the French Wars of Religion. On returning to Scotland he became principal of the University of Glasgow where he reformed the syllabus on anti-scholastic humanist lines and emphasized the teaching of biblical languages.[38] He swept St Mary's with the same reforming brush, intending that it would be 'an Anti-Seminarie [...] to the Jesuist Seminaries, for the course of Theologie'.[39] This is borne out by the surviving *theses theologicae* from 1592–1602 which are obviously Calvinist in character (for example, one addressed the idolatry of the mass while

34 Ibid., pp 76, 169, 188.
35 Raymond Gillespie, *Reading Ireland: Print, Reading and Social Change in Early Modern Ireland* (Manchester: Manchester UP, 2012), p. 62.
36 University of St Andrews Library, *Acta rectorum* 4 (UYUY305/3), fo. 131r.
37 Stephen J. Reid, *Humanism and Calvinism: Andrew Melville and the Universities of Scotland, 1560–1625* (Aldershot: Ashgate, 2011), p. 150.
38 James Kirk, 'Melville, Andrew (1545–1622)', *ODNB*.
39 James Melville, *The Autobiography and Diary of Mr James Melvill [...] with a Continuation of the Diary*, ed. Robert Pitcairn (Edinburgh: The Wodrow Society, 1842), p. 76.

another argued that the pope was the anti-Christ).[40] It was certainly a change for Quin to study at an institution where Aristotle's authority was questionable.[41] He would have been aware that Melville held that papists were led by the spirit of the serpent and that he had a horror of the fact that 'Jesuistes, Seminarie Preists, and uther emissars of the Antichryst crape in the countrey': Quin must have had some explaining to do to demonstrate that he was not one of these.[42]

Why did Quin move to St Andrews? His decision may have been rooted in some reason lost to history such as a conversation with a Scottish student or traveller. Robert Turner's family originally came from St Andrews, but it is unthinkable that Turner would have sent him there, given his anxieties when Quin was merely visiting the local court.[43] St Andrews was so different from Ingolstadt that the possibility must be admitted that there were two well-travelled Irish Walter Quins studying abroad in the 1590s. However, this seems to be only a remote possibility.

Since Quin's work was so political, and as he later appears in English intelligence reports, it might be thought that he was in St Andrews covertly. In Quin's time in Scotland Catholics and Catholic agents were, to the distress of Melville, a continuous presence, even in the most exalted of circles. During his international negotiations about the succession to the English throne, James was in contact with the pope and other Catholic powers.[44] Despite the king's complaints about the Jesuits, and their alleged involvement in the 1593 conspiracy of the Spanish blanks (in which Scottish noblemen treated with Phillip II to restore the old faith), when the queen converted to Catholicism James appointed her confessor, Robert Abercrombie SJ, as keeper of hawks.[45] Other court positions were also filled by Catholics: the Princess Elizabeth's governess, the countess of Linlithgow, was notorious for her refusal to adhere to reformed religion, and Alexander Seaton, earl of Dunfermline and James' chancellor, merely conformed outwardly to the Kirk while receiving the sacraments of communion and confession in his household.[46] James was content to have loyal or useful Catholics

---

40 Reid, *Humanism and Calvinism*, pp 184–5.

41 For Melville's education and Aristotle, see Kirk, 'Melville'. Melville did not, however, abolish Aristotle from St Andrews: Reid, *Humanism and Calvinism*, pp 54, 139, 191, 262.

42 Melville, *Autobiography*, p. 265.

43 Anthony Wood, *Athenae Oxonienses*, ed. Philip Bliss (3rd ed.; 4 vols, London: F.C. and J. Rivington, 1813–20), iii, p. 680.

44 W.B. Patterson, *King James VI and I and the Reunion of Christendom* (Cambridge: Cambridge UP, 1997), p. 39; Maurice Lee, Jr, 'The Gowrie Conspiracy Revisited' in Maurice Lee, Jr (ed.), *The 'Inevitable Union' and Other Essays on Early Modern Scotland* (East Linton: Tuckwell Press, 2003), p. 103.

45 Michael J. Yellowlees, *'So Strange a Monster as a Jesuiste': The Society of Jesus in Sixteenth-Century Scotland* (Colonsay: House of Lochar, 2003), p. 150. For James and the Jesuits, see also ibid., 126, 135.

46 Kate Aughterson, 'Livingstone, Helen, countess of Linlithgow (d.1627)', *ODNB*; Maurice

around him, so Quin's previous beliefs and perhaps even discreet enduring ones, would not have alienated him. Later, Quin married in the Anglican church and he baptized and buried his children in it, but for someone who been educated by fervent Catholics and by fervent Calvinists, for someone who had studied canon law, he rarely wrote about religious topics and when he did so they were mostly neutral, conventional lines about the divine favour shown towards the royal family.[47]

1 Quin's signature (reproduced courtesy of the University of St Andrews Library, UYUY305/3, fo. 131r).

Because Quin wrote about the controversial topic of James VI's succession to the English throne, he is in the unusual position of being a poet whose first collection, *Anagrammata*, is recorded in intelligence reports. Quin first appears in these in the correspondence of the English diplomat Robert Bowes who had been the English representative in Scotland before 1583 and who remained involved in Scottish affairs (he returned as ambassador in 1596).[48] In a letter of 27 November 1595 from his secretary, George Nicolson, Bowes was informed: 'Here is such making of "cokelandes" and verses and emulations as I fear still troubles, notwithstanding the intent of agreements [...] The [the paper is accidentally torn here, but the word may be "Irishman"] quin seems to be very simple suppose his verses be not so'.[49] This was followed on 4–5 December by a communication from a different correspondent, Dr James MacCartney, who informed him of the arrival at court of 'Gualterus Quinnus', 'an Irish gentleman' who has 'spoken the King divers times'.[50] MacCartney did not consider Quin to be simple; instead, he describes him as 'learned and courtly and well travelled'.

Lee, Jr, 'King James's Popish Chancellor' in Maurice Lee, Jr (ed.), *The 'Inevitable Union' and Other Essays on Early Modern Scotland* (East Linton: Tuckwell Press, 2003), pp 145–57.

47 Because the question of Quin's religious beliefs has not been resolved, the notes on his texts that have been provided in this volume flag up any issues touching on religious affiliation.

48 C.A. McGladdery, 'Bowes, Robert (d.1597)', *ODNB*; Alan Haynes, *Invisible Power: The Elizabethan Secret Services, 1570–1603* (Stroud: Alan Sutton, 1992), pp 31–2.

49 *CSP, Scotland* (1898–1969), xii, p. 65. 'Cokelandes' is a version of 'cockalane', a satire (see *OED*, where its first recorded instance is 1605).

50 Ibid., xii, p. 79.

Certainly the visitor had caught the attention of the monarch to whom he delivered a 'treatise of poesie', with the result that the royal secretary was given orders to maintain him: 'what with speaking with the man and what by reading of the verses [...] the King is become incredibly rejoiced'.[51]

Shortly afterwards, a third English agent, John Colville, wrote about Quin in a letter of 12 January:[52]

> There is also another Irishman here called Walter Quin, a fine scholar. He has presented at New Year day to His Majesty an oration touching his title which is well accepted and he placed at the Master [of the] Household's table and to be rewarded and kept. This oration is kept quiet, yet I had it about two hours and have extracted the substance thereof which shall be sent by my next.[53]

Colville obtained a copy of Quin's work, which he sent Bowes in a letter dated 17 January, remarking that Quin 'is jealously looked on' because his oration identified Elizabeth's successor.[54] Quin had chosen his subject well. James' eagerness to assert his claim to the throne of England was all the more keen after the appearance of a book that had played down his right of succession, advancing instead the claims of Philip II's daughter, the Infanta Isabella. *A Conference About the Next Succession to the Crown of England* (Antwerp, 1594), which had been written under the name the name R. Doleman, was in fact the product of Robert Parsons SJ and his circle, one of whom may have been Stanihurst (a reminder, if one were needed, of how much Quin's milieu had changed). The book had enraged the king, and anything that might be employed against it could count on a favourable royal reception.[55]

James may also have welcomed the support of an Irishman as it was in keeping with his claim to the rule of the three kingdoms, a note Quin was careful to sound.[56] The king's political interests had accompanying historical elements: in a sonnet he described himself as a 'happie Monarch sprung from Ferguse race', a reference explained in *The Trew Law of Free Monarchies* (1598) in which James, drawing on Hector Boece's *Chronicles of Scotland*, notes:

---

51 Ibid.
52 See Rob Macpherson, 'Colville, John (1542?–1605)', *ODNB*.
53 *CSP, Scotland*, xii, p. 120.   54 Ibid., p. 125.
55 Lennon, *Richard Stanihurst*, p. 50.
56 At other times the court had welcomed an Irish harper and an Irish poet: Amy L. Juhala, 'The Household and Court of King James VI of Scotland, 1567–1603' (Unpublished PhD thesis, University of Edinburgh, 1999), pp 188, 307. One writer has even detected the possibility, in his use of the imagery of the king as spouse of his kingdoms, of the influence of a Gaelic tradition which James may have known from conversation with Quin: Michael J. Enright, 'King James and His Island: An Archaic Kingship Belief?', *Scottish Historical Review*, 55, 159 (1976), 29–40 at 39.

This Ile, and especially our part of it, being scantily inhabited, but by very few, and they as barbarous and scant of civilitie, as number, there comes our first King Fergus, with a great number with him, out of Ireland, which was long inhabited before us, and making himselfe master of the countrey, by his owne friendship, and force, as well of the Ireland-men that came with him, as of countrey-men that willingly fell to him, he made himselfe King and Lord.[57]

The multilingual Quin would have been at home where courtiers could speak six languages and 'most poets and musicians either were foreign or had attended university in France, Italy or Holland'.[58] The dangers of court life that Turner had warned against would both have schooled him and provided him with conversation in Edinburgh.

In 1598 we learn from the correspondence of Nicolson and Cecil of a book that the former believed might have been written by Quin, although if it was, it has not survived. It was a reply to *The Faerie Queene*, 'Spencer's book whereat the king was offended'.[59] James had been affronted at Spenser's allegorization of his mother as Duessa, the epitome of duplicity.[60] He complained about it to the English ambassador and demanded that the author should be punished, but nothing came of this.[61] Quin's book, it seems, could be the only reparation the king could enjoy but it is unknown whether it was ever finished.

Nicolson also writes of 'a book in Latin made by Walter Quin the Irishman [...] concerning the King's title to England that it may be dispersed to foreign princes'.[62] (He also opines that Quin would be open to bribery.)[63] However, sensitive to the political import of the volume's contents, the king's printer, Robert Waldegrave, was refusing to print it. Waldegrave was well acquainted with controversy, having fled England after printing the Martin Marprelate tracts (satires on the Elizabethan church). In Scotland in 1594 he had printed Melville's *Principis Scoti-Britannorum natalia* (*The Lineage of the Scoto-Britannic Prince*), with its prophecy of the unification of Scotland and England and this prompted

---

57 *Selected Writings*, pp 123, 269.
58 Juhala, 'Household and Court of King James VI', p. 7.
59 *CSP, Scotland*, xii(1), p. 167.
60 James may not have primarily been thinking of his mother's reputation, but instead may have been concerned that he was tainted by this association and that it might affect his succession to the English throne: Jonathan Goldberg, *James I and the Politics of Literature: Jonson, Shakespeare, Donne, and Their Contemporaries* (Stanford: Stanford UP, 1989), p. 3.
61 Richard A. McCabe, 'The Masks of Duessa: Spenser, Mary Queen of Scots, and James VI', *English Literary Renaissance*, 17, 2 (1987), 224–42; Andrew Hadfield, *Shakespeare, Spenser and the Matter of Britain* (Basingstoke: Palgrave Macmillan, 2004), pp 122–36.
62 *CSP, Scotland*, xii(1), p. 167.
63 Ibid., xiii(1), p. 168.

Elizabeth to send a personal reprimand via Bowes.[64] Waldegrave defended himself with an unlikely claim to the effect that as Melville's book was in Latin he had not understood what he was printing. When Quin's book came along he hoped he had some leverage that might help him get permission to return to England and Nicolson describes him as 'almost weeping and wishing that for avoiding of this [the printing of the book] he might have liberty to return to his own country, which being granted to him he would return and leave all here to themselves to print as they could'.[65] A little over three months later Nicolson opines that Quin's book, along with another one on the succession, 'are sent out of the country to be printed, for of this long time the printer has not been dealt with for printing of them',[66] and shortly afterwards Cecil received word from another correspondent that the succession had been the subject of a book by 'one Quin (Guen) an Irishman that is in St Andrews, pedagogue to the young Earl of Mar'.[67] What became of this book? There is no evidence that it was eventually published abroad. Perhaps it remained in manuscript. More likely its printing was simply very delayed and it became *Sertum poeticum* (1600), a copy of which was forwarded to Cecil, who by then must have needed no prompting about the identity of Walter Quin.[68]

The storm over the delayed printing of Quin's book was driven by the king. No-one recorded what Quin himself thought, although it is reasonable to assume that he welcomed the royal endorsement. On the evidence of what he wrote it is clear that what mattered to Quin was the impact of his writing in a fairly narrow but powerful world. In recent years the importance of manuscript circulation in early modern Scotland and England has received a good deal of attention, and it is no longer the case that a manuscript is regarded as a work that did not get printed. Quin came from a society where manuscript transmission was particularly prized and he found himself in one where it could earn him his living.[69] Only two of his manuscript works survive (*Anagrammata* and *Recueil*), but he mentions the fact that *Bernard Stuart* first circulated in manuscript form in French. The extant printed works may not, therefore, give a correct picture of Quin's writing career. It may well be that important texts await discovery in a royal collection or that they have disappeared, having served their purpose four hundred years ago.

In the meantime Quin still attended the university and must have spent time at Stirling Castle, the home of the earl of Mar. His duties were extended from

---

64 Katherine S. Van Eerde, 'Robert Waldegrave: The Printer as Agent and Link Between Sixteenth-Century England and Scotland', *Renaissance Quarterly*, 34, 1 (1981), 40–78 at 68.

65 *CSP, Scotland*, xii(1), p. 167.

66 Ibid., xiii(1), p. 216.

67 Ibid., p. 219.

68 Ibid., xiii(2), p. 752.

69 For Ireland, see Gillespie, *Reading Ireland*, p. 11.

those of teaching the earl's son to being one of the tutors of Prince Henry, who was born into the succession controversy and was named for his ancestor Henry VII: the occasion was marked by Melville's *Principis Scoti-Britannorum natalia*, which predicted that the child would unite Britain, a sentiment that Quin would echo.[70] As a reward for this consistent support, Quin's position in the prince's household became a permanent one and thus Quin moved south with him when James at last ascended his longed-for throne.

PRINCE HENRY'S TUTOR

In January 1596 a committee known as the Octavians was appointed by the king to supervise the royal finances and to cut back spending. One of the consequences of this was that Prince Henry's household was reduced to seventy people.[71] Quin kept his position and this, and the fact that James was genuinely interested in the prince's studies, suggests that his appointment was not a sinecure, although it is not clear precisely what Quin taught.[72] In the records of Henry's funeral it is as a 'teacher of musicke to the Prince' that Quin was allowed 7 yards of mourning livery in addition to 4 yards for his servant (for the same occasion, the principal musicians were allowed 8 yards of cloth while the dancing master, the trumpeters and the drummers received only 4 yards – this gives some indication of where 'Mr Quin' came in the order of things).[73] Although this is certainly what he was paid for, this may have been a nominal designation as there is no evidence that Quin taught or even had a particular fondness for music. On the other hand, he went on to produce multi-lingual works for the royal princes along with historical and philosophical texts, so his teaching may have been wider than his official title suggests.

In terms of surviving texts, Quin's service under Henry was a fallow period during which he wrote two sonnets and an epithalamium to celebrate the marriage of William Alexander (in 1601), as well as a sonnet for Alexander's *Tragedie of Darius* (1603), and in 1609, an Italian sonnet in praise of Alfonso Ferrabosco, one of the court musicians. Finally, a longer Italian poem – Quin's only adventure in humour – was one of the many verses collected in Thomas Coryate's *Crudities* (1611). At the pinnacle of the prince's public career, his creation as

---

70 Malcolm Smuts, 'Prince Henry and His World' in Catharine MacLeod (ed.), *The Lost Prince: The Life and Death of Henry Stuart* (London: National Portrait Gallery, 2013), p. 20.

71 Juhala, 'Household and Court of King James VI', p. 70.

72 James VI and I, *Letters of King James VI & I*, ed. G.P.V. Akrigg (Berkeley: University of California Press, 1984), p. 219.

73 Andrew Ashbee (ed.), *Records of English Court Music* (8 vols, Snodland: Ashbee, 1986–96), iv, p. 36.

prince of Wales, Quin was only, so far as we know, in the background: imagery that had been used in connection with Henry's father pervaded the occasion, and Ben Jonson's masque *The Speeches at Prince Henry's Barriers* quoted Quin's anagram of the king's name, 'claims Arthur's seat'.[74] Quin can hardly have been idle, however, as he was paid £50 a year and, in 1610, Henry granted Quin the office of examiner of the Exchequer Court at Chester (that is the right to claim fees for the examination of court witnesses).[75]

Although Francis Bacon remarked on Henry's loyalty to 'the masters and tutors of his youth',[76] the precariousness of Quin's position can be seen in the career of Josuah Sylvester, the merchant turned poet with whom he worked on *Lachrimae Lachrimarum* (1612). Despite the fact that Sylvester's translations of Du Bartas were to be greatly admired, and were purchased in folio editions in the early seventeenth century, his dedications of them to King James received no monetary reward.[77] Between 1608 and 1612 he received an income from Henry, but the prince's death was a severe reversal.[78] Again, he attempted to attract the favour of the king (as well as writing for Charles and Elizabeth), but this did not yield enough to keep him out of poverty. Eventually he abandoned his hopes of earning a living by his pen and moved to Zeeland in the Netherlands where he ended his life as a secretary to the Merchant Adventurers in Middleburg.[79]

When Henry died in 1612 Quin did not go the way of Sylvester, which must have been a particular relief, since on 30 August, he had married another royal servant, Ann Leigh.[80] Instead, he passed into Charles' household and although he may not then have known it, this was a crucial moment for his service to the Stuarts as, like Henry, Charles was loyal to his family's servants and when he became king the people he replaced for the most part yielded to mem-

---

74 Timothy Wilks, 'Introduction' in Catharine MacLeod (ed.), *The Lost Prince: The Life and Death of Henry Stuart* (London: National Portrait Gallery, 2013), pp 11–17; Ben Jonson, *The Complete Masques*, ed. Stephen Orgel (New Haven, CT: Yale UP, 1969), p. 143.

75 Ashbee (ed.), *Records of English Court Music*, iv, pp 27, 211, viii, p. 59. The Exchequer Court had its roots in the Palatinate of Chester: R. Stewart-Brown, 'The Exchequer of Chester', *The English Historical Review*, 57, 227 (1942), 289–97.

76 Cited in Wilks, 'Introduction', p. 11.

77 Jane Rickard, 'The Cultural Politics of Translation: King James VI and I, Du Bartas and Josuah Sylvester' in David J. Parkinson (ed.), *James VI and I, Literature and Scotland: Tides of Change, 1567–1625* (Leuven: Peeters, 2013), pp 114–15.

78 Leila Parsons, 'Prince Henry (1594–1612) as a Patron of Literature', *Modern Language Review*, 47, 4 (1952), 503–7 at 504–7.

79 Susan Snyder, 'Du Bartas, Guillaume de Salluste' in A.C. Hamilton (ed.), *The Spenser Encyclopedia* (rev. ed.; Toronto: University of Toronto Press, 1997), p. 80.

80 Percival Boyd, 'Boyd's Marriage Index', *SoG Data Online* (Society of Geneaologists, 2011), www.sog.org.uk/search-records/search-sog-data-online, accessed 13 Apr. 2014; 'England Marriages, 1538–1973', *FamilySearch* (Church of Jesus Christ of the Latter-day Saints, 2014), https://familysearch.org, accessed 17 Jan. 2014.

bers of his household as prince of Wales.[81] At the obsequies for James I, 'Walter Quinne who waited on the King [Charles I] at the time of his Scooling' once again received 7 yards of cloth with an additional 4 yards for his servant.[82]

CHARLES, PRINCE AND KING

In Prince Charles' household Quin continued to draw his £50 a year (there are records for 1614 and 1626).[83] In 1629 he was paid £50 wages and £50 board wages by the lord steward.[84] The annual sum of £100 would appear in various ways for the rest of his life, and it was eventually inherited by his wife, his son and then his son's widow.[85] Calculating the actual revenue of royal officials is complicated by the fact that there were forms of income other than their salary (for example, entitlements to meals and to levy fees, and the receipt of gratuities), that some offices had to be bought and that some expenses associated with them were paid for personally.[86] In consequence, comparing Quin's allowance of £100 with those of other office holders is not straightforward. In the 1630s, the secretary of state and the cofferer each received about £2,000 while at the other end of the scale, the king's barber had an income of £280 and a messenger earned something in excess of £55.[87] In this decade, a craftsman earned 30d. a day while a building labourer's wage was 16d.[88]

In addition to his £100, Quin derived other income from his privileged position and this was for the most part tied up with Irish affairs. In 1629 the Signet Office sent a letter to the justices of Ireland to the effect that Quin was to receive the revenues of the monastery of St John the Evangelist in Waterford for a yearly rent of £40 (the priory was a twelfth-century Benedictine foundation whose community had dwindled to eight members by the time of its suppression.)[89] Furthermore, they ordered

> that search shall be made in Berminghams Tower [in Dublin Castle] for all records showing the King's title to the lands &c. of the dissolved monastery of St John the Evangelist in Waterford, which, according to

---

81   G.E. Aylmer, *The King's Servants: The Civil Service of Charles I, 1625–1642* (2nd ed.; London: Routledge & Kegan Paul, 1974), p. 257.

82   Ashbee (ed.), *Records of English Court Music*, iii, p. 5.

83   Ibid., iii, p. 167, v, p. 5, viii, p. 59.   84   Ibid., v, p. 5.

85   NA, SP 16/306, fo. 14. For the posthumous payments, see below.

86   Aylmer, *King's Servants*, pp 203–39.   87   Ibid., pp 204–7.

88   Jeremy Boulton, 'Wage Labour in Seventeenth-Century London', *The Economic History Review*, 49, 2 (1996), 268–90 at 279.

89   Aubery Gwynn & R. Neville Hadcock, *Medieval Religious Houses: Ireland* (London: Longman, 1970), p. 108.

the report of Walter Quin, are detained from the King. These lands &c. shall then be granted to Walter Quin, to be held in free and common socage for a rent of 40*l.*, to be paid in half-yearly instalments.[90]

Quin had received royal bounty, but it was difficult to realize. As Charles wrote to the lord justices of Ireland: 'we are informed by our trusty and well-beloved servant Walter Quin' that 'possessions, lands, tenements and hereditaments [...] are concealed and the profits thereof detained from us'.[91]

In 1632 Quin petitioned the king for the 'licence for the sole making of Tobacco pipes throughout all your Kingdome of Ireland' for a term of thirty-one years at a yearly rent of £10.[92] This was intended 'for ye better support and maintenance of ye petitioner and his wife [...] and of their children'. Charles granted Quin's request 'out of his special favour to this Petitioner and to his Wife, beeing both his ancient servants'. This went untypically well. The same year Quin made a complaint to the Court of Wards who judged that the debts owed him by the late James Sedgrave had been discharged and that the king was entitled to the future profits of Sedgrave's estate while his heir was a minor.[93]

It is clear that as well as being a teacher and writer Quin was involved in various other business dealings. The extent of them can be seen in a scheme he unsuccessfully proposed in 1623 when the Privy Council considered the 'petition of Walter Quin, gentleman' for 'a graunt under the great seale for the transporting of twoe hundred thousand sheepes' pells and lambs pells yearely out of the kingdome of Irelande into partes beyond the seas dureing the tearme of one and twentie yeares'. However, 'theire Lordships are of opinion that the petitioner's suite is very unfitt to be granted and that the petitioner should forbeare to trouble his Majestie or this Boarde and further herewithall'.[94]

How did Quin propose to handle 200,000 fleeces? Some hint may be had from an undated petition to King Charles about 'Peter Quyn a Merchaunt of Dublyn' who had been detained at Liverpool for the possession of dangerous books.[95] As Quin cannot forget 'the bond of nature' with his relative, he is obliged 'not to forsake him'. He asks the king to write to the mayor of Liverpool with instructions to make full restitution of his nephew's goods. Evidently Quin was still in contact with his Dublin family. Their position was better suited to trading, or even for ascertaining local information about the pos-

---

90 *CSP Domestic, Charles I* (1858–93), i, p. 488.
91 *Calendar of Patent and Close Rolls of the Chancery in Ireland, of the Reign of Charles the First [...]*, ed. James Morrin (Dublin: HMSO, 1863), p. 499.
92 BL, Add. MS 69915, fo. 58.
93 *CSP Domestic, Charles I*, i, p. 646.
94 *Privy Council* (1932), pp 478–9.
95 BL, Add. MS 69915, fo. 60.

sessions of a Waterford priory. Given his dealings with Ireland, it would be surprising if he himself had not returned there on occasion.

What was Quin's principal occupation? Understandably there is a bias here
to consider him as an author, but again, as under Prince Henry, it must be
observed that his extant output is not prodigious, although it is at once uniform
and varied. It is uniform insofar as it is mainly taken up with works for the royal
family. He celebrates both Charles' creation as prince of Wales and his marriage.
In doing so, his works range from *Elogium serenissimi regis*, a broadsheet in which
the praise of James and Charles takes the form of single word columns of text,
to a long (at least for Quin) history of a Franco-Scottish soldier in the Italian
wars. At this time he also produced *Recueil*, a French collection of the sayings of
Henry IV for Queen Henrietta Maria, and *Corona virtutum*, a neo-Stoic flori-
legium, Quin's only work that was reprinted abroad.

In his last extant poem he provided a commendatory verse for Thomas
Herbert's *Travels* that is signed 'Walt. O-Quin Armig.', which shows that he was
a gentleman ('armiger' did not imply he had a coat of arms: in the Stuart period
its technical definition was often put aside, and it was acceptable for a gentleman
to adopt it, although this could be challenged). It was common to regard men
with MA degrees as gentlemen, and even the Privy Council had considered him
a gentleman in 1623 while they were rejecting his mercantile plans.[96]

ENGLISH FAMILY

Quin's family life in London can only be imagined from the bare records of fact
that remain. The one poem that seems to be about the Quin family comes not
from Walter but from Arthur Johnston whose 'On the Death of Anne Quin in
Childbirth' was included in his *Epigrams* (1632).[97] Whatever its precise date, it is
too early to refer to Quin's wife, so he may have had a daughter called after her
mother, or, by that time an Anne could have been married to one of his sons.

Quin's own marriage took place in the parish of St Martin in the Fields but
the Quins must have lived in the parish of St Mary the Virgin (Church Street,
Twickenham). In this church James and Mary were baptized (on 14 March
1620 and 19 October 1623),[98] and Lucy and Walter Jr were buried (on 21
February 1625 and 11 May 1629).[99] An entry in the *Administration Act Books* of

96 I owe this information to David White, Somerset Herald at the College of Arms. The college
    has no record of a grant of arms to Quin. See also Aylmer, *King's Servants*, pp 261–2.
97 The text can be found in the Appendix, p. 267.
98 St Mary the Virgin, Twickenham, 'Register of baptism', DRO/174/A/01, item 002, 36, 38.
99 St Mary the Virgin, Twickenham, 'Register of burials', DRO/174/A/01, item 002, 127. For
    Walter, see St Mary the Virgin, Twickenham, 'Register of burials', DRO/174/A/01, item

the Prerogative Court of Canterbury for 2 December 1640 lists Walter Quin, the administration of whose estate was to pass to his widow Anne.[100] (An administration was used when the deceased had left no will. It allowed a named person – a family member or creditor – to distribute the moveable goods of the estate.)

After Quin and his wife had died, another son, John, petitioned the king on his own behalf as well as that of a 'distressed' sister, that since his parents 'were ancient servants to the Royal Family' and his father 'had an allowance of 100l. per annum' that the king would continue this allowance during his own lifetime.[101] John's suit was successful as there is a record of his having been paid the pension in 1660. Subsequently, his widow Ann applied to receive it (along with its arrears).[102]

John may have exaggerated his distress in order to extract money from the royal coffers, but it seems unlikely that he was wealthy.[103] His father's liminal status is seen in the career of his son James (1620–59) who was a Queen's Scholar at Westminster School, a feeder school for Christ Church, Oxford, where he matriculated in December 1639.[104] He received his BA in 1642 and his MA in 1646.[105] He followed his father in being a neo-Latin poet and contributed to university anthologies in celebration of Charles' marriage (*Epithalamia Oxoniensa*, 1625) and in praise of the king (*Eucharistica Oxoniensia*, 1641).[106] James' royalist sympathies had him expelled from the university in 1648.[107] Apparently he

---

002, 129; 'Register of burials', DRO/174/A/01, item 003, 47 (note that there are two MS copies).

100 NA, PROB 6/17, fo. 170.

101 NA, SP 16/306, fo. 14. The date of the petition is uncertain. *CSP* suggests 1635, but this is impossible, as Quin is explicit that his parents are dead: *CSP Domestic, Charles I*, x, p. 2.

102 Undated petitions of 1670 in *CSP Domestic, Charles II* (1860–1939), x, p. 626. A Mrs Anne Quinn is listed as an actress in Charles II's Theatre Royal in 1676–7: NA, 'Records of the lord chamberlain and other officers of the royal household', LC 3/28 (203); 'Lord chamberlain's department: miscellaneous records, great wardrobe', LC 5/62 (1).

103 In 1643 a John Quin was the secretary of George Goring, earl of Norwich and vice-chamberlain of the king's household: NA, SP 84/157, fo. 229.

104 Joseph Welch (ed.), *The List of the Queen's Scholars of St. Peter's College, Westminster* (2nd ed.; London: G. W. Ginger, 1852), p. 113. James' life is included in Lee and McGinley, 'Quin'.

105 Joseph Foster, *Alumni Oxonienses: The Members of the University of Oxford, 1500–1714* (2nd ed.; 2 vols, Oxford: Parker and Co., 1891–92), p. 1225.

106 *Epithalamia Oxoniensia in auspicatissimum, potentissimi monarchae Caroli [...] cum Henr[i]etta Maria, aeternae memoriae Henrici magni Gallorum regis filia, connubium* (Oxford: John Lichfield & William Turner, 1625), sig. H3; *Eucharistica Oxoniensia: in exoptatissimum & auspicatissimvm Caroli [...] serenissimi & clementissimi regis nostri e Scotia reditum gratulatoria* (Oxford: Leonard Lichfield, 1641), sig. C3.

107 Montagu Burrows (ed.), *The Register of the Visitors of the University of Oxford, from A.D. 1647 to A.D. 1658* (Westminster: J. B. Nichols and Sons, 1881), p. 489.

died in a crazed condition in his bedmaker's house in Pennyfarthing Street, and was buried in the cathedral of Christ Church. Anthony Wood had some acquaintance with him, and hath several times heard him sing with great admiration. His voice was a bass, and he had great command of it. It was very strong and exceeding trouling [rolling], but he wanted skill, and could scarce sing in consort. He had been turned out of his student's place by the visitors; but being well acquainted with some great men of those times, that loved music, they introduced him into the company of Oliver Cromwell the protector, who loved a good voice, and instrumental music as well. He heard him sing with very great delight, liquored him with sack, and in conclusion said: 'Mr Quin, you have done very well, what shall I do for you?' To which Quin made answer with great complements, of which he had command with a great grace, that 'your Highness would be pleased to restore him to his student's place;' which he did accordingly, and so kept it to his dying day.[108]

Although this is doubtless touched by Wood's usual colour, its outline is probably true. James inherited his education but not enough money to live outside the university. He had been brought up by a gentleman to be a gentleman, but one who depended on the favour that came from acquaintance with the powerful: 'Mr Quin, you have done very well, what shall I do for you?'

---

108 Wood, *Athenæ Oxonienses*, i, p. 39. Abbreviations expanded and spelling modernized. For Cromwell's love of music, see Antonia Fraser, *Cromwell: The Lord Protector* (New York: Grove Press, 1973), p. 464.

Note on the texts and apparatus

The aim of this edition is to gather together the writings of Walter Quin and to present them in an accessible form. To this end, the decision to provide translations of texts written in languages other than English was an easy one. The question of the modernization and regularization of the texts was more challenging. This is not the place to launch into a wholesale discussion of a topic that has provoked much debate. Philip Gaskell has argued that modernization is 'undesirable' since it obscures puns and ambiguities and 'deprives the work of the quality of belonging to its own period'.[1] A similar stance is taken by the excellent *Penguin Book of Renaissance Verse*, which departs from the practice of most other volumes in the Penguin Classics series by eschewing modernization so that the reader is presented with a version of the texts that 'existed at about the time when they were written' and not an editor's 'imposition of sense and structure which may distort poetry's meaning and effect'.[2] At the same time, this has not prevented the anthology from jettisoning typographical features (such as capitalization and the use of italics), eliminating long s, and silently expanding contractions, a compromise that others have cogently rejected.[3]

While Gaskell is adamant in condemning the modernization of texts from the eighteenth century onwards (as their original features are usually not such that they are a significant obstruction to comprehension), he will allow that in sixteenth- and seventeenth-century texts, old spelling 'is liable to put off non-specialist readers' and 'that we have all read Shakespeare and the 1611 Bible in modernized texts without coming to much harm'.[4] This last observation is certainly as true as the acknowledgment that Shakespeare and the King James Bible require old spelling versions in addition to modernized ones: because of the cultural importance of these works there is a demand for such editions; furthermore, their subtlety of language increases the possibility that modernized texts either impose misinterpretations or erase interesting ambiguities. It is no slight

1   Philip Gaskell, *From Writer to Reader: Studies in Editorial Method* (Oxford: Clarendon Press, 1978), p. 8.
2   David Norbrook & H.R. Woudhuysen (eds), *The Penguin Book of Renaissance Verse* (2nd ed.; London: Penguin, 1993), p. 71.
3   Michael Hunter, *Editing Early Modern Texts: An Introduction to Principles and Practice* (Houndmills: Palgrave Macmillan, 2009), p. 91.
4   Gaskell, *From Writer to Reader*, p. 8.

to Quin to observe that the first edition of his work should seek the widest audience possible and that there are few, if any, places where the process of modernization implemented in this book endanger the polysemy of his texts. One final untidy consideration was taken into account when deciding to modernize the text: many people interested in an old spelling edition will be able to read most of Quin's work on *EEBO* (the availability of electronic texts of Quin's works is listed in their headnotes). This is a theoretically lame rationale but one which carries some pragmatic force.[5]

As this edition deals with manuscripts and non-English works it would have been defensible to have employed different sets of editorial principles. The manuscripts, for example, are not as easily available to those interested in an original spelling text. Works in languages other than English are translated here, and thus available to general readers, so in their original language, their orthography and punctuation could have been preserved. This would only have been slightly confusing (if at all). However, the rationale for modernizing the texts of the manuscripts is the same as that for modernizing printed sources, and between the poles of those who can and cannot read texts in neo-Latin or early modern French and Italian, there is a sizeable constituency who can do so with the combination of a translation and a modernized text. In consequence, a consistent approach to editing has been adopted throughout.

This edition works on the basis of individual copy-texts. The extant manuscript works are unique, and consequently pose no problem. The printed sources exist in several copies and sometimes in several editions. In all cases an example of the first edition of the work has been used. Although various copies of the first edition have been examined (principally to ensure that they were in fact the same edition and to check for anything indicating their provenance or for marginalia), no attempt has been made to collate these. The process of modernization would in any event erase most distinctions arising from stop-press corrections or press variants. Although there are *prima facie* justifications for choosing first editions as copy-texts, these need not be aired since in practice there are no substantial differences between editions. Even where Quin himself laments the carelessness of his printer, the resulting errata are minor.[6]

EDITORIAL PRINCIPLES

The application of these principles has been flexible. To preserve features such as metre and rhyme, or to make sense of some of the anagrams that Quin

5 Stanley Wells deals more robustly with the automatic rejection of modernized editions in Stanley Wells, *Re-editing Shakespeare for the Modern Reader* (Oxford: Clarendon Press, 1984), pp 5–31.
6 *Corona virtutum* (1613), sig. H11r.

employs, it has occasionally been necessary to make exceptions to the procedures explained below. Where necessary, footnotes explain editorial decisions.

Orthography and capitalization have been modernized and regularized. Common early modern English words have been retained. In some cases this still leaves the reader with words whose meanings are unfamiliar, but in the English texts these are marked with an obelisk† and can be found in the glossary at the end of the book (texts that have translations are not glossed as the translations should provide the key to unfamiliar words). The use of j/i, v/u and long s have been modernized. Ligatures (for example, 'œ') have been separated. Abbreviations and contractions have been silently expanded. Punctuation has been modernized in two ways: (i) punctuation has been translated into modern conventions, for example, quotation marks have been inserted where, in the copy-text, there was a colon followed by a capital letter; (ii) in a small number of cases the punctuation has been changed. Since this can significantly change the meaning of the text this has been done conservatively. Printers' errors have been silently corrected. Editorial additions are indicated by square brackets.

The copy-texts are well preserved, but where their readings are doubtful they have been compared with other examples of the same edition.

TYPOGRAPHY, SCRIBAL FEATURES AND MISE-EN-PAGE

Original stanzas, paragraphs and line indents have been retained. Minor corrections in manuscripts (for example, where the scribe crossed out a letter and substituted another) have not been indicated but more substantial ones are listed in the notes. Italics, font changes and drop, block and small capitals have been removed except where they are used to highlight the elements of an anagram or for special emphasis, in which case italics are employed here. Marginal notes are recorded in the footnotes. Paratextual elements are not reproduced, although where they are judged significant they are described.

TITLES

With the exception of the details of the copy-text (see below), the titles of early-modern book-length works are presented in the same way as modern ones. Long early modern titles are sometimes truncated (this is indicated with ellipses). Titles solely in languages other than English are capitalized in accordance with the conventions of the relevant language.

The majority of Quin's poems have no titles or, when they do, they have headings which are generic (for example, 'Idem in obitum eiusdem serenissimi principe'). This edition provides titles that clearly distinguish one poem from another. In doing so, Quin's own ones have been retained where possible. When a work has no suitable title, one has been supplied, and this is indicated by square brackets.

FOOTNOTES

Although some of the footnotes are textual, the vast majority of them are explicatory. Textual notes are keyed to the original language text only. For the convenience of a variety of readers, historical and literary references have been explained, and although some will find this otiose, it should not prove obtrusive. Information that has been provided in the introductions to a text is usually not repeated in the footnotes, but footnotes have sometimes been repeated to avoid unnecessary cross-referencing.

HEADNOTES

The introductions in the headnotes to Quin's works provide details of their contexts and any necessary background information. They also supply details of the copy-text. For printed sources this includes bibliographical details in the form:

> Author, *Title*. Edition. Place of Publication: Publisher, Date. Size/format. *ESTC* number (number of copies listed in *ESTC*). *USTC* number for books published in Germany (number of copies listed in *USTC*). Library, call number.

Descriptions of manuscripts are in the form:

> Author, *Title*. Library, call number. Size. Number of folios.

Where relevant, the details of the copy-texts are followed by information regarding all further seventeenth-century printed copies (of all or part of a work) and any notable modern editions, including electronic versions. The titles of copy-texts retain their original spelling, capitalization (with block capitals used for small capitals) and punctuation.

TRANSLATIONS

Translations of texts follow immediately after their originals and their titles are marked with a [T]. The translations aim to be literal but readable (the position of verbs in Latin can often make it impossible to translate poetry line by line without using jarring syntax). Phrases added in the translation to clarify a work's sense appear in square brackets. Proper nouns have sometimes been silently substituted for pronouns for ease of reading.

Conscious of my own limitations, I have sought assistance with the translations, thus the Latin texts have been supplied by Dr David Butterfield, while Prof. Eiléan Ní Chuilleanáin and Prof. Cormac Ó Cuilleanáin provided me with the Italian ones. As parts of these translations have been reworked, any deficiencies in them must be laid at the door of the editor.

DATES

In the time period covered in this book there were two systems of dating. To align the calendar and solar years, in 1582 Gregory XIII introduced a reform (subsequently called 'New Style'), which skipped ten days of that year's October, made provision for leap years and specified that a new year was to be counted from 1 January (rather than Lady Day, 25 March). New Style was in use in Ingolstadt when Quin was there; however, because of religious differences it was not adopted in England, Scotland and Ireland until 1752, although in 1600 Scotland began dating the beginning of a new year on 1 January.[7] Note that although official publications used Old Style, for other works printers frequently began the year on 1 January.[8] Dates in this edition are given in Old Style unless otherwise noted.

---

7   For this paragraph, see C.R. Cheney & Michael Jones (eds), *A Handbook of Dates for Students of British History* (new ed.; Cambridge: Cambridge UP, 2000), pp 17–19, 236–41.
8   *STC*, i, p. xxxviii.

WORKS

I

From Robert Turner's *Oratio et epistola* (1590)

An Oration and Letters is a memorial for Martin von Schaumberg (1523–90), prince-bishop of Eichstätt and *ex officio* chancellor of the University of Ingolstadt. The bishop was an enthusiastic supporter of the Catholic reformation who sought to implement the decrees of the Council of Trent in his diocese without alienating his Protestant neighbours.[1] The bulk of the volume is taken up by writings in his memory, consisting of an oration and letters addressed to Cardinal William Allen by Robert Turner (1547–99).[2] Turner was born in Devonshire and having studied at Douai (where he was ordained) he went to Rome with John Lesley, bishop of Ross, where he studied at the Jesuit German College. He was appointed to the newly founded Tridentine seminary in Eichstätt by von Schaumberg. In 1582 he joined the University of Ingolstadt where he served as rector in 1584–5.[3] During this time he considered himself an exile for the sake of his faith.[4] For reasons that are unclear, he was forced to leave the university two years later, and once again von Schaumberg became his patron as he appointed Turner a parish priest. After the bishop's demise, Turner quit the diocese, eventually finding employment as the Latin secretary to Archduke Ferdinand II (an alumnus of Ingolstadt), at his court in Graz, where he died.

The volume begins with a letter by Turner addressed to the bishop of Eichstätt and a poem by Edmund Hollings MD (a Yorkshire-born convert to Catholicism who had studied at Douai, Reims and Rome).[5] Quin's epigrams follow and are headed: 'Epigramma Gualteri Guinni Angli in obitum ejusdem reverendissimi et illustrissimi Domine Martini episcopi Eystetensis' (The Epigrams of Walter Quin, Englishman, on the Death of the Aforesaid Most Reverend and most Illustrious Lord Martin, Bishop of Eichstätt). The other contributors to the volume are

1   Ernst Reiter, 'Martin von Schaumberg', *Neue Deutsche Biographie* (Bayerischen Staatsbibliothek, 1990), www.deutsche-biographie.de/sfz58605.html, accessed 28 Nov. 2013.
2   For Turner's date of birth (not in *ODNB*), see Iva, Kurelac 'Robertus Bonaventura Britanus (Robert Turner) and the Lost Manuscript of Dinko Zavorovi 's *De rebus Dalmaticis*', *Journal of Croatian Studies*, 48 (2007), 98–113 at 111.
3   Peter E.B. Harris, 'Turner, Robert (d.1599)', *ODNB*; Alois Knöpfler, 'Turner, Robert', *Allgemeine Deutsche Biographie* (Bayerischen Staatsbibliothek, 1895), www.deutsche-biographie.de/pnd128565101.html, accessed 28 Nov. 2013.
4   George Wolff (ed.), *Die Matrikel Der Ludwig-Maximilians-Universitat: Ingolstadt-Landshut-Munchen, Teil 1* (Munich: J. Lindauersche, 1937), cols 1145–6.
5   Thompson Cooper & Sarah Bakewell, 'Hollings, Edmund (*c.*1556–1612)', *ODNB*.

Mathias Mairhofer SJ (professor and pro-dean of the theology faculty at Ingolstadt) and Philipp Menzel (the professor of medicine).

Copy-text

Robert Turner, *ROBERTI TVRNERI* | *DEVONII* | *Oratio & Epistola* | *de Vita & Morte* | *REVERENDIS-* | *SIMI ET ILLVSTRISSI-* | *MI DN. MAR-TINI A SCHAVM-* | *BERG, Principis & Episcopi EYSTADI-* | *ANI: illa in funere 3. Non. Iul. An. 1590.* | *Eystadii habita: haec scripta* | *Romam ad* | *Reverendissimu[m] & Illustrissimum* | *Dn. GVLIELMVM ALANVM* | *S. R. E. Cardinalem.* | *Subnexum est Clarissimi viri D. PHILIPPI* | *MENZELLI, Medicinæ Doctoris & Professoris* | *Ingolstadiani carmen de eâdem re* | *elegantissimum.* Ingolstadt: Wolfgang Ederus, 1580 [actually 1590]. 8°. *USTC* 691241 (7 copies). BL, General Reference Collection 697.a.59.

There was another printing of this work in 1590 (*USTC* 691242 [3 copies]). Their texts of Quin's poetry are identical, although their page decorations are slightly different. Digital copies of both printings are available at the Bavarian State Library (www.bsb-muenchen.de).

[Vir quantus cecidit fatali cuspide mortis?] [sig.)(7r][6]

Vir quantus cecidit fatali cuspide mortis?
  Teutonici cecidit gloria quanta soli?
Praesul erat, princepsque simul: fortuna nec illi
  Hoc peperit, virtus sed veneranda, decus.
Tam pius ille fuit, tanto splendore refulgens;   5
  Praesul, ut ambigeres, anne dynasta foret.
Praesulis officium tanta pietate gerebat;
  Principis ut munus vix obiisse putes.
Principis et gessit munus tam splendide, ut illud
  Pontificem credas vix potuisse pium.   10
Pontifices pauci quod sunt, paucique dynastae,
  Inclytus hic heros solus utrumque fuit.

[How Great a Man Has Fallen by the Fatal Spear of Death?] [T]

How great a man has fallen by the fatal spear of death? How great a glory of the German land has fallen? He was a bishop and prince simultaneously: fortune did

---

6 German printers often used inverted parentheses)(for signing preliminaries: R.A. Sayce, 'Compositorial Practices and the Localization of Printed Books 1530–1800', *The Library*, 21 (1966), 1–45 at 9.

not procure this honour for him, but his venerable virtue. He was so pious, shining with such splendour, that you would doubt as to whether he was a bishop or a sovereign. He carried out the office of bishop with such piety that you would scarcely suppose that he had received the position of prince, and he performed the role of prince so splendidly, that you would believe a pious bishop could hardly have done this. Because there are few bishops, and few sovereigns, he alone was a renowned hero in both roles.

[Coelicolis, vitam dum corpore tectus agebat] [sig.)(7v]

Coelicolis, vitam dum corpore tectus agebat,
    Martinus placuit, terricolisque simul.
Hinc cum coelicolis, exutus corpore, vivit
    Mente, et terricolis nomine vivus adest.

[While he Lived his Life] [T]

While he lived his life, when possessed of a body, Martin pleased both the dwellers in heaven as well as those on earth. Henceforth, his body cast aside, he lives in his mind with heaven's inhabitants, and in name he is present with the inhabitants of earth.

Ad revendum Turnerum [sig.)(7v]

Est, Turnere, tibi decus ingens gloria tanti
    Praesulis; est illi buccina tanta decus.

For Reverend Turner [T]

Turner, the glory of so prodigious a bishop is a great ornament for you. So great a fanfare is an honour for him.

2

From Joannes Croesselius' *Parentalia anniversaria* (1591)

Johann Egolf von Knöringen (1537–75), bishop of Augsburg, studied at Ingolstadt and later donated more than six thousand printed volumes as well as his manuscript collection to the university, and these became the foundation of a new library.[1] He took a harsh stance against his diocese's Protestants and Jews and engaged in a protracted quarrel with the Jesuits.[2] *Parentalia anniversaria* marked the twenty-fifth anniversary of his death.[3]

Johann Krösel (c.1555–1633) was a student at and subsequently the librarian of the University of Ingolstadt. His literary aspirations are attested by his *Poemata* of 1585. In 1595 he moved to Graz where he became the librarian of Archduke Ferdinand II (an alumnus of Ingolstadt) and a tutor of the duchess.[4] This may link him to the circle of Robert Turner (see p. 41). Certainly, Krösel owned two books written by Turner, in addition to a volume by Edmund Hollings, a contributor to Turner's *Oratio et epistola*.[5] He published *Parentalia anniversaria* in 1590 and it was followed by an expanded edition in the following year.

In addition to Krösel's own work, the second edition contains epitaphs by various people associated with Ingolstadt including two poets laureate of the Holy Roman Empire: a former professor of poetry, Johannes Engerd (d. c.1587), and Valentin Rotmar (d. 1581), a former professor of rhetoric.[6] The other contributors were three doctors of law (Johannes Lescher, Johannes Ritter and

1   Helmut Wolff, *Geschichte Der Ingolstäder Juristenfakultät, 1472–1625* (Berlin: Duncker & Humblot, 1973), p. 71.

2   Friedrich Roth, 'Johann Egolf Von Knöringen', *Allgemeine Deutsche Biographie* (Bayerischen Staatsbibliothek, 1905), www.deutsche-biographie.de/pnd100118747.html, accessed 1 Mar. 2014.

3   *Parentalia* originally refers to a Roman festival of the dead and is here the equivalent of a eulogy.

4   Hans Zotter, 'Bibliotheca Craesseliana: Johannes Krösel Aus Vilseck' (1983), http://sosa2.uni-graz.at/sosa/druckschriften/druckschriften/g-craesseliana.php, accessed 25 Jan. 2014.

5   Ibid.

6   Engerd and Rotmar were laureated in 1572 and 1575/6 respectively: John L. Flood, *Poets Laureate in the Holy Roman Empire: A Bio-Bibliographical Handbook* (4 vols, Berlin: Walter de Gruyter, 2006), pp 485, 1754; Georg Westermayer, 'Engerd, Johannes', *Allgemeine Deutsche Biographie* (Bayerischen Staatsbibliothek, 1877), www.deutsche-biographie.de/pnd116503610.html, accessed 28 Nov. 2013; Georg Westermayer, 'Rotmar, Valentin', *Allgemeine Deutsche Biographie* (Bayerischen Staatsbibliothek, 1889), www.deutsche-biographie.de/pnd119810311X.html, accessed 28 Nov. 2013.

Daniele Paggaeus), a *candidatus* of law (Konrad Rittershuis), *Magister* Philipp Metzenhausen and *Magister* Johannes Hacker. Quin's is the last poem in the volume.

Copy-text
Joannes Croesselius, *PARENTALIA ANNIUERSARIA | REVEREN- | DIS- SIMO ET ILL- | VSTRISSIMO PRINCIPI | AC DOMINO, DN. IOANNI EGOL- | PHO À KNOERINGEN,* Episcopo *AVGV- | STANO* amplissimo, *Bibliothecæ Academicæ | apud INGOLSTADIENSES Fundatori bene- | ficentissimo, Principi & patrono optimo, opti- | mæ recordationis debitæq; gratitudinis ergô fa- | cta, & apophoretorum loco Patribus Academi- | cis oblata, Idib. Decemb. Anno instauratæ | salutis M. D. XCI.* Ingoldstadt: David Sartorius, 1591. 4°. USTC 682765 (3 copies). Munich, Bayerischen Staatsbibliothek (Bavarian State Library), Res/4 Jes 1.

This copy has been digitized by the Bayerischen Staatsbibliothek at: http://nbn-resolving.de/urn/resolver.pl?urn=urn:nbn:de:bvb:12-bsb00025117-7. It is also linked from *USTC*.

Gualteri Guinni Hyberni I.U. studiosi epigramma, in ejusdem reverendissime episcopi Knoeringeri laudem [p. 15]

Magnificae potius quam verae laudis amantes,
  Qui post fata suum vivere nomen avent;
Hoc sibimet statuis, obeliscis, amphitheatris,
  Et mausoleis perpetuare student.
Sed spes fallit eos: nam laus haec vana, ruente   5
  Mole, ruit, nec dum mole cadente, cadit.
Quanto tu melius (praesulter maxime) famam
  Non tibi, sed meritum grande parare volens?
Anglipolitanum, ductus pietate, librorum
  Gymnasium ditas dum locuplete penu: 10
Cujus opes ditant hos, qui commercia tractant
  Cum Musis, quavis hos et in arte juvant.
Unde velut dulci sumunt ex fonte liquorem,
  Quo possint avidam saepe levare sitim.
Hoc, quo relligio per te, Musaeque fruuntur   15
  Non minus annosum marmore munus erit.
Amphitheatra cadent, obelisci, altique colossi,
  Virtutis steterint cum monumenta tuae.
Cumque sepulta decus venantum fama jacebit:
  Nomen ad astra tuum postera secla ferent.   20

Epigram of Walter Quin, Irish Student of Law, in Praise of the
Aforementioned Most Reverend Bishop von Knöringen [T]

Lovers of magnificent rather than true praise, who wish their names to live on
after their deaths, desire to be perpetuated by statues, obelisks, amphitheatres and
mausoleums for themselves. However, their hopes delude them, for this praise
is vain: when a building collapses, it collapses; when the structure no longer falls,
it still decays. But how much better is it that you, most excellent three-time
leader, desire not to acquire fame for yourself, but a grand reward? Being led by
piety, you fill the University of Ingolstadt with a rich provision of books whose
wealth enriches those that have dealings with the Muses and helps them in any
given art. Therefore, just as they draw liquid from a sweet fountain by which
they could often alleviate their avid thirst, this, which religion and the Muses
enjoy through you, will be a gift no less enduring than marble. Amphitheatres,
obelisks and tall colossi will fall when the monuments of your virtue will stand;
and when the fame of those who hunt glory will lie buried, ages to come will
carry your name to the stars.

3
Anagrammata in nomen Jacobi sexti (1595)

This manuscript is composed of an opening epigram, four anagrams with their associated sonnets (two in English and one each in Italian and French) and a long French verse dialogue. Pairs of anagrams and their poems are also to be found in Quin's *Sertum poeticum* (1600) in which some of the poems of *Anagrams on the Name of James VI* have been reworked.

The poetry in *Anagrammata* is explicitly political as it was designed to support the claims of James VI to the throne of England. Apart from James' inherent virtues, Quin taps into a revived Scottish regard for King Arthur (a genealogy of the Stuarts existed that traced their line back to him) by means of variations of anagrams of James' name that can be transformed into such phrases as 'claimes Arthur's seat' (borrowed by William Camden and Ben Jonson) and 'qui est la? César, Artus'.[1]

The poems' controversial topic led to their preservation in a copy sent by Dr James MacCartney to Robert Bowes on 5 December 1595 (see the Introduction, p. 22). Bowes had been the English ambassador to Scotland and MacCartney was one of his agents while Bowes was absent from Edinburgh. Ultimately the poems ended up in London in the possession of Sir Robert Cecil (1563–1612), then a member of the Privy Council and head of one of the principal English intelligence rings. Sir Robert doubtless found them particularly interesting as the Cecil family is mentioned in unflattering terms in the closing work. William Cecil, Lord Burleigh (1520–98), is represented as a fox who is only concerned for his own and his children's advancement, and not for the good of the realm.[2] As it happened, from about 1601, Robert Cecil (by then secretary of state) became one of the

---

1   William Camden, *Remaines of a Greater Work, Concerning Britaine [...]* (London: by G[eorge] E[ld] for Simon Waterson, 1605), p. 153. Jonson uses it in *The Speeches at Prince Henry's Barriers*: *The Complete Masques*, ed. Stephen Orgel (New Haven, CT: Yale UP, 1969), p. 143. For the Stuart genealogy, see Murray G.H. Pittock, *Poetry and Jacobite Politics in Eighteenth-Century Britain and Ireland* (Cambridge: Cambridge UP, 1994), pp 15–17; N.J. Higham, *King Arthur: Myth-Making and History* (New York: Routledge, 2002), p. 238. As these authors point out, Scottish attitudes to Arthur were vexed by the fact that Henry VII had used him as a basis for a claim to be the overlord of Britain.

2   As both William and Robert were prominent politicians at this time, it is the reference to the fox enriching his children that clarifies which one is being spoken of (see below, p. 59). Cecil-as-fox is perhaps too obvious to be considered Quin's coinage and it can later be found in Jonson's *Volpone* (wr. 1606): Ian Donaldson, *Ben Jonson: A Life* (Oxford: Oxford UP, 2011), pp 139–40.

principal English supporters of James' succession. During James' English reign, Cecil was created earl of Salisbury and was appointed lord treasurer while his brother Thomas was made earl of Exeter.[3] In these circumstances *Anagrammata* must have become a source of discomfort for Quin.

Copy-text

Walter Quin, *ANAGRA[M]MATA* | *IN NOMEN IACOBI SEXTI,* | *SERENISS[IME] SCOTO-* | *RVM REGIS,* | *VARIIS LINGVIS INVENTA,* | *ATQ[UE] ETIAM EARUNDEM* | *LINGUARUM VER-* | *SIBVS ET ME-* | *TRIS EXPRESSA. A Gualtero Quinno hiberno, qui hoc deuotissimi animi, et* | *obsequii sui pignus, eidem Pio, Invicto, et Clementissimo* | *Principi, su[m]ma animi demissione dedicat* | *et consecrat.* London, NA, SP 52/57, doc. no. 79.[4] This is a sewn booklet of 16 folios measuring 210x155mm written in brown ink on paper. The pages have been ruled in ink to box off the body of the text and pro-vides guideline for titles.[5] Several pages have stamps from The Public Record Office and Her Majesty's State Paper Office. The booklet was written by one scribe who, for the most part, used an italic hand for poetry in Latin, French and Italian and secretary hand for English texts. The manuscript's folios have been clearly and consistently numbered in black ink in modern times and these page numbers have been used here.

Anagrammata has been printed (with some errors) in the *Calendar of State Papers* and an electronic facsimile is available in *State Papers Online.*[6]

[Cum superis reges communi iure fruuntur][7] [p. 639]

Cum superis reges communi iure fruuntur:
   Regibus, ut superis, numen inesse solet.
Numina magna velut superorum nomina produnt:

---

3 David Loades, *The Cecils: Privilege and Power Behind the Throne* (Kew: National Archives, 2007), pp 178, 221, 237.

4 There are various reference numbers given in SP 52/57 as it is currently bound. As well as a document number (the only consistent system in the volume), fo. 1 is numbered 171 and 633.

5 The rulings differ slightly from page to page. There are two vertical lines 15mm and 20mm from the left and right margins respectively. There are three horizontal lines, one 50mm from the bottom of the page, one 10mm from its top and one 18mm from its top. These create a thin band of 8mm, which is used to accommodate most of the poems' titles.

6 *CSP, Scotland*, xii, pp 80–6; *State Papers Online*, ed. Stephen Alford & John Miller (Gale Cengage Learning, 2014), http://gale.cengage.co.uk/state-papers-online-15091714/part-i.aspx, accessed 5 Apr. 2014.

7 In *The Trew Law of Free Monarchies*, James describes monarchy as the 'forme of government, as resembling the Divinitie, [that] approacheth nearest to perfection': *Selected Writings*, p. 260.

Omina sic regum nomina saepe ferunt.
Hinc tibi tam felix in nomine volvitur omen,   5
    Coelitus o regnis pluribus orta salus.
Quod variis linguis ex nomine ducitur arte
    Omen te superis innuit esse parem.
Ergo bonis avibus, tua quo te gloria ducit,
    Jacobus rex sic ratum nominis omen erit.   10

[Kings Enjoy a Law Shared with the Gods] [T]

Kings enjoy a law shared with the gods: divine power tends to be present in
them as well as in deities. Just as the divine powers of the gods manifest great
signs, so the names of kings often bear tokens; therefore, such a blessed omen is
contained in the king's name, one who is heavenly born, the salvation to many
kingdoms. The significance that is skilfully drawn from your name (in various
languages) asserts that you are equal to the gods; consequently, with the good
auspices to which your glory leads you, King James, the signification of your
name will be ratified.

[Victor ovans, collis domitis virtute superbis] [p. 641]

Carolus Jacobus Steuartus
Victor, salvus, carus stabo

Victor ovans, collis domitis virtute superbis,
    Clara trophaea feram, sceptra, perenne decus.
Salvus, et incolumis superabo pericula mille,   5
    Exortus variis gentibus ipse salus.
Carus ero superis, carus mortalibus: ipsi
    Victorem victi me facilemque colent.
Stabo cardinibus virtutum innixus, et astra
    Sublimi feriam vertice victor ovans.   10

[Triumphant victor] [T]

Charles James Stuart: as triumphant victor, I will remain beloved.

As triumphant victor, having tamed proud necks through my virtue, I will bear
splendid trophies, sceptres and eternal honour. Safe and unharmed, I will overcome a thousand dangers, having sprung forth as the salvation for various races.

I will be beloved of the gods and dear to mortals: they who vanquished themselves will revere me as the unquestionable victor. I will endure, relying upon the foundation of my virtues, and being the triumphant victor I will touch the stars at their sublime peak.

[L'accorto, giusto re ama, o Inghilterra][8] [p. 643]

Carlo Giacomo Stuarte
Ama l'accorto, giusto re

L'accorto, giusto re ama, o Inghilterra,
Che ti vien' da cieli benigni offerto,
Re tuo per dritto di sangue, e per merto   5
Degno d'esserlo più d'ogn' altr' in terra.
    Egli ti sarà sempre e'n pace, e'n guerra,
Padre benigno, guardian' fido, e certo;[9]
E ti reggerà qual nocchier' esperto,
Che la nave in buon porto e guida e serra.   10
    Ma s'alcun tuo, non già figlio amante,
Anzi traditor' disleale ed ingiusto
Vorrà impedirlo, a se dara impacci.
    Ch'a domarlo magnanimo, e bastante,
Proveràllo, non meno *ch'accorto, e giusto*:   15
Ma felice te, se l'ami, el'abbracci.

[Love the Wise, Just King O England] [T]

Charles James Stuart: love the wise, just king.

Love the wise, just king O England, who is offered to you by kind heaven, your king by right of blood, and by merit, worthy to be so more than any other on earth.

    He will be to you always in both peace and war, a kind father, a faithful and sure protector; and he will rule you like a skilful helmsman who guides the ship to a safe port and haven.

---

8   Compare 'L'accorto, giusto re ama, o nobil regno' in *Sertum poeticum*, p. 75.
9   For James as doctor and as *pater patriae*, see *Selected Writings*, pp 262, 272–3, 281, 328; Alan
    Stewart, *The Cradle King: A Life of James VI & I* (London: Chatto & Windus, 2003), pp 206–
    7.

But if one of yours, not indeed a loving son, rather a disloyal and unjust traitor, attempts to prevent him, he will make trouble for himself.

For magnanimous and sufficient to master him, he will find him no less just than wise: but happy you if you love him and embrace him.

[A Worthy Peerless Prince Claims Arthur's Seat][10] [p. 645]

Charles James Stuart
Claimes Arthur's seat

A worthy peerless prince claims Arthur's seat,
Born to the same by heavenly providence.
No force, no sleight, no vain claim or pretence   5
This worthy wight† can of his right defeat.
   For with his right, he is of might so great,
Through God's especial favour and defence,
As he can chastise treacherous offence,
And down the pride of foes, and rebels beat.   10
   In his just claim none else will him resist,
Save base and wicked wretches, deadly foes
To virtue, honour, peace and unity.
But God, and kingdoms, who will him assist,
With his own virtue, will in spite of those   15
Him raise to Arthur's seat and monarchy.

[Cease Lets Arthur I am, of Britain King] [p. 647]

Charles James Stuart
Cease lets,† I am Arthur

Cease lets Arthur I am, of Britain king,
Come by good right to claim my seat, and throne,
My kingdoms severed to rejoin in one,   5
To mend what is amiss in every thing.
   To root out discord, whence much woe doth spring,
To renew chivalry almost foregone,
To relieve virtue, which for want doth moan,

10 Compare 'A Peerless Pearl and Prince Claims Arthur's Seat' in *Sertum poeticum*, p. 74.

[51]

All former bliss to this my land to bring.   10
    Who doth me overthwart,† not holding me
For Arthur, my name let him turn,† and spell:
The truth hereof then shall he soon espy.
    But better this by trial men shall see:
Arthur in bounty, who deserveth well,   15
In courage Arthur my foes shall me try.

[Qui est là? César, Arthus, princes de grands honneurs][11] [p. 649]

Charles Jaques Stuart
Qui est là ? César, Arthus

Qui est là ? César, Arthus, princes de grands honneurs,
Desquels l'un de l'État des Romains se fait maître,
Et en Bretagne vint ses trophées à mettre,   5
Et l'autre fut des rois de Bretagne la fleur.
    Ces deux se sont conjoints en un prince plein d'heur,
Lequel Dieu a voulu roi de Bretagne naître,
Et l'ornant des vertus royales l'a fait être
Digne de ce royaume, et de toute grandeur.   10
    Que si quelque mutin poussé d'envie, et rage,
À lui s'ose opposer, d'un *César* le courage
Et l'heur éprouvera, mais à son grand malheur.
    Et ceux, qui volontiers lui prêteront hommage,
Exempts de tout péril, d'encombre, et de dommage,   15
D'un Arthus goûteront la clémence, et douceur.

[Who Is There? Caesar and Arthur, Princes of Great Honour] [T]

Charles Jaques Stuart: who is there? Caesar and Arthur.

Who is there? Caesar and Arthur, princes of great honour; one of whom made himself master of the Roman state and came to Britain to plant his victory trophies; and the other of whom was the flower of British kings.
    These two are linked in one fortunate prince whom God wished to be born king of Britain, and he made him gilded by royal virtues, worthy of this kingdom and of every greatness.

---

11 Compare 'Qui est là? Arthus sacré, roi de la Grande Bretagne' in *Sertum poeticum*, p. 74.

If some mischievous one, driven by envy and rage, dares to oppose him to test the bravery and the good fortune of a Caesar, it will only be to his great misfortune.

Moreover, those who willingly pay him homage will be free of every danger, misadventure and injury: they will taste the clemency and mildness of an Arthur.

Discours sur la même anagramme, en forme de dialogue entre un zélateur du bien public et une dame, laquelle représente le royaume d'Angleterre [p. 651]

ZÉLATEUR: Toi, dame en tous endroits du monde renommés,
Vainqueresse jadis, et princesse nommée
Non seulement des eaux, et îles du ponant ;
Mais du royaume aussi des fleurs se couronnant,
De ton palais royal fait qu'on ouvre la porte   5
Au roi, qui l'heur ancien, et honneur te rapporte.

DAME: Qui est ce roi, dis-moi. *Qui est là ?*

                ZÉLATEUR: *César, Arthus.*

DAME: Noms des princes prisés pour leurs rares vertus,
Et qui par leurs beaux faits ont acquis tant de gloire,
Que, sans flétrir jamais, fleurira leur mémoire ;   10
Desquels l'un me vainquit, et mit en désarroi,
Et l'autre fut du tout mon grand monarque, et roi.
Mais comment peuvent-ils en ce lieu-ci se rendre,
Si tant de temps passe, leurs corps furent en cendres
Réduits, et leurs esprits, montés là-haut aux cieux,   15
Triomphent immortels, changés en demi-dieux ?

ZÉLATEUR: Certes ils n'y sont pas en propres corps et forme,
Ni comme ceux, lesquels, suivant l'erreur énorme
D'un vieux rêveur, passaient les esprits des humains
Faisaient de corps en corps, assignaient aux plus sains,   20
Et parfaits en vertu, venant leur tour et heure
De retourner en corps, la plus noble demeure.
Que s'il était ainsi, deviner on pourrait,
Qu'avec *Arthus*, *César* ici se trouverait.
Mais en ce prince seul tous deux au vif se montrent   25
Au nom, heur, et vertu duquel ils se rencontrent.

[53]

DAME: Le présage me plaît : mais aussi je le crains :
Car la mémoire j'ai d'icelui, qui des freins
Tant de peuples brida, et entr'autres moi-même :
De quoi me souvenant deviens de frayeur blême.   30

ZÉLATEUR: Trop vaine et ombrageuse, Angleterre, est ta peur.
Ce César est tout tien ; rassure-toi le coeur.
Car en cette île même il a pris sa naissance :
Joint qu'en lui se voit bien la naïve ressemblance
D'ARTHUS, et d'autres rois, ses très nobles aïeuls,   35
Qui ont haussé ton nom et honneur jusqu'aux cieux.
Allez, allez renards, et nommez l'étranger,[12]
Par quenouille cuidans l'État sous vous règne.
Quoi ? L'héritier plus proche, et certain, et viril,
Issu d'un père anglais, natif d'une même île,   40
Faut-il qu'il soit par vous, pour étranger forclos,
Et que l'état royal soit dans vos parcs enclos ?
Jugez-vous étranger le roi d'une île même,
Jadis toute sujette à même diadème ?
Étrange serait-il, que sous un même chef   45
Ces deux membres unir se dussent derechef ?
Si vous vous fondez sur royale ordonnance,
Ainsi que prétendez faut-il pas qu'on balance
Toute ordonnance telle au poids de l'équité,
Du bon sens de l'auteur, et de sa volonté ?   50
Ou bien faut-il tenir pour lui ce qu'en devise
[Ce]Cil, qui a son butin, non au bien public vise ?
Qui soutiendrait qu'aucun des Henri, et Edouard
Eut ordonné qu'au gré de ces loups et renards
Dussent être forclos les lions de sa race,   55
Âne se montrerait de très mauvaise grâce.
Mais toi, très noble dame, envers ton sang royal
Ayant toujours montré le coeur bon et loyal,
Permettras-tu qu'un tas des loups, renards et ânes,
Qu'on ait braire et hurler de leurs bouches profanes   60
Contre droit et raison et toutes saintes lois,
Puissent à leur plaisir t'instituer des rois ?
Non feras : car je sais que ta brave noblesse,
Qui n'a pas moindre los de foi que de prouesse,
À joug indigne d'eux on ne s'asservira :   65

12 The foxes refer to the Cecils, in particular Lord Burleigh (see headnote).

Ains parti bien plus sûr, et louable élira,
D'embrasser pour son roi ce prince magnanime,
Qui mérite, que fleur de noblesse on l'estime.
Ni ton bon peuple aussi, qui toujours los avait
En embrassant parti de s'accoster au droit,   70
Voudra quitter sa foi et loyauté anciennes,
Pour suivre autre parti, ou cause, que la sienne.
Que si quelques mutins regimber oseront,
Et en sa juste cause à lui s'opposeront,
En lui éprouveront d'un *César* la vaillance   75
Et l'heur, en châtiant leur folle outrecuidance.
Mais ses sujets loyaux, qui le reconnaîtront,
Et qui, sans regimber, à lui se soumettront,
Sentiront par effets d'un *Arthus* la clémence,
La justice, le soin paternel, la prudence.   80
Enfant il a sucé ces royales vertus
(Dont rarement on voit les princes revêtus),
Du lait, et doux nectar des Muses et Minerve ;
Et en a fait au coeur précieuse conserve ;
Pour toujours, maintenir en santé et vigueur   85
Soi-même, et ses sujets, lesquels avec douceur,
Comme membres et fils, étant leur chef et père,
Traitera, les gardant du mal et vitupère.
Et craindre ne faudra que nouvelle grandeur,
Comme à d'autres ferait, lui face enfler le coeur,   90
Qui est très bien muni de vertu et constance
Contre les vents légers d'une vaine arrogance.
Joint aussi qu'il ne faut, que ce titre et pouvoir
Lui fasse de nouveau apprendre son devoir.
Car en l'art de régner il est déjà grand maître,   95
Puis qu'il vint à régner presqu'aussitôt qu'à naître.
Les peuples, que déjà il gouverne, compris,
Avec toi, Angleterre, en une même purpris,
Sous son sceptre royal, et son obéissance,
Des fruits de sa vertu reçoivent jouissance.   100
Vivant en tel repos, en biens si plantureux,
Qu'onques leurs devanciers n'ont été plus heureux.
Et bien que quelques-uns poussés d'envie et rage
En ces pays ont cuidé susciter maints orages :
Si a il tellement renversé leurs desseins,   105
Domptant et bridant ces furieux des freins,

Qu'il en demeure à eux perte, malheur et honte ;
À lui heur et honneur qui jusqu'aux astres montent.

    Aussi aux plus grands rois et princes d'outre-mer
Ses mérites le font tant prisé et aimé ;   110
Que d'eux il est jugé très digne d'être prince
Non d'un royaume seul, mais de maintes provinces.
Et s'acquitte envers tous si bien de son devoir,
Qu'heureux, et triomphant souhaitent de le voir.

    Mais surtout, Angleterre, il s'acquitte, et comporte   115
Si bien envers les tiens, qu'à eux jamais la porte
De sa grâce et faveur ne se vient à boucher.
Donc comme père, et prince, il leur doit être cher.
Plusieurs preuves ont eu par longue expérience
De sa grâce envers toi, bonté et patience,   120
Mais une seulement te veux ramentevoir
(Jaçoit que souvenance en dois toi-même avoir),
C'est que si proche étant de ton riche héritage,
Et du sexe viril ayant eu l'avantage,
Contre ta reine, ou toi il n'a rien attenté ;   125
Ains a bénignement toujours patienté,
Attendant le temps moeurs, auquel, sans préjudice
De ta reine vivant, il puisse entrer en lice.
Et quoi qu'aucun cerveau bouillant et furieux
Tâchaient de l'enaigrir, disant qu'injurieux   130
Envers lui quelques-uns de tes ministres furent,
Et que du tort reçu porter la peine dussent :
Ils n'ont su toutefois contre toi l'irriter,
Ni faire que comme eux vint à se dépiter.
Ains lorsqu'eux s'efforçaient d'émouvoir un orage   135
À l'encontre de toi, il empêcha leur rage ;
Et comme médecin sage, doux, et bénin,
T'apprêtas l'antidote encontre leur venin.
Quoi donc, très noble Dame, en oubli peux-tu mettre
Les mérites si grands de ton bon prince et maître ?   140
Savais-tu souhaiter autre que lui pour roi ;
Même qu'à lui de droit tu dois hommage et foi ?
Si à autre que lui présentais ta couronne
On te pourrait blâmer, comme ingrate et félonne :
Et folle et malheureuse on te pourrait juger,   145
Pour vouloir sans merci tes membres outrager.
Car si pour roi voudrais autre que lui t'élire,

De Dieu et des humains te pourchasserais d'ire,
Et sentirais l'effort de ce prince irrité,
Se vengeant justement de ton iniquité,   150
Alors, après plusieurs massacres et carnages,
Dégâts, saccagements, et infinis outrages,
De supporter le joug contrainte encore serais,
De quoi avec raison plaindre ne te savais.
Et qui être pourrait des autres la maîtresse,   155
Servante deviendrait en misère et détresse.
Alors ces fins renards, et ces terribles loups,
Qui contre le lion t'animeraient des coups,
Et blessures de mort sauver ne te sauraient,
Ains de leur propre peau seulement soin auraient,   160
Mais ca ne plaise à Dieu que leurs fiers appétits
Et desseins d'amasser trésor pour leurs petits
Te puissent onc induire à causer ta ruine,
Irritant contre toi la justice divine,
Et le juste dédain de ce prince vaillant,   165
Contraint de maintenir son droit en bataillant.
Mais ton Dieu sentira envers toi plus propice,
Si ne crois en Ce Cil, qui pousse d'avarice,
Et désir d'agrandir ses petits renardeaux
Veut, comme fin renard, rendre les autres veaux,   170
Tâchant de les armer par paroles fardées
Contre le grand lion, comme bêtes bardées.
Ne te laisse Angleterre à tel galant brider ;
Aincois agents d'honneur t'offre, pour te guider ;
Qui te conseilleront de te rendre et soumettre,   175
De gaieté de coeur à ton vrai prince et maître.
Sous lequel heur, honneur, et pouvoir croîtront
Et plusieurs pays aussi chef te reconnaîtront.
Et n'y aura puissance au monde, tant soit grande,
Qui, sans se repentir, encontre toi se bande,   180
Donc ce prince embrassant te jettera entre ses bras.
Ce faisant ton état ancien recouvrira
Aincois l'augmenteras, et en biens plantureuse
Seras de tous prisée et réputée heureuse.

DAME: Toi qui m'as mon état et devoir remontrés,   185
N'as qu'avec mon avis et désir rencontrés.
J'ouï déjà chanter de plusieurs les louanges

De ce prince, approchant de la vertu des anges
En continence, rare en tous, mais plus en grands,
Qui vont souvent sans bride après Vénus courant ;   190
Sa prudence bien mûre, hardiesse et vaillance ;
Sa justice, tenant en main juste balance ;
Sa douceur envers tous, sa largesse et bonté ;
Envers Dieu éternel sa rare piété ;
Ses dons d'un rare esprit, savoir et éloquence,   195
Desquels l'a enrichi le ciel en affluence ;
Avec tant d'autres los, que de les raconter
Serait comme vouloir les étoiles compter.
Dont je ne m'ébahis, si son nom lui présage
De l'honneur de *César* et d'*Arthus* le partage,   200
Et mon royaume aussi, par l'un d'eux conquis,
Et par l'autre de droit, comme héritage, acquis.
     Par quoi non seulement à lui je me veux rendre ;
Mais le supplie aussi mon sceptre vouloir prendre ;
Et régir mes enfants avec grâce et douceur,   205
Ainsi qu'il a fait ceux de l'Écosse, ma soeur,
Et ensemble avec nous bien fort lui recommande
Nos cousins, les enfants de notre soeur Irlande ;
Le priant, qu'il nous mette en paix et union,
Retranchant d'entre nous toute dissension,   210
Et toute occasion de haine et de rancune,
Afin que devenons trois sous un chef une.
Et sous ce même chef d'un accord si heureux
Puissions cueillir les fruits très doux et savoureux.
Rendant grâce à Dieu qu'envers nous pitoyable   215
Il nous ait élargi trésor si désirable.
Et le prions vouloir punir avec rigueur
Ceux, qui s'efforceront de nous troubler cette heure.
Enfin le supplions qu'à louable police
Il règne nos enfants par prudence et justice.   220

[Discourse on the Same Anagram, in the Form of a Dialogue between a
Partisan of the Public Good and a Lady Who Represents the Kingdom of
England] [T]

PARTISAN: Lady, you are renowned in all parts of the world, a victor in times
past and named princess not of the western seas and isles only; the kingdom of

flowers also crowns you. Open the door of your royal palace to the king who brings back you old fortune and honour to you.

LADY: Tell me who this king is. Who is there? PARTISAN: Caesar, Arthur.

LADY: Names of princes valued for their rare virtues, who by their good deeds achieved such great glory that their memory will flower without ever withering: one of these vanquished me and made me helpless and of all the other was my greatest monarch and king. However, how can they return to this place here when so much time has passed that their bodies have been reduced to ash and their spirits are gone up high into the heavens, triumphant immortals, changed into demi-gods?

PARTISAN: Indeed, they are not here in their own body and form, nor are they like those who, according to the great error of an old dreamer, human souls transmitted from body to body, arriving in healthier ones perfect in virtue, until their turn and time comes to be incarnated in the noblest body, as a final residence. If this were so, one could guess that Caesar would here be found with Arthur. However, only in this prince [James VI] do these two appear in life; in his name, fortune and virtue are they met.

LADY: This portend pleases me, but I also fear it, because the memory I have of him who bridled so many people with reins, including, amongst others, myself. Remembering this makes me become pale with fear.

PARTISAN: England, your fear is very vain and oversensitive. This Caesar is all yours; reassure your heart. After all, in this very island he was born: joined in him alone can be seen the native resemblance to Arthur and the other kings, his very noble forebears, who raised your name and honour to the heavens. Go! Go you foxes, and call him a foreigner, believing the state to be under the reign of your distaff.[13] What? The nearest heir, sure and virile, the issue of an English father, native to this very island; must it be that by you he is debarred as though he were a foreigner, and that royal estate is only to be found in your enclosed parks? Would you consider a king from this very island that was once all subject to the same crown to be a foreigner? Would it be unusual that once again these two members should unite under one leader? If you are founded on a royal ordinance as you claim, should you not balance every ordinance with the weight of equity, the true sense of the author and his intention? Or must one take in his place the currency of Cecil who aims for loot for himself rather than for the public good?

---

13   The foxes refer to the Cecils, in particular Lord Burleigh (see headnote).

One who would not have supported Henry or Edward was ordered by the will of these wolves and foxes to debar the lions of his race, to show himself an ass of very bad grace. However, you, very noble lady, having always shown a good and loyal heart towards your royal blood, will you allow the crowd of wolves, foxes and donkeys that we have bray and yell from their propane mouths against right and reason and all holy laws, to be able to set up kings at their pleasure? You will not do it, because I know that your brave nobility which has no less honour from faith than from prowess, will not enslave yourself to an unworthy yoke. On the contrary, you will elect the more sure and praiseworthy party, embrace as your king this magnanimous prince who deserves it, whom you esteem as a flower of nobility. Nor will your worthy populace either, who always had honour, in embracing the party who approaches right, want to abandon its faith and ancient loyalty to follow another party or cause than its own. If some mutineers dare to rebel and oppose him in his just cause, they will encounter in him the valour and good fortune of a Caesar in his punishing of their mad presumption. On the other hand, his loyal subjects who recognize him and who, without balking, submit themselves to him, will feel by the effects of the clemency, justice, paternal care and prudence of an Arthur. As a baby he suckled on these royal virtues (in which princes are rarely endowed), the milk and the sweet nectar of the Muses and of Minerva; and in his precious heart he stored up these things, to keep himself and his subjects in eternal health and vigour, subjects whom he will treat with mildness, like family members and sons (being their head and father), affectionately guarding them from evil and spite. And do not fear that new grandeur will swell his heart as it would others, because he is well furnished with virtue and constancy against the breezes of a vain arrogance. Added to this, he will not on account of that title and power have to learn his duty as if for the first time, because he is already a great master in the art of ruling, having come to rule almost as soon as he was born. The peoples whom he already governs comprise with you, England, the same domain; under his royal sceptre and his command, the fruits of his virtue are enjoyed. Living in such ease, so fortunate in good things, their ancestors' good times were not more felicitous. And although, in these countries, a few people driven by envy and rage, have thought to arouse many a storm, as he reversed their plans to such a degree, taming and bridling these furies with reins, halting them to their loss, misfortune and shame, his fortune and honour rises up to the stars.

In addition, the greatest kings and princes from overseas value and love his merits so highly that he is judged by them very worthy to be prince not alone of one kingdom, but of many a province, and he performs all of his duty so well that they wish to see him happy and triumphant.

Moreover, towards England and the English he especially acquits and conducts himself so well that he will never shut the door of his grace and favour to

them. Thus, like a father and prince he must be dear to them. By long experience, you have received many proofs of his grace, bounty and patience towards
you, but I wish to remind you of one only (although it is something that you
must recall yourself): that is, being so near to your rich patrimony, and the male
sex having had the advantage, he never made an attack against your queen or
against you, but with goodwill was ever patient waiting for the proper time
when, without prejudice to your living queen, he could come into contention.
And that none were there but hotheaded and furious brains stained with bitter-
ness who said offensive things against him; amongst these were some of your
ministers and they alone should be responsible for this wrong. Nevertheless, they
did not know how to provoke him against you nor to do anything so that like
themselves, he came to harm himself. Instead, at the time that they had exercised
their powers to stir up a storm against you, he stopped their rage, and like a wise
doctor, mild and benign, he gave you an antidote against their poison. How
then, very noble lady, can you forget such great merits of your good prince and
master? Would you know how to wish someone other than him as king, while
he has the right to your homage and faith? If you presented your crown to
someone other than him one could reprimand you for being an ingrate and traitor; one could judge you to be foolish and unfortunate thus to mercilessly wish
to affront your people. Because if you would like to elect another as king, and
to feel the will of this prince in his annoyance revenge himself justly on you for
your iniquity, after many massacres and slaughters, injuries, pillages and infinite
outrages, then you would still have to bear the yoke of compulsion, about
which you would not know how to complain reasonably, and she who could be
mistress of others, would become a servant in misery and distress. Then those
fine foxes and these awful wolves who impel your shots against the lion[14] would
not know how to save you from mortal injuries, but they would only take care
of their own skins; moreover, it would not please God that their proud appetites
and their plans to amass wealth for their children could one day mislead you to
bring about your ruin, stirring divine justice against you as well as the just disdain of this valiant prince, constrained to maintain his right in battle. But your
God will feel more favourably towards you if you do not believe in Cecil, who,
driven by greed and the desire of aggrandizing his little foxes, wishes, like a true
fox to turn the others into dumb animals, attempting through his loaded words
to incite them into taking arms, like barded beasts, against the lion their master.
England, do not let yourself be bridled by such wooing! Instead, I offer you men
of honour to guide you; who counsel you to render honour and submit with
gladness of heart to your true prince and master. You will grow under this happiness in honour and power and what is more many countries will recognize

14 James VI's coat of arms had a shield with a lion rampant (an element of the royal arms of
    Scotland).

you as leader. In addition, with this prince embracing you soundly in his arms there will be no earthly power, no matter how great, which without repenting themselves of it will band against you. Moreover, you will recover your previous state after which you will add to it, and in copious good things you will be esteemed by all and renowned as happy.

LADY: You who have shown me again my estate and duty, have not only answered my opinion and desire. I already hear sung the many praises of this prince, approaching the virtue of the angels in self-restraint, rare in everyone, but even more so in the great, who often wish to run after Venus without constraint. His seasoned prudence, bravery and valour; his justice, having in hand impartial scales; his mildness to all, his largesse and generosity; his uncommon piety towards the eternal God; his gifts of a rare spirit, knowledge and eloquence, with which heaven has enriched him in abundance; with so many other praises that to enumerate them would be like wishing to count the stars. I would not be dumfounded, therefore, if his name were an omen of his share in the honour of Caesar or Arthur, as well as in my kingdom (which was conquered by one of these two, and was the other's by right), acquired as an inheritance.

Consequently, not only do I wish to give myself to him, but I also beg him to desire to take my sceptre; to govern my children with grace and mildness just as he does those of my sister Scotland, and together with us strongly commend him to our cousins, the children of our sister Ireland; requesting him that he establishes us in peace and union, removing from amongst us all dissention as well as all occasion for hatred and rancour, in order that we become three united under one leader. Moreover, under this same leader of a harmony so fortunate, we might gather very sweet and succulent fruits, giving thanks to God who would enlarge such desirable treasure for us pitiable ones. And praying him to consent to punish rigorously those who aggravate the troubles of the times. Finally, we beg him [James] that with his praiseworthy rule he governs our children by prudence and justice.

4

Sertum poeticum in honorem Jacobi sexti (1600)

A Garland of Poems in Honour of James VI has two distinct subjects. The printed texts of Quin's *In nuptiis* derived from two earlier manuscript works and it seems likely that *Sertum poeticum* is also composed of two works The first part deals with James' right of succession to the English throne and in support of this Quin has recourse to themes from his *Anagrammata*, which most obviously appear in poems that can be seen as variants of their manuscript predecessors (since we know that James studied the latter carefully, it may not be fanciful to see some of his influence in their rewriting). *Sertum poeticum* retains the earlier references to King Arthur and its preface explains that the author wishes his use of anagrams of names as omens to be taken seriously. The preface also stresses 'the daily wars and disasters' of the Wars of the Roses between the houses of Lancaster and York. These were finally ended by the accession of Henry VII, a Lancastrian who married Elizabeth of York, and who founded the Tudor dynasty. Since Henry VII's daughter Margaret married James IV of Scotland, James VI also unites Lancaster and York in his person and is thus fitted to take the throne of England in peace.

The second part is a series of poems related to the Gowrie Conspiracy of August 1600 (so these verses were produced quickly and dealt with the latest court news). It is made up of epigrams and sonnets celebrating the king's escape from danger and praising those who came to their monarch's aid. The preface and most of the poems are written in Latin. In part this may have been with an eye to an international audience, as James wanted to encourage foreign support for his succession to Elizabeth I and *Sertum poeticum* is appropriately flattering about his virtues.

The Gowrie Conspiracy remains an enigmatic episode in James' life. Fortunately, since Quin's poetry is based on the official version of the events of August 1600, it is unnecessary to deal with all the speculations regarding what actually happened and, instead, some background to the alleged conspirators, the Ruthven family, along with the king's version of the events (as published *cum privilegio regio* by Robert Charteris), provide the necessary context for Quin's poems.[1]

---

1   *Gowreis Conspiracie: A Discourse of the Unnatural and Vyle Conspiracie Attempted against the Kings Majesties Person at Sanct-Johnstoun Upon Twysday the 5. Of August 1600* (Edinburgh: Robert Charteris, 1600). For the Gowrie Conspiracy, see Maurice Lee, Jr, 'The Gowrie Conspiracy Revisited' in Maurice Lee, Jr (ed.), *The 'Inevitable Union' and Other Essays on Early Modern*

Quin points out that the Ruthven family had produced three generations inimical to the king. Patrick, the third lord Ruthven (*c.*1520–66), and his son William (*c.*1543–84) were among the chief actors in the 1566 plot against Mary, Queen of Scots, during which her secretary, David Riccio, was dragged from the pregnant queen's presence and murdered in an adjoining room.[2] William, having been pardoned, rose in royal favour and became treasurer and the first earl of Gowrie. In 1582, however, during the Ruthven Raid, he seized the 16-year-old king and headed an administration that lasted a little less than a year. In 1583 he was suspected of plotting another coup and was found guilty of treason and witchcraft, for which he was beheaded.[3] On the death of William's eldest son, his second son, John (*c.*1578–1600), became the third earl. Gowrie was well-regarded by the English government and, during a visit to London, met the queen on a number of occasions (so his subsequent execution required justifications such as Quin's as long as the question of Elizabeth's succession was in the balance).[4] On returning to Scotland, Gowrie opposed some of the king's plans for taxation. It was at this stage that the events of the Gowrie conspiracy took place.

According to the king, on Tuesday 5 August, Alexander Ruthven, Gowrie's younger brother, approached him in the stables at Falkland Palace with a story of a suspicious, cloaked man carrying a large pot of gold whom Ruthven had met the previous evening. This gold was now secured at Gowrie House in St Johnstoune (Perth), and Ruthven asked that the king come and inspect it. James eventually believed that it was possible that 'it had been forraine gold, brought home by some Jesuites or practising Papistes',[5] so after the hunt he made up his mind and decided to accompany Ruthven to Gowrie House. The hunting party, which included the duke of Lennox and the earl of Mar, arrived in Perth in the early afternoon and Ruthven rode ahead to give his brother notice of the impending visit. At Gowrie House, after some delay, the king was given a meal in a private chamber while those accompanying him were fed in the hall. After this, the unarmed king and Ruthven went alone to a small room where a man waited whose dagger Ruthven took, holding 'the poynt of it to the kings breast'

Scotland (East Linton: Tuckwell Press, 2003), pp 99–115; Amy L. Juhala, 'Ruthven, John, Third Earl of Gowrie (1577/8–1600)', *ODNB*; Amy L. Juhala, 'Ruthven, Alexander, Master of Ruthven (1580?–1600)', *ODNB*. For other writers' treatment of the affair, see the references in the introduction to Adam King, *Ad Iacobum sextum Scotorum regem a nefaria fratrum Ruvenorum coniuratione divinitus servatum soteria (1601)*, ed. Jamie Reid Baxter, The Philological Museum, www.philological.bham.ac.uk/king (2008), accessed 11 Apr. 2014.

2   Alan Stewart, *The Cradle King: A Life of James VI & I* (London: Chatto & Windus, 2003), p. 9.

3   Sharon Adams, 'Ruthven, William, Fourth Lord Ruthven and First Earl of Gowrie (C.1543–1584)', *ODNB*.

4   The biographical information on the third earl is taken from Juhala, 'Ruthven, John', *ODNB*.

5   *Gowreis conspiracie*, sig. A3v. For an overview of the printing of King James' narrative, see the introduction to King, *Soteria* (2008).

and announcing his intension of revenging the execution of his father.[6] Before acting on this, leaving the king under guard, Ruthven went to consult his brother, but when he returned and made to bind the monarch, in the ensuing struggle James managed to call for assistance through an open window. In the courtyard below, the hunting party was assembling; having been told that James had already departed, they were about to follow him. Hearing the cries of their lord they fought to get to his prison. The first to reach him was the king's page, John Ramsay, who, followed by Sir Thomas Erskine, Dr Hugh Herries and a servant, gained access to a spiral staircase through an outer door. Ramsay attacked Ruthven, who, beaten back, was killed by Erskine. When Gowrie arrived on the scene he was run through by Ramsay. In the meantime, Lennox and Mar had spent half an hour frantically trying to break down a double door through which they had seen the king passing while they were dining. By the time they arrived, the fighting was over, and they found the king and his men kneeling down and 'his Majesty out of his own mouth thanked God of that miraculous deliverance and victory, assuring him selfe that God had preserved him from so dispaired a perril for the perfiting of some greater worke'.[7] The Ruthven brothers were tried posthumously: during the proceedings witnesses attested that Gowrie had dabbled in magic.[8] The malefactors' bodies were quartered.

Copy-text

Walter Quin, *SERTVM POETICUM,* | *IN HONOREM IA-* | *COBI SEXTI SERENIS-* | *SIMI, AC POTENTISSIMI* | *SCOTORUM REGIS,* | *A GVALTERO QVINNO DVBLINIENSI contextum.* Edinburgh: Robert Waldegrave, 1600. 4°. *ESTC* S110577 (three copies). BL, General Reference Collection C.175.d.42.

The coat of arms of James VI and Queen Anne appear on the verso of the title page. The text, albeit illegible in places, is available on *EEBO*.

[Qui tibi plus uni, quam cunctis, optime regum] [p. 1]

Qui tibi plus uni, quam cunctis, optime regum,
    Debeo, post superos, quos bonitate refers,
Grati animi saltem specimen dare gestio; nulla
    Sors mihi det referam cum tibi parte vicem.

6   *Gowreis conspiracie*, sig. B4r.
7   Ibid., p. sig. C2v.
8   Ibid., pp sigs C4r–C7r. Gowrie's interest in Hebrew recalls the work of Heinrich Cornelius Agrippa whom King James had referred to in the preface to *Daemonologie* (1591, 1597): *Selected Writings*, p. 151.

SERTVM POETICVM,

IN HONOREM IA
COBI SEXTI SERENIS-
SIMI, AC POTENTISSIMI
SCOTORVM REGIS,

A GVALTERO QVINNO DVBLINIENSI contextum.

EDINBVRGI,
EXCVDEBAT ROBERTVS WA
grave Typographus Regius 1600.
Cum Priuilegio Regio.

2 Title page of *Sertum poeticum* (© The British Library Board, General
Reference Collection, C.175.d.42).

Sed specimen tale est, dant quale, ob dona rependunt   5
    Aurea qui summo florea serta Iovi.
Sertum est hoc etiam, variis e floribus arte
    Textuit inculta quod mea Musa tibi.
Clara tuae gentis videas hic symbola, flores
    Ante alios, albam, purpureamque rosam.   10
Laeta tibique, tuisque notes hic omnia, laudes
    Iure tuas; superos et tibi propitios.
Ergo tui decoris monumentum hoc accipe sertum,
    Grati animi certum pignus idemque mei.[9]

[I Who Owe More to You Alone Than to Anyone Else] [T]

I who owe more to you alone than to anyone else, greatest of kings (with the exception of the gods, whom you imitate in benevolence), desire to at least give a token of my gratitude, since I have no opportunity to repay you in your own coin. This, then, is the sort of token given by those who repay supreme Jove for his golden gifts with floral garlands. This too is a garland made of various flowers, one which my Muse wove for you with uncultivated skill. Here you may clearly see the symbols of your family, the white and the red roses surpassing other flowers. You may note here everything that is pleasing to you and yours, the praises that you deserve, and the gods who are propitious to you. Accept, therefore, this garland as a testimony of your honour and a sure pledge of my gratitude and of me.

Praefatio [Sertum poeticum] [p. 2]

Virorum aliquot ingenii, ac literarum amoeniorum laude praestantium exemplo anagrammata quaedam, et carmina eadem explicantia, serto huic intexta, in lucem editurus pauca mihi praemittenda censui, quibus nonnulla in iis minus forte perspicua illustrentur. Inprimis vero, quod attinet ad ipsa nomina, quae anagrammatismis, et versibus occasionem, argumentumque praebuerunt, animadvertendum est non ea me sola serenissimi regis, ac principis eius filii, quae vulgo usurpantur, nomina delegisse (haec autem sunt Iacobus, et Henricus) sed iis etiam alia duo, cum gentilitio nomine Stuarto addidisse, nomina nimirum Caroli, et Friderici; quorum illud serenissimus rex a Carolo nono Galliarum rege, hoc illustrissimus princeps a Friderico rege Daniae in sacro lustrico accepit.

---

9   This poem is signed: 'Majestati tuae aeternum devinctus ac devotus, Gualterus Quinnus' ('Your Majesty's eternally obliged and devoted Walter Quin').

Quae ut adiungerem maxime visum est rationi consentaneum. Si quid enim ominis e nominibus capiendum, id potius ex primo impositis, ac gentilitiis (eorum, qui in hoc genere optime versati sunt, exemplo) quam (quod a nonnullis fieri video) e nominibus tantum vulgo usurpatis, honorumque titulis adiunctis eliciendum iudico. In nominibus autem ipsis nullam mihi permisi licentiam literam aliquam vel addendi, vel detrahendi, vel etiam immutandi nisi quod alicubi pro Stuarto, Steuartum (ut non raro scribi solet) ad anagrammata quaedam commodius excogitanda, scripserim; uti etiam eadem de causa Fredericum pro Friderico; quo utroque modo nomen hoc apud probatos authores scriptum deprehendi.

Primum anagramma occasionem praebet carmina quaedam pangendi de rosarum insignibus, ac de iure, quo rex noster serenissimus eadem sibi vendicat. Quae ut facilius intelligantur, sciendum est duas in Anglia fuisse familias e regia stirpe Eduardi Tertii oriundas, Eboracensem nimirum, et Lancastriam; quae de regni iure infestis animis, ac armis decertantes diversis insignibus dissidium hoc suum testatum esse voverunt, Eboracensi rosam albam, Lancastria vero rubram usurpante.

Nec prius ortis hinc diuturnis bellis, et cladibus, utrique familiae, ac toti regno funestis, finis, aut modus est impositus, quam Henricus septimus, Lancastriae familiae princeps, Elizabetam, Eduardi quarti filiam natu maximam, domus Eboracensis haeredem, felicissimis auspiciis coniugem sibi adscivit. Qua ratione factum est, ut utraque familia in unam coaluerit. Ex his vero nuptiis ortum habuerunt Henricus octavus, pater serenissimus reginae Elisabetae iam regnantis, et duae filiae. Quarum natu maior Margarita Iacobo quarto Scotorum regi, eoque vita functo, Archibaldo Douglassio Angusiae comiti nupsit. Huius autem Margaritae ex utroque coniugio haeres est rex hic noster serenissimus ac proinde proxime post reginam Elisabetam (in qua deficit Henri octavi proles) utriusque rosae insignia, et quicquid in utriusque familiae haeredem haereditario iure cadere potest merito sibi vendicat.

Secundi anagrammatis, et versuum illud explicantium sensus ex regiorum Scotiae insignium inscriptione Anglica 'in defense' (cuius haec altera 'nemo me impune lacesset', numismati Scotico impressa interpres esse potest) atque ex veteri illustrium virorum insignia et symbola in scutis exprimendi more facile elucescet. Hunc ego morem intuens, dum inter alia scuti regii insignia Anglica etiam recenseo, leones voco, quos plerique leopardos, scriptorum aliquot insignium authoritatem secutus.

In anagrammate tam Anglico, quam Gallico nominis serenissime regis occurrit nomen Arthuri, quem Britanniae regem fuisse celeberrimum historiae, ac monumenta vetera testantur.

Atque haec quidem ea sunt, quae in sequentibus minus fore perspicua iudicavi. Eo autem lubentius eadem explico, ut lector intelligat quae de rosis, et Arthuri nomine in anagrammatismis occurrunt serenissimo regi vel maxime congruere. Quamobrem si oblata mihi tam opportuna occasione, quae ad illum iure

spectant ominatus, ac precatus illi fuero, neminem non prorsus iniustum, et
iniquum iniquo id animo laturum mihi plane persuadeo.

Preface [*Sertum poeticum*] [T]

When, following the example of several men of better intellect and learning
who are outstanding in merit, I was about to publish some anagrams with poems
to explain them woven into this garland, I thought that I should add a few
things in a preface, by means of which some perhaps less evident matters among
them may be clarified. In particular, as regards the actual names that have provided the opportunity and argument for the anagrams and verses, one should
note that I did not choose only those names of the Most Serene King and his
son, the prince, that are commonly used (that is, James and Henry); rather I sup-
plemented them with another two along with the family name of Stuart; which
is to say, the names of Charles and Frederick (the former of which the Most
Serene King received from Charles IX, king of France, while the latter the Most
Illustrious Prince received from Frederick, king of Denmark, at his baptism). It
seemed a very sensible idea to add these, for if any omen should be drawn from
the names, I judge from the precedent of those who are well versed in this genre
that this should be elicited primarily from their first names and family names
rather than (as we see done by some) from the names that are commonly
employed and from the titles of honours added to them. In the names themselves I have not allowed myself the licence of adding or taking away a letter, or
even of changing one, except that I have written in some places 'Steuart' for
'Stuart' (as tends to be written quite often) in order to work out the anagrams
more conveniently. In the same way I have written 'Frederick' for 'Friderick',
which I have found written in both ways in reliable authors.

The first anagram provides an opportunity for composing some poems about
the insignia of roses and about the right by which the Most Serene King claims
these for himself. In order that these may be more easily understood, one should
know that there were two families in England springing from the royal line of
Edward III, namely that of York and that of Lancaster. These fought over the
authority of the kingdom with hostile wills and weapons and they solemnly
promised that their dispute be attested by different insignia, with York adopting
the white rose and Lancaster the red.

And no end or restraint was imposed upon the daily wars and disasters that
arose from this which were fatal to both families and to the whole kingdom,
before Henry VII (the prince of the family of Lancaster), joined Elizabeth (the
oldest daughter of Edward IV, heir to the house of York) to himself as wife by
the most happy auspices. This was done in order that each of the two families
came together as one. From this marriage Henry VIII, father of the Most Serene

Queen Elizabeth who now reigns, and his two daughters, took their origin. The elder of these two, Margaret, married James IV, king of the Scots, and after he had died, Archibald Douglas, the earl of Angus. The heir of this Margaret (from either of the marriages) is our Most Serene King, and next Queen Elizabeth (in whose person the line of Henry VIII ceases), thus King James rightfully adopted for himself the insignia of both roses and whatever could fall by the law of inheritance to the heir of either family.

The sense of the second anagram and the verses that explain it is from the English inscription on the royal coat of arms of Scotland, 'In defens' (the second motto, 'may no one harm me with impunity', can be deciphered on Scottish coins) and will easily be explained by the old custom of printing the insignia and symbols of famous men on coats of arms. Bearing in mind this custom, I also consider *inter alia* the insignia of the English royal coat of arms (that is, lions, which many people – following the authority of some famous writers – call leopards).

In the English and French anagrams on the name of the Most Serene King, the name of Arthur occurs, whom histories and ancient records testify was a very famous king of Britain.

These then are the things that I thought would be less clear in what follows. I am all the more ready to explain these matters in order that the reader understands that those things which appear in the anagrams pertaining to roses and the name of Arthur very closely fit the Most Serene King. For this reason, if so timely an opportunity be offered me, I shall have wished and prayed for the things that are rightly the king's own, I am fully persuaded that no one is so completely unjust and iniquitous as to exhibit this with an iniquitous spirit against me.

[Bis rosa Scotus] [sig. B1r][10]

Carolus Iacobus Stuartus
Cultu, aura bis rosa Scotus

Bis rosa cultu, aura Scotus, mireris ut ipsum
    Multimodi decoris nomen habere notas.
Bis rosa, cum praestet *cultu* virtutis, et *aura,*   5
    Quae quavis *aura* gratior inde fluit.
Bis rosa, candenti tam quae decorata notore est,
    Quam quae purpureo grata colore rubet.
Bis rosa, progenuit *rosa* quam Lancastria nexu
    Sacro Eboracensi conciliata *rosae.*   10
Bis rosa, ut Angligenam, Angligenum bis origine dicas

10 This section is headed 'Anagramata, in nomen serenissimi regis' ('Anagrams on the name of
     the Most Serene King'). The anagrams that follow are numbered.

Et decus, Anglorum est nam *rosa* primus honos.
Cum *rosa* sit toties et *cultu*, et amabilis *aura*,
   Sitque prior reliquis stirpe, et honore *rosis*;
Non illi tribues in amoena rosaria iure   15
   Ius summum, decoris praecipuumque locum?

[A Scottish Rose Twice Over] [T]

Charles James Stuart: a Scottish rose twice over, in cultivation and in vital air.

A Scottish rose twice over, in cultivation and in vital air, such that one is amazed at the marks of manifold honour in his very name. A rose twice over, since he is outstanding in his cultivation of virtue and his vital air flows from him more pleasantly than any other breeze. A rose twice over, both that one which is decorated with a bright white gleam and that one which glows pleasantly with a red colour. A rose twice over, which the Lancastrian rose engendered, joined by a sacred bond to the rose of York. A rose twice over: you would say it is English-born (English-born twice over through its origin and nobility), for the rose is the foremost honour of the English. Since he is a rose which is dear in its cultivation and vital air so many times over, and is more distinguished than other roses in family and honour, will you not rightly assign to him in lovely rose-gardens the utmost right and the principal position of honour?

[Clarus scuto abavis ortus] [sig. B1v]

Carolus Jacobus Stuartus
Clarus scuto abavis ortus

Clarus scuto abavis ortus vero omine dici
   Nonne, ut transposito nomine, iure potes?
Profiteare tui cum scuti in fronte tibi esse   5
   Pectus, et arma, quibus ius tueare tuum:
Natus et ipse atavis cum rex tot regibus alti
   Sanguinis in scuto symbola clara geras.
Hinc tibi maiorum centum, septemque gerenti
   Sceptra Caledoniae sit leo grande decus.   10
Cui cumulum ingentem superaddunt inde leones,
   Angli quos abavi regni habuere notas,
Cumque rosis horum candentia lilia regni
   Francorum, generis symbola prisca tui.
Nec citharas, scuto quas addit Hibernia, trinas   15
   Indecores decori quis putet esse tuo,

Haec regni antiqui cum sint insignia, regum
  Unde Caledoniae fluxit origo vetus.
His abavis auctus, clarisque insignibus, heros
  Inclute, grateris tu tibi iure, licet,   20
Hoc tibi sed gratere magis, virtutibus addas
  Maiorum decori quod decus ipse tuis.

[Illustrious in Coat of Arms and Ancestors] [T]

Charles James Stuart: illustrious in coat of arms and ancestors.

Without doubt by a true omen, as well as by the transposition of your name, you can truly be said to be illustrious in coat of arms and ancestors. Since you announce on the front of your arms the breast and the weapons by which you defend your right; since, furthermore, you are born from so many kings of high blood and bear these clear symbols on your arms; therefore let a lion be the great honour of Scotland for you who bear the sceptres of one hundred and seven forefathers.[11] The English lions provide a grand addition, which your ancestors had as their kingdom's markers, and which along with the roses and the white lilies of the kingdom of the French are the ancient symbols of your race. Nor would the three lyres, which Ireland adds to the coat of arms, be thought unbecoming of your honour, since these are the insignia of this ancient kingdom, from which the venerable origin of Scottish kings emanated.[12] Made greater by these ancestors and distinguished insignia, renowned hero, you may rightly congratulate yourself, but you should congratulate yourself more for adding honour to your ancestors' honour through your own virtues.

[Orta salus ubi tu coruscas] [sig. B2r]

Carolus Iacobus Stuartus
Orta salus ubi tu coruscas

Ceu gemini fratres, atroce minante procella
  Naufragium, nautis sidera grata micant:
Sic quoque tu populis, quos iactavere tumultus,   5
  Affulgens affers, numinis instar, opem.
Arguit hoc diuturna quies, regnante fruuntur
  Qua te Scotigenae post fera bella tui.

11 The list can be found in the Scottish history of James' tutor: George Buchanan, *Rerum Scoticarum historia* (Edinburgh: Alexander Arbuthnot, 1582).
12 For the conquering of Scotland by the Irish King Fergus, see the headnote.

Eventurum aliis populis hoc auguror ipsum,
  Qui iam naufragii caeca pericla timent.   10
Augurer id faciunt data iam documenta, elementis
  Quodque tui felix nominis omen inest.
Nempe his *orta salus ubi tu*, rex clare, *coruscas*
  Dicitur: o tua sit lux diuturna precor.

[Prosperity Arises Where You Gleam] [T]

Charles James Stuart: prosperity arises where you gleam.

Just as the twin brothers (the stars that are welcome to sailors),[13] gleam when a
fierce squall threatens shipwreck, your radiance brings divine help to a people
whom disturbances have thrown into chaos. This is proven by the present peace
(succeeding fierce wars), that your Scotsmen enjoy during your reign. I foretell that
this will befall the other peoples who now fear the unseen dangers of shipwreck.
Therefore, I predict that the proofs that have now been given do this, as does the
happy omen in the letters of your name. Of course it is said of you, famous king,
that prosperity arises where you gleam: I pray that your light be long-lasting!

[Tu victor salvus, carus stabis] [sig. B2v]

Carolus Iacobus Stuartus
Victor salvus, carus stabo

Tu victor salvus, carus, rex inclyte, *stabis*:
  Nempe hoc a superis nominis omen habes.
Victor ovans virtute tuos pessundabis hostes,   5
  Inde relaturus sceptra, perenne decus.
Salvus, et incolumis quaevis discrimina vinces,
  Exortus variis gentibus ipse salus.
Carus eris superis, *carus* mortalibus: ipsa
  Flectentur meritis ferrea corda tuis.   10
Stabis et ut defixa solo radicibus altis,
  Ac caelo attollens florida palma comam.

---

13 King James had written of 'the Seamans starres, and there Twinnis bright' in his translation of
    Du Bartas' *The Uranie, or Heavenly Muse* (in *The Essayes of a Prentise*, 1584): James VI and I, *The
    Poems of James VI of Scotland*, ed. James Craigie (2 vols, Edinburgh: William Blackwood &
    Sons, 1955, 1958), i, p 21, l. 50.

[Unharmed Victor, You Remain Beloved] [T]

Charles James Stuart: as the unharmed victor, I will remain beloved.

You, the unharmed victor, famous king, will remain beloved. Truly, you have this omen in your name from the gods. Glorying as victor, you will ruin your enemies by your virtue and you will thereby regain the sceptre, an everlasting honour. You will conquer all dangers, unharmed and unimpaired, having sprung forth as the symbol of prosperity from various races. You will be beloved of the gods and mortals: even iron hearts will be swayed by your merits. You will also remain fixed in the ground by deep roots, like a verdant palm raising its foliage to the heavens.

[A Peerless Pearl and Prince Claims Arthur's Seat][14] [sig. B3r]

Charles James Stuart
Claimes Arthur's seat

A peerless pearl and prince *claims Arthur's seat*
Borne to the same by heaven's most high decree,
Thereon to sit and rule, as monarch great,   5
In whom all righteous claims united be.
The highest branch of Albion's royal tree
He is, and first of roses white, and red;
Whose happy union made all England free
From bale and mischief, which their discord bred.   10
To win his right his courage void of dread
With God and man's assistance he shall bend;
And under foot as conqueror shall tread
The pride of such as shall with him contend.
    So to King *Arthur's seat* attain he shall   15
    Whereto by name and claim the heavens him call.

[Qui est là? Arthus sacré, roi de la Grande Bretagne][15] [sig. B3v]

Charles Jaques Stuart
Qui est là ? Arthus sacré

Qui est là ? Arthus sacré, roi de la Grande Bretagne,
Surmontant l'autre *Arthus* en vertu et bonheur ;

14 Compare 'A Worthy Peerless Prince Claims Arthur's Seat' in *Anagrammata*, p. 51. For the
    'peerless pearl', see Mt 13:45–6.
15 Compare 'Qui est là? César, Arthus, princes de grands honneurs' in *Anagrammata*, p. 52.

[74]

À qui par don du ciel ait apprêté l'honneur 5
De commander partout de la Norvège à l'Espagne.
    Le pêcheur orcadais, et de la grande campagne
L'île au midi bornant le riche moissonneur,
Et la patrie irlandaise de gaieté de coeur
Hommage lui feront ; si grand heur l'accompagne. 10
    Par lui seul de ces trois s'éteindra le discord,
Source de leur malheur, et un heureux accord
Fera fleurir sous lui leurs campagnes, et leurs villes.
    Adonc d'eux à bon droit doit être désiré,
Le règne bienheureux de cet *Arthus sacré*, 15
Par droit, et par destin grand monarque des îles.

[Who Is There? Sacred Arthur, King of Great Britain] [T]

Charles Jacques Stuart: who is there? Sacred Arthur.

Who is there? Sacred Arthur, king of Great Britain, surpassing the other Arthur in virtue and good fortune; one who by heavenly gift is prepared to command honour everywhere from Norway to Spain.

The Orkney fisherman, the wealthy harvester of the great plain bounded in the middle island, and the homeland of the Irish, with joy of heart render him homage with great happiness.

By him alone will these three extinguish their discord, the source of their misfortune; and a joyful harmony will blossom under him in their countrysides and towns.

Thus, they have the right to wish for the fortunate reign of this sacred Arthur, by law and by destiny the great monarch of the islands.

[L'accorto, giusto re ama, o nobil regno][16] [sig. B4r]

Carlo Giacomo Stuarte
Ama l'accorto, giusto re

L'accorto, giusto re ama, o nobil regno,
Ch'il ciel ti da per tuo ben e onore,
Re tuo per dritto, e per merto e valore 5
Più di qualunqualtro d'esserlo degno.
    Amalo, ch'ei ti sia appoggio e sostegno

---

16 Compare 'L'accorto, giusto re ama, o Inghilterra' in *Anagrammata*, p. 50.

Ne rischi, e rimedio ad ogni dolore:
Ei ti sia qual' nocchier, chi senz' errore
Conduce in porto il travagliato legno.   10
    La prudenza sua ti sia buon timone
Per reggerti, e per indirizzarti al porto
Sua giustizia per calamìta avrai.
    Però se brami salvo e senza guai
Giunger in buon porto, egl'è ben ragione   15
Ch'ami questo tuo *re giusto, e accorto*.

[Love the Wise, Just King O Noble Kingdom] [T]

Charles James Stuart: love the wise, just, king.

Love the wise, just king O noble kingdom, whom heaven gives you for your
good and honour, your king by right, and by merit and valour, more worthy
than any other to be so.

    Love him, that he may be your prop and upholder in danger, and cure for
every sorrow: and let him be to you as the helmsman, who unerring, guides into
port the battered vessel.

    Let his prudence be to you a good rudder to govern you, and in directing
you to the port you will have his justice as a lodestone.

    Therefore if you long to arrive safe and trouble-free in a good harbour, there
is strong reason that you should love this wise just king of yours.

[Arthuri in sede futurus crescis] [sig. B4v][17]

Henricus Fridericus Steuartus
Arthuri in sede futurus crescis

Innumeris proavis, quos ampla Britannia reges,
    Gallia quosque habuit, nobilis orte puer;
Regum et quos coluit, cum Teutone, Cimber, Hibernus   5
    Quos memoratque suos, inclyta progenies,
Caelitum munus, magnorum dulce parentum
    Pignus, regnorum spesque decusque trium
Orbis flos, et honos, *Arthuri in sede futurus*
    Crescis, id a superis nominis omen habes.   10

17 This section is headed 'Anagrammata, in Nomen Illustrissimi Principis' (Anagrams on the
    Name of the Most Illustrious Prince).

Crescis, ut occulto quam crescere cernimus aevo
    Praecipuum nemoris planta futura decus.
Qui iam principibus praefulget laude coaevis,
    Crevit in immensum sic pater ante tuus.
Ille tibi *Arthuri* sceptrum, cum sede, parabit;   15
    Ille tibi morum, regni erit ille typus.
Ocia longaevus populis cum fecerit ille,
    Auxerit et superum clarus honore choros,
Arthuri solium scandes tu nomine nonus,
    Invictaque geres sceptra paterna manu,   20
Et patrem referes meritis, virtutibus, aevo:
    Augurium eventu sit precor usque ratum.

[You Grow Up Destined for the Throne of Arthur] [T]

Henry Frederick Stuart: you grow up destined for the throne of Arthur.

From innumerable ancestors, magnificent kings of Britain and France, have you sprung noble boy, rulers venerated by the Teuton, the Cimbri and the Irishman.[18] You are counted as their own, a noble progeny, a gift of the gods, a sweet pledge of great parents and the hope and glory of three kings. You are the flower and honour of the world; you grow up destined for the throne of Arthur: you have this omen in your name given by the gods. You grow up like a plant which we see grow in its hidden age, fated to be the outstanding glory of the forest. You now shine with praise from your fellow princes, just as your father before you grew great. He will prepare the sceptre and throne of Arthur for you: he will be the model for your character and rule. Since through his long life he brought peace to his people and through his fame he increased the honour of the chorus of gods, you will ascend the throne of Arthur as the ninth in name bearing your father's sceptres in your invincible hand, and you will resemble your father in your merits, virtues and longevity: I pray that this prophecy will be for ever fulfilled in its outcome.

[Suis charus fidenter recturus] [sig. Cr]

Henricus Fredericus Stuartus
Suis charus fidenter recturus

Servandi incolumes sese, populosque regendi
    Ad libitum reges anxia cura tenet.

18 The Teutons and the Cimbri were Germanic tribes. The latter were from north Jutland and so here recall the Danish family of Queen Anne. See *OCD*.

Hinc numerosus eos ambit, stipatque satelles,   5
    Immensae hinc illis accumulantur opes,
Urbibus hinc arcesque hinc agris castra minantur:
    Fisci hinc, lictorum, carnificisque metus.
Sed non praesidis his, vel terroribus aeque
    Rex est ac populi tutus amore sui,   10
Ergo Britannorum imperii sibi regis haeres
    Gratetur merito, spem foveatque bonam.
Elogium cuius virtutis tale, futuri
    Ac regni auspicium nominis omen habet.
Namque *suis charus fidenter* dicitur ille   15
    Recturus, fausto nominis augurio.

[Dear to His People and Destined to Rule Courageously] [T]

Henry Frederick Stuart: dear to his people and destined to rule courageously.

Kings are gripped by the uneasy cares of keeping themselves from harm and of ruling their peoples as they please, hence numerous attendants surround and crowd them, and immense wealth is accumulated by them; therefore, citadels encroach on cities and war camps encroach on fields and there is a dread of taxation, of magistrates and of the executioner. However, a ruler is not as safe by means of these defences or fears as he is through the love of his people. Thus the king's heir, the heir to the British empire, deservedly congratulates himself and fosters good hope. This praise of virtue and prophecy of rule is contained in the omen of his name, for he is said to be destined to be dear to his people and to rule courageously, in accordance with the happy augury of his name.

[Fierce, Hardy, Earnest, True, Thou Named Art] [sig. Cv]

Henrie Frederic Steuart
Fierce, hardi, earnest, true

Fierce, hardy, earnest, true, thou named art,
O prince extract from kings of high degree;
Whose lion as the heavens to thee impart;[19]   5
So they a lion's heart impart to thee:
That thou thereby mayst *fierce* and *hardy* be

19 The lion refers to the prince's coat of arms.

The pride and fury of thy foes to tame;
    And keep thine own from all annoyance free:
Wherein, and in all actions worthy fame   10
Thou shalt be *earnest*, as foreshoweth thy name.
True shalt thou be, as doth the same declare.
In actions truth shall keep thee free from blame:
Truth of thy words, and thoughts shall be the square.†
    Thus being found, *fierce, hardy, earnest, true*,   15
    Thou shalt win glory to thy merits due.

[Fruit hérité rendras, prince sorti d'un père] [sig. C2r]

Henri Frédéric Stuart
Fruit hérité rendras

Fruit hérité rendras, prince sorti d'un père,
Et de l'estoc royal de tant des grands aïeux.
De la vertu desquels les enlevant aux cieux,   5
Comme de leur état, seras propriétaire.
    Mais de tous ceux desquels le fruit tant salutaire
Tu viens à hériter, rapporteras le mieux
Ton père, et le septième *Henri* victorieux,
Qui t'a laissé son nom, et sceptre héréditaire.   10
    Ainsi qu'eux, tu rendras le doux *fruit hérité*
De justice, et bonté, de paix avec planté,
De tous biens aux nations de cette Grande Bretagne.
    Comme un surgeon fruitier, qui en haut s'étendant
De son estoc natif force, fruit va rendant   15
Pour nourrir ceux, desquels il orne la campagne.

[You Will Yield Inherited Fruit] [T]

Henri Frederick Stuart: you will yield inherited fruit.

You will yield inherited fruit, prince sprung from a father, and of the royal stock of such great ancestors. You will be the possessor of the virtue which, like their state, they won from heaven.

    However, of all those of whom the fruit is so beneficial from whom you will inherit, you will profit most from your father and from the victorious Henry VII who left you his name and his hereditary sceptre.

Together with them you will yield the sweet inherited fruit of justice, goodness and peace with stability, for the good of all of the nations of this Great
Britain.

[You are] like a fruit sapling which stretches itself on high from its trunk with
its native force, yielding fruit to nourish those for whom it adorns the countryside.

[Nympha Caledoniae] [sig. C2v]

Elisabeta Stuarta
Salutaris, et beata

Nympha Caledoniae natarum maxima regis
    Optatum et felix nominis omen habet.
Namque *salutaris* ferturque *beata* futura   5
    Nomine, cum divis laudem habitura parem.

[Maiden of Scotland] [T]

Elizabeth Stuart: prosperous and blessed.

The greatest maiden of the daughters of the king of Scotland has a desirable and
prosperous omen in her name. For she is said to be destined to be prosperous
and blessed in name, and to have praise that is equal to that of goddesses.

[A Blest Sweet Heart, O Nymph of Noble Kind] [sig. C2v]

Elisabeth Stewart
A blest sweet heart

A blest sweet heart, O nymph of noble kind,
Thou art, as showeth thy name by presage clear;
A blessing by the heavens to earth assigned,   5
As heart to be accounted sweet and dear.
A blest sweet heart, thy nurse and such as near
Were to thy cradle gan† thee first to greet.
Thy royal parents oft with smiling cheer
Have named their *heart* both *blest*, and *sweet*.   10
This use they also for a greeting meet

Who now thy beauty though in blossom see:
But when the same by growth shall be complete,
And shall with virtues rare adorned be;
    Then all, but one, a king, thine above all,   15
    A *blest sweet heart* shall thee account and call.

De illustrimo principe primum ex arce Sterlinensi in publicum prodente [sig.
C3r]

Qua primum egreditur tectis regalibus hora
    Spectandus princeps, arva et aprica petit,
Venantem augustum patrem comitatur, alumnum
    Qui cupit agnoscat Cynthia casta suum.
Venator felix, tanto auspice, prodit eunti   5
    Tres quoque ductores omnia fausta ferunt.
Casu hinc Angligenae, et simul accurrentis Hiberni,
    Ducitur inde equitans Scotigenaeque manu.
Auspice nempe velut patre, et ducentibus istis,
    Primum exit, captas spectat ovansque feras: 10
Sic tria sceptra, quibus trinis hi gentibus orti
    Ductores subsunt, auspice patre, geret.

On the Most Illustrious Prince's First Entry into Public from Stirling Castle [T]

At the time he first leaves the royal palace and seeks the fields and sunny spots,
the prince accompanies his august father – he who wants chaste Cynthia to recognize him as her heir – as he hunts.[20] The fortunate hunter with great auspices
leads forth three commanders who bring with them all prosperity: as he rides it
happens that an Englishman, and hastening beside him, an Irishman, and a
Scotsman lead him by the hand. Of course, when with his father as protector
and with these leaders, he first came out, he observed and rejoiced in the animals he had captured: thus with his father as protector he will bear the three
sceptres, sprung from these three races.

[In 19 Iunii] [sig. C3v]

In 19 Iunii serenissimi regis. 19 Februarii illustrissimi principis eius filii. 19
Augusti filiae eiusdem natu maioris, ac 19 Novembris filii natu minoris diem

20 'Cynthia' = Elizabeth.

natalem, ultimum hunc etiam regis serenissimi ac serenissimae reginae congressu
primo notabilem.

Natalis numero tibi par, natisque duobus,
    Et natae, o heros, lux data mensis erat.   5
Quaeque tuo nato lux candida mense Novembri
    Posterius genito lucis origo fuit,
Aspectu alloquio, gratisque amplexibus ante
    Coniugis ut primum tu fruerere dedit
Illa novem decies, cum luna secuta calendas   10
    Viseret Antipodas, fulsit amoena dies.
Haud reor augurio numerus caret ille secundo:
    Est nec enim samii vana sophia senis.
Hic iungit numerus decadi nonum: illius ingens
    In paribus laus est, huius in imparibus.   15
Namque monas decadis velut est coeuntis origo;
    Sic numeris auctis est et origo decas.
Qui deni a totidem geniis volvuntur in axe
    Orbes vim decadis, grande decusque notant.
Nonus in imparibus numeris plenissimus exit: 20
    Utque trias felix, sic quoque trina trias.
Hunc ornant numerum genii super astra beati;
    Quorum ait esse novem fama vetusta choros.
Commendant pariter Musae; quibus addito Phoebum:
    Ac decimus nono fiet honoris apex.   25
Sive paris spectes igitur, sive imparis omen;
    Seu magis hic numerus iunctus uterque placet:
En superi, rex magne, tibi, prolique vicissim
    Hoc numero spondent maxima quaeque tuae.
Pignus et esse sui voluere favoris, eodem   30
    Quod toties numero teque, tuosque notent.

[On 19 June] [T]

On the birthday of the Most Serene King on 19 June; of the Most Illustrious
Prince, his son, on 19 February; of his elder daughter on 19 August; of his
younger son on 19 November; this last too being notable for the first union of
the Most Serene King and Most Serene Queen.[21]

---

21 Quin is correct in saying that the king was born on 19 June, Prince Henry on 19 Feb., Princess
    Elizabeth on 19 Aug. and King Charles I on 19 Nov., although some sources give 16 Aug. as

The same birthday in number of the month has been given to you, O hero, to your two sons and to your daughter. This splendid day of the month was the origin of life for the son subsequently born in the month of November. Before this, it allowed you to enjoy for the first time the appearance, conversation and welcome embraces of your wife. That lovely day had shone nineteen times, when the moon, following the Calends[22] saw the Antipodes; that number is not, I think, devoid of a second prophecy, for it is not the idle wisdom of the old man of Samos.[23] This number joins nine to ten: there is great praise for the former in even and for the latter in odd things. For one is just like the start of the ten that goes with it, and so is ten the beginning of larger numbers. Those ten orbs which are turned by so many deities on their axis denote the force and great glory of ten. Nine comes out most fully in odd numbers, and just as three is prosperous, so also is three times three. The blessed deities furnish this number above the stars, of which ancient fame says there are nine choruses. The [nine] Muses likewise commend this, to whom Phoebus should be added, and ten will be the peak of honour for nine. Therefore, you will see either the omen of the even or the odd; either number added to these is the more pleasing. Look, great king, the gods promise by this number all of the greatest things to you and your offspring in turn, and they have wished it to be the pledge of their favour that they designate you and yours so often by the same number.

De tumultibus aliquot regis serenissime virtute, eloquentia, et prudentia sedatis
[sig. C4r]

Manibus ore canem infestum, rictuque trifauci
    Tres tribus heroes perdomuere modis.
Robore prostratum domuit Tirynthius heros,
    Invitum subigens vincula dura pati.
Sic demulsit eum dulcedine carminis Orpheus,   5
    Stratus ut illius sterteret ante pedes.
Illum Anchisiadi subiecit provida cura,
    Offas in rabidam coniiciendo gulam.
Macte heros animi, tribus his heroibus unum
    Te triplici hac praestas tu quoque laude parem;   10
Magnanimum pectus, facundum os, provida cui mens
    Aemula dat Stygii monstra domare canis.

the date of Elizabeth's birth: see Ronald G. Asch, 'Elizabeth, Princess (1596–1662)', *ODNB*.
22 The calends is the first day of the month.
23 Aristarchus of Samos, third-century BC astronomer.

On Some Disturbances Quelled by the Virtue, Eloquence and Prudence of the Most Serene King[24] [T]

In three ways, three heroes utterly subdued the dog that ravaged the underworld with his mouth and threefold jaw:[25] the Tirynthian hero[26] subdued him when he was laid low by Hercules' strength, overcoming one that was unwilling to endure harsh chains; so did Orpheus soothe him with the sweetness of song, so that when the dog was laid before his feet Orpheus could proceed [into Hades]; and the prudence of Aeneas overcame him by throwing morsels of food into his ravenous throat. Hero of outstanding spirit, you alone show yourself to be equal to these three heroes by your threefold hope. Your magnanimous spirit, eloquence and prudence allow you to conquer the opposing monsters of the dog of Styx.

Carmen gratulatoriam coram serenissime rege in gymnasio S. Salvatoris Andraeapoli recitatum [sig. C4v]

Qualis Apollo, diu populo responsa petenti
Divina ex adytis fundentem oracula sacris
Regis quem Pataraea, Clarosve, aut Delphica tellus
Detinuit, tandem curarum taedia longa
Lenire exoptans secessus quaerit amoenos   5
Parnassi, Aonias ultro invisitque sorores;
Illae adventantem laetum paeana canentes
Excipiunt, meritoque Deum venerantur honore:
Talis ades nobis, sibi quos dignatur alumnos
Annumerare chorus, tu, praestantissime regum,   10
Prae cunctis aliis Phoeboque, adamate choroque;
Ipse etiam redamans Phoebumque chorumque vicissim,
Post data iura tuis, et pacis commoda parta,
Qua populos inter longe, lateque iacentes,
Quos fera bella premunt regum ambitione nefanda,   15
Munere sola tuo fruitur gens Scotia felix:
O felix nimium, sua si bona norit, et unde

---

24 As Jamie Reid Baxter has pointed out to me, this refers to the rioting in Edinburgh that began on 17 Dec. 1596, 'which was in reality an attempted coup d'état spread out over several days': Julian Goodare, 'The Scottish Presbyterian Movement in 1596', *Canadian Journal of History*, 45 (2010), 21–48.

25 Cerberus, the three-headed dog that guards the entrance to Hades.

26 Hercules.

Proveniant recolat memor illa Deique, tuique.
    Cum reliquas regni te non piguisset obire
Pervigili cura partes, et nostra vicissim   20
Est tibi visa tuae schola pars haud infima curae,
Hic te nempe iuvat plantaria crescere pulchra:
Quae foveat Phoebi calor, irriget unda perennis
Castalidum fontisque quaeque erigat aura favoris
Dia tui, fructus ut laude ferentia dignos   25
Virtutum reliquo sint firma columina regno,
Fulcra tuis rebus, laudum ornamenta tuarum.
    Et favor iste tuus (nihil ambigo) submovet acres
Pectoribus stimulos iuvenilibus: ardor at ingens
His iuga virtutum scandendi celsa tuarum   30
Crescat ab exemplo virtutum: namque monarcha
Cum prius imperio fueris cogente solutus,
Quam cunis (fieri qua libertate iuventus
Pronior in vitium solet, et male sane teneri
Sirenum illecebris) studium virtutis, et artes   35
Es tamen ingenuas amplexus sponte: nec illas
(Grex ut rudit iners) indignas esse putasti
Principis ingenio; sed non cessante labore
A reptas avide didicisti: nec tibi primis
Castalidum fontem sat visum atingere labris,   40
Pectoris inde sitim ni saepe bibendo levasses.
Unde sit ut dulci tibi iam videamus ab ore
Nectar, et Ambrosiam placide manare, recessu
Seu tibi fons Pegasi saliat sub pectoris imo.
Quid, quod et astrictis numeris te vena benigna   45
Ingenii summis exaequat laude poetis;
Culta perorantis nec non facundia linguae
Aequiparat, quibus applaudens dat concio palmam?
Seu iuvat aut populi fando sedare tumultus,
Seu quid religio, quid rectum poscat, et usus,   50
Aut mystas dubios, dubiumve docere senatum
Eloquii vis magna tui: sed maior habenda
Vis sophiae praestans, animique sagacis acumen;
Luminis et radiis mens illustrata superni,
Suspiciens caelum, rectum illuc iterque capessens.   55
Ut cynosura, tibi lux haec divina refulget;
Quae te per scopulos, syrtes, aestusque tuetur
Incolumem, nec te Sirenum cantibus ullis,

Circaeisve dolis captum, Scyllaeve furentis
Latratu infesto discrimina saeva minanti   60
Attonitum e recto patitur deflectere cursu
Tutius utque tuos tecum deducere possis
In placidum portum, regnandi caelitus artes
Sunt tibi concessae, virtutum et copia, dotes
Quae tanto superant reliquorum pondere; quanto   65
Tu tibi subiectis, fortunae culmine praestas.
Has ego si decorare putem me posse canendo,
Illi sim similis qui lychno adiungere posse
Splendorem Phoebi radiis se somniet amens.
   Haec cano pauco tamen non hac spe lusus inani,   70
Sed quia iusserunt te compellare Camenae
Dignatum subiisse suum, rex optime, fanum,
Teque insigne suis monstrare exemplar alumnis,
Ad iuga Parnassi quem contendendo sequantur;
A quo nec dubitent Musarum dotibus aucti   75
Praemia se meritis, et digna labore laturos.
   Macti animis, o vos, divini Heliconis alumni,
Ad decus accendat vos, et virtutis amorem
Principis exemplum, quo secula nulla tulerunt
Conspicuumve magis, magis aut imitamine dignum.   80
Vos favor illius, vos praemia certa laborum,
Utilibus patriae quae Marte, vel arte futuris
Apparat ad tantum decus excitet, ipse benigne
Principis aspectus, grata et praesentia reddat
Vos alacres merito subeunda ad culmina Pindi,   85
Doctae ubi dent vobis cytharas, et plectra sorores,
Regis ut eximii decus immortale canatis.
   Sed tibi quas grates referemus, amabilis heros,
Pro meritis in nosque tuis, doctasque Camenas;
Haud equidem reor ingratas tibi posse referri   90
Carminibus grates: nobis sed carmina desunt
Digna tuis meritis, digna auribus: auspice Phoebo,
O utinam nobis te pangere digna liceret,
Teque tua Phoebo digna celebrare Camena.
Improbus at fundo cur irrita vota. Precari   95
Quae tibi, quae populis fausta et felicia multis
Auguror eventura iubet pietasque, fidesque;
Nempe tuo generi quae regia sceptra, tuisque
Debentur meritis, ea mox tibi Caelitus aucto

Adveniant, altoque animo sors undique quadrans: 100
Ut virtute tua quaecunque Britannica regna
Aut mala divexant, terrentve aliunde pericula
Propuliata tuos mox avertantur in hostes:
Auspice te populis ut oborta luce salutis,
Alma hos longaevus placidaque in pace gubernes: 105
Serus ut ad superos evectus, et aurea nato
Sceptra tuo tradens, linguis, plectrisque canoris
Vox ubicunque sonet, vel Musa, canaris in aevum.

A Congratulatory Poem Recited in the Presence of the Most Serene King in St Salvator's College in St Andrews [T]

Just as Apollo (who occupied the land of Lycia, Claros or Delphi as he poured out divine oracles from the holy sanctuaries to those who had been protractedly seeking answers), eventually chooses to soothe the long-standing weariness of his cares by seeking out pleasant retreats, and of his own accord visits the Aeonian sisters[27] who happily receive him when he arrives, singing their paeans, and worshiping God with rightful honour; such a person are you in our presence, most excellent of kings, whom the Chorus[28] deigns to count among their disciples, who are beloved before all others both of Phoebus and of the Chorus. You, for your part, love Phoebus and the Chorus in return, according to the rights given to your people and the benefits of peace they have obtained by which among people living far and wide, whom fierce wars press because of the nefarious ambition of kings, the Scottish race alone in its prosperity enjoys your gift: oh too fortunate are they, if they know your gifts and recall from where they come, being mindful of God and of you!

Since it was not a source of regret for you to visit with your most vigilant care the remaining parts of the kingdom, and our school did not seem to you to be the smallest part of your care, here it certainly pleases you that beautiful plants grow, which the heat of Phoebus fosters, and a continual wave flows from the font of the Muses, which the divine breeze of your favour raises up so that the columns of virtue which bear fruits worthy of your praise are firm for the rest of the kingdom, relying upon your resources as ornaments of your praises.

Moreover, that favour of yours (I have no doubt) applies keen spurs to young hearts: a great desire to climb the lofty peaks of your merits increases in them from the example of your virtues: for you were freed from power at the instance of a monarch, before you were freed from swaddling cloths (by which freedom youths tend to be more prone to vice, and indeed to be caught to their

27 The Muses.   28 The Muses.

[87]

detriment by the snares of Sirens), yet you embraced the study of virtue and the noble arts of your own accord: nor did you think that these were unworthy of a prince's intellect (as the indolent herd bellows), but with unceasing labour you avidly acquired knowledge; nor did it seem enough for you to touch the font of the Muses with your lips for the first time, unless you often quenched your thirst from there by drinking. Therefore it happens that we now see nectar and ambrosia drip gently from your sweet mouth and the spring of Pegasus leaps from the innermost recess of your heart. What of the fact that in tightly bound metres your bountiful talent makes you through its praise the equal of the most gifted poets and that the cultivated eloquence of your tongue in your speeches likens you to those men to whom the applauding audience give the victory palm? Whether it pleases you to quell popular disturbances by speaking, or to teach doubtful mystics or the doubtful senate that which religion, right, and experience demands,[29] the force of your eloquence is great; but your outstanding force of wisdom should be regarded as greater, as should the acumen of your shrewd mind which is illuminated by the rays of heavenly wisdom, since it looks heavenward and obtains the true path to there. Like a guiding star, this divine light shines for you and preserves you safely through rocks, through quicksand, and through swells, and it does not let you be captured by any songs of the Sirens or tricks of Circe, or be stunned by the hateful bark of raging Scylla[30] as it threatens savage dangers, and it does not let you deviate from the right course. So that you can convey your own people with you more safely into a peaceful port, skills in ruling have been divinely granted to you, and the host of virtues, which gifts overcome the great weight of others as much as you surpass your subjects in the height of fortune. If I imagined that I could adorn these with my poetry, I would be like the man who dreamt in his folly that he could join the splendour of Phoebus' rays to a lamp.

I sing these few things, however, not because I am deluded by this somewhat idle hope, but because the Camenae[31] ordered you to condescend to bring yourself into their shrine, most excellent king, and to show yourself as an outstanding example to their disciples, so that they may follow you in climbing the heights of Parnassus; and having been augmented by you with the gifts of the Muses they should not doubt that they will win prizes worthy of their merits and toil.

Blessed in mind, you disciples of divine Helicon,[32] may the example of a prince of which no age has brought forth anyone more notable or more worthy

---

29 A reference to James' struggles with his nobles and with the Kirk.

30 In *The Odyssey*, the Sirens tried to lure sailors to their doom with their enchanting song. Near them lived Scylla, a six-headed monster. The sorceress Circe was indeed wily, although she is slightly out of place here as she helped Odysseus escape the Sirens and Scylla.

31 Goddesses of springs and fountains later equated with the Muses.

32 A mountain sacred to the Muses.

of imitation, kindle you to glory and to the love of virtue. May his favour and the sure rewards for your labours stir you to the great glory which he provides for those who will be beneficial to the fatherland in war or in art. May the kindly regard of the prince and his welcome presence render you suitably eager to enter upon the peaks of Pindus[33] where the learned sisters may give you lyres and plectrums so that you may sing of the immortal glory of an exceptional king.

I do not think, dear hero, that the thanks which I give to you for your deeds to us and your Camenae, can be rendered ungrateful in poetry, but I am devoid of compositions worthy of your merits and worthy of your ears: under Phoebus' guidance, I wish I could compose poems deserving of you, and celebrate you with your Camena that is worthy of Phoebus. But why do I, wretched, pour forth empty wishes? Both piety and faith order me to pray for those fortunate and happy things which I think will happen to you and to many peoples. Of course, those royal sceptres that are owed to your family and your merits may soon come to you, being augmented by divine power, with fate responding to your profound mind in all respects, so that through your virtue the British king-doms may either vanquish evils or frighten off the evils that arise from elsewhere and turn them promptly against your enemies, so that under your guidance, once the light of salvation has arisen for these peoples, you in your long life may govern them in gentle and placid peace so that when in old age you are taken up to the gods, and hand over your golden sceptre to your son, a voice may sound out from all quarters with tongues and melodious plectrums, or a Muse; and you may be sung of for ever.

Ad Deum optimum maximum ob serenissimum regem e variis periculis, praesertim vero ex insidiis Perthi nuper vitae illius structis feliciter ereptum
[sig. D2v]

Coelitum rector, Deus alme, laetis
Qui supernarum celebratus hymnis
Mentium caeli resides suprema
    Clarus in arce;
Tu regas solus licet, et gubernes   5
Orbium motus rapidos, meatus
Siderum, pulchri nitet inque celso
    Quicquid Olympo:
Infimi mundi tamen et caduci

---

33 Pindus is glossed as a 'hill consecrate to Apollo, and the Muses' in 'A table of obscure words' at the end of *The Essayes of a Prentise* (1584): James VI and I, *Poems*, i, p. 93.

Res tuo nutu moderaris omnes; 10
Nec, quod excelsus dominere summis,
    Negligis ima.
Inter haec curas hominum salutem:
In quibus regum tibi summa cura est,
Qui tuum nomen, referuntque numen 15
    Munere celso.
Omnis hoc aevi monumenta, nostri et
Iam recens saecli documenta firmant.
Hoc ratum tu prae reliquis in uno
    Principe reddis; 20
Nempe Iacobo, modo qui Britannos,
Qui polum spectant, regit, et favente
Te, sitis est mox reliquis ad austrum
    Iura daturus.
Matris huic vindex fueras in alvo 25
Tu pius, quando in gravidam minaci
Voce, vultu, armis, manibus ruebat
    Turba scelesta.
Mox et in cunis posito fuisti
Praestita clemens ope sospitator, 30
Cum tetendisset laqueos parentum
    Proditor illi.
A dolis, et vi puerum tegebas
Usque, nec per tot fera bella, turbas
Et graves praedam fieri sinebas 35
    Insidianti.
Plurimis aevo reliquo periclis
Dextra eum texit tua, perduelles
Inque eum saeva rabie ruentes
    Saepe repressit. 40
Nuper at quam te Deus, o benignum
Vindicem sensit, neque vim timentem,
Nec dolos cum vi peterit dolosa
    Proditor atrox.
Tum tua summa bonitate fretus 45
Viribus nixum, magicisque technis,
Vicit, et victor merito cadentem
    Vulnere vidit.
Hunc tibi acceptum referens triumphum
Tum tibi verbis, animoque grates 50

Reddidit tanti memor is futurus
  Usque favoris.
Nos at illius famulos, et omnes,
Quos regit miti imperio, Britannos
Debitas par est tibi gratulantes   55
  Dicere laudes.
Nam salus, et pax peritura nobis,
Si (quod avertas Deus alme) fraudi
Praeda rex esset, manet usque firma,
  Sospite rege.   60
Sospitem semper bonus ergo serves,
Quem tibi charum documenta monstrant
Esse, quae quondam toties, recenter
  Quaeque dedisti.
Neu sinas unquam vel aperta vis hunc   65
Opprimat, vel fraus laqueis dolosis:
Hostium sed te, Deus, usque perstet
  Vindice, victor.

To Almighty God on Account of the Most Serene King's Being Fortunately
Saved from Various Dangers, Especially from the Ambush That Was Recently
Set upon His Life at Perth [T]

Ruler of the heavens, loving God, who, attended by the happy hymns of celestial minds reside in your glory in the utmost citadel of heaven.

Although you alone rule and govern the swift motions of the planets, the
courses of the stars and whatever shines beautifully on lofty Olympus,

Yet you control by your nod all affairs of the fleeting world below; but
although you rule the loftiest affairs on high, you do not neglect the lowliest.

Among these, you look after the health of men, among whom your care for
kings who repay your name and your godhead with noble service is foremost.

The chronicles of all this age and the proofs of our most recent age confirm
this. You ratify this in the case of one ruler before others,

Namely in James, who rules the Britons of the north, who with your favour
is soon to give laws to the rest of them, those living in the south.

You had been an attentive guardian of his mother in the womb, when a
wicked crowd fell upon her during her pregnancy with threatening voice, mien,
weapons and hands.[34]

34 Patrick, third lord Ruthven, was one of the chief actors in the 1566 plot against the pregnant
  Mary, Queen of Scots.

Moreover, you were his merciful saviour by providing aid to him once laid soon after in swaddling clothes, when a traitor to his parents aimed the noose at him.

You continually protected the boy from treachery and violence, and you did not allow him after so many fierce wars and grave disturbances to become prey to the waylayer.

Your right hand protected him from many dangers in his remaining years and often checked assailants who rushed against him in savage frenzy.

Only recently as he sensed that you, God, were his kindly protector and thus did not fear violence, a fierce traitor attempted treachery with deceitful force.

Then, relying upon your utmost goodness, he conquered one who came against him with power and magical arts, and as victor he saw his enemy fall with a deserved wound.

In reporting this triumph obtained by you he then returned thanks in words and mind, being ever mindful of such great favour.

But it is also right that we and all the British servants he rules with his merciful power celebrate and speak of your praises.

For prosperity and peace will perish among us if (please avert it, loving God) the king were to fall prey to deceit, whereas it will remain for ever firm should the king be safe.

Therefore in your goodness may you always keep him who is dear to you safe, as you have done so recently and on so many other occasions.

May you never allow either open force or deceit with its treacherous snares to overcome him; but, through your protection, God, may he continually remain the conqueror of his enemies.

Epigrammata de multis notatu dignis, quae in serenissimi regis periculo, et liberatione contigerunt[35]

I: [Dum venare feras][36] [sig. D4v]

Dum venare feras, ferus, en, venator, et atrox
    Occulta laqueos, rex, tibi fraude struit.
In quibus incautum te (pro scelus) implicat; et iam
    Illius, ecce, parant te laniare canes:
Eriperis cum tu praesenti numine divum;   5
    Atque perit captus casibus ille suis.

35 'Epigrams on Matters Worthy of Note Which Have Concerned the Danger and Freedom of the Most Serene King' [sig. D4v]
36 The epigrams are numbered in the copy-text (albeit with some printing errors).

I: [While You Hunted Wild Beasts] [T]

While you hunted wild beasts, look O king, a wild and fierce hunter lays snares for you with hidden treachery! In these he ensnares you unwittingly (oh the crime!), and now look, his dogs prepare to tear you apart, but you are snatched away by the favourable power of the gods, and the captured enemy perishes through his own misfortunes.

II: [Aurum pollicitus tibi perfidus insidiator] [sig. D4v]

Aurum pollicitus tibi perfidus insidiator
    Intentat iugulo ferrea tela tuo.
Sed male vertit ei scelus hoc, Iove vindice: ferro,
    Incolumi nam te, iustius, ipse perit.
Unde tuo (licet imprudens, nolensque) relinquit   5
    Plus fisco, fuerat quam tibi pollicitus.

II: [A Treacherous Plotter Promised You Gold] [T]

A treacherous plotter promised you gold while he aimed[37] iron weapons at your throat. However, he injuriously turned this crime against himself, as by Jove's protections, it was he himself who more justly perished by the sword and no harm was done to you. He thereby (albeit unintentionally and unwillingly) left more to your treasury than he had originally promised to you.

III: [Credulus es nimium visus] [sig. D4v]

Credulus es nimium visus, rex optime, fratrum
    Dum sceleratorum te sinis arte capi.
Nullius id fecit sed mens sibi conscia noxae,
    Et meritis fratrem freta in utrumque tuis.
Nec reor id factum sine numine, quo brevis esset,   5
    Quale malum fuerat, sic metus ipse mali.

III: [You Seem to Be Too Credulous] [T]

You seem to be too credulous, Most Excellent King, when you allow yourself to be captured by the craft of wicked brothers. However, your mind, innocent

---

37 The Latin verbs are in a mixture of the present and the past tense. In the translation these have been regularized for ease of comprehension.

of the harm intended to it, did this, relying on your kindnesses to both siblings.[38] Nor do I think this happened without divine guidance since the fear of evil, such as the evil was, was brief.

IV: [Exceptum hospitio patriae patremque] [sig. E1r]

Exceptum hospitio patriae patremque, suumque
    Munificum dominum Gourius ense petit.
Impietate lares hac impiat, atque penates,
    Praesidem et hospitii provocat ille Iovem,
Expiat inde lares, Iovis et vindicta penates,   5
    Dum monstrum hoc oreo victima rite cadit.

IV: [The Father of the Fatherland Received with Hospitality] [T]

Gowrie attacks the father of the fatherland, his munificent lord, having received him with hospitality. Through this impiety towards the deities of hearth and home he provokes Jove, the guardian of hospitality. Therefore Jove's revenge expiates the gods of hearth and home, while this monster justly falls as his victim.

V: [Proditor atrox] [sig. E1r]

Vincula carnificem referens dum proditor atrox
    Intentat manibus, rex venerande, tuis;
Magnanimum pectus tibi tum magis aestuat, illud
    Quam mortem intentans dum pugione petit.
Nempe decus vitae iusto dum pondere praefers,   5
    Tu toleranda minus vincula morte putas.

V: [Savage Traitor] [T]

The savage traitor emulates the executioner when he aims to enchain your hands, venerable king. Your magnanimous breast is then in greater turmoil than

---

38 'His Majestie could never suspect anie harme to be intended against his Hienes by that young gentleman [Ruthven], with whome his Majestie had ben so well acquanited': *Gowreis conspiracie*, sig. A8r.

when he came at you seeking your death with a dagger. Without doubt, as long you prefer the glory of a just life to this burden, you consider that chains are less tolerable than death.[39]

VI: [Non stupeat] [sig. E1r]

Non stupeat quivis quem solum, tecto et inermem
    Inclusum, armatos vincere posse duos.
Praestitit hoc, heros, plusquam mariana refulgens
    In te maiestas, ore sophia fluens;
Celsi animi virtus; auctae in discrimine vires;   5
    Et superum, qui te protegit usque favor.

VI: [Let No One Be Amazed] [T]

Let no one be amazed that one person shut up alone can defeat two armed men covertly and be kept safe.[40] This was achieved, O hero, by the majesty brighter than the sea that shines in you, by the wisdom that flows from your speech, by the virtue of your lofty mind, by your greater control in a crisis, and by the favour of the gods which always protects you.

VII: [Semotos comites] [sig. E1r]

Semotos comites a principe Gourius optans,
    Patraret melius, tectius utque scelus,
Asserit his regem iam discessisse: sequuntur
    Hi subito, regem qua praeiisse monet.
Pergentes qua ducit eos ex voce querentis   5
    Principis agnoscunt iam scelus ante latens.
Unde sui sceleris, nolens licet, ipse fit index:
    Principis hoc vindex tu, Deus alme, facis.

VII: [Separated Attendants] [T]

Gowrie, choosing [a moment when] attendants [were] separated from the monarch so as to achieve a better and surer crime, claimed that the king had

---

39 When Ruthven went to tie up James, 'his Majestie [...] said, he was borne a free king, and should die a free king': ibid.

40 James fended off Alexander Ruthven and his servant (see headnote).

now left them. They immediately followed where he directed them that the
king had gone. As they went on where he led, the voice of the prince calling
them alerted them that a crime was being concealed before them and, therefore,
although unwillingly, Gowrie became the betrayer of his own felony. You,
loving God, the protector of the ruler, brought this about.

VIII: [Ad regem comites aditu perrumpere] [sig. E1v]

Ad regem comites aditu perrumpere noto
   Dum certant, clausum hos et remoratur iter;
Postremi tantum penetrant sibi limine ad illum
   Quatuor ignoto, suppetiasque ferunt;
Debellantque hostes, numero, armis, viribus, usu,   5
   Arte quibus nullo teste fuere pares.
Illis ergo viaeque ducem, pugnaeque, salutis
   Et regi authorem quis neget esse Deum.

VIII: [While Attendants Strive to Break Through to the King] [T]

While attendants strive to break through to the king by a known way, the
unknown route holds them up. At last four gain entrance through a doorway
unfamiliar to them and bring help.[41] The enemies wage war in numbers, arms,
strength, experience and skill in which their equals have never been witnessed.
Who will then deny that the leader of the king's course, the general of his battle
and the protector of his health is God?

IX: [Impietas Ruthveni concita Diris] [sig. E1v]

Qua luce impietas Ruthveni concita Diris,
   Fretaque praestigiis, insidiata tibi est,
Hac illum Nemesis iure ulta est, teque periclis
   Eripuit merito cura benigna Dei.
Namque tua is voluit quem reddere caede nefastum,   5
   Numinis hunc festum reddis honore diem.

41 Lennox and Mar tried to get to the king through a door they had seen in the castle (thus it is
    both known and unknown). In the meantime, John Ramsay led a small party through a
    quicker way to reach James (see headnote).

IX: [Impiety Was Stirred up by the Furies of Ruthven] [T]

On the day that impiety was stirred up by the Furies[42] of Ruthven, trusting to tricks as it lay in ambush for you, Nemesis[43] rightly avenged him and the benign care of God rightly saved you from danger. For the day which he had wanted to render unholy by your slaughter you make festive by the honour of God.

X: [Propitium Martem sibi credidit usque futurum] [sig. E1v]

Propitium Martem sibi credidit usque futurum
    Ruthvenus, quoniam sic cecinere magi.
Unde die saevi signato nomine Martis
    Ausus inauditum est impius ille nefas;
Fraudibus e medio sacrum, et vi tollere regem,   5
    Secula cui meritis nulla tulere parem.
Carmina sed magica elusit, spemque illius aequo
    Qui Martem imperio, caeteraque astra regit:
Hinc sibi, non regi, Martem portendere mortem
    Tartara Ruthvenus sensit ad ima ruens.   10

X: [He Believed That Mars Would Always Be Favourable to Him] [T]

Ruthven believed that Mars would always be favourable to him,[44] since the prophets had sung of this; therefore, on the day that bears the name of savage Mars that impious man dared an unheard of crime, namely through trickery and force to do away with the holy king, one to whose merits no age has brought forth an equal. However, the magic spells and intent of that man were eluded by the king who with just power rules Mars along with the other stars. Therefore, as Ruthven fell into the depths of Tartarus, he realized that it was for him and not for the king that Mars portended death.

XI: [Regibus esse ratus Perthum fatale] [sig. E2r]

Regibus esse ratus Perthum fatale, sibique
    Ruthvenus, genti propitiumque suae,

---

42 The *Dirae* are described as 'Thre furies of hell, Alecto, Megera and Tesiphone' in 'A table of obscure words' at the end of *The Essayes of a Prentise* (1584): James VI and I, *Poems*, i, p. 92. The king had translated a section of Du Bartas' *The Divine Weeks* which was titled 'The Furies': *Selected Writings*, pp 53–93.

43 Nemesis is the goddess of righteous indignation and the check on human presumption.

44 Mars, god of War, gave his name to *dies Martis* (Tuesday).

Struxit ibi insidias regi, dominoque scelestas
    Praestigiis fretus, subsidiisque loci.
Sed spes lusit eum, versumque (ut debuit) omen;   5
    Criminis ultorem sensit et esse Deum.
Namque illum Perthi, Ruthvenorumque superbam
    Obruit, incolumi rege, ruina domum.

XI: [Thinking That Perth Was Fatal to the King] [T]

Thinking that Perth was fatal to the king but propitious to him and his family,
Ruthven, relying on trickery and the soldiers at the place, sprung a wicked
ambush there against his sovereign and lord. However, his hope deluded him
and the omen turned against him (as it should have): he realized that God was
also an avenger of his crime, for at Perth ruin overcame him and the proud
house of the Ruthvens without harm to the king.

XII: [Rex, tua cum virtus] [sig. E2r]

Rex, tua cum virtus, oritura salusque Britannis
    Inde foret geniis invidiosa malis;
Saepe tuae filium vitae resecare nefandis
    Artibus, ac magiae vi studuere suae.
Mancipia ast illis fuerant plerumque ministri   5
    Infima, quae vili spe potuere capi.
Quorum ubi vidissent coepta irrita, vilibus uti
    Mancipiis aptum non satis esse rati,
Stirpe legunt, opibus, fama elatumque ministrum,
    Inflatum ingenii, corporis atque bonis;   10
Virtutum specie, ficta ac pietate tegentem
    Perfidiam, atque animi crimina dira sui.
Talis Ruthvenus, diris agitantibus illum,
    Te patrem patriae vique, doloque petit.
Sed Deus, ecce, tui, patriaeque miseratus ab alto   15
    Aethere fit vindex, ceu fuit ante, tuus.
Utque malos genios in te quos ante ciebant
    Exitium in proprium praecipitasse patet:
Ruthvenus, salvo sic te, cacodaemonis aestu,
    Ut reliqui, casu sed graviore ruit.   20

XII: [Your Virtue, O King] [T]

Since your virtue, O king, and the prosperity that will arise for the Britons are consequently a source of envy for evil minds, they have often desired to cut off the thread of your life using their unspeakable arts and the power of their magic. However, the evil ones had the lowliest servants and attendants, those who could be seized by base ambition. When they saw the vain attempts of such people they thought that it would not be sufficient to employ base servants, thus they choose an accomplice that is of high birth, wealth and fame, one considerable in intellect and bodily gifts, who could conceal his treachery and the dire crimes of his mind by means of his virtuous appearance and feigned piety. Such a man is Ruthven, who at the instigation of the Furies attacks you, Father of the Fatherland, with violence and trickery. But look! God, taking pity on you and the fatherland from heaven on high, becomes your protector as before. And just as it is clear that the bad minds that had stirred themselves up against you before fell headlong to their own destruction, so Ruthven, with you thus saved, falls by the tide of the evil spirit, just as the others have, but with a graver misfortune.

XIII: [Gourius et vulgo fuit, et se iudice, magnus] [sig. E2v]

Gourius et vulgo fuit, et se iudice, magnus:
  Clarus erat peregre; clarus et ille domi.
Fucata specie virtutum pluribus annis
  Aucupat hoc folers hinc sibi, et inde decus.
Sed vera ac solida regem virtute nitentem   5
  Dum, quo fit maior, vique, doloque petit:
Crimine tam faedo vel puncto temporis illi
  Gloria, res, animus, vita, domusque perit.

XIII: [Gowrie Was Adjudged Great by Common Consent and by Himself] [T]

Gowrie was adjudged great by common consent and by himself: he was famous abroad and he was famous at home.[45] The cunning man seeks glory for himself from here and there through the counterfeit appearance of many years' virtues. But while he attacks by force and trickery a king who shines with true and solid virtue in order that he will become greater, at that very moment in time his glory, fortunes, spirit, life and household perish through so foul a crime.

45 A reference to Gowrie's warm reception in London (see headnote).

XIV: [Quos scenae tragicae insignes spectare cothurnos] [sig. E2v]

Quos scenae tragicae insignes spectare cothurnos,
    Audire et procerum tristia fata iuvat,
Ruthvenum spectent, modo quem Fortuna fovebat,
    Tollebatque suae culmina ad alta rotae,
Moxque suum in regem carum superisque, bonisque   5
    Egit praecipitem Tartara ad ima scelus.
Sed quibus eventus comici plaususque theatri,
    Post dubios casus, cernere mente placet,
Sint spectatores regis, modo cuius honestum
    Ruthveni insidiae, ac vis petiere caput;   10
Caelitus erepto sed cui nunc inde Britanni
    Applaudunt populi, cunctaque fausta vovent.

XIV: [Those Whom It Delights to Watch the Tall Boots of the Tragic Stage]
[T]

Those whom it delights to watch the tall boots[46] of the tragic stage and to hear the sad fates of elders should watch Ruthven, whom Fortune once fostered and raised to the high peaks of her wheel, and whose crime against a king that was dear to the gods and to good men, drove him headlong into the depths of Tartarus. However, those whose mind it pleases to view comic events and the applause of the theatre after doubtful fortunes should be spectators of the king, whose honest head Ruthven attacked with ambushes and force, but whom the people of Britain now applaud and to whom they pray for all blessed things now that he has been saved by divine fortune.

XV: [Si Deus, o heros, tibi pieridesque faventes] [sig. E3r]

Si Deus, o heros, tibi pieridesque faventes
    Te vatem a teneris excoluere suum;
Harum si numeris sic sacra oracula pandis
    Illius, ut stupeant qui tua scripta legunt;
Sique, velut reliquis sublimi culmine praestas,   5
    Si reliquos vatum laude in utraque praeis:

---

46 Such boots were worn by actors in Classical tragedies. See *Horace: Satires, Epistles and Ars poetica*, ed. and trans. H. Rushton Fairclough (Cambridge, MA: Harvard UP, 1929), *Ars poetica*, l. 80.

Quid mirum hoc? vatem fore te portendit in alvo
Inclusum vates tum tua facta parens.
Namque a Ruthvenis iam tum te vim sibi factam
    Ulturum vere vaticinata fuit.   10

XV: [If God and the Peridies Who Favour You] [T]

If God and the Pierides[47] who favour you, O hero, cultivated you as their bard
from tender beginnings, if you thus compose in their metres his sacred oracles
so that those who read your writings are amazed, and if, just as you surpass
others by your lofty height, you precede the rest of bards in praise for either:
what wonder is this, that your parent, a bard, predicted that you would be a bard
when enclosed in the womb, and then predicted your deeds. For it was truly
prophesied then that you would now avenge the violence done against you by
the Ruthvens.

XVI: [Dum gravidae matri intentarunt] [sig. E3r]

Dum gravidae matri intentarunt, et tibi nondum
    Ruthveni nato vique, doloque necem
Illa suoque, tuoque simul commota periclo
    Vindictam urgentes fudit ad astra preces.
Numine mox afflata mea iacet, inquit, in alvo,   5
    Qui iustus tanti criminis ultor erit.
Ecquis non merito credat tum vaticinatam;
    Cum faciat dictis exitus ipse fidem.
Mortuus exul avus, caesi pater, atque nepotes
    Fatales poenas namque dedere tibi.   10
At (ne cui saevus, vel tu videaris iniquus)
    Hi periere dolis, criminibusque suis.
Sic voluere Dii, te labe carere, parentis
    Auguriumque tuae sic tamen esse ratum.

XVI: [When They Threatened a Pregnant Mother] [T]

While the Ruthvens threatened through violence and deceit to slaughter a
pregnant mother and her unborn son, she, moved at once by the danger to her
and her son, poured forth prayers to the stars that urged revenge. Soon she

47 The Muses.

says, 'Moved by divine favour there lies in my womb someone who will be the just avenger of so great a crime'.[48] Would anyone believe that this was then not deservedly prophesied, when the very outcome gives credibility to what was said? The exiled grandfather is dead, the father and descendants slaughtered, for they were fatally punished by you. However, lest you seem cruel or unfair to anyone, these perished through their deceit and crimes. Thus did the Gods will it, that you be devoid of blame, and yet the prophecy of your mother be ratified.

XVII: [Ter tua Ruthvenae infando] [sig. E3v]

Ter tua Ruthvenae infando, rex, crimine gentis
    Aetate in triplici vita petita fuit.
Matris adhuc gravidae cum gestareris in alvo,
    Illam vi petiit, teque scelestus avus.
Mox adolescenti tibi truso natus in arcem   5
    Exitii peperit, dedecorisque metum.
Vicit avi, patrisque scelus sed dira nepotum
    Impietas ficta sub pietate latens:
Dum te aetate virum, meritis patriaeque parentem
    Fraudibus e medio tollere, vique parat.   10
Talibus ast ausis gens haec scelerata quid egit.
    Te nisi maiorem ut redderet ipsa ruens.

XVII: [Abominable Crimes] [T]

Thrice was your life attacked, king, by the abominable crimes of three different generations of the family of Ruthven. When you were still gestating in the womb of your pregnant mother their wicked grandfather attacked her and you with force. Later, his son engendered the fear of destruction and shame for you, an adolescent thrust into a castle. Nevertheless, the dire impiety of the descendants surpasses the crimes of the grandfather and father: lurking beneath his feigned piety, while he prepares to do away with you by deceit and force, you a man in age, and father of the fatherland in merits. Whatever this wicked race did with such acts of daring, as it falls it can do nothing but make you greater.

48 See Stewart, *Cradle King*, pp 9–10.

XVIII: [En salvus, carus iam stas, rex inclyte, victor][49] [sig. E4r]

Carolus Iacobus Stuartus
Victor salvus, carus stabo

En salvus, carus iam stas, rex inclyte, *victor,*
   Omen ut innuerat nominis ante tui.
Ante pedes strato hoste tuos, ubi perfidus ille   5
   Te petit insidiis, sternere vique parat,
Stas victor salvus, tanto ereptusque periclo,
   Ut stupeant, *salvum* qui modo stare vident.
Carum te superis tua sat testatur ab illis
   Supra hominum nascens spemque, fidemque salus.   10
Et sibi te *carum* populi testantur ovantes,
   Gratantesque tibi pectore, et ore tui;
Quique tui iam spe, tales re moxque futuri,
   Plaudunt, stesque diu tu sibi *salvus,* avent.

XVIII: [Look, Unharmed Victor] [T]

Charles James Stuart: as unharmed victor, I will remain beloved.

Look, unharmed victor, you now remain beloved, famous king, as the omen of
your name had intimated beforehand. With your enemy laid before your feet,
when that traitor attacks you with his ambush and prepares to lay you low with
force, you remain the unharmed victor, and you have been saved from so great
a danger that those who see you now remaining unharmed are amazed. Your
prosperity, which arises beyond the hope and faith of men, testifies sufficiently
that you are beloved of the gods. Moreover, the people rejoice and testify that
you are dear to them and congratulate you in heart and countenance; those who
now and in the near future will be such in hope and in deed applaud you and
desire that you will be unharmed for them.

XIX: Ad illustras equitem, Thomam Areskinum[50] [sig. E4v]

O equitum decus eximium, tua quanta periclo
   In domini virtus, enituitque fides?

---

49 This is the first poem of a section entitled 'In anagrammatismum nominis serenissimi regis huic
   argumento pulchre convenientem' (On an Anagram of the Name of the Most Serene King,
   Which Agrees Beautifully with This Argument).
50 This is the first poem of a sequence headed 'Ad equites auratos serenissime regis propugna-

Dum properas vitae illius fraude insidiantem
  Ulcisci vitae prodigus ipse tuae;
Insidiatorem sociis hinc, indeque septum   5
  Intrepido aggressus pectore sternis humi:
Mox avulsus eum, sociosque a rege repellis,
  Dum, rege incolumi, saucius ille cadit.
Clarius at niteat quo virtus tanta, fidesque,
  En, tua fida gerit dextra utriusque notam.   10

XIX: For the Illustrious Knight, Thomas Ereskine [T]

Exquisite glory of knights, how much of your virtue and faith shone out amidst
the danger to your master? While you hasten to avenge one who is deceitfully
plotting against your life, you yourself abound in your life. Attacking the plotter (who is surrounded by allies on all sides), you lay him low on the ground
with your intrepid courage. Next, having torn yourself away, you drive him and
his allies back from the king, and while he falls wounded, the king suffers no
harm. However, in order that such great virtue and faith shine brighter; see,
your faithful right hand carries the mark of both!

XX: Ad clarissimum equitem, Hugonem Herrisium, serenissimi regis medicum[51] [sig. F1r]

Quod Phoebi excultus sis artibus, anxia curis
  Pectora, quae morbis corpora et aegra levant,
Te rex iure suis, vir clare, adscribit, alumnum
  Phoebaeum Phoebi cultor et ipse fovet.
Sed non hoc regi solo es tu nomine carus: 5
  Te quoque pro meritis nunc amat ille novis.
Marte salutarem nam te, velut arte, probavit,

---

tores' (For the Golden Knights That Fight for the Most Serene King). Thomas Erskine, first
earl of Kellie, was educated with King James and had been a gentleman of the bedchamber
since 1585. He was wounded in the hand during the Gowrie episode: David Stevenson,
'Erskine, Thomas, first earl of Kellie (1566–1639)', *ODNB*. See 'To the Noble Knight Sir
Thomas Areskine', p. 107.

51 Sir Hugh Herries of Cousland (which was granted to him from the Gowrie estates) was a royal
    doctor who had served the king abroad: 'Act in favour of Sir Hugh Herries', 20 Nov. 1600
    (NAS, PA2/16, fos 17v–19r) in Gillian H. MacIntosh et al., *The Records of the Parliaments of
    Scotland to 1707* (University of St Andrews, 2014), http://www.rps.ac.uk, accessed 1 Mar. 2014.
    See 'To Sir Hugh Herries, Knight, and Physician to His Majestie', p. 108.

Oppugnaret eum cum scelerata manus.
Macte igitur virtute, novis nova praemia debet
   Rex tibi pro meritis, munificusque dabit.   10

XX: To the Most Famous Knight, Hugh Herries, Physician to the Most Serene King [T]

Because you are cultivated in the arts of Phoebus, which alleviate hearts anxious with cares and bodies sick with illness, the king rightly describes you, O celebrated one, as a disciple of Phoebus among his men, and the worshipper of Phoebus cherishes him too. Now your name is dear to the king for more than this since he also loves you for your recent deeds. For when a wicked hand attacked him it was proved to him that you are beneficial in combat as well as in medicine. Therefore, blessed in virtue, new gifts are owed to you by the king for your new deeds and in his munificence he will give them.

XXI: Ad nobilem equitem Iohannem Ramisaeum[52] [sig. F1r]

Flos iuvenum, mire favet, en, tibi dux tua virtus,
   Huic fortuna comes te fovet inque sinu.
Alma tibi virtus dederat mentemque, fidemque;
   Qua domino tuleras promptus, et acer opem.
Primus ei vindex fieres, indexque latentis   5
   Tu sociis aditus, fors tibi mira dedit.
Plus dederit virtus, an fors tibi, nescio, nulli
   Largitam iuveni plus sed utramque scio.

XXI: To the Noble Knight John Ramsay [T]

Flower of youths, see, your virtue, your leader, wondrously favours you, and fortune, your companion, favours you in your courage. Nourishing virtue gave you the mind and faith by which you readily and keenly brought help to your lord. By wondrous fortune you were his first protector and the revealer of secret entrances to his allies. Whether virtue or good luck played a larger part, I do not know, but no other youth has more of these lavished on him.

---

52 John Ramsay, later earl of Holderness. During the Gowrie conspiracy Ramsay was the first rescuer to succour the king. He was knighted that year by his grateful monarch: Alan R. MacDonald, 'Ramsay, John, earl of Holdernesse (*c.*1580–1626)', *ODNB*. See 'To Sir John Ramsay, Knight', p. 108.

Of the Danger Wherein His Majesty Was Lately at Saint Johnstone, and of His Happy Delivery[53] [sig. F1v]

The gifts to thee imparted from above,
The peace and wealth thence flowing to this land,
O sacred prince, thee to envy did move,
And to conspire thy death the Stygian[54] band.
A traitor meet they chose to take in hand   5
This vile attempt, one decked† with nature's parts,
And virtues counterfeit, which rightly scanned†
Were mere illusions, and but juggler's† arts,
Men's eyes to soil, and to bewitch their hearts.
This traitorous juggler laid a snare for thee: 10
But God, who all thy enemies overthwarts,†
Himself entrapped therein, and made thee free.
    For he, even he it was that did thee shield,
    And win against the Stygian band the field.

To the Most Honourable Lord, the Duke of Lennox[55] [sig. F2r]

As to thy sovereign prince, renowned lord,
Thou art by band of blood, and nature near;
So doth in sundry virtues your accord
Make thee to him, him to thee also dear.
This lately in his danger did appear;   5
When thou with him in presage, doubt, and care
Did'st sympathize, ere treason waxed clear.
First thou him heard'st complaining in the snare,
Thy grief did then thy faithful love declare:
Thy running eke† with speed to make him free;   10
Wherein thou didst no pains, nor peril spare,
'Till him thou didst in wished safety see.

53 St Johnstone is another name for Perth.
54 Infernal (by association with the River Styx). The earliest attestation of this in *OED* is 1601.
55 Ludovick Stuart, having surrendered his title to his French patrimony of Aubigny, was the
    second duke of Lennox. He was a close confidant of the king and served as a gentleman of the
    bedchamber, a privy councillor and (during James' absence for his marriage), governor of
    Scotland: Rob Macpherson, 'Stuart, Ludovick, second duke of Lennox and duke of
    Richmond (1574–1624)', *ODNB*. Lennox was the most important courtier accompanying the
    king to Gowrie's house and thus he is the first dedicatee in a sequence that follows social rank
    rather than the importance of the role the dedicatee played in James' rescue.

Then did ye both at joyful meeting prove
A new enkindled flame of mutual love.

To the Right Honourable the Earl of Mar[56] [sig. F2v]

True honour's pattern, who had present been,
When as our king in danger was of late;
Towards him thy true and faithful love had seen,
As well as traitors' treachery, and hate.
For when by fraud they did you separate,   5
And him assailed, then he with ruthful sound
Thy help imploring in that hard estate,
O how his voice thy heart did thrill and wound?
The passage to him clos'd thou having found
Didst break it up, to come to his relief.   10
He being safe, thy joy did then abound
No less, then did before thy bitter grief.
    Such was thy love, thy faith, thy grief, and mirth
    In his supposed death, and second birth.

To the Noble Knight Sir Thomas Erskine[57] [sig. F3r]

From ancestors of high and noble stem,
O worthy knight, great praise to thee doth flow.
Yet from thine own desert to thee, and them
Far greater honour and renown doth grow.
For when as traitors sought to overthrow   5
Our sacred king, and murder him with shame,
His voice his peril making thee to know,
Thou didst him rescue, to thy endless fame,
And win a stout and faithful champion's name.
To witness which thy service, thou dost bear   10

56 Like his cousin Thomas Erskine, John Erskine, earl of Mar, had been educated with King
    James. In 1592 he had married Ludovick Stuart's sister and when Prince Henry was born in
    1594 Erskine was given custody of him: Julian Goodare, 'Erskine, John, eighteenth or second
    earl of Mar (*c*.1562–1634)', *ODNB*. During the Gowrie episode the king called to Mar for aid.
    Mar was one of the people who broke down a door barring them from the king (who, in the
    meantime, had been succoured by Thomas Erskine who had reached James via a different
    route). Quin was attached to the earl's household.
57 See 'Ad illustram equitem, Thomam Areskinum' (p. 104) and its notes.

In thy right hand a token of the same,
More glorious far, than ought that hand can wear:
　　For that so oft as men the same shall view,
　　It will thy virtue's praise, and fame renew.

To Sir John Ramsay, Knight[58] [sig. F3v]

Thy virtue, and good fortune have conspired,
O worthy youth, a doubt in me to breed,
Which of them twain is most to be admired:
For when I mark thy valiance indeed,
In words thy wisdom, and in taking heed　　　　　　　　5
To stop the traitors that pursued our king,
Thy faithful love whence did the rest proceed,
Thence doth a heap of many wonders spring.
But seeing how thy fortune did thee bring
Him first to aide, and slay his chiefest foes,　　　　　　10
Thy fortune seemeth such a wondrous thing,
As which exceeds I cannot well disclose.
　　But well I wote† yet youth was never seen,
　　That hath more virtuous, and more happy been.

To Sir Hugh Herries, Knight, and Physician to His Majesty[59] [sig. F4r]

Thy learning, chiefly in the chief of arts
Found out by Phaebus[60] for the health of man,
With wisdom joined, and sundry worthy parts,
Renown to thee in foreign countries won,
And moved thy prince, who judge uprightly can　　　5
Of men's deserts, a choice to make of thee
(When to perceive thy merits he began)
A help by physic for his health to be.
Such hast thou proved in more than that degree.
For thou didst help from traitors' rage and might　　10

58　See 'Ad nobilem equitem Johannem Ramisaeum' (p. 105) and its notes.
59　See 'Ad clarissimum equitem, Hugonem Herrisium, serenissimi regis medicum' (p. 104) and its notes.
60　Epithet of Apollo, god of healing and the father of Aesculapius, the Greek god of healing (see l. 14).

His life, and health to keep by manhood free,
Receiving glorious wounds even in his sight.
 For which men shall thee to thy endless fame,
 His Asclepius, and his knight proclaim.

 Aux chevaliers, qui ont aidé à sauver la vie de sa majesté [sig. F4v]

L'honneur d'un chevalier sage, vaillant, et preux,
Gît tout en servant Dieu, son prince, et sa patrie.
Qui sert bien l'un des trois, ainsi que le convie
Son serment et devoir, se peut nommer heureux.
 Quel donc est votre heur, chevaliers valeureux,   5
Qui service à tous trois par vertu accomplie
Avez fait, en sauvant à votre roi la vie
Contre les fiers assauts des traîtres furieux ?
 Dieu a été servi par un si grand service
Fait à son lieutenant sacré, et bien aimé ;   10
Et votre paix, étant pour choir en précipice,
Avec lui garantit bien peu d'être estimée.
 Donc de votre vertu, loyauté, et vaillance
 Recevrez des tous trois la juste récompense.

 To the Knights Who Helped Save His Majesty's life [T]

The honour of a wise knight, valiant and brave, lies wholly in serving God, his prince, and his country. He who serves any one of these three well, as well as spurring him to his oath and duty, can call himself happy.

 What, therefore, is your happiness brave knights who by skilled virtue gave service to all three by saving the life of your king from the proud assaults of furious traitors?

 God has been served by such great service on behalf of his sacred and greatly beloved lieutenant; and with him secure, your country, about to fall into a chasm, can be considered healthy.

 Therefore, for your virtue, loyalty and courage, all three of you will receive fair recompense.

[109]

5

Poems for the marriage of William Alexander and Janet Erskine (1601)

The Hawthornden manuscripts preserve an 'Epithalamium by Walter Quin' for the marriage of William Alexander. Immediately following this are two anonymous sonnets celebrating the same occasion and it seems likely that these are from Quin's pen.

The owner of the manuscript (in whose hand Quin's poems were copied) was William Drummond (1585–1649), laird of Hawthornden. Drummond corresponded with Scottish writers at the London court and he was particularly friendly with William Alexander. He himself was a poet, pamphleteer and historian, and three of his poems appeared alongside Quin's contribution to *Mausoleum* (1613, see p. 125), a verse compilation commemorating the death of Prince Henry. Drummond also owned a copy of Quin's *Sertum poeticum* as well as editions of William Alexander's *Darius*, for which Quin supplied a sonnet.[1]

William Alexander of Menstrie (1577–1640) had little of the celebrity he would later enjoy when, in 1601, Quin wrote an epithalamium in celebration of his marriage to Janet, the daughter of Sir William Erskine.[2] In 1603 Alexander published *Darius*, the first of *The Monarchik Tragedies*, and Quin provided commendatory verses for it (see p. 114). Alexander returned the favour in 1619 with a panegyric for Quin's *Bernard Stuart* (p. 264). In the meantime, Alexander had published extensively and had pursued a profitable public career that resulted in a knighthood and his appointment as master of requests for Scotland. Subsequently he was involved in schemes to colonize the New World and was given several important crown offices before being created viscount and then earl of Stirling.

Copy-text

Papers of William Drummond. NLS, Hawthornden MS 2065, fos 44–7. 298x185mm. Written in Drummond's secretary hand. In the nineteenth century Drummond's manuscripts were bound in fifteen volumes.[3] Quin's poem appears

---

1   R.H. MacDonald (ed.), *The Library of Drummond of Hawthornden* (Edinburgh: Edinburgh UP, 1971), pp 169, 187.
2   David Reid, 'Alexander, William, first earl of Stirling (1577–1640)', *ODNB*.
3   David Laing, 'A Brief Account of the Hawthornden Manuscripts in the Possession of the Society of Antiquaries of Scotland: With Extracts, Containing Several Unpublished Letters and Poems of William Drummond of Hawthornden', *Archaeologia Scotica*, 4 (1857), 56–116, 225–40.

in volume 13 (xii+154 folios), which contains poems in Latin, English, French and Italian by a number of authors (but principally by William Fowler).[4]

The epithalamium was printed by David Laing in 1857 and both the epithalamium and the sonnets are included in the *Works* (1921) of William Alexander.[5]

Epithalamium by Walter Quin for the Marriage of William Alexander and Janet Erskine [fo. 44r]

Lo, here a youth of young men paragon,
Lo, there a nymph the honour of her sex,
By happy lot combined together soon
By love which doth not them by crosses vex;
For with delay the flower of youth doth waste,   5
    O Hymen come, and knit this couple fast!

Yet never Hymen didst thou couple link
That was more meet to be together bound,
Whatever thing praiseworthy we may think
Both in their age and sex in them is found;   10
Therefore as they and we thee call in haste,
    O Hymen come, and knit this couple fast!

Most comely shape and feature doth adorn
Both with proportion like and symmetry,
And under planets like they have been born   15
With manners like and virtues' sympathy,
As he, so she is gentle, wise and chaste,
    O Hymen come, and knit this couple fast!

To them both Phoebus and the sisters nine
Impart their heavenly gifts abundantly: 20
To him their sweetest ditties† they assign,
To her their sweet and pleasant harmony;[6]

---

4   The contents of the manuscript are listed in William Fowler, *The Works of William Fowler, Secretary to Queen Anne, Wife of James VI*, ed. Henry W. Meikle et al. (3 vols, Edinburgh: Blackwood, 1940), iii, pp xlvi–xlviii.

5   Laing, 'Hawthornden manuscripts', 234–6; William Alexander, *The Poetical Works of Sir William Alexander, Earl of Stirling*, eds L.E. Kastner & H.B. Charlton (2 vols, Edinburgh: Scottish Texts Society, 1921–9), i, pp 444–6.

6   William composed lyrics that Janet played on her lute. See the sonnets that follow, below.

Then that this double sweetness we may taste,
    O Hymen come, and knit this couple fast!

With sweet and heavenly Muse allureth he   25
And doth contend and please the rarest wits,
Her lute, with which his Muse doth well agree
Of passionate minds doth ease the raging fits
And cheereth such as into dumps[7] are cast.
    O Hymen come, and knit this couple fast!   30

Therefore since he and she so sympathise
In outward parts and qualities of mind,
And in all points that may to love entice,
As she alone is meet his heart to bind
And he to loose her maiden belt from waist,   35
    O Hymen come, and knit this couple fast!

Dame Juno, patroness of wedlock's band,
Delightful Cupid, with thy mother clear,
Bright Phoebus with the Muses, be at hand,
To grace and honour those your darling dear,   40
And when from hall to chamber they be past,
    O Hymen come, and knit this couple fast!

Then let not shame nor mother's tender love
Nor pity fond of any maid her mate,
Hold back the bride from field where she shall prove   45
Victorious after but a small debate.
And when with bridegroom's arms she shall be clasped,
    O Hymen come, and knit this couple fast!

With favour great of powers celestial,
With parents' blessing and especial joy,   50
With kind assent of friends and kindred all,
Without envious grudging or annoy,
With love and concord, that may ever last,
    O Hymen come, and knit this couple fast!

---

7   *OED* explains 'dump' as 'a fit of melancholy or depression', but it can also be 'a mournful or
plaintive song', so, given the bride's musical ability, Quin may be punning here.

[In Wedlock's Yoke Now Love and Hymen Tie] [fo. 47r]

In wedlock's yoke now love and Hymen tie
Two of the sacred sisters darling dear,
In whom the greatest glory doth appear
Of their inventive art and harmony.
His muse which doth aloft like eagle fly   5
To sharpest sight makes his perfection clear,
The hearts of such as hear her, by the ear
She ravisheth with her sweet melody.
Thus love and Hymen patrons of delight
Most fitly join the Muses' pleasant arts,   10
When as those two in wedlock they unite
That matchless are for these and other parts;
    Which moveth love and Hymen them to match
    In spring of age and with so good dispatch.

[Most Worthy Couple, Happy Is Your Lot] [fo. 47r]

Most worthy couple, happy is your lot
Above all lovers' fortune, since for aye
In flower of youth, and without all delay
Ye are combined and bound with Hymen's knot.
    Strange is your hap† that love no sooner shot   5
Into your hearts his darts, that wound and slay,
And with mishaps men's rising hopes betray,
But he his balm applies where he you smote.
    What cause could work this strange and rare event,
If not that th'one of you with heavenly Muse,   10
And th'other with harmonious instruments,
Doth let† him that he can no rigour use;
    Hath so him charmed with wonderful delight
    As for reward he doth you thus requite?

6

From William Alexander's *The Tragedy of Darius*
(1603)

In 1610 Quin had written in celebration of Alexander's marriage (see *Alexander and Erskine*). Like Quin, Alexander was looking for royal notice and thus he dedicated his verse drama *Darius* to James VI. Drawing on the ten-book history of Alexander the Great by Quintus Curtius Rufus (first/second century), the Scotsman tells the story of Darius III of Persia whose armies were defeated by the Macedonian hero. The play's theme of treason may have echoes of the Gowrie Conspiracy (see *Sertum poeticum*), and Quin would have found its neo-Stoicism congenial.[1]

The sonnet (signed 'W. Quin') is based on a well-known episode from Plutarch's *Lives*, the visit of Alexander of Macedon to Achilles' tomb (an episode that Quin draws on again in his *Recueil*).[2] Quin's comparison of William Alexander to Homer strikes the modern ear as exaggerated, but it was not unusual at the time: John Murray (d. 1615), the other person who supplied a commendatory verse for *Darius*, lauded its author above Sophocles, Euripides and Aeschylus.[3]

Copy-text

William Alexander, THE TRAGEDIE | OF DARIUS. | By VVilliam Alexander | of Menstrie. Edinburgh [London]: Robert Waldegrave, 1603.[4] 4°. *ESTC* S104386 (seven copies). NLS, Special Collections, Mf. 99.

1 Astrid Stilma, 'William Alexander, King James and Neo-Stoic Advice to Princes in *The Monarchik Tragedies*' in David J. Parkinson (ed.), *James VI and I, Literature and Scotland: Tides of Change, 1567–1625* (Leuven: Peeters, 2013), pp 239–41.

2 Plutarch, *Plutarch's Lives*, trans. Bernadotte Perrin (11 vols, London: Heinemann, 1914–26), vii, p. 263. King James reworks the same episode in a 1584 letter to Lord Burleigh, and Henry Lok used it as the basis of a sonnet which prefaced *His Majesties Poeticall Exercises at Vacant Hours* (1591): James VI and I, *Letters of King James VI & I*, ed. G.P.V. Akrigg (Berkeley: University of California Press, 1984), p. 59; James VI, *The Poems of James VI of Scotland*, ed. James Craigie (2 vols, Edinburgh: William Blackwood & Sons, 1955, 1958), p. 105.

3 Little that can surely be attributed to Murray has survived and little is known of his life. Alienated from King James, but enjoying the esteem of several of his fellow poets, he died in poverty: Helena Mennie Shire, *Song, Dance & Poetry of the Court of Scotland Under King James VI* (Cambridge: Cambridge UP, 1969), pp 181–6.

4 *ESTC* marks this as a false imprint actually printed by Waldegrave in London. See also Emma Va. Unger & William A. Jackson (eds), *The Carl H. Pforzheimer Library: English Literature 1475–1700* (rev. ed.; 3 vols, New Castle, DE: Oak Knoll Press, 1997), p. 8.

The text of *Darius* is available on *EEBO*. Quin's poems prefaced *Darius* when the play was collected in Alexander's *The Monarchick tragedies* (1604), but they were omitted from Alexander's *Recreations with the Muses* (1637).[5] Quin's anagram on Alexander's name was printed in Gerald Langbane's *An Account of the English Dramatick Poets* (1691).[6]

[When as the Macedonian Conqueror Came] [sig. A4v]

When as the Macedonian conqueror came
To great Achilles' tomb, he sighed, and said:
Well may thy ghost, brave champion, be appayed,
That Homer's Muse was trumpet of thy fame.
    But if that monarch great in deeds and name,   5
Now once again with mortal veil arrayed,
Came to the tomb where Darius hath been laid,
This speech more justly sighing might he frame:
    My famous foe, whom I less hate, than pity,
Even I, who vanquished thee envy thy glory,   10
In that such one doth sing thy ruin's story,
As matcheth Homer in his sweetest ditty;
    Yet joy in that he Alexander hight,†
And sounds in they o'erthrow my matchless might.

In nomen authoris Guilielmus Alexander, anagramma [sig. A4v]

I, largus melle exunda.
Tetrasticon.

Cum tibi det genius, Musa, ingeniumque, poesis
    Floribus e variis Attica mella legas;
I, largus melle exunda, mellit aque funde   5
    Carmina: sic facias nomine fata jubent.

5 William Alexander, *The Monarchick Tragedies* (London: V[alentine Simmes] [and G. Elde] for Edward Blount, 1604), sig. A2r; *The Monarchick Tragedies* (London: Valentine Simmes for Edward Blount, 1607), sig. A2v; *The Monarchick Tragedies* (London: William Stansby, 1616), sig. G2r; William Alexander, *Recreations with the Muses: By William Earle of Sterline* (London: Thomas Harper, 1637).

6 Gerard Langbaine, *An Account of the English Dramatick Poets [...]* (Oxford: George West and Henry Clements, 1691), p. 5.

An Anagram on the Name of the Author, William Alexander [T]

You who are bountiful in honey, go pour it out: A quatrain.

Since your genius and intellect permit you, Muse, may you collect Attic honey from the various flowers of poetry. You who are bountiful in honey, go pour it out; pour forth honeyed poems: the fates order you to do this [a fact] witnessed by your name.

7
From Alfonso Ferrabosco's *Lessons* (1609)

The son of an Italian musician, Alfonso Ferrabosco II (*c.*1575–1628) was born in England. He was a composer and viol player, and in 1604 was made an extraordinary groom of the privy chamber in recognition of his instruction of Prince Henry in music (a role in which he encountered Quin).[1] He collaborated with Ben Jonson for court masques and wrote music for several of Jonson's plays. In 1609 he published a book of *Ayres* dedicated to the prince. The death of Henry did not impede his promotion as he was given a post as a senior musician in the household of Prince Charles in 1617.[2] *Lessons* is dedicated to Henry Wriothesley, the third earl of Southampton. Quin's poem is signed 'Gual: Quin', and as the earl was a well-known literary patron (who spoke Italian), Ferrabosco may have been obliging his colleague as much as Quin obliged him with his praise. *Lessons'* other commendatory verse was written by Jonson.

Copy-text
Alfonso Ferrabosco, *LESSONS* | *FOR* | *1. 2. And 3. Viols.* | *BY* | *Alfonso Ferrabosco*. London: Thomas Snodham for John Browne, 1609. 2°. *ESTC* S117687 (one copy). BL, Music Collections K.8.h.1.

The text is available on *EEBO*.

In lode dell'arte e dell'autore [sig. A2v]

S'ogni arte tanto più da noi s'apprezza,
Quanto ha più nobil senso per oggetto,
E quanto n'e più degno il soggetto,
Vince l'altre arti armonica dolcezza.
Quella a dar gusto e contento s'avezza,   5
Al nostro udir, de sensi il più perfetto;
Per soggetto h'a numero uguale, e retto,
E di bella aria, e tuoni la vaghezza.
Questa arte dunque essendo di tal merto,
Alfonso mio, chi d'Orfeo porti il vanto,   10

---

1   He and Quin appear in the same salary records, for example in Andrew Ashbee (ed.), *Records of English Court Music* (8 vols, Snodland: Ashbee, 1986–96), viii, p. 71.
2   Andrew Ashbee, 'Ferrabosco, Alfonso (*c.*1575–1628)', *ODNB*.

Convien pregiarti, e questi tuoi concenti;
Tanto più ch'essi con doppio concerto,
A gl'istrumenti attando il dolce canto,
Di piacer doppio ne appagan le menti.

In Praise of the Art and the Author [T]

If every art is the more prized by us the more noble the sense it has for [its] object, and the more worthy its subject is; harmonious sweetness triumphs over the other arts.

This always gives relish and pleasure to our hearing, the most perfect of the senses; its subject is equal and proper rhythm and the grace of lovely air and sounds.

This art then being of such merit, my Alfonso who bears the fame of Orpheus,[3] one must prize you, and these harmonies of yours

All the more, as they with doubled harmony adapting sweet song to instruments delight our minds with double pleasure.[4]

---

3   Orpheus – the legendary Greek lyre player, who was so skilled that his music affected animals, trees and rocks – is an obvious figure to employ in praise of a musician; however, in this case it is particularly apt as Alfonso's work was written for lyra-viol and even a modern commentator can observe: 'it is from the lyra solos that we can perhaps best form an impression of Ferrabosco's artistry on an instrument which, in his hands, seemed like the Jacobean equivalent of Orpheus' lyre': John V. Cockshoot & Christopher D.S. Field, 'Ferrabosco: (5) Alfonso Ferrabosco (ii)', *Grove Music Online. Oxford Music Online* (Oxford UP, 2013), www.oxfordmusiconline.com/subscriber/article/grove/music/09507pg5, accessed 1 Mar. 2014.

4   There may be a pun here as a section of Ferrabosco's work was for two instruments. See ibid.

8

From Thomas Coryate's *Coryate's Crudities* (1611)

Thomas Coryate (1577?–1617) was a member of Prince Henry's household where he entertained others with his buffoonery.[1] In 1608 he went on a continental tour, which provided the material for his lengthy and privately printed *Coryate's Crudities* (1611). Coryate's text is preceded by commendatory works in several languages written by about sixty writers (including Jonson, Donne, Hugh Holland, Inigo Jones and Michael Drayton). These were frequently derogatory since Henry, to whom the book was dedicated, insisted that all the commendatory material that Coryate was given was printed regardless of how it reflected on the author. The expense involved in producing the volume and the list of those who provided its panegyrics indicate its courtly origins, so it is easy to see why Quin was involved in it. Quin's poem – his only humorous one – contains satirical references to Coryate's adventures, so he was familiar with them before their publication. Later in 1611, the prefatory works (including Quin's poem) usurped Coryate's own narrative when they appeared independently of his travels in *The Odcombian Banquet*.[2] In the copy-text, Quin's poem is headed: 'Incipit Gualterus Quin. In lode del l'autore' and ends 'Explicit Gualterus Quin'.

Copy-text

Thomas Coryate, CORYATS | Crudities | Hastily gobled up in five | Moneths trauells in France, | Savoy, Italy, Rhetia, com[m]only | called the Grisons country Hel- | vetia aliàs Switzerland, some | parts of high Germany, and the Netherlands; | Newly digested in the hungry aire | of ODCOMBE in the County of | Somerset, & now dispersed to the | nourishment of the trauelling Mem- | bers of this Kingdome. London: W[illiam] S[tansby], 1611. 4°. *ESTC* S108716 (forty-five copies). Oxford, Balliol College Library, 575 b 6.

An edition is available on *EEBO*. Quin's poem was reprinted in *The Odcombian Banquet*.[3]

---

1 For the details of Coryate's life summarized here, see Michael Strachan, 'Coryate, Thomas (1577?–1617)', *ODNB*; Katharine A. Craik, 'Reading *Coryats Crudities* (1611)', *Studies in English Literature, 1500–1900*, 44, 1 (2004), 77–96.

2 In 1612 John Taylor produced a satire on Coryate's panegyrists but he did not mention Quin: *Laugh, and be Fat: or, A Commentary upon the Odcombyan Blanket* ([London?]: [W. Hall?], 1612).

3 *The Odcombian Banquet: Dished Foorth by Thomas the Coriat, and Serued in by a Number of Noble Wits in Prayse of his Crudities and Crambe Too* ([London]: [by George Eld] for Thomas Thorp, 1611), sig. G3r.

La cornamusa di Gualtero Quin [sig. E3v]

Se'l gran guerrier, chi tanto fece e scrisse,
Se stesso, e 'l mondo insieme ingarbugliando,
Per commandar a tutti, mentre ei visse,
De' suoi gran vanti andava trionfando;
    Ben è ragion, *Tom-asino* galante,   5
Ch'altiero e bravo tu ti pavoneggi,
Poiché nel far, e scriver stravagante,
Vinci il gran Giulio, non che lo pareggi.
    Di quel, ch'egli ebbe in parecchi anni oprato
Con schiere armate, scrisse un libricciuolo: 10
Ma dal cervello tuo un libraccio è nato
Di quel, c'hai fatto in pochi mesi solo:
    Latino e Greco sapeva esso assai;
Ma dell'inglese era affatto ignorante:
Tu'l vinci in questo, e pur d'avanzo sai   15
Greco e Latino, per far un pedante.
    Un gran rumor e terribile fracasso
Fece ei, per metter sottosopra il mondo:
Di dar da rider con sollazzo e spasso
A tutti, fù de' tuoi disegni il fondo.   20
    Molte migliaia di schiere nemiche
Morir ei fè con lancie, dardi, e stocchi:
Mai non ti piacquer archibugi, ò picche,
Nè morte alcuna, fuor che de pidocchi:
    Quei chi scamparon l'unghie tue prigioni   25
Portasti addosso: come quel guerriero
Di squadre morte i principi e padroni
Menossi avanti trionfante e altiero.
    Ei vincitor ascese in Campidoglio,
Con pompa e boria, in carro trionfale: 30
Contadinesco carro senza orgoglio
Per trionfar ti piacque; manco male.
    Colui mostrando, come andava ratto
Nel vincer, scrisse, *Io venni, vidi, vinsi*:
L' hai detto meglio tu vincendo il patto,   35
Che ti fe scorrer e quinci, e costinci.
    Francia, Lamagna, Italia, Helvetia, Rhetia,
Non scorse già senza armi quel bravaccio;
Come scorresti tu ratto a Venetia,

E indietro a casa tua con poco impaccio. 40
    Solo un villan tedesco, ubriaco, e tristo,
Con bastonate ben ti pestò gli ossi:
Forse ch'ei sceso dal vecchio Ariovisto
Di casa Giulia pensò che tu fossi.
    Ma per disgrazia se'n valor attivo 45
A Giulio alcun sopra te desse il vanto;
Egli è pur forza ch' in valor passivo
Voto e sentenza egli dia dal tuo canto.
    Né suoi viaggi gran fatica ei prese,
Non però senza cavai, muli, e cocchi: 50
Tu sempre andavi a pie, mal in arnese,
Vincendo i cingani, staffieri, e scrocchi.
    Elquel ch'a schivo havria per morbidezza,
Bastotti un par di scarpe in quel viaggio,
Che rattoppasti spesso con destrezza; 55
Di lesinesca industria vero saggio.
    Questa lode anc' hai di buon lesinante
(Di che quel prodigo non fu mai degno)
Ch'una camicia e veste, da buon fante:
Sola portasti allor senza aschio, ò sdegno. 60
    Parsa a lui peste saria la tua rogna,
Che nel grattarla dandoti sollazzo,
Ballar ti fè come al suon di zampogna,
O violin di quel francese pazzo.
    L'avrian ucciso i tuoi stenti, e disagi 65
Nel mangiar, bever, dormir, appiccarti
Pulci, pidocchi, e cimici malvagi,
Guastar le gambe, e 'l culo scorticarti:
    Nel travagliar col corpo il capo ancora,
Quindi il cervello ognora lambiccando; 70
Per ciascun passo, che pria facesti, ora
Righe altrettante dal cervel stillando.
    S'ei questi affanni mai sofferti avrebbe,
Manco gl'affronti, onte,[4] e scorni, ch'omai
Non senti sordo e cieco, soffrirebbe; 75
Trastullo a te si fan pur questi guai.
    Poiché in oprar, dunque, e 'n patir l'agguagli,
Anzi lo vinci, *Tom-asino* invitto,

---

4 'Onte' (a variant of 'onta') is a conjectural emendation for the copy-text's 'ente', which is
    unintelligible. The editor is grateful to Ian Campbell Ross for this suggestion.

Qual cornamusa si gonfi, e travagli,
Chi vuol cantarti con decoro e dritto.   80

The Bagpipe of Walter Quin [T]

If the great warrior who wrote and did so much, bamboozling both himself and
the world, so as to be the boss of everyone in his lifetime, triumphed with his
great achievements;

It is quite right, gallant *Tom-ass* that you should peacock it lofty and bold
since in doing and writing wild things you beat great Julius rather than just being
[his] equal.

Of what he had done in many years with armed troops, he wrote a little
book:[5] but from your brain a monster-book is born of what you did in only a
few months:

Latin and Greek he knew sufficiently, but he was wholly ignorant of English:
you beat him in this, and then you know quite enough Greek and Latin to
make a schoolmaster.

A great clamour, a terrific uproar, he made, to turn the world upside-down:
to raise laughter with fun and amusement for all, was the basis of your designs.

Many thousand of enemy troops he did to death with spears, arrows and
swords: but you did not love arquebuses or pikes nor any killing except for lice:

Those that escaped your capturing nails you carried with you: just as that warrior had the princes and chieftains of slaughtered armies led before his triumph.

He ascended as victor to the Capitol, with pomp and show in a triumphal car:
a peasant cart with no ostentation pleased you to triumph in; a good job too.

He showed how rapid he was in victory, writing *veni, vidi, vici*:[6] you said it
better, bettering his challenge which had you rushing hither and yonder.

France, Germany, Italy, Switzerland, Rhetia, that bully overran, but not
unarmed; as you ran over rapidly to Venice, and backwards to your home with
little hindrance.

Only a German peasant, drunken wretch, hammered your bones well with
his stick: perhaps he descended from old Ariovistus and thought you were of the
Julian house.[7]

But if, unfortunately, in active valour one might give Julius a higher place

---

5   Julius Caesar's *Commentaries on the Gallic Wars*, to which Quin refers to again below.
6   Caesar's famous 'veni, vidi, vici', recounted in his biographies by Plutarch and Suetonius:
    Plutarch, *Plutarch's Lives*, trans. Bernadotte Perrin (11 vols, London: Heinemann, 1914–26),
    vii, p. 563 [50]. Suetonius, *The Twelve Caesars*, trans. Robert Graves (Harmondsworth:
    Penguin, 1970), p. 25 [37]. Quin uses Caesar as a serious parallel in *Bernard Stuart*.
7   There is an account of how Ariovistus, a Germanic king, was driven out of Gaul by Caesar in
    Caesar's *Commentaries*.

than you, it cannot be denied that in passive valour he must give his vote and verdict on your side.

He took great trouble in his travels but not without horses, mules and chariots: you travelled always on foot, dressed in rags, outdoing all gypsies, grooms and scroungers.

And, scorning all outward signs of luxury, you needed only one pair of shoes on that journey, that you often mended dextrously, truly accomplished in miserly industry.

Another praise you earned as a prime scrimper (of which that prodigal was never worthy), was that like a good soldier you wore one shirt and one coat all that time without grudge or scorning.

Your itch would have seemed a plague to him, and your pleasure in scratching it made you dance as if to the sound of the pipe or that mad Frenchman's little viol.

Your privations would have killed him, and your troubles with food, drink, sleep, picking up fleas, lice and dangerous bugs, breaking your legs and flaying your arse:

Battering your body and your head as well, and then racking your brains without cease; for every step that you had taken, now distilling matching verses from your brain.

If he had ever suffered these labours, much less the affronts, indignities and scorns (which deaf and blind you don't feel), he would have suffered. Even these afflictions seem like trifles to you.

Since you in active and passive achievement are his equal, and you even surpass him, *Tom-ass* unconquered, let this bagpipe swell and strain, which wishes to sing of you fittingly and rightly.

9

From Josuah Sylvester's *Lachrimae Lachrimarum* (1612)

In 1612, the sudden illness and death of Henry, Prince of Wales, gave rise to national mourning. Sylvester's *Distillation of Tears*, with its description of the prince as *Panaretus* ('all virtuous'), does not seem excessive in the context of 'close to fifty different volumes of memorial writing – including elegies, epicedia, epitaphs, emblems, impresa, devices, meditations, sermons' that followed on the prince's demise.[1]

Josuah Sylvester (1563–1618) was and is best known as the translator of the works of Guillaume de Salluste, lord Du Bartas (see the Introduction, p. 27). Much of his work was dedicated to King James and between 1608 and 1612 he was patronized by Prince Henry (to whom he first dedicated a work in 1605).[2] It was natural, therefore, that Sylvester would produce a volume lamenting the death of Henry, and although measured in terms of numbers of pages of text Quin is a co-author of *Lachrimae Lachrimarum*, both its title page and the diminishing space given to Quin's work in subsequent editions clearly demonstrate that the initiative was Sylvester's.

Copy-text

Josuah Sylvester, LACHRIMAE LACHRIMARVM | or | The Distillation | of Teares | Shede | For the vntymely Death | of | The incomparable Prince | PANARETVS. | by Iosuah Syluester. London: Humfrey Lownes, 1612. 4°. ESTC S118065 (nineteen copies). BL, General Reference Collection C.194.a.1114.[3]

The work is strikingly presented: it has a xylographic black title page with white lines. Its poems (surrounded by images of skeletons) are printed on the recto sides with black mourning pages (relieved only by an image of Henry's coat of arms) on their facing versos. This kind of visual metaphor was not uncommon in elegies for the prince.[4] A copy of this edition is available on *EEBO*.

---

1   J.W. Williamson, *The Myth of the Conqueror. Prince Henry Stuart: A Study of 17th Century Personation* (New York: AMS Press, 1978), p. 171.
2   Leila Parsons, 'Prince Henry (1594–1612) as a Patron of Literature', *Modern Language Review*, 47, 4 (1952), 504–7.
3   From the collection of Sir Thomas Grenville (1755–1846), whose name is stamped on the binding.
4   Catharine MacLeod et al. (eds), *The Lost Prince: The Life and Death of Henry Stuart* (London: National Portrait Gallery, 2013), pp 171–2.

There is a second edition of this work from 1612 (ESTC S118066) with the same title page and a different border (one that includes a figure in a winding cloth as well as the skeletons) and a nearly identical text (for example, *STC* notes that it has 'Caedars' for 'Cedars' on sig. A3r). *STC* notes the possibility that there may have been mixed sheets or impositions in the first two editions.

Sylvester's volume was obviously popular. Humphrey Lownes printed a third edition in 1613 (*ESTC* S125682), which was reissued that year (*ESTC* S118067).[5] Both included Quin's 'Occidit ante diem' and 'Il fior de principi' but omitted his English and French poems. Their place was taken by other poets' 'sundrie funeral elegies' including works by members of the prince's household (Dr Joseph Hall, one of the chaplains, and Henry Burton, the clerk of the closet) as well as by John Donne and his friends (Hugh Holland, Sir Henry Goodere and Sir William Cornwallis the younger).[6]

'Lo here intomb'd' and 'Occidit ante diem' are also to be found (attributed to Quin) in the anonymously compiled *Mausoleum or, the Choisest Flowres of The Epitaphs, Written on the Death of the Never-Too-Much Lamented Prince Henrie* (Edinburgh: Andrew Hart, 1613), sig. A2r. The *Mausoleum* texts vary slightly in spelling and punctuation. Quin's two poems appear in the opening page of the collection and are followed by three verses by William Drummond. Although it may appear initially that this is a Scottish collection, there are poems by the English writers Hugh Holland, Robert Allyne, George Chapman and William Rowley.

The Prince's Epitaph, Written by His Highness' Servant, Walter Quin [sig. C1r]

Lo here entombed a peerless prince doth lie,
In flower and strength of age surprised by death,
On whom, while he on earth drew vital breath,
The hope of many kingdoms did rely;
    Not without cause: for heavens most liberally   5
To him all princely virtues did bequeath,
Which to the worthiest princes here beneath
Before had been allotted severally.
    But when the world of all his virtues rare
The wished fruit to gather did expect,   10
And that he should such glorious works effect,

5   The latter is described by *ESTC* as 'another state of *STC* 23577.5, with quires B and C in another setting' while *STC* says that it is 'another issue' of *STC* 23577.5.

6   John Donne, *The Complete Poems of John Donne*, ed. Robin Robbins (2nd ed.; Harlow: Pearson Education, 2010), p. 761.

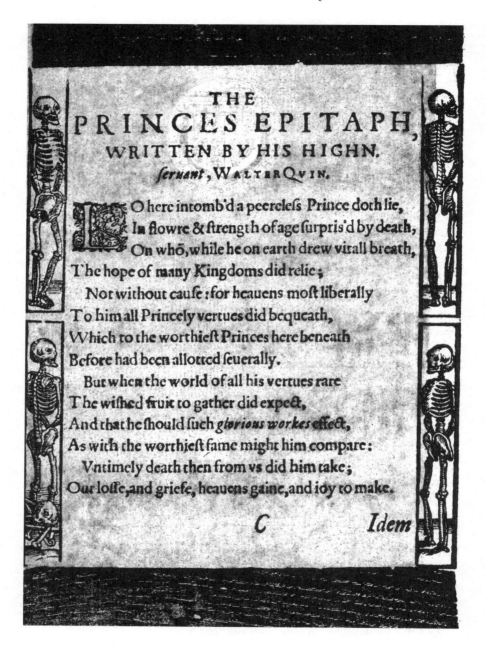

THE PRINCES EPITAPH,
WRITTEN BY HIS HIGHN.
seruant, WALTER QVIN.

LO here intomb'd a peereless Prince doth lie,
In flowre & strength of age surpris'd by death,
On whō, while he on earth drew vitall breath,
The hope of many Kingdoms did relie;
    Not without cause : for heauens most liberally
To him all Princely vertues did bequeath,
Which to the worthiest Princes here beneath
Before had been allotted seuerally.
    But when the world of all his vertues rare
The wished fruit to gather did expect,
And that he should such *glorious workes* effect,
As with the worthiest fame might him compare :
    Vntimely death then from vs did him take;
Our losse, and griefe, heauens gaine, and ioy to make.

C   *Idem*

3 Josuah Sylvester's *Lachrimae Lachrimarum*, sig. Cr (© The British Library
Board, General Reference Collection, C.194.a.1114).

As with the worthiest fame might him compare:
    Untimely death then from us did him take;
Our loss, and grief, heaven's gain, and joy to make.

[Occidit ante diem iuvenum flos] [sig. C2r]

Occidit ante diem juvenum flos, gloria stirpis
Regalis, patriae spes, columenque suae.
Occidit ante diem, patri populisque Britannis
Flendus et his junctis foedere, amore, sacris.
Occidit ante diem gesturus principe digna,   5
Accelerasset ei ni fera parca necem.
Occidit ante diem, virtutis et ubere fructu,
Et mundum exemplo funere destituens.
Occidit ante diem, si vota et commoda spectes
Publica, vel vitam si brevitate notes.   10
Sin vitam spectes partam illi morte perennem,
Haud iam, par superis, occidit ante diem.

[He Perished Before His Time] [T]

He perished before his time, the flower of youth, the glory of the royal line, the hope and mainstay of his native land.

He perished before his time, a man to be mourned by Britain and her people and by those joined to them by treaty, love and rites.

He perished before his time, a man destined to do deeds worthy of a prince, had fierce fate not hastened his death.

He perished before his time, leaving behind virtue and rich success and, with an exemplary death, the world.

He perished before his time if you consider his pledges and services to the public, or if you observe the brevity of his life;

However, if you consider the eternal life obtained by him in death, as one fit for heaven, then he has not perished before his time.

[Tant plus qu'un bien est grand, et rare en excellence] [sig. C3r]

Tant plus qu'un bien est grand, et rare en excellence,
Et que la jouissance en a plus de plaisir ;
Tant plus ainsi la perte en a de déplaisir,

Et se fait regretter avec impatience.
    Ceci se montre assez en la fruition,   5
Qu'avons eu d'un grand prince, en tous bien admirable ;
Et en sa triste mort, d'autant plus déplorable,
Que rare de tout point fut sa perfection.
    Tant l'eurent la Nature, et la Vertu ensemble,
Et la Fortune aussi de leurs dons enrichi,   10
Que de quelle des trois il fut le plus chéri,
De pouvoir bien juger malaisé il me semble.
    De l'estoc plus ancien d'entre les rois extrait,
Il fut si bien doué des dons de la nature
En corps, et en esprit, que jamais créature   15
N'a été de son art chef-d'oeuvre plus parfait.
    D'elle il eut beauté, la grâce, et bienséance,
Force, adresse, esprit vif, et invincible coeur,
Grandeur et majesté mêlée avec douceur,
Que reluire on voyait en sa contenance.   20
    La Vertu voyant par Nature apprêter
Un si riche sujet, l'enrichit davantage
Et la rendant pieuse, tempérée, preux, et sage,
Lustre, clémente, et pleine de largesse et bonté.
    Cette même Vertu lui fait les arts apprendre,   25
Par lesquels un grand prince à bien régir en paix,
Et à bien soutenir de la guerre le fait ;
Quand il en a besoin, capable se peut rendre.
    La Fortune envers lui favorable aussi fut
Sur les plus chers mignons lui donnant l'avantage :   30
Car trésors et grandeurs et le riche héritage
De maints pays et royaumes, et maintes villes il eut.
    Il semblait que ces trois avec telle largesse
L'ayant de tous leurs dons à l'envie étrenné,
Par la faveur du ciel il fut au monde né,   35
Pour vivre un siècle entier de gloire, heur, et liesse ;
    Et pour faire jouir aux siens l'exemple et fruit
De ses faits vertueux et en paix, et en guerre ;
Et étendre son los aux bornes de la terre,
Où notre hiver été, notre jour se fait nuit.   40
    Ô que le monde avait bien besoin de sa vie !
Car il servait d'épée, et bouclier aux amis ;
De terreur, et de fléau contre les ennemis ;
De rempart assuré, et d'ancre à sa patrie ;

D'appui, et de défense à son père royal ;   45
À sa mère d'honneur ; de miroir à son frère ;
D'ornement à sa soeur ; aux princes d'exemplaire ;
De merveille et de joie à tout peuple loyal.

    Mais, hélas, ce grand prince en la fleur de son âge,
Et de notre espérance (Ô triste coup de ciel !)   50
Nous a été ravi : dont en sel notre miel
Se change, et notre joie en deuil, regret, et rage.

    Ô ciel à quelle fin nous prêtas-tu ce bien,
Ce joyau non pareil, ce miroir de noblesse,
Pour nous l'ôter si tôt ? Et que ce coup nous blesse,   55
Nous foudroie, et fracasse, et réduit presqu'en rien !

    À quelle fin je vois : c'est pour prendre vengeance
De nos méchancetés, et horribles méfaits,
Que si cruellement tu décoches tes traits
Sur nous pauvres chétifs, et misérable engeance.   60

    Trop bon pour nous il fut : reprendre il t'aura plu
Ton cher gage, duquel avons joui naguère,
Afin d'en embellir tes plus belles lumières,
Et de le réunir à son céleste feu.

    Mais envers toi, cher prince, ô quel devoir nous reste-t-il ?   65
Avec toi nous faut-il nous réjouir du sort,
Que t'est échu au ciel, des bienheureux le port ?
Ou regretter ta mort aux tiens par trop funeste ?

    L'un, et l'autre serons : t'applaudir il convient
En ce que tu jouas si bien ton rôle au monde,   70
Et là viens à revivre où tout bonheur abonde,
Et où tout deuil en joie à convertir se vient.

    Mais tant plus que nous fuit ta vie douce et chère,
Et qu'en fleur d'ans la mort nous te vint arracher,
Les rênes d'autant plus nous convient-il lâcher   75
Au deuil, en regrettant notre perte et misère.

[The More That a Good Person Is Great and Rare in Excellence] [T]

The more that a good person is great and rare in excellence, taking pleasure in
his health, all the more then is the displeasure in a loss that is to be regretted
impatiently.

    This is sufficiently demonstrated in the fruition which we had of a great
prince – in everything admirable – and in his sad death, all the more appalling
since he was in all points perfect.

He was given so much by Nature, and Virtue together with Fortune also enriched him with their gifts, that it seems difficult to judge rightly which of the three prized him most.

Descended from the oldest kingly origins, he was so generously endowed in body and mind with the gifts of Nature, that there was never a creature that was of her art a more perfect masterpiece.

From her he received beauty, grace and decorum, strength, skill, liveliness of spirit and invincible courage; greatness and majesty mixed with mildness, the light of which was visible in his countenance.

Virtue, seeing that Nature had prepared such a rich subject, enriched him more and made him pious, temperate, chivalrous and wise, bright, merciful and full of generosity and bounty.

This same Virtue made him learn her arts, by which a great prince can reign well in peace, and, when necessary, be made capable of withstanding well the burdens of warfare.

Fortune had been more generous to him than she had been to her most cherished ones, because he received treasures, dignities and a rich inheritance of many a country and kingdom, as well as many a town.

It seems that these three with great generosity wished to give him all their gifts, since by heaven's favour he was born in the world to live for a whole century in glory, honour and jubilation;

And to give the advantage of his example and the fruit of his virtuous deeds (both in peace and in war); and to spread his praise across the land, where our winter was, our day was turned to night.

O the world surely had need of his life! Because he acted as sword and shield to friends, as a terror and scourge against enemies, and as a sure rampart and anchor for his country;

As a prop and defence of his royal father, an honour to his mother, an example to his brother, an ornament to his sister, a pattern for princes, a marvel and a joy to all loyal people.

But alas, in the flower of his age and of our hope, this great prince (O sad blow of heaven!) was robbed from us, thus our honey is changed to salt and our joy to mourning, regret and rage.

O heaven, to what end did you take this good thing from us, this unparalleled joy, this mirror of nobility removed from us so soon? O but this blow wounds us, strikes us down, smashes us and reduces us to near nothing!

I know the explanation: it is to take revenge for our wickedness and horrible misdeeds, that you so cruelly shoot your lightning at our poor, puny and miserable race.

He was too good for us, you wished to take him back to you (your dear pledge from which we recently benefitted), in order to embellish your most beautiful lights and to rejoin him with his celestial fire.

So, dear prince, what duty towards you remains to us? Must we rejoice with you because your fate is heaven, the port of the blessed, or regret your death by keeping to deepest mourning?

We will do both: it is proper to applaud you in that you played so well your earthly role, and you come to life again there where every good fortune abounds, and where all mourning will be turned into joy.

But, the more that your dear and sweet life flees away from us and all the more because in the bloom of your years you were plucked from us, it behooves us to abandon all feelings to mourning, lamenting our loss and wretchedness.

[Il fior' de principi nel fior' de gl'anni] [sig. D3r]

Il fior' de principi nel fior' de gl'anni
E delle nostre speranze, ora è colto
Dalla spietata morte (ahi lasso) e tolto
A noi dolenti e miseri Britanni.
    A nessun' popol' mai diè tanti affanni   5
Morendo alcun' gran principe, per molto
Ch'ei fosse amato, quanti il nostro sciolto
Dal corpo ci lascia e dolori, e danni.
    Dal ciel pareva ch'ei ci fosse dato,
Perché del padre successor nel regno   10
Fosse, e felice, e chiaro e'n pace, e'n guerra.
    Ma ci vien tolto (ohimè) dal ciel irato.
A danni nostri; perché di se degno
Stimolo, e'indegna esser' di lui la terra.

[The Flower of Princes in the Flower of His Age] [T]

The flower of princes in the flower of his age and of our hopes is now cut down by pitiless death (alas), and taken away from us suffering wretched Britons.

No people were ever afflicted with such pain when any great prince died, no matter how much he was loved, as much as ours, unbound from the flesh, leaves us full of pain and injured.

From heaven it seemed he had been given to us, so that he should be his father's successor in the kingdom; fortunate, and famous in peace and war.

But to our cost he has been taken from us (alas) by angry heaven, because he was esteemed worthy of heaven, and the earth unworthy of him.

[131]

Corona virtutum principe dignarum (1613)

This volume deals with the virtues appropriate to a ruler (it is in the mirror-for-princes genre) and is dedicated to Prince Charles. It principally consists of quotations about virtues drawn from Classical sources and two short biographies of just Roman emperors whose deeds and characters could be profitably emulated. It is a work that reflects Quin's neo-Stoicism. Charles was fond of quoting aphorisms, many of which were based in neo-Stoic philosophy, so Quin's book may have answered to (or been partially formative of) a developing taste.[1]

The first and main part of the book (pp 1–136) contains eleven chapters dealing with virtue, vice, religion, prudence, justice, clemency, faith, modesty, generosity, temperance and fortitude. It draws on a wide range of Latin sources including Aulus Gellius, Ammianus Marcellinus, Ausonius, Boethius, Cassidorus, Cato the Elder, Catullus, Cicero, the *Historia Augusta* (see below), Horace, Juvenal, Livy, Lucan, Ovid, Perseus, Petronius, Plautus, Pliny, Propertius, Sallust, Seneca, Suetonius, Tacitus, Tibullus, Terence, Valerius Maximus and Virgil. These are augmented by a smaller number of Greek authors whose quotations are translated into Latin (Aristotle, Epictetus, Euripides, Hesiod, Plutarch, Strobaeus, Thucydides and Xenophon).

Quin explains his method in his address 'To the reader': 'I have applied nothing but connecting passages, as a sort of cement to link together the sentences of authors and I did this as sparingly as possible […] I have added to the Latin maxims those of the Greeks, but they have been rendered into Latin.' He acknowledges his debt to Justus Lipsius' *Politicorum sive civilis doctrinae libri sex qui ad principatum maxime spectant* (*Six Books of Politics or Political Instruction Which Especially Concern Monarchy*, 1589). In Lipsius, book I deals with the role of virtue in community, book II with the virtues desirable in princes, while books III and IV deal with prudence (books V and VI deal with military matters, and were thus less relevant to Quin). Lipsius organized his volume like a commonplace book or a prose *cento* (a poem composed of quotations from others' work), a format that Quin also adopted.[2] Although Quin regarded Lipsius as 'a man of

---

1   Richard Cust, *Charles I: A Political Life* (Harlow: Pearson Education, 2007), p. 17. The long-term effects of the championing of Marcus Aurelius by Quin and others are discussed in Reid Barbour, *English Epicures and Stoics: Ancient Legacies in Early Stuart Culture* (Amherst: University of Massachusetts Press, 1998), pp 172–4.

2   Justus Lipsius, *Politica: Six Books of Politics or Political Instruction*, ed. and trans. Jan Waszink (Assen: Royal Van Gorcum, 2004), pp 55–8.

singular intellect, judgment and learning' (see 'To the Reader', below), King James had condemned his religious inconstancy in the 1599 edition of *Basilicon doron*, but the excision of this passage from subsequent editions suggests that Lipsius was to be tolerated.[3] In any event, Quin must have judged that James would not have felt his work to be inappropriate for the education of the prince of Wales, and his admiration for Lipsius was shared by many admirers in Scotland and England, both Protestant and Catholic.[4]

The second part of *Corona* is composed of two biographies. The life of Antoninus Pius (pp 137–43) appears with the title 'De vita et virtutibus Antonini Pii imperatoris, e Julio Capitolino, et Aurelio Victore excerpta maxime memorabilia.' Pages 145–63 are taken up with an account of the philosopher-emperor Marcus Aurelius: 'De vita et virtutibus Marci Antonini philosophi, imperatoris, ex Dione, Julio Capitolino, Vulcatio Gallico, Herodiano, et Aelio Lampridio excerpta, et in ordinem digesta maxime memorabilia.' Quin's chief source for these biographies is the fourth-century collection known as the *Historia Augusta*. The date and authorship of this work have been disputed by modern scholars, but it was originally attributed to six writers, three of whom Quin mentions: Julius Capitolinus, Vulcacius Gallicanus and Flavius Vopiscus.[5] The *editio princeps* of the *Historia* was printed in 1475 and subsequent editions include one by Erasmus (1518). Continued interest in the work is attested by the edition of Janus Gruter (1611), but Quin is more likely to have known the influential edition by Isaac Casaubon (1603), which was dedicated to Henry IV.[6] Casaubon's notes could have supplied Quin with material from Sextus Aurelius Victor (*fl.* 360–90) for the biography of Antoninus Pius, and with quotation from Cassius Dio (*c.*164–post-229) for his life of Marcus Aurelius.[7] Herodian of Syria (third century) does not feature in Casaubon's section on Marcus Aurelius (although he is cited elsewhere), but his Greek *History of the Roman Empire* that had appeared in a Latin translation by Politian (who had also translated Epictetus) in 1493 was reprinted throughout the sixteenth and seventeenth centuries and was published in an English translation by Nicholas Smith *c.*1556.[8]

3   *Selected Writings*, p. 245.

4   For the latter point see J.H.M. Salmon, 'Seneca and Tacitus in Jacobean England' in Linda Levy Peck (ed.), *The Mental World of the Jacobean Court* (Cambridge: Cambridge UP, 1991), p. 171.

5   *OCD*. The *Historia* is the only evidence for the existence of these writers.

6   David Magie (ed.), *The Scriptores Historiae Augustae* (3 vols, Cambridge, MA: Harvard UP, 1991), i, p. xxxvii.

7   See, for example, Isaac Casaubon, *In Aelius Spartianum, Julium Capitolinum, Aelium Lampridium, Vulcatium Gallicanum, Trebellium Pollionem, & Flavium Vopiscum: emendationes ac notae* (Paris: Ambrose and Hieronymus Drouart, 1603), pp 105, 111, 112, 125–9.

8   Herodian of Antioch, *History of the Roman Empire*, trans. Edward C. Echols (Berkeley: University of California Press, 1961), p. 8. Both Cassius Dio and Herodian are sources of the

In the early modern period, the *Historia Augusta*, the works of Cassius Dio and of Herodian of Syria identified Marcus Aurelius as a paradigm of good rule and an explicit adherent of Stoic philosophy.[9] King James had thought well enough of him to gift a volume on his life to the library of St Andrews and, as such, he was a suitable model for Charles I.[10]

Copy-text

Walter Quin, CORONA | VIRTVTVM | PRINCIPE DIG- | NARVM, | Ex variis Philosophorum, Histo- | ricorum, Oratorum, & Poetarum | floribus contexta, & con- | cinnata, | In vsum D. CAROLI Magnae | Britanniae, & Hiberniae Principis | Illustrissimi, Cornubiae, Eboraci, | & Albaniae Ducis. | Cui adiuncta sunt de vita, & vir- | tutibus duorum ANTONINORVM, | PII, & MARCI maximè me- | morabilia è variis histo- | ricis excerpta. London: John Bill, 1613. 12°. ESTC S115532 (six copies). BL, General Reference Collection 721.a.44.

This was one of Quin's most popular works and there were three subsequent editions: two impressions set from the same plates by John Bill (1615 and 1617), one printed by Elsevier in Leiden (1634) and one by Havenstein (Hanover and Frankfurt, 1678).[11] *Corona* also appeared in Etienne de Melles et al., *Steph. de Melles [...] Ethica particularis* (1670).[12] The 1613 edition is to be found on Google Books. All of the English editions are available on *EEBO*.

This edition includes Quin's introductory material in prose and verse, but it does not reproduce the rest of the work, which is a collection of quotations or, in the case of the imperial lives, a digest of well-known sources.

Historia Augusta: Geoff W. Adams, *Marcus Aurelius in the Historia Augusta and Beyond* (Lanham, MD: Lexington Books, 2012), pp 22–3.

9   Jill Kraye, 'Marcus Aurelius and Neostoicism in Early Modern Philosophy' in M. van Ackeren (ed.), *A Companion to Marcus Aurelius* (Malden, MA: Wiley-Blackwell, 2012), p. 516.

10 David Allan, *Philosophy and Politics in Later Stuart Scotland: Neo-Stoicism, Culture and Ideology in an Age of Crisis, 1540–1690* (East Linton: Tuckwell Press, 2000), p. 34 n. 20.

11 The full details of these editions can be found in the bibliography.

12 The page introducing the work reads: 'Gualteri Quinni De virtutibus principis. Opus ex praestantissimorum authorum floribus & sententiis contextum. Ad Carolum Magnae Britannae principem' (Walter Quin, the Virtues of a Prince: A Work Composed from the Best Parts and Opinions of the Most Excellent Authors. For Charles, Prince of Great Britain). It does not include the opening epistle and poem addressed to Prince Charles and the biographies of the emperors: Etienne de Melles et al., *Steph. de Melles [...] Ethica particularis seu institutiones privaae, oeconomiae, et politiae [...] annexa ejusdem opera et studio duo opuscula: I. Celsi [...] princeps ex. C. Tacito; Q. Quinni de virtutibus principis [...]* (Paris: Dionysius Thierry, 1670), pp 337–481.

Illustrissimo principi [sig. A2r][13]

Post illum ego si tibi in hoc genere meum aliquid offerrem, ne et impudens et imprudens optime actum agerem pessime, meque cunctis merito deridendum propinarem.

Caeterum cum ad virtutem in te promovendam operam quoque meam conferre cupiam, nec de meo quicquam te dignum mihi suppetat, virtutum principe dignarum coronam, e variis optimorum authorum floribus in usum tuum contextam et concinnatam tibi offero.

Cui maxime memorabilia de vita et moribus duorum principium (quorum alter alteri, ut in imperio, sic in omni virtutum genere successit) attexere visum est operae pretium; ut una et monitis, et exemplis erudiri possis.

E sacris literis, et patrum scriptis quae huc faciunt theologis excerpenda relinquo; cum ipse sacra illotis (quod aiunt) manibus attingere non ausim.

Quod si virtutem principi tantopere commendent tam sententiis suis authores hic citati, quam exemplo principes a me commemorati, utrique fere omnes non nisi naturae ac rationis lumine illustrati, quanto studio princeps, cui religionis etiam Christianae lux affulsit, virtutem par est amplectatur? Unde operam hanc meam tibi ad virtutem incitamento aliqua ex parte futuram spero. Hanc vero, et quamvis aliam grati animi significationem debere me profiteor cum patris tui serenissimi in me favori, ac de me iudicio (qui octodecim abhinc annis me in familiam aulicam admissum, et benigne sublevatum postea et illustrissimo tuo fratri felicis memoriae, et tibi ipsi in studiis aliquam operam navare voluit) tum etiam tuae in me ab infantia tua perpetuae benignitati. Si opella haec mea ad animi tui cultum usui tibi fuerit, et tibi, et reipublicae magnopere gratulabor. Faxit Deus ut votis meis successus respondeat, et ut virtute, ac felicitate principum optimo et felicissimo cuique par evadas.

Celsitudini tuae,

Aeternum devinctus ac devotus famulus, et cliens, Gualterus Quinnus.

Most Illustrious Prince [T]

Most Illustrious Prince, willingly and full of gratitude do I recognize the many indications of your lofty and famous intellect: your outstanding genius, your generous mind, your candour and your kindness shine forth even upon your

13 The volume opens with a quotation from Seneca's *De beneficiis* (*On Benefits*): 'Plus proderit, sit pauca praecepta sapientiae teneas, sed illa in promptu tibi, et in usu sint, quam si multa quidem didiceris; sed illa non habeas ad manum' (sig. A1v; 'it is much better to have only a few philosophical teachings that are nevertheless known to you and in regular employment, than to learn a great deal of knowledge that is not to hand'). See Seneca, *Seneca: Moral Essays*, ed. and trans. John W. Basore (3 vols, London: Heinemann, 1964), iii, p. 454 [vii.1.3].

very countenance. However, whatever things remain still to be praised in you should be thought of as the sparks or seeds of virtue rather than virtues themselves. For in order that they flourish in you and are fruitful, you must have judgment that matures with age and careful cultivation of the mind united with heavenly grace. Nor indeed is there a lack of people who diligently cultivate that mind, since besides those to whose faith and prudence the care of educating and instructing you has been assigned and who discharge their task in a praiseworthy manner, the pieces of advice from your most serene father – both in word and in writing – inform you, in particular that golden book about the kingdom[14] which was worthy of so great a king as its author (as a measure of its esteem by everyone everywhere, its translation into many languages and its frequent publication are more than enough attestation).

If after that I thought I could offer anything of my own in this genre, I should impudently and imprudently act very badly, and present myself to be rightly mocked by others with good reason.

But since I also desire to apply my own efforts to promoting virtue in you, and since there is nothing of mine that is worthy of you which is available, I will offer a garland of virtues worthy of a prince, woven and arranged together for your use from the various flowers of the best authors.

It seemed a good idea to append to these the most memorable facts about the life and characters of the two leaders [Antoninus Pius and Marcus Aurelius] (the latter of whom succeeds the former in all kinds of virtues, just as he does in ruling), so that you may be educated at once by their advice and example.

I pass over those things that concern this topic that are to be gathered from the sacred authors by theologians, since I myself have not dared to touch them with unwashed hands so to speak.[15]

But if the authors cited here recommend virtue to the prince by their opinions just as the leaders praised by me do by their example (both of whom are almost entirely enlightened by the light of nature and of reason),[16] with how much enthusiasm is it right that the prince, on whom the light of the Christian religion has also shone, embraces virtue. Therefore, I hope that my efforts will in some respect be a spur for you towards virtue. I acknowledge that I owe you this, along with any other indication of gratitude, both for the favour and good opinion of me of your most serene father (who, eighteen years ago, admitted me into his family court, generously raised me up and afterwards desired that I

---

14 The 'golden book' is King James' *Basilicon doron*.

15 Although Lipsius quotes sparingly from biblical and theological sources, he does do so: Lipsius, *Politica*, pp 129–30.

16 Christians were persecuted during the reign of Marcus Aurelius and he mentions them in a derogatory manner in his *Meditations*. This was a block to his adoption by Christian Stoics: Kraye, 'Marcus Aurelius', p. 518.

devote some energy in study to your most illustrious brother of blessed memory and to you yourself), and also for your continual kindness towards me from your infancy. If this little work of mine should be of any use in cultivating you, I heartily rejoice both for you and for the state. May God grant that the outcome match my prayers, and that you emerge in virtue and in blessedness equal to any of the best and most blessed rulers.

To Your Highness, from your eternally dedicated and devoted servant and dependant, Walter Quin.

[Floribus et variis, en, haec tibi texta corolla est] [sig. A4v]

Floribus e variis, en, haec tibi texta corolla est,
    Carole, regnorum spesque, decusque trium.
Hac redimitus eris virtutum insignis honore;
    Quae cumulent variis teque, tuosque, bonis
Teque haec si decoret nunc aevi in flore corona;   5
    Regali ornabit laurea iuncta virum.

[Look, This Garland Has Been Woven for You from Various Flowers] [T]

Look, this garland has been woven for you from various flowers, Charles, the hope and the honour of the three kingdoms. You will be crowned with this, being illustrious because of the honour of your virtues, which pile various benefits upon you and your family. If this garland adorns you now in the flower of your life, so will the laurel wreath, one joined with the crown, adorn the man.

Ad lectorem [*Corona virtutum*] [sig. A5r]

Erunt fortassis qui supervacuam operam hanc meam, post illud a Iusto Lipsio in hoc ipso genere ingenio, iudicio, et doctrina singulari *Politicorum* elaboratum opus, existimabunt. Nam et illum dicent de virtute principis egisse. Egisse quidem agnosco, sed ut de una tantum parte *Politicorum*: ac proinde visum illi satis, si pauca tantum libaret ex variis authoribus, quae virtutem principi commendarent. Cum autem quod illi perexigua pars argumenti fuerit totum mihi sit, danda fuit opera, ut uberius, ac pleniori (quod aiunt) manu flores hinc, inde legerem in usum principis nostri virtutum documentis diligentius erudiendi. Quid hac in re praestiterim, aliorum esto iudicium. Quod autem non de virtute tantum, sed etiam de vitio in genere egerim, cum de singulis tantum virtutibus, non de vitiis seorsim agam, ratio est, quod materiam ad prius illud utcunque praestandum authores mihi suppeditaverint, ad posterius hoc non item. Nec etiam apposite, aut concinne de singulis virtutibus agere potui, quin et coniunctim cum illis de vitiis mihi fuerit agendum. De meo nihil nisi connexiones, tanquam caementum quoddam, ad vinciendas inter se authorum sententias adhibui, easque quam potui parcissime, operam dans ubicunque commode licuit, ut id auctores ipsi facerent. Graecorum sententias duntaxat Latine redditas Latinis attexui; cum et brevitati studerem, et ad eum quem proposui mihi finem id sufficeret. Is autem non alius est, quam principis nostri, in eoque reipublicae bonum: quod utrique mecum a Deo precatus. Vale.

To the Reader [*Corona virtutum*] [T]

There will perhaps be those who will think this effort of mine superfluous, after *Politics*, that work which was undertaken by Justus Lipsius, a man of singular intellect, judgment and learning in this field, for they will say that he treated the virtue of a ruler. I acknowledge that he did this, but that this was only in one part of *Politics*, and it seemed to him to be sufficient if he gathered only a few things from various authors that recommended virtue to a prince. Since what was a very small part of his argument is all of mine, pains must be taken to collect more copiously and with, as they say, a fuller hand, flowers from here and there for the purpose of more diligently educating our prince through examples of virtues.[17] Let what I have achieved in this respect be judged by others. As to the fact that I have dealt not alone with virtue, but also with vice in its kind, although I treat virtues individually but not the vices, my rationale is that the authors supplied me with the requisite material for treating the former in any way whatever, but do not do likewise for the latter. Nor could I treat appropriately or harmoniously individual virtues without also treating vices in conjunction with them. For my part, I have applied nothing but connecting passages, as a sort of cement to link together the sentences of authors and I did this as sparingly as possible, taking as much pain throughout as I fittingly could so that it is as if the authors themselves were doing this. I have added to the Latin maxims those of the Greeks, but they have been rendered into Latin, since I have striven for brevity and this sufficed for the goal I set myself: which is nothing other than the good of our prince and of the state, both of which you have, with me, beseeched from God. Farewell.

---

17 Despite Quin's statement that he is collecting with 'a fuller hand', Lipsius' long work draws from a similiar range of authors. See Lipsius, *Politica*, pp 254–8.

Elogium serenissimi regis (1616)

This broadsheet consists of two five-column acrostics based on the names of King James and Prince Charles. Because of the ephemeral nature of such works, Latin verse broadsheets have rarely survived. They had their origins in the universities and were frequently occasional (in celebration of royal events), two generalizations that fit well with what we know of Quin.[1] In this instance it seems likely that he was celebrating the creation of Charles as prince of Wales (see the dating of the copy-text below). In the seventeenth century, broadsheets were frequently commissioned and subsidised 'and they generally reflected elite-to-middling cultural concerns'.[2]

Note that in keeping with the rest of this edition, u/v has been regularized, but in the copy-text v is always used as the initial letter (as can be seen from Illustrations 4 and 5).

Copy-text

Walter Quin, *ELOGIVM SERENISSIMI* | *REGIS,* | *CARMINE ACROS-TICO, CVIVS SINGVLI* | *versus quinque vocabulis constant, totidem Columnis* | *nomen eiusdem complectente.* [London]: [George Purslow], [1616]. Broadsheet. *ESTC* S94817 (two copies).[3] NLS, RB.s.2272(2).

There are no details of the publisher or date. *STC* suggests it was printed in London by Purslow (*c.*1620) and, as the decorated borders of *Elogium* match those of *Bernard Stuart*, this seems likely.[4] The copy bound in NLS, Advocates MS 33.2.31, fos 138–9, is lightly annotated and bears the signature 'By Mr James Seaton, Minister of Logy.' James Seaton was minister of Logie (also known as

---

1   Angela McShane, 'Ballads and Broadsides' in Joad Raymond (ed.), *The Oxford History of Popular Print Culture: Vol. I, Cheap Print in Britain and Ireland to 1660* (Oxford: Oxford UP, 2011), p. 353; J.W. Binns, *Intellectual Culture in Elizabethan and Jacobean England: The Latin Writings of the Age* (Leeds: Francis Cairns, 1990), pp 75–6. A partial list of extant Latin broadsheets can be found in ibid., 483.

2   McShane, 'Ballads and Broadsides', p. 362.

3   Note that there are errors in *ESTC*'s records of the copies in the NLS as it lists the same copy twice and omits another copy in the library's manuscript collection. I am grateful to Anette Hagan, senior curator of Rare Book Collections at the NLS, for bringing this to my attention (as well as for alerting me to the question of the borders used here and in *Bernard Stuart*). I would not have seen the copy in the Advocates collection without her patient responses to my queries.

4   Purslow had used the elements of this border before 1616, for example in Bartholomew Chamberlaine, *The Passion of Christ, and the Benefites Thereby* (London: George Purslow, 1615).

ELOGIVM SERENISSIMI
REGIS,

CARMINE ACROSTICO, CVIVS SINGVLI
versus quinque vocabulis constant, totidem Columnis
nomen eiusdem complectente.

Iacobus Monarcha Magnæ Britanniæ.

IMperio	Iungens	Insignibus	Imá,	Iubendo
Auxiliari	Auras	Animantibus,	Astraque,	Amanter
Commisit	Capitum	Ciuilia	Corpora	Curæ
Omnipotens	Opifex	Orbisque	Orientis	Origo.
Bellaces	Bellosque	Beans	Bonitate	Britannos,
Vnius	Vnanimes	Voluit	Virtute	Vigentis,
Scotigenæ	Summi,	Sese	Submittere	Sceptris.
Magnifico	Musis	Memorandus	More	Monarcha
Oceano	Occiduis	Occlusis	Obtigit	Oris.
Nemo	Nobilior	Natus:	Nam	Nobilitatem
Accipit	Antiquis	Ab	Auis,	Aborigenibusq;
Regnorum	Radijs	Redimitam:	Regna	Regendo
Ciuica	Cernatur	Complecti	Commoda,	Clarus
Hæres	Heroum,	Harpyarumq;	Hostis	Hiantum,
Atque	Aliena	Animis	Atrocibus	Arripientum.
Munificus,	Mitis,	Moderata	Mente	Modestu
Affulgens	Artes	Amat:	Admirandaq;	Agenti
Gloria	Gestorum	Generose	Gaudia	Gignit.
Numine	Neglecto,	Natales,	Nobile	Nomen
AEacides	AEquans	AErumnas	AEstimat	AEquus.
Bellica	Bellonæ,	Belli	Barathrumq;	Beatus
Repressit,	Regnis	Requie	Redeunte	Refectis.
Iudicis	Improbitas	Iura	Infringentis	Iniquè
Tundetur,	Themidis	Tanto	Tutore	Tuente
Aras,	Astræamque	Aula	Amplexabitur	Almam.
Nulla	Nefandorum	Nobis	Nocumenta	Nocebunt,
Nauarcho	Nostræ	Nitenti	Numine	Nauis.
Indigetes	Igitur	Iouis	Imperitando	Imitator
AEtherios	AEquans	AEquabitur	AEtheris	AEuo.

4 *Elogium serenissimi regis*, left side (NLS, RB.s.2272(2) © The National Library of Scotland).

VOTVM

EIVSDEM GENERIS CARMINE ACROS-
tico Illuſtriſſimi Principis nomen iterante.

Carolus Princeps Walliæ.

CArole,	Conſtanti	Cœlum	Conamine	Cultus
Artibus	Aſcendas,	Animoſis	Auſibus	Auctus:
Recturus	Recta	Ratione	Regare:	Regendis
Occiduis	Oris	Orienſque	Optabilis,	Opto,
Lætificaturo	Laté	Loca	Lumine	Luſtres:
Vſque	Voluptatum	Vites	Virtute	Venena,
Sirenum	Suaueſque	Sonos,	Scelerataq;	Saxa:
Pectore	Prudenti	Præſtes,	Probitate,	Piaque
Relligione:	Regat	Recturum	Regula	Recta
Iuſtitiæ:	Iuris	Iungas	Illuſtribus	Imos
(Nemine	Neglecto)	Nexu;	Noxiſque	Nocentum
Compreſsis,	Curans	Ciuilia	Commoda,	Clarus
Emineas:	Expers	Erroris	Et	Experiaris
Propitios	(Precibus	Placato	Patre	Potenti
Spirituum)	Superos	Semper,	Sortemque	Secundam:
Viribus	Vlturus	Violentos,	Victor	Vbique
Victores	Vincas	Vera	Virtute	Vetuſtos:
Accenſis	Animis	Affectu	Ardentis	Amoris,
Læteris	Lucens	Longè	Latéque,	Lyriſque
Laurigerûm,	Linguis,	Lepidis	Laudere	Libriſque:
Inde	Immortalis	Iuſſu	Iouis	Indigitatos
AEtherios	AEques,	AEternumq;	AEtheris	AEuum.

Difficiles haud ipſe nugas hæc eſſe negarem,
His niſi materiem Nomina tanta darent.

G. Q.

5 *Elogium serenissimi regis*, right side (NLS, R.B.s.2272(2)) © The National Library of Scotland).

Blairlogie) near Stirling from 1610 until the end of 1616.[5] Since *Elogium* addresses Charles as prince of Wales, a title he acquired in November 1616, it seems likely that the broadsheet was produced to mark the occasion. *EEBO* reproduces the copy-text. The author's name is given as 'G.Q.', so it cannot with certainty be ascribed to Quin (see p. 208).

Elogium serenissimi regis, carmine acrostico, cuius singuli versus quinque
vocabulis constant, totidem columnis nomen eiusdem complectente

Iacobus monarcha Magnae Britanniae

Imperio	Iungens	Insignibus	Ima,	Iubendo	
Auxiliari	Auras	Animantibus,	Astraque,	Amanter	
Commisit	Capitum	Civilia	Corpora	Curae	
Omnipotens	Opifex	Orbisque	Orientis	Origo.	
Bellaces	Bellosque	Beans	Bonitate	Britannos,	5
Unius	Unanimes	Voluit	Virtute	Vigentis,	
Scotigenae	Summi,	Sese	Submittere	Sceptris.	
Magnifico	Musis	Memorandus	More	Monarcha	
Oceano	Occiduis	Occlusis	Obtigit	Oris.	
Nemo	Nobilior	Natus:	Nam	Nobilitatem	10
Accipit	Antiquis	Ab	Avis,	Aborigenibusque	
Regnorum	Radiis	Redimitam:	Regna	Regendo	
Civica	Cernatur	Complecti	Commoda,	Clarus	
Haeres	Heroum,	Harpyarumque	Hostis	Hiantum,	
Atque	Aliena	Animis	Atrocibus	Arripientum.	15
Munificus,	Mitis,	Moderata	Mente	Modestus	
Affulgens	Artes	Amat:	Admirandaque	Agenti	
Gloria	Gestorum	Generose	Gaudia	Gignit.	
Numine	Neglecto,	Natales,	Nobile	Nomen	
Aeacides	Aequans	Aerumnas	Aestimat	Aequus.	20
Bellica	Bellonae,	Belli	Barathrumque	Beatus	
Repressit,	Regnis	Requie	Redeunte	Refectis.	
Iudicis	Improbitas	Iura	Infringentes	Inique	
Tundetur,	Themidis	Tanto	Tutore	Tuente	
Aras,	Astraeamque	Aula	Amplexabitur	Almam.	25
Nulla	Nefandorum	Nobis	Nocumenta	Nocebunt,	
Nauarcho	Nostrae	Nitenti	Numine	Navis.	

5 Hew Scott (ed.), *Fasti Ecclesiae Scoticanae: The Succession of Ministers in the Church of Scotland from the Reformation* (vol 4, new ed.; Edinburgh: Oliver and Boyd, 1923), p. 355.

| Indigetes | Igitur | Iovis | Imperitando | Imitator |
| Aetherios | Aequans | Aequabitur | Aetheris | Aevo. |

An Elogium of the Most Serene King, in an Acrostic Poem, Each of Whose Verses Consists of Five Words, Containing His Name in As Many Columns[6] [T]

James, monarch of Great Britain

Uniting the lowest and the distinguished through his empire, by ordering the winds and the stars to help the living, he lovingly cared for the well-being of his citizens to care for their lives. The omnipotent artist and the origin of the eastern world, blessing the warlike and beautiful Britons with prosperity, he wanted them all to thrive through the virtue of one man, and to submit themselves to the sceptres of the greatest Scot. This monarch is to be commemorated by the Muses in magnificent fashion, who has reached the western shores bounded by the ocean. No one nobler has been born, for he receives his nobility from his ancient ancestors and native inhabitants, crowned by the rays of kings. By ruling kingdoms he may be seen to have brought about civic benefits, a famous heir to heroes, and an enemy of gaping harpies and of those who with fierce characters snatch others' goods. Munificent, gentle and modest through his moderate mind, in his splendour he loves the arts, and the admirable glory of his deeds liberally engenders joys for the man who did them. Without exception he equals the lineage, noble name, and toils of Achilles and judges them with equanimity. In his blessedness he has repressed the bellicosity of Bellona[7] and the abyss of war, so that peace returns to the kingdoms he has repaired. The wickedness of a king who unjustly infringes the laws will be quashed: with so great a guardian protecting the altars of Themis[8] the palace will embrace loving Astraea.[9] With the captain of our ship exerting his power, no harm from the wicked will harm us. Therefore, one who is an imitator of Jupiter in his rule equals the ethereal deities and will live for all eternity.

Votum eiusdem generis carmine acrostico illustrissimi principis nomen iterante

Carolus princeps Walliae

| Nauarcho | Nostrae | Nitenti | Numine | Navis. |
| Carole, | Constanti | Coelum | Conamine | Cultus |

6   An elogium is a 'a brief summary of a person's character', usually positive: *OED*.
7   Roman goddess of war.
8   Goddess personifying justice.
9   'Starry maiden' is a reference to Elizabeth I.

Artibus	Ascendas,	Animosis	Ausibus	Auctus:	
Recturus	Recta	Ratione	Regare:	Regendis	
Occiduis	Oris	Oriensque	Optabilis,	Opto,	
Laetificaturo	Late	Loca	Lumine	Lustres:	5
Usque	Voluptatum	Vites	Virtute	Venena,	
Sirenum	Suavesque	Sonos,	Scelerataque	Saxa:	
Pectore	Prudenti	Praestes,	Probitate,	Piaque	
Religione:	Regat	Recturum	Regula	Recta	
Iustitiae:	Iuris	Iungas	Illustribus	Imos	10
(Nemine	Neglecto)	Nexu;	Noxisque	Nocentum	
Compressis,	Curans	Civilia	Commoda,	Clarus	
Emineas:	Expers	Erroris	Et	Experiaris	
Propitios	(Precibus	Placato	Patre	Potenti	
Spirituum)	Superos	Semper,	Sortemque	Secundam:	15
Viribus	Ulturus	Violentos,	Victor	Ubique	
Victores	Vincas	Vera	Virtute	Vetustos:	
Accensis	Animis	Affectu	Ardentis	Amoris,	
Laeteris	Lucens	Longe	Lateque,	Lyrisque	
Laurigerum,	Linguis,	Lepidis	Laudere	Librisque:	20
Inde	Immortalis	Iussu	Iovis	Indigitatos	
Aetherios	Aeques,	Aeternumque	Aetheris	Aevum.	

Difficiles haud ipse nugas haec esse negarem,[10]
His nisi materiem nomina tanta darent.

A Prayer of the Same Kind in an Acrostic Poem that Repeats the Name of the
Most Illustrious Prince [T]

Charles, prince of Wales

Charles, you may ascend to heaven by your own efforts, cultivated in the arts
and magnified by brave and daring deeds. You who are destined to be ruled by
right reason: and should be chosen to rule in western and eastern lands, may
you, I hope, range widely over these places with your light that will bring happiness. May you, through your virtue, continually avoid the poisons of pleasures,
the sweet sounds of Sirens and the wicked rocks. May you be eminent in your
prudent heart and in excellence, and be pious in religion. May the right rule of
justice govern you who are destined to govern. May you unite the lowest to the

---

10 In Seaton's copy, this line has been amended in pen to read: 'Difficiles nugas haud ipse haec
   esse negarem.'

lofty by the bond of law, and having suppressed the dangers of the harmful may you care for civil benefits and emerge in glory. Being without error may you also enjoy ever prosperous gods (once your powerful father has been placated by the prayers of the spirits), and a favourable fate. May you wreak revenge on the violent by force, and as a victor in all respects may you overcome all old victors through your true virtue. Having stirred up spirits through the influence of a burning love as you shine far and wide, may you be happy and be praised by the lyres of the laurel-wearers, by their eloquent tongues and balances: therefore, by the order of Jupiter, may you equal the immortal and aethereal deities and the eternal age of aether.

I myself would not deny that this would be difficult if such a great name as yours did not offer the basis for it.

12

The Memory of the Most Worthy and Renowned Bernard Stuart (1619)

This work has its origins in two previously circulating manuscript works by Quin that are otherwise unattested. In the preface he explains that his account of Bernard Stuart had originally been written in French (and therefore calls to mind *Recueil*) while the poems that follow were 'directed and presented to the prince's highness at his creation' (thus they were written in 1616). Quin explains that he included the latter in *Bernard Stuart* as they were 'contained in so few leaves'. From a survey of English books available in Dublin in Quin's time Raymond Gillespie concludes that 'history and law are clearly predominant'.[1] This may have had some influence on Quin's decision to write an historical work.

Bernard (or Bérault) Stuart (1452/3–1508) was the son of John (d. *c.*1469), second lord of Aubigny.[2] Bernard Stuart's grandfather, Sir John Stewart of Darnley (*c.*1390–1429), fought with the French against the English. His military successes earned him the lordship of Aubigny and the right to quarter his arms with those of the French royal house.

Bernard joined the king's Scots guard in his teens and in 1483 was promoted to the command of a company of lances: ten years later he was captain of the entire guard. He acted as an ambassador of the French crown to James III and James IV, as well as to several Italian potentates and governments. However, he is best remembered for his military achievements. He fought at Bosworth (1485) on the side of the future Henry VII, and with King Ferdinand of Aragon at the capture of Granada (1492), but most of Quin's account of Stuart's life deals with his campaigns in Italy and some knowledge of these is necessary to follow the narrative.

Charles VIII of France had inherited a claim on the throne of Naples through the Angevins.[3] In search of military glory and with the encouragement of various Italian allies, he decided to press his claim and in mid-1494 he led an army (which

1 Raymond Gillespie, *Reading Ireland: Print, Reading and Social Change in Early Modern Ireland* (Manchester: Manchester UP, 2012), p. 62.
2 The biographical information on Stuart in this introduction is based on Philippe Contamine, 'Stuart, Bérault (1452/3–1508)', *ODNB*; Berault Stuart, *Traité sur l'art de la guerre*, ed. Elie de Comminges (La Haye: Martin Nijhoff, 1976), pp ix–xxxii. See also Douglas Gray, 'A Scottish "Flower of Chivalry" and his Book', *Words*, 4 (1974), 22–34.
3 The account of Charles VIII's campaign in Italy is digested from Michael Mallett & Christine Shaw, *The Italian Wars, 1494–1559: War, State and Society in Early Modern Europe* (Harlow: Pearson, 2012), 6–34.

included Stuart and his men) into Italy. The French army's progress down the Mediterranean coast was swift as, with its enormous size, it was eventually given free, albeit grudging, passage through Milan, Florence, Siena and Rome (Stuart had been one of the ambassadors who had facilitated this in advance of Charles' entry into Italy). Any resistance the French army met with was easily crushed. In the face of this, Alfonso II of Naples (d. 1495) abdicated and took himself and the royal treasury to Sicily, leaving his son Ferdinand II (Ferrandino, d. 1496) to defend his new kingdom. Ferrandino was not able to rally Naples and he was forced to flee. Although fortresses in the kingdom and in the city itself put up some resistance, Charles VIII was able to take possession of Naples in February 1595.

Charles could not stay in Naples indefinitely as he needed to return to France. He began his journey home in May and left Naples in the hands of his viceroy, Gilbert de Bourbon, count of Montpensier. In addition, he left Frenchmen − including Stuart, who was made count of Acri and marquis of Squillace − in charge of key offices and fortresses. In exile, Ferrandino had enlisted the support of Spain and Venice, and around the time that Charles was departing from his newly acquired territory, Gonzalo Fernández de Córdoba landed in Calabria with Ferrandino's new army. Gonzalo, known as 'the Great Captain', is a significant figure in Quin's history, not only because the two men met in battle, but also because the fame of the Spaniard is contrasted by Quin with the undeserved obscurity of Stuart.[4]

Gonzalo's initial encounter with Stuart, at the First Battle of Seminara (1495), went badly for the Spaniard and the French were victorious. However, things were not going as well for the French elsewhere since, in the midst of a popular uprising against them, Ferrandino returned to Naples, Montpensier fled the city to join Stuart, and shortly afterwards the French garrison surrendered. In 1496, after the capture of Montpensier at Atella, the French quit their last foothold in the Kingdom of Naples and Stuart was allowed retreat to France. Ferrandino had not long to enjoy his reconquest as he died later that year and his uncle Frederick (r. 1495–1501) took the throne.

In 1498 when Louis XII succeeded Charles VIII, French attention turned again to Italy.[5] The following year, Louis' army attacked Ludovico Sforza in Milan and the victorious monarch followed in its wake. After Louis had returned home, Sforza managed to retake the city for a brief period before he was captured and French government reimposed on his city. The new French regime included two lieutenants-general, one of whom was Stuart.

In 1500 Louis and Ferdinand of Aragon agreed to divide Naples − to which they both had a claim − between them. In June 1501 Stuart left Milan to march

4 Plutarch's *Parallel Lives* may have inspired Quin to pair the two military leaders.
5 The information on Louis XII's relationship with Italy is taken from Mallett and Shaw, *Italian Wars*, pp 47–69.

on Naples while Gonzalo once again landed in Calabria. King Frederick withdrew from Capua to Naples, and was captured by Stuart. Frederick was sent to France and, to Stuart's dissatisfaction, Louis d'Armagnac, duke of Nemours, was appointed viceroy of the kingdom. Stuart requested and was denied leave to quit Naples. Soon, as Louis and Ferdinand's commanders quarrelled over jurisdictions, Stuart was in the field again, defeating the Spanish at the Second Battle of Seminara (1502) and at the Battle of Terranova (1502). In April of the following year, Stuart was the leader of the main force at the Third Battle of Seminara, where the Spanish were victorious. Shortly afterwards, Nemours was defeated at Ceringola and Stuart was taken captive. After the Spanish occupied Naples, Stuart was imprisoned in the city in Castle Nuovo. Following a further victory by Gonzalo, the French garrison at Gaeta surrendered and under the terms of the consequent treaty French prisoners, including Stuart, were released. On returning to France, with the exception of Stuart, the French found that their monarch was incensed at their incompetence.

The French expulsion from Naples did not affect Louis' rule over Milan. Stuart accompanied a royal visit in 1507 during which there was an incident that Quin notes. While he was ill – Stuart's illnesses are remarked on several occasions – as a mark of esteem for his service at Granada, he was visited by Ferdinand of Aragon and his old rival, Gonzalo, who had come to meet Louis. Once again, Quin can contrast the regard in which Stuart was held abroad with his obscurity in his native land.

Quin knows some of the details of Stuart's last years from John Lesley (see below). Having decided to go on pilgrimage to the shrine of Saint-Ninian in Scotland, he was given permission by Louis XII to leave France at the head an embassy to James IV. Arriving in Edinburgh in 1508, he was greeted by a generous monarch. Having discharged his official duty, Stuart proceeded with his pilgrimage. He got no further than Costorphine (a village west of Edinburgh that is now in the city's suburbs) and the house of a friend, Sir James Forrester, and there he died. His title was inherited by his daughter's husband (and his own cousin), Robert Stewart (c.1470–1544). Quin also refers to the distinction of Robert's career: he was captain of the king's Scots guards, a marshal of France, and a combatant at the Battle of Marignano (1515), where Francis I defeated an army of Swiss mercenaries opposing the French occupation of Milan.[6]

Sources

Quin's text emphasizes his use of source material (he frequently supplies side notes as references), and explains his historiographical method, so the authors he draws on are summarized here.

6   ODR.

PHILIPPE DE COMMINES (OR COMMYNES, c.1447–1511) was born in Flanders and brought up at the Burgundian court, from which he defected to the service of the French crown. He is best known for his *Mémoires*, which, within fifty years of the publication of their complete edition in 1552, had been translated into Latin, English, Dutch, German and Italian.[7] Quin's side-notes indicating his use of *Mémoires* read 'Hist.', suggesting the title of their English translation, *The Historie of Philip de Commines Knight, Lord of Argenton* (which had appeared in several editions since its first printing in 1596), however, the differences in wording suggest that Quin translated it for himself.[8]

BERNARD DE GIRARD DU HAILLAN (1537–1610) was a court historiographer whose best-known work was *L'histoire génerale des rois de France* (*A General History of the Kings of France*, 1576). Although a careful seeker after source-material and respected by his contemporaries (and by Quin), his treatment of what he discovered was at times credulous.[9] The title of Du Haillan's *Recueil d'avis et conseils sur les affaires d'Estat tirés des Vies de Plutarque* (*A Collection of Opinions and Counsels on Affairs of State Taken from the Lives of Plutarch*, 1578) is reminiscent of Quin's Plutarchian treatment of Henry IV in *Recueil*.

PAOLO GIOVIO (1486–1552), bishop and man of letters, is one of the sources that Quin most frequently draws on. His *Historiarum sui temporis* (*History of His Time*) was printed in two volumes that appeared in 1550 and 1552. Although Giovio's *Histories* sold well and were translated into Italian, French, German and Spanish, their method attracted much scholarly criticism, including that of a scholar Quin greatly admired, Justus Lipsius, who found Giovio 'untrustworthy in judgement and fidelity'.[10]

Giovio's life of Gonzalo Fernández de Córdoba was commissioned by the great captain's son-in-law, who wished to defend the reputation of a soldier who had eventually been suspected by Ferdinand of Aragon of harbouring desires for the Neapolitan crown.[11] It appeared in Giovio's *Illustrium virorum vitae* (*Lives of Illustrious Men*, 1549; Italian translation by Ludovico Domenichi, 1550).

FRANCESCO GUICCIARDINI (1483–1540) was a Florentine historian. Under the patronage of the papacy he was, variously, governor of Modena, Reggio, Parma

7   Adrianna E. Bakos, 'Commynes, Philippe de' in Paul F. Grendler (ed.), *Encyclopedia of the Renaissance* (6 vols, New York: Charles Scribner's Sons, 1999), ii, p. 58.

8   Phillippe de Commynes, *The Historie of Philip de Commines Knight, Lord of Argenton*, trans. Thomas Danett (London: Ar. Hatfield for I. Norton, 1596), p. 315.

9   Arlette Jouanna et al. (eds), *Histoire et dictionnaire des guerres de religion* (Paris: Robert Laffont, 1998), pp 856–8. J.H.M. Salmon, *Essays in the Intellectual and Social History of Early Modern France* (Cambridge: Cambridge UP, 1987), pp 130–1.

10 T.C. Price Zimmermann, *Paolo Giovio: The Historian and the Crisis of Sixteenth-Century Italy* (Princeton, NJ: Princeton UP, 1995), pp 263–5.

11 Ibid., pp 65, 224.

and Bologna as well as lieutenant general of the papal army. His *Storia d'Italia* (*History of Italy*), covering the period 1492–1534, was published posthumously.[12] It was translated via French into English by Sir Geoffrey Fenton in 1579 (with two more editions before 1618 and numerous abridgements). Fenton gave 'an anti-Catholic twist to Guicciardini's anti-clericalism, introducing patriotic and moralizing inflections at odds with the original's cool objectivity'.[13] He also mangled d'Aubigny's name ('Eberard Daubigny'), so it is unsurprising that Quin did not choose to use the English translation.[14]

JOHN LESLEY (1527–96) studied for his doctorate in canon and civil law at Paris before returning to his native Scotland. A privy councillor, he was a valued advisor to Mary, Queen of Scots, who appointed him to the bishopric of Ross. His intrigues on behalf of his queen when she was in Elizabeth's custody led to his imprisonment in the Tower. On his release he went to Paris and from there he proceeded (in the company of Robert Turner) to Rome as Mary's ambassador to the pope. While he was there, he published *De origine moribus, et rebus gestis Scotorum* (*The Origins, Customs and Deeds of the Scots*, 1578, published in a Scottish translation by James Dalrymple in 1596). Back in France, where he remained until his death, he urged Esmé Stuart, the sixth lord Aubigny, to try to convert James VI to Catholicism.[15]

CLAUDE MALINGRE, SIEUR DE SAINT-LAZARE (1580–1653), was an historian whose work was derivative; however, the title page of his *Histoire chronologique* (*Chronological History*, 1617) would have caught Quin's eye as it advertises the book's treatment of the alliances of France and Scotland, the services the Scots rendered to the French monarchy, and the founding of the Scots guards.[16]

JUAN DE MARIANA SJ (1536–1624) was an historian and political philosopher. His *Historia de rebus Hispaniae* (*History of Spanish Affairs*) was published in 1592 and extended to thirty books in its 1605 edition. In Quin's milieu, Mariana was better

---

12 *ODR*.

13 Peter France (ed.), *The Oxford Guide to Literature in English Translation* (Oxford: Oxford UP, 2000), p. 484.

14 Francesco Guicciardini, *The Historie of Guicciardin Containing the Warres of Italie and Other Partes [...]*, trans. Geoffrey Fenton (London: Richard Field, 1599), p. 23.

15 Rosalind K. Marshall, 'Lesley, John (1527–1596)', *ODNB*; John Leslie, *The Historie of Scotland*, trans. James Dalrymple, ed. E.G. Cody (2 vols, Edinburgh: William Blackwood & Sons, 1888, 1895), i, pp xvii–xxii. Lesley had presented a vernacular *History of Scotland* to Queen Mary in 1571, and although Quin might have seen it in manuscript, it was not printed until the nineteenth century.

16 Patrick Dandrey (ed.), *Dictionnaire des lettres françaises: le xviie siècle* (2nd ed.; Paris: Fayard, 1996), p. 805. For references to Aubigny, see Claude Malingre, *Histoire chronologique de plusieurs grand capitaines, princes, seigneurs, magistrats, officiers de la couronne, et autres hommes illustres...* (Paris: Adrian Tiffaine, 1617), pp 40, 45.

known for his *De rege et regis institutione* (*The King and the Instruction of the King*, 1598), a work in the advice to princes tradition that controversially sanctioned tyrannicide in extreme cases. Mariana was regarded as having provided an intellectual under-pinning both for the assassination of Henry IV and the Gunpowder Plot.[17] As recently as 1616, King James had associated him with both regicide and parricide.[18]

JEAN DE SERRES (1540–98) was a Calvinist pastor, a translator and an historian. He had provided the Latin translation in Henri Estienne's edition of Plato's works (1578), the first two volumes of which were dedicated respectively to Queen Elizabeth and James VI. His *Commentariorum de statu religionis et reipublicae* (*Commentary on the Condition of Religion and the State*, 1571) was a well-known work, subsequently enlarged and reissued many times. Quin is drawing here on his *Inventaires géneral de l'histoire de France* (*A General Inventory of the History of France*, 1597), which was also available to him in English, having been translated by Edward Grimeston. He was made one of the royal historiographers by Henry IV.[19]

For all Quin's knowledge of Stuart, there are two noteworthy omissions from his list of sources. If he knew of it, he would surely have mentioned Stuart's *Traité sur l'art de la guerre* (*Treatise on the Art of War*), as it would have added scholarly to martial achievements. Quin is also silent both about the ballad William Dunbar composed to welcome Stuart to Edinburgh and the elegy he wrote after his death.[20] It is possible, however, that if Quin had heard of Dunbar's work he might have ignored this inconvenient fact, since it would have diluted his claim that Stuart had been ignored in his home land.

Copy-text

Walter Quin, THE | MEMORIE | OF THE MOST | WORTHIE AND RE-|KNOWMED BERNARD STVART, | *Lord D'Aubigni renewed.* | *Whereunto are added* | *Wishes presented to the Prince at his* | *Creation. By Walter Quin, Seruant to his Highnesse.* London: George Purslow, 1619. 4°. ESTC S110563 (three copies). NLS, RB.s.2272(1).

17 ODR; William S. Maltby, 'Mariana, Juan de' in Hans J. Hillerbrand (ed.), *The Oxford Encyclopedia of the Reformation* (4 vols, Oxford: Oxford UP, 1996), iii, pp 7–8.

18 Harald Ernst Braun, *Juan de Mariana and Early Modern Spanish Political Thought* (Aldershot: Ashgate, 2007), p. 9.

19 S.K. Heninger, Jr, 'Sidney and Serranus' Plato' in Alfred F. Kinney (ed.), *Sidney in Retrospect: Selections from English Literary Renaissance* (Amherst: University of Massachusetts Press, 1988), pp 27–31. Whether Quin read de Serres' work in English or French cannot be known. The passage he uses is to be found in Jean de Serres, *A General Inventorie of the History of France from the Beginning of that Monarchie, unto the Treatie of Vervins, in the Year 1598 [...]*, trans. Edward Grimeson (London: George Elde, 1607), p. 336.

20 William Dunbar, *Poems* (1998), pp 100, 177–9. Dunbar's eulogy ends with an acrostic stanza which Quin would have found very much to his taste.

The title page includes the name of the book's author ('By Walter Quin, servant to his Highnesse') and a quotation from Horace's *Odes*: 'Dignum laude virum Musa vetat mori.'[21] William Alexander provided a sonnet dedicated 'to his worthy friend Master Walter Quin' [A4v] (see p. 264). The current *EEBO* text is severely defective as several of its pages are missing.

To the Prince My Most Gracious Master [sig. A2r]

I yours in zealous love and due respect,
Great prince, to you present, as yours by right
This true memorial of a worthy knight;
Whom as your own you cannot but affect:
   Sith† both your royal lineage by him decked,†   5
As him it honoured, and his virtues bright,
That early show in you their orient light,
Your rays on him, and his on you reflect.
   Vouchsafe therefore to view with gracious eye
These verses, though not worthy of your view   10
As mine, yet in respect that they renew
His fame, and yours, as his, become thereby.
   So favour still may the celestial powers
   And worthiest Muses honour you, and yours.

Preface [*Bernard Stuart*] [sig. A3r]

The memorable virtues and actions of the renowned Bernard Stuart, lord d'Aubigny, recorded in sundry histories, although but incidentally and in several places, have invited, yea incited me by a collection of them, and of what else I could learn concerning him by written records and credible relations of honourable persons, to renew his memory, which I did first in French; for that from his youth he having served two French kings, and been the most worthy and victorious of all the commanders employed by them in their wars, yet are his virtues and brave exploits more sparingly and slightly recorded by French writers, than by those of the Italian and Spanish nation against which he warred. And now have I done the same in English, for that, albeit he were born of an illustrious family in one of the kingdoms of Great Britain, and deserved well of them both, as it is testified by good records, and by Lesley, bishop of Ross, in his Latin history of Scotland, yet is he scarcely remembered in any other public

---

21 'If a man is worthy of praise, the Muse does not let him die': *Horace: Odes and Epodes*, ed. and trans. Niall Rudd (corr. ed.; Cambridge, MA: Harvard UP, 2012), p. 242 [iv.8.28].

history of either of them. But if any shall read his memorial written by me in French, find in it some points of difference from this, let him know that it is not in any point of history, but only in some amplifications which I have endeavoured to better in this, being my latter labour.

The reason which induced me thus to write, rather in verse than in prose, was because what I could gather being not sufficient for a competent relation of his life in prose, I might with more liberty and congruity enlarge the same in verse by digressions and other amplifications, which notwithstanding I have used moderately, rather to confirm and illustrate than to sophisticate the truth, his worth having been such as it needeth not any forged commendation, and it being my desire that these my verses should rather want the praise of a right poem, than of a true memorial. In respect whereof I have forborne to make use of the testimonies of the aforementioned Lesley, and of Malingre, a French chronicler, when as they name him marshal of France, and viceroy of Naples (albeit these titles might add much to his reputation) sith† I find by more authentic and approved histories, that he had neither of both these places.

This my respect to truth will the better appear by a collection of the most notable places of histories concerning him added to this his memorial, the defects whereof, I hope the discreet reader will censure the more favourably, for that undertaking this task, I have not put my scythe (as the by-word is) into any other man's harvest, but rather, gleaning and gathering what others have left unreaped, have performed an office due to the memory of so worthy a person and suitable to the duty which I owe his royal, and most honourable lineage. And although I presume not to think that in these my homely verses I have hit the mark proposed in that sentence of Horace, 'omne tulit punctum, qui miscuit utile dulci': 'All readers him approve, that with delight | Doth profit interlace, when he doth write', yet I have aimed thereat, and hope that they will not seem altogether unpleasant or unprofitable to the courteous and judicious reader, to whose censure I submit them.[22]

The Memory of the Most Worthy and Renowned Bernard Stuart, Lord d'Aubigny, Renewed [sig. Br][23]

I

If after death to men, whose virtues rare
And worthy actions memorable are,
Posterity immortal honour owe

22 *Horace: Satires, Epistles and Ars poetica*, ed. and trans. H. Rushton Fairclough (Cambridge, MA: Harvard UP, 1929), *Ars poetica*, l. 343.
23 The poem has side-notes indicating its historical sources. As these are all repeated in Quin's

Which from the Muses' powerful art doth flow,
For their reward; and that provoked thereby   5
Brave minds apace in virtue's race may hie†
To honour's jail: such fame is due by right
To Bernard, lord of Aubigny, that bright
Like to a star did shine in virtue's sphere
Among their worthiest knights that ever were: 10
Who yet hath not received his honour due
In prose or verse from any of the crew
Of all those learned clerks, that did adorn
That ancient kingdom wherein he was born,
Or that, wherein he was free denizen,   15
And to whose kings great service he had done.
For more than their records, the history
Of Italy and Spain, his memory
(Though only by the way) doth celebrate:
Whereas by wars he did exasperate   20
And much annoy their princes and their states,
Against the crown of France associates
His virtues and his acts heroical,
As also strange his fortune may we call;
Sith† he from foreigners among his foes   25
Received hath greater honour, than of those,
Who him for country's sake and his deserts
Should honour and extoll with grateful hearts.
   I this neglect abhorring, and inflamed
With love of his transcendent worth have framed   30
These virtues to renew his memory,
And leave a pattern to posterity.
But of his life no treatise having found,
Whereon with method this discourse to ground,
Like to th'industrious bee, which here and there,   35
From sundry flowers, that growing anywhere
She finds, doth gather honey less or more,
Her honeycomb that she therewith may store
So I from sundry nations' histories
Have of his virtues, wars, and victories,   40
Culled and compiled this short memorial,

appendix, 'A Short Collection […]', they are omitted here. The poem is in two parts (clearly
indicated by the dropped capitals in the copy-text): part numbers have been added here to
clarify this.

Not fabulous, nor hyperbolical,
Though couched in verse too homely to set forth
A subject of such dignity and worth;
That such a Muse to grace it would require,   45
As the renowned Mantuan did inspire.[24]
    In Scotland was he born a younger brother
To the ancient earl of Lennox, whom no other
Of all that kingdom brave nobility
Surmounted in illustrious dignity,   50
For that he from the royal stem did spring
Ennobled with the surname of his king.
This noble graft foreshowed in spring of youth
What he would prove in age's riper growth.
He comely was and graceful outwardly,   55
With active strength endured, and towardly
In wit and disposition: so as he
Began betimes such as he ought to be;
And to ensure himself to every game
And exercise, that best his birth became,   60
Misspending not of time the precious treasure
In sloth, in riot, or unlawful pleasure;
Wherein we see our youths themselves to wallow:
And truly had he not begun to follow
Thus early in his springtime virtue's lore,   65
In riper years such had not been the store
And harvest of his virtue as it grew.
For as we see a vessel that is new
With any liquor seasoned to retain
Long time the smack thereof; so it is plain   70
That both the virtue and the vice also
Of youth, men hardly grown in years forgo:
Yea both of them do rather grow than cease
In their possessors, as their years increase
But more than virtue vice doth on us seize   75
Because the same our fancies best doth please.
Then Bernard, being such by inclination,
And also by his virtuous education
And practice may we call both wise and blest,   80
That had the skill, and will to choose the best.

24 The choice of Virgil is an obvious one. King James had ended *Basilicon doron* with a quotation
    from 'that sublime and heroicall poet': *Selected Writings*, p. 258.

    Like Hercules, who being of that age[25]
Did show himself both virtuous and sage,
When as two women in a forked way
Him met, the one faire seeming, gaudy, gay,
Perfumed, powdered, painted, by her arts   85
To lust enticing the beholder's hearts:
The other shamefaced, modest in attire
And truly faire and lovely, yet the fire
Of lust abating with an awful eye.
The former from the left hand shamelessly   90
Before her better stepping, said to him:
'Brave youth, if to this woman stern and grim
Thou ear doth give, and wilt her footsteps tread,
In a most irksome way she will thee lead
With great turmoil, and dangers manifold   95
In summer's parching heat, and winters cold
Through many a thorny steep and craggy ground:
Wherein no pleasing mates are to be found,
But savage beasts, and monsters fell, to whom
In end a woeful prey thou shalt become.   100
But if thou wilt resolve to go with me
In this my way, thou shalt be wholly free
From all such toil and danger, passing still
Through flowery fields and meadows, where at will
Thou mayest most pleasant company enjoy,   105
And all delightful sports without annoy:
Where Venus joined with Bacchus at thy hest
Shall entertain thee as their welcome guest.'
These charming words and pleasing baits so wrought,
As to her bent well-nigh she had him brought.   110
    But the other comely matron, that did stand,
As th'entring of the way on the right hand,
This seeing, said to him: 'O noble youth,
Let not the sugared words come from the mouth
Of this deceitful strumpet thee incline   115
Her steps to follow, and abandon mine.
Her beauty is but false and counterfeit,

---

25 In the Renaissance the literary and artistic representation of Hercules' choice of virtue at the crossroads was a common one, and he was admired for his moral rather than his physical strength: Anthony Grafton et al. (eds), *The Classical Tradition* (Cambridge, MA: Belknap Press, 2010), p. 427.

Though to the view and sale she forth it set:
Mine see thou mayest, although to please thine eyes
I use no curious art, without disguise   120
True and unstained to be: which to they view
Her inward falsehood, and my truth may show.
As painful, dreadful, dangerous my path,
Yes and pernicious she traduceth hath,
Hers vaunting to be pleasant and secure,   125
And such as might all joy to thee procure.
In both she a most shameless liar is;
For that my path, though painful, leads to bliss
And glory: yea that pains thereof are sweet
For that with solid inward joys they meet.   130
Whereas her way, though pleasant she it name,
Leads to destruction, infamy and shame;
The pleasures thereof being such as beasts
Enjoy, her sports of Venus, and her feasts
Of Bacchus being poison to the health   135
Of mind and body, and the wrack of wealth
And honour. Both our ways, and ends (of which
No mention made was by this guileful witch)
They that do follow either her or me,
Such by experience find at length to be.   140
I therefore for thine honour and avail
Wish in advising thee I may prevail.
    Voluptuousness and virtue so did strive
Him after them to draw: which did him drive
Into a great quandary for a while,   145
His fancy to her, that would him beguile,
Inclining, but his reason to the other,
Who sought his welfare, as a loving mother.
But reason ruling fancy, virtue won
The victory: so as he soon begun   150
To tread her path: whereby he did attain
To endless bliss and glory, virtue's gain.
Young Bernard so did virtue's counsel take
And vice with all her pleasant baits forsake.
    He had occasion in his youth to pass   155
To France from Scotland, whither called he was
By John his uncle, who before his death
Did by his will to him as heir bequeath

Of Aubigny the lordship, with the rest
Of those domains that he in France possessed,[26]   160
And which he most deservedly had won
By valiant, wise and faithful service done
To Charles, then king, who having had a proof
Thereof much to his honour and behooft†
In many a conflict, chiefly in the fight   165
Of Baugé, wherein many a noble knight[27]
With princely Clarence died, to grace him more,
Adjoined to the arms he had before
His own three royal lilies in a field
Of azure, quartered in his coat and shield   170
Of arms, to him a glorious ornament,
And to his house an honour permanent.
His noble nephew bent to act his part,
As he had done by acts of martial art
Renown and honour went about to win,   175
And shortly did so much excel therein,
As he among the valiant'st knights renowned
For valour was, as also worthy found,
When as he did in riper years increase,
For skill and judgments both in war and peace   180
Of great employments. Which in peace he had
When Charles his master with intent to add
New tied of friendship to the former band
Of ancient league, which without breach did stand
Twixt France and Scotland, thither to that end   185
Ambassador did him appoint and send:
In which his embassy he did approve
To both those kings his prudence, faith, and love.
    Great also grew in warfare his command
When he was chosen captain of that band   190
Of his own warlike nation, that contained
A hundred men of arms, and had obtained
That honour first of all the companies,

26 Quin is in error here. Bernard was the son of John Stuart (d. *c.*1469), the second lord of
    Aubigny.
27 John Stewart of Darnley, Bernard Stuart's grandfather, played a prominent part in Franco-
    Scottish victory at the Battle of Baugé, where the English forces were defeated and their leader
    (the duke of Clarence, the king's brother) was killed: Alastair J. Macdonald, 'Stewart, Sir John,
    of Darnley (*c.*1380–1429)', *ODNB*.

Which of that kind did since in France arise:
Whose princes no disparagement it hold   195
To be as captains of those bands enrolled.
He of this charge, and of each high degree
Of honour worthy showed himself to be,
As did by many his brave deeds appear:
Whereof much one by right should him endear   200
To all Great Britain, and throughout the same
Immortal glory purchase to his name.
        Which was, that he with warlike power from France
Did come to England, Henry to advance,
Long thence exiled, and but in name and show   205
Then Richmond's earl, who when he overthrew
And slew the crookback tyrant in the field,[28]
Rich England's sceptre gloriously did wield:
The help of this his champion wise and stout
Both in his passage full of dread and doubt,   210
And in the battle having happily
Been such, as much he furthered was thereby.
        It seemeth then to have been heaven's intent,
That he in Scotland born, and by descent
Of kingly race, should for a Scottish king   215
Sprung from the royal stem, whence he did spring,
Who both Great Britain's sceptres now doth sway,
Prepare to this great monarchy the way.
        O how both nations of this famous isle
Are by this union blest! which doth exile   220
From them all discord and unpleasant jars
With all the harms and woes of former wars
Them tying fast with concord's happy bands,
And giving them occasion hearts and hands
To join in serving both one sovereign lord,   225
And for their mutual profit to afford
All fruits of love and friendship th'one to th'other,
As if they were the children of one mother
Joined by this union, for which thanks they owe
To him, from whose support such help did flow   230
To royal Henry, who the roses twain
Made one by wedlock, whence proceeds again

28 At Bosworth (1485), Henry Tudor defeated Richard III. Quin notes the Tudor ancestry of
    James VI in *Anagrammata* and *Sertum poeticum*.

This second union more than th'other blessed,
Made by a king sprung hence, of kings the best,
Appointed by heaven's high and blest decree   235
Sole monarch of Great Britain first to be,
As well by virtue's purchase having right
Thereto, as by inheritance; whose might
Is equalled by his goodness, and goodwill
Is guarded by Minerva's arts and skill.   240
Whose prudence linked is with piety,
With justice, and unfeigned sincerity;
Whose justice is by mercy qualified;
Whose courage is by wisdom modified;
Whose majesty with modesty is decked;†   245
Whose worth is less in show, than in effect,
Like Phoebus, whom, the brighter is his light,²⁹
The less we see, his rays so dim our sight.
And as he doth to all this worldly frame
Impart his beams to benefit the same: 250
So doth our Phoebus well with all men deal,
As an efficient cause of public weal
To subjects, neighbours, and confederates,
As likewise to all other Christian states,
Sith† he by wisdom mediates their peace,³⁰   255
And thereby their commerce and wealths increase.
And as he happy in his person is,
So in his issue is he blest ywis;†
As in his princely son, both of his feature,
And physiognomy the lively portraiture,   260
As also of the beauty of his mind,
Who to all kinds of virtues well inclined
Such buds of them doth yield in spring of youth,
As promise us in age's riper growth
The virtues rare and deeds heroical   265
A fruitful harvest, whereby win he shall
The name of Albion's Charlemagne,
When on his father's throne he come to reign.
Who in his daughter fair is blest likewise
From all the worthiest of her sex the prize   270
Of honour winning by her worth, whereby

29 Phoebus Apollo was god of the sun as well as the god of poetry.
30 King James' motto was *Beati pacifici* (see Mt 5:9: 'blessed are the peacemakers').

She doth procure to her elector hie†[31]
Much happiness, as by her bringing forth
Such princes, as may for their blood and worth.
When th'emperor's election shall be free,   275
As well elected as electors be,
And daughters, matches fit for France's flowers,
Rome's eagles spread, or Castile's stately towers.
But cease to range thus any more, my Muse,
And by thy homely chanting to abuse   280
The praises of such sacred majesty,
Though it to honour, duty do thee tie,
Yea, and the present subject thee invite,
And (going on where thou dids't leave) indite†
To me his worthy deeds, whom we may bless   285
As instrument of so great happiness.
      When as King Henry crowned and settled was,
Lord d'Aubigny back into France did pass:
Whereby the king and his nobility
His valour, wisdom and felicity   290
In his late action was with great applause
Extolled and magnified: and for that cause
He worthy was esteemed of greater charge
And place; wherein, as in a field more large,
Or theatre, he might his martial skill   295
And prowess use and exercise at will.
Whereof a fit occasion shortly came:
For Charles then king th'eight being of that name,
Encouraged by his heat and strength of youth,
And by ambition (whose enormous growth   300
Exceedeth in that age) more hardy made,
Resolved the realm of Naples to invade:
Which to the dukes of Anjou appertained
Some ages past, but then from them detained
Was by th'usurping house of Aragon.   305
And Sforza, duke of Milan, egging on
Charles to this action, him to be therein
More forward moved. But ere he would begin
This enterprise, not thinking ought more needful
And requisite, than that he should be heedful   310

31 Elizabeth Stuart, wife of the Frederick V, count palatine of the Rhine and an elector of the
    Holy Roman Empire.

And provident in choosing men expert
To lead his army, merely for desert,
And not through favour, d'Aubigny, thought he
A stranger were, he did appoint to be
One of the chief and for that he was fit   315
For great affairs of state, as having wit
And judgment them to manage prudently;
The pope and other states of Italy
By embassy of persons eminent
In place and worth desiring to his bent   320
As friends to draw, of four, whom to that end
He chooseth, chief our Bernard doth he send.
Who to the pope, and to his purple crew
In consistory met doth wisely show
In few and weighty words his master's right;   325
Them boldly wishing not to try his might
As enemies opposed to his ends,
But rather to deserve his love as friends.
With sundry other potentates likewise
He treating in like sort did them advise.   330
Whereof some by his words persuaded were,
And some more backward put in doubt and fear.
But shortly after more their terror grew,
When he himself presented to their view
An army leading against Ferdinand   335
Of Naples prince: who from his father's land
Would have diverted by prevention sly
Bellona's tumults into Lombardy.[32]
But this our champion his design did cross,
And homeward him repelled with grief and loss.   340
Whereby his father greatly damnified,
And therewithal extremely terrified,
No heart, no hope, no hap had to withstand
King Charles then coming to invade his land.
Who with his forces brought from France, and those,   345
Which valiant Bernard having tamed his foes
Brought to him, peaceably to Naples went,
Where without opposition his intent
Of conquering the same he did effect

32 Bellona is the Roman goddess of war.

So speedily, as he in the respect   350
Might into France have written, ere by fame
It had been known: 'I came, saw, overcame.'[33]
    But by a league then made, through jealousy
And fear of this his strange felicity,
Between the chief Italian potentates   355
Against him, thereby to secure their states,
He backward into France apace did hie,†
The danger of their arms conjoined to fly.
But he rewarded, ere he did depart,
Lord d'Aubigny, who acted had his part   360
More wisely, stoutly, happily than any
Of his commanders; yea and, although many
They were, alone more than they all had done
In furthering him to all that he had won,
By his embassage, and when hard he held   365
To the Aragonian prince and him repelled:
As also when of late with forces sent
Into Calabria, he with good event
And expedition conquered all the same   370
Even to the city Regium called by name.[34]
    The king him gave, to better his estate,
A goodly earldom, and a marquisate,
And of that realm's high constable the place,
The more thereby him to advance and grace,   375
Together with Calabria's government,
The next in honour and commandment
To that of all the kingdom; wherein he
Monpensier placed, a prince of high degree.[35]
    All this he did, not only to reward   380
This worthy lord, but also in regard
He knew, that when his gifts he thus did sow,
Thence to himself such fruits should after grow
Of honour, service, and fidelity,

33 Caesar's famous 'veni, vidi, vici', recounted in his biographies by Plutarch and Suetonius:
    Plutarch, *Plutarch's Lives*, trans. Bernadotte Perrin (11 vols, London: Heinemann, 1914–26),
    vii, p. 563 [50]. Suetonius, *The Twelve Caesars*, trans. Robert Graves (Harmondsworth:
    Penguin, 1970), p. 25 [37]. Quin also uses this in 'La cornamusa di Gualtero Quin', p. 120.
34 Reggio di Calabria is a port on the Strait of Messina in the toe of Italy.
35 Gilbert de Bourbon (d. 1496), count of Montpensier, led the advance guard of King Charles'
    army and was subsequently made viceroy of Naples: Mallett and Shaw, *Italian Wars*, pp 20–1.

As he with great increase should gain thereby.   385
And in effect right so to pass it came:
For d'Aubigny himself did ever frame
To honour him, and serve him faithfully
In war and peace with care and industry,
And with unfeigned love and ardent zeal   390
Both to his good and to the public weal.
In his Calabrian government appeared
This to be true, while there the helm he steered:
Where still to work his master's good he sought:
And what he could for public good he wrought,   395
That people ruling with much equity,
With moderation and with lenity:
So as when they his goodness tried and proved,
He was by them much honoured and beloved,
Thought they were demi-Grecians, and defamed   400
As factious and rebellious, yea and named
Devils by nickname old, as yet they are.[36]
Such force have virtues eminent and rare
In rulers, as the stubbornest they allure,
And them to love and reverence procure.   405
And for his sake (so much they him respected)
They to the French the better were affected:
Nor any in the realm surmounted them
In loyalty to the French diadem.
    The power whereof awhile there being great   410
Was much diminished by the king's retreat;
But more by reason of his dalliance
And negligence, when he returned to France.
King Ferdinand, that had a long time hovered
And lurked to save himself, thereby recovered   415
Both strength and courage, and was heartened more
By new supplies, which from the Spanish shore
Came to assist him under the command
Of that Consalvo surnamed Hernand,
To whom as eminent in worth and fame,   420
The Spaniards of 'Great Captain' gave the name.
The king his forces having with his own
Conjoined, and thereby the more hardy grown,

36 Naples had been described as 'a paradise inhabited by devils' since the sixteenth century:
   Benedetto Croce, *Uomini e cose della vecchia Italia* (2 vols, Bari: G. Laterza, 1927), i, p. 70.

Into Calabria passeth in all haste:
Where th'Angevin's possessions he doth waste,[37]   425
And all subverts that would his passage stop;
Like to the torrent from the mountain top
Down falling after stormy snows and rains,
Which over-flowing all the lower plains,
Trees, bridges, cottages and country towns   430
With violence down bears, subverts and drowns.
  But d'Aubigny, whose courage like a rock
Or bulwark strong did nothing fear the shock
Of this his furious force, himself prepares
Him to encounter, yea and stoutly dares   435
His passage finding out by wise foresight,
To meet him, hie† apace, and with him fight.
Near to the walls of Seminare he found[38]
Him, and his Spanish champion so renowned,
With all their army, which did his surpass   440
In number far: but such the valour was,
Which he himself, and all his warlike crew
Of Frenchmen and North-Britains† then did show,
As they defeated quite their enemies:
Whose leaders, though themselves both stout and wise   445
They showed, yet to escape by flight were fain,
The king in danger being to be slain,
Or taken through the falling of his steed,
When faithful Altavile in this his need[39]
His horse to him, and for him gave his life.   450
Thus our brave warrior in this warlike strife
To his immortal honour overcame
A king, and a commander of such fame,
As was Consalvo, whose worth and valiant deeds
Of Spain's renown and greatness were the seeds.   455
  But Fortune of his glorious victory
Or rather of so great prosperity

37 France's claim on Naples came through the Angevins.

38 In June 1495 in the First Battle of Seminara, despite being heavily outnumbered, Stuart defeated the Spanish and Neapolitan forces of the newly arrived Gonzalo Fernández: Stuart, *Traité*, xvii–xix.

39 Giovanni, a Capuan nobleman (the brother of Bartolomeo, count of Altavilla), gave King Ferdinand II his own horse: Donald J. Larocca, 'A Neapolitan Patron of Armor and Tapestry Identified', *Metropolitan Museum Journal*, 28 (1993), 85–102 at 87–8.

Of the French nation growing envious,
The course of his exploits victorious
Stopped by a sickness troublesome and long,   460
Which on him seized: wherein as she did wrong
His glory, so much woe thereby she wrought
To the French side, which to decay was brought,
Not having chieftains, able to withstand
The reinforced assaults of Ferdinand,   465
And of Consalvo, that did the French assail,
And everywhere against them did prevail.
The viceroy, Lord Monpensier without doubt
Was both a noble personage and stout,
But not so circumspect and provident,   470
As needful was, such dangers to prevent.
Wherewith Lord d'Aubigny, that then diseased,
With sickness lay, was vexèd and displeased,
As also seeing that no new supply
Came from the king, who living carelessly   475
In pleasure suffered by his negligence
To be lost, which with so great expense
Of treasure, yea with care and toil sustained
Even by himself he rather bought than gained.
But this his champion (although ever true   480
And faithful to him, much displeased he grew
That his affairs were in so evil estate)
Yet seeing that with providence and fate,
Which wrought this change, he should but strive in vain,
Himself in end to yield thereto was fain;   485
When of his long disease not wholly rid
By true relation understand he did
How that the Lord Monpensier, having lost
The field, and with the remnant of his host
Besieged in Atella, did agree[40]   490
And solemnly capitulate that he
With all his Frenchmen should that land forsake:
And therefore he not able head to make
To th'Aragonian forces, nor to mend,
What was by others marred, did condescend,   495
Though much against his stomach, to be tried

40 Montpensier surrendered Atella, a town in the province of Potenza and his last foothold in the Kingdom of Naples, in July 1496: Mallett and Shaw, *Italian Wars*, pp 33–4.

To th'articles already ratified.
And seeing that no hope to him was left,
Since he was wholly of his means bereft
Of doing service to his king, or good 500
To those distressed Neapolitans, that stood
Well-minded and affected to him still;
He used his best endeavours and good will
To save that remnant of the French, that were
Surviving to their woes and dangers there. 505
Then as among the first he thither passed,
So in departing was he of the last.
    Much was he graced, when back to France he came,
Both by the king, and those, to whom by fame
His virtues rare and eminent were known, 510
Which by his worthy actions he had shown,
As trees do show their goodness by their fruit:
Which to him chiefly made them attribute
What victories and honour had been won,
And whatsoever other good was done 515
In Naples by the Frenchmen, as the blame
Of all the losses, crosses, woes, and shame
By them sustained to others they imputed.
Yea by the king he was so well reputed,
As he was like to send him back again, 520
That kingdom lost by arms to reobtain.
    But he surprised being in his flower
And strength of age by death, which doth devour
As well the young and lust, as the old,
And is as much with kings as subjects bold; 525
To him succeeded Louis, the twelfth by name,
Who willing to enlarge his power and fame,
Assembled a great army, by the force
Thereof to drive away usurping Sforze
From Milan, which as rightful heir he claimed, 530
And for that armies are as bodies maimed
Without commanders valiant and expert
Three did he choose, as men of best desert,
To lead his army: whereof chief in worth
And place was d'Aubigny: who setting forth 535
Towards Lombardy, when thither he arrived,
Th'usurper of his chiefest towns deprived

By force or composition, put to flight
His army, and himself bereft of might
And courage he compelled likewise to fly   540
From Milan: whither soon the king did hie,†
To take possession of that goodly state,
Commanders valiant, wise and fortunate
Reputing them, who thus did him invest,
But this our noble knight above the rest.   545
    Whereof sufficient proof he shortly gave;
When by this conquest he began to have
Both more desire, and greater hope again
By arms the realm of Naples to obtain.
But judging nothing else so requisite   550
For this his purpose, as that opposite
Th'ambitious Spaniard to it should not be,
The conquest of that land he did agree
To share with him, who did thereto pretend
A title, as he did, and in his end   555
Of growing greater did with him consent.
And knowing well that to the same intent
He was to choose for leading of his host
A fit commander, such a one as most
Could further his attempt, of d'Aubigny   560
He made election: who both warily
And valiantly with speed did through the lands
Of foes, and doubtful friends conduct his bands;
The Roman columns much endamaging,
That then assisted th'Aragonian king.   565
Whose army in his passage come to let†
His troops from passing Gariglian he met.[41]
But when to pass the river he did think,
To set on them, he saw his horsemen shrink:
Whom thus he loudly did rebuke and taunt,   570
To egg them on. Yet lately oft did vaunt,
That you are alone without our footmen's aid
Your enemies would daunt: yet now afraid
Of them you are: which must your honour wrongs.
O let it not be said, that in your tongues   575
Your courage lies, not in your hands and hearts!

41 The River Garigliano meets the sea at Minturno, between Rome and Naples.

But bravely act of valiant men the parts,
And show that you can do as well as speak.
His words them made wroth with themselves, to wreak
Their anger on their foes; whom furiously   580
They charged, defeated, and compelled to fly.
He Capua did besiege, and quickly take.
Averse, and Nole durst not against him make[42]
Resistance, but themselves did to him yield.
King Frederick would neither sword, not shield   585
More use against him, so much terrified
He was, and by his prowess damnified.
Wherefore he by experience in the reign
Of Charles well having learned, how humane
And true he was, some sent to treat with him,   590
That found him not in countenance sour or grim
Nor harsh in words, but meek and mild in both,
To help him willing, and to grieve him loath.
When they his answer back to him did bring,
It pleased him so (if ought could please a king,   595
That from a throne was forcèd to descend)
As he resolved in vain not to defend
His kingdom, but to trust his faithful word,
And rather try his goodness, than his sword.
He therefore with himself did Naples, head   600
Of all his kingdom, yield to him, instead
Thereof his promise taking, that in France
The king should give him princely maintenance.
Which, with his letters, and no more he having
Him to assure, and from him no more craving;   605
So much did on his faithfulness rely,
As into France he went immediately.
Where to him was allotted by the grant
Of Louis the king more than the covenant
Required, which he had made with d'Aubigny.   610
Whose faith and trust this much doeth magnify,
That thus a king his enemy to it
His honour, state, and safety would commit.
    When of the kingdom by his arms pursued
His master's part he with the king subdued,   615

---

42 Capua, Aversa and Nola are towns near Naples. Stuart's victory at Aversa was followed by a
    massacre of its inhabitants: Stuart, *Traité*, p. xxv.

Whilst he in Naples stayed, he showed his care
Of public-weal, and his discretion rare,
In settling that disordered government,
And choosing men in wisdom eminent,
Learned in the laws, and from corruption free,   620
Both senators and judges there to be.
And as to cherish martial men his place
Did summon him; so likewise did he grace
Them, that devoted to the Muses were:
Of whom Pontanus, who then flourished there,[43]   625
Renowned for learning he did much regard,
And with his gifts and favours him reward:
So as for governing with judgment sound
As well in peace, as wars he was renowned,
Experience joined with his capacity   630
In him begetting such sufficiency.
And truly no less praise, yea more by right
Is due to him that doth by reason's light
And virtue's lore commands a state in peace,
Than to him, that by arms doth it increase.   635
For government in peace requires more art,
And virtue than in war, wherein her part
Oft more than virtue we see Fortune play.
Yea, to th'ambition, which doth warriors sway,
Oft opposite is virtue, which requires   640
A moderation due in their desires:
Whereas how much his virtue is the greater,
That rules in peace, he rules so much the better;
And as he justly merits, hath therefore
Of happiness and praise the greater store.   645
Yet I confess, that he, who doth excel
In both these kinds of rule, deserveth well
A double praise for this his double worth.
But few such worthies Nature bringeth forth.
Our Bernard such to be in either kind   650
Both the Neapolitans and French did find.
    But his commanding in the highest place

43 Giovanni Pontano (1426/9–1503) was a humanist and diplomat. His fame was such that the
    Neapolitan Academy was later called the Accademia Pontaniana. It is of more than passing
    interest that Aubigny's virtues were displayed in his patronage of a neo-Latin poet who wrote
    about Fortune: *ODR*.

Was of continuance over-short a space
For him, to act his part in furthering
The public-weal, and service of the king: 655
The duke of Nemours being thither sent,[44]
As viceroy, there the king to represent.
Yet also then, though second in degree
And place, himself he ever showed to be
In great achievements the most eminent,   660
As by the sequel it is evident.

II

About that time King Ferdinand of Spain
Consalvo sent, with forces to obtain
The share to him allotted in that land
Who so prevailed, as none could him withstand,
When as with arms he did the same invade;   5
His conquest the more easy being made
By d'Aubigny, who did subdue the king,
And stately Naples to subjection bring.
But both those nations proud and insolent,
In humours and conditions different,   10
Contending for their bounds began to jar:
Whence did arise betwixt them open war.
Wherein on the French party for a while
The better having Fortune seemed to smile,
And as in former times our d'Aubigny   15
More stoutly, skilfully, and happily
Than any other did in war command:
So did he at this season, when in hand
He took the third part of the host to lead
Into Calabria lately conquered   20
By great Consalvo; for he hence did chase
By force the Spaniards, and in every place
Thereof prevail: wherein availed him much
His reputation in that country such
For martial deeds, and civil government,   25
When in those parts he had commandment,

44 Louis d'Armagnac, duke of Nemours, was appointed viceroy of Naples in 1501. His military
    command ended with his death at the Battle of Ceringola in Apr. 1503 when the French were
    defeated by Gonzalo: Mallett and Shaw, *Italian Wars*, pp 64–5.

As they against the Spaniards did rebel,
And joined their arms with his them to expel.
Yea, such as were the greatest of them all,
And of that kingdom's peers the principal,   30
Who did his worth and virtues best discern,
Joined with him: as the princes of Salerne,
And Bisignan, with the earl, to whom Milet[45]
Did appertain: whom envy did not lett†
From serving under his command in field: 35
In so great estimation him they held,
And so him loved: whereof he had a proof
Soon after to his honour and behoof.†
    For Hugo de Cardon from Sicily[46]
With puissant forces coming furiously   40
Into Calabria, therein to annoy
The French, and if he could, them to destroy,
Our worthy warrior, who with watchful eye
Did see, yea and foresee what th'enemy
Did, or intended, joined in haste together   45
His forces, and with greater haste them thither
He led, where he to find his foes did look;
And through unhaunted ways his journey took
Of purpose, unawares them to surprise:
Which wisely he effected in such wise,   50
As unexpected he did on them set.
Yet so their courage did Don Hugo whet
By his courageous deeds, and words, as they
His deeds did follow and his words obey.
Which made the combat, many being slain   55
On either side, so doubtful to remain,
As d'Aubigny, whose eye was in all parts,
Perceiving that his footmen's hands and hearts
Began to faint, and that they did recoil,
The Spanish footmen striving them to foil,   60

45 Bernardino Sanseverino, prince of Bisignano (in Naples), his brother, the count of Mileto, and
their cousin, Antonello Sanseverino (d. 1499), prince of Salerno, welcomed the French army
into Italy in 1494: Francesco Tatò (ed.), *Enciclopedie on line*, www.treccani.it (Istituto della
enciclopedia italiana, 2014), accessed 1 Mar. 2014.

46 Don Hugo de Cardona was one of the Spanish captains. He died at the Third Battle of
Seminara (1503): Antonio Rodríguez Villa (ed.), *Crónicas del Gran Capitán* (Madrid: De Bailly,
1908), p. 283.

Commanded Grigni with his horsemen light[47]
Those Spaniards to assail: which of the fight
The fortune changed twixt both infantries.
But seeing that their hearts did eftsoones† rise
Encouraged by their valiant men of arms,   65
With his North-Britains† brave, that no alarms
Nor arms could terrify, he them assailed,
And breaking them, against their host prevailed;
Which utterly in the end he put to flight.
As at this time his skill joined with his might   70
Made him victorious, so did it likewise
In many another warlike enterprise
Of conflicts, and of taking towns and forts:
Which, seeing† story† shortly them reports
But as his meanest actions, I omit,   75
As acts of greater fame to match unfit.
But after this his famous victory
Her fickleness and mutability
Did Fortune show: for full of fraud and guile
She on the Spaniards now began to smile,   80
But on the Frenchmen spitefully to frown,
And, as she raised them up, to cast them down.
He being chief upholder of that side,
To which this misadventure did betide
Through Fortune's alteration, did partake   85
With them therein: yet could not that him make
Faint-hearted: yea, in this to his behoof.†
Did Fortune's frowning turn, that for a proof
It served, the more his virtue to refine,
And for a foil the more to make it shine.   90
      For truly courage in adversity
Appearing greater magnanimity
And worth in the owner shows, than when it is
Accompanied with Fortune's seeming bliss:
As pilots do in storms their art and skill   95
Far better show, than having wind at will.
Some in renown of valiancy† do flourish,
While Fortune with her favours doth them cherish,
Who, if she frown on them, will play the parts

---

47   Claude de Grignan, who died in 1502 at the Battle of Terranova (see below).

Of men dejected and deprived of hearts.   100
And if it chance (which seldom chance we see)
That he, who valiant is, still happy be
In his attempts: yet, in his good success
Her share and portion Fortune claiming, less
Appears his courage, than if he thereby   105
Should Fortune daunt and vanquish manfully.
For though Timoleon so favoured were[48]
By her, as evermore, and every where
He had success, so as the fame to show,
A painter him with nets towns taking drew: 110
Yet was he not therefore so much esteemed
As many warriors not so happy deemed.
    Oh how I much admire that worthy king,
Renowned Bruce, whom Fortune, envying[49]
His glory, more than once in wars did cross   115
And forced him to retire with grief and loss!
Yet could she never force him to forsake
His brave designs, nor him faint-hearted make,
Who did from all occasions great and small
Draw motives, to stir up himself withal.   120
For when he once a spider weaving viewed,
That oftentimes her broken web renewed,
Till she had weaved it wholly; then shall I,
Said he, demean myself less constantly,
In that which doth concern my country's good,   125
And mine own right by Fortune's spite withstood,
Than doth this vermin when it thus doth weave?
No, no: for all the affronts, that I receive
From Fortune, to her shall not make me yield,
Nor as a coward quit my sword or shield,   130
Till my foes shall vanquish, and her might,
And win the kingdom that is mine by right.

---

48 A Corinthian general, Timoleon (fourth century BC) expelled tyrants from Syracuse and other
    parts of Sicily. He subsequently defeated a Carthaginian army invading the island. Plutarch
    writes of him that 'all his successes were ascribed by him to fortune [...] Moreover, in his
    house he built a shrine for sacrifice to Automatia, or Chance, and the house itself he conse-
    crated to man's sacred genius': 'Timoleon' in Plutarch, *Lives*, vi, p. 347 [36].
49 Robert I ('the Bruce') (1274–1329), king of Scotland. *ODNB* notes that it was Sir Walter Scott
    who 'first put into circulation the subsequently well-known story of Bruce and the spider' and
    speculates that Scott's source was an unpublished manuscript by David Hume of Godscroft
    (1558–1629x31): G.W.S. Barrow, 'Robert I (1274–1329)', *ODNB*.

So spoke, so did he; and thought his attempt
From many dangers great were not exempt,
Yet he by valiant constancy therein   135
Did Fortune vanquish, and a kingdom win.
Lord d'Aubigny, who to his royal race
Was near in blood, and whom the heavens did grace
As they did him, with magnanimity
In overcoming Fortune's enmity,   140
Perceiving, that the Spaniards did begin
Upon the Frenchmen daily ground to win,
Their strength decreasing, and no new supply
From France arriving them to fortify,
Desired of his own party the decay,   145
And the others growing, if he could, to stay.
Wherefore new forces, that from Spain were sent
His province to invade, to meet he went,
The rather for that he did understand,
That their commander died when they did land;   150
Which twixt their other chieftains strife did breed,
Who should to him as general succeed;
As also that their troops for want of pay
Through mutiny were like to shrink away:
He them encountered near to Seminare: 155
Whereby his skilfulness and prowess rare
Before a famous victory he won
(Then seconded by Fortune as her son)
Against Consalvo, and King Ferdinand.
But now, though he his army did command   160
With skill and courage; yet the unluckiness
And faintness of the French his happiness
Surmounting, he was driven to leave the field;
But not through faintness or despair to yield
To Fortune, as her thrall: for his retreat   165
Was to a fortress strong by art and feat:
Where he sustained valiantly the brunt
Of engines, canons, mines, and what is wont
In sieges and assaults most to be used;
And summoned, yea with threats, to yield refused;   170
Until their chieftains did to him relate,
How that Consalvo the viceroy had of late
Slain, and defeated in a bloody fight

His army: of which news with greater light
He had of some to know it by him sent,   175
To yield himself to them he was content:
With covenant that him in free custody
They keeping should release his company,
Such was his goodness and his earnest care,
That better than he did his friends should fare.   180
But when himself to yield he thus did grant,
To show that this misfortune could not daunt
His noble mind, not aught impair his worth,
He coming to the Spanish captains forth
In garments rich of tissue† was arrayed,   185
And with a look not cloudy nor dismayed
But clear and cheerful thus to them he spake.
    'I see that fickle Fortune to forsake
Our side, that earst† she cherished, not content,
To persecute and ruin it is bent.   190
I therefore it account an humour vain
To rail against her, and a madness plain
To struggle with her: sith† by doing so
Nought should be gotten, but increase of woe.
Then more against her will I not repine,   195
Or wrestle, but to Providence divine,
Whereby she ruled is, myself apply;
As do I must, and do it willingly.
Yet though she never so much lower and frown
Against our side, and me, my courage down   200
To cast or quail she shall not have the power,
Nor for her crosses make me wail, or lower.
Wherefore with patience I me yield to you,
Whom she does cherish as her darlings now;
And do this favour only of you crave,   205
That, as already these my fellows have
Of you the grant of freedom, so they may
Enjoy it without hindrance, or delay.'
Thus did he to his enemies approve
His courage brave, and to his friends his love.   210
    Two noble youths there being then with them,
His kinsmen, sprung from Scotland's royal stem;
(That after worthy chieftains were esteemed)
Who to bemoan too passionately seemed

Their own mischance, and that of all their side,   215
Desiring that by reason they should guide
Their passions, them thus greatly taxed he.
'Dear kinsmen, I am grieved thus you to see
Dejected and disheartened, who should prove
Of valiant courage, patterns fit to move   220
All noble youths the same to imitate;
Not suffering any chance unfortunate
Your manly courage womanly to make,
Or thus yourselves, like women, to betake
To tears and wailing. What? Thus will you wrong   225
That ancient royal stock, whence you are sprung,
As from it to degenerate so much,
Or wrong your country's honour; which is such,
As Britains have the old Romans' property
And praise, to act and suffer valiantly?   230
Let courage then such tenderness remove
From you, and (as it much doth you behove†)
Let reason, without too much grief or fear,
All Fortune's changes make you stoutly bear;
Especially in war, wherein more rife   235
They are, than in the remnant of our life:
Since by experience oft it hath been seen,
That they which have one day victorious been,
Another day, yea and perhaps the same
Have lost the field, such is Bellona's game.   240
And therefore as on Fortune to rely
Too much ye ought not; so you are to fly
Of her, or of yourselves a base distrust:
Yea bravely strive to vanquish her ye must,
And make her by your valiancy renewed   245
As friendly to you, as she now is shrewd.'
Thus both in deeds and words he made appear
His courage and his virtue bright and clear,
As well when Fortune's storms did him assail,
As when her favours most did him avail.   250
He prisoner in Naples did remain,
Till, when the war was ceased, to France again
He was to go with other men of worth.
To them Consalvo at their setting forth
Did offer horses with much courtesy   255

[177]

For their return: for which our d'Aubigny
Him thanking, thus did answer him: 'My lord,
Since that your bounty doth to us afford
To bear us horses, we would have them strong,
That they to France may carry us along,   260
And hither back.' Consalvo what he said
Well understanding, thus him straight repaid:
'Return, when it shall please you, lords, for I
Towards you will use like liberality,
Both horses and my passport giving you   265
As willingly, as I you give them now.'
There words their quickness in conceit did show,
And noble minds, such as are found in few.
Yet show they most his magnanimity,
Who thus could jest in his adversity.   270
If we the warriors of their time compare
With them, among them all they peerless are.
    Such by two famous kings esteemed they were,
Soon after meeting at Savona: where
King Louis of France inviting to a feast   275
The king of Spain, Consalvo as guest
With him invited, and most courteously
Him using, did extol and magnify
The worthiness that did in him abound,
His martial deeds, and victories renowned.   280
All which his jealous king did little please.
Louis, peradventure knowing his disease,
Thus to increase it, did Consalvo grace.
King Ferdinand behindhand in this case
Was not with Louis: but as Louis of his train   285
The worthiest warrior chose; so he again
Desirous choice of such a guest to make,
Among the French our d'Aubigny did take
For such, and in like sort him entertained.
To whom this honour high his merits gained,   290
Though he a Britain were, and in degree
To princes, dukes, and peers that chanced to be
There at that time inferior far, so bright
Did virtue shine in this renowned knight.
The favour of these monarchs to these twain   295
Was of their matchless worth a witness plain.

But if them both we do compare together
(Which fitly may be done) both th'one and th'other
Were younger brethren of two noble lords;
To whom in what inheritance affords   300
Inferior being, more they were than mates
To them by their own purchase of estates,
And honour made by their industrious care,
And by their virtues eminent and rare.
For industry, which both did help to raise,   305
Lord d'Aubigny deserves the greater praise:
Sith† he no Frenchman being, could in France,
By industry himself so much advance:
Where th'other great in his own country grew,
Graced by a queen, that him to action drew.   310
In virtue both excelled, yet different were
In that our Bernard's virtue was sincere;
Where th'others having still a glistering† show,
Sometimes more artificial was than true.
Both th'one and th'other of a noble mind,   315
And truly generous to have been we find.
Yet when on both malignant Fortune frowned,
More courage did in d'Aubigny abound.
With prudence both were plentifully stored:
Yet taxed and branded is the Spanish lord   320
For craft and breach of faith in histories;
Which th'other name no less upright than wise.
For valiance, that like in both was found,
Among the valiantest both may be renowned.
In martial skill they may be paralleled,   325
And justly for great captains both be held:
Although to win that name, th'one Fortune's aid
Had more than the other: for Consalvo swayed
And ruled, as best him pleased, the Spanish side:
Where d'Aubigny so could not rule and guide   330
The French, another being then viceroy.
Yet did he so the power he had employ,
As in both wars made for that kingdom, none
Of all that led the French, but he alone,
Won any great and famous victory,   335
As witnesseth that age's history.
Whereby this truth is also testified,

[179]

That not Consalvo, so much magnified
So oft victorious was in field as he.
For besides lesser conflicts, battles three   340
He won, the first of them at Seminare;
Wherein Consalvo had of the less his share
With Ferdinand then king; at Gariglian[50]
The next against King Frederick's host he won;
The third, near to Terine: whereas but twice[51]   345
Consalvo in battle ranged† (although the price
Thereof was all that kingdom) vanquished
The French by Nemours, and Gonzaga led.[52]
This of our warrior Giovio more doth tell,
That after the mischance, which him befell   350
But once in war, of Fortune he complained,
That him, who had twelve victories obtained,
Since he in Britain, and in France betook
Himself to war, she thus in end forsook.
Whereby appeareth how this noble knight   355
By silence is defrauded of his right:
As also we may well thereby observe,
That oftentimes such men as best deserve,
Are less than men of less desert respected,
And in their fame, as otherwise neglected.   360
     But this to him the rather hath arrived,
For that almost continually he lived
In foreign lands, and all his famous deeds
In them achieved: where seldom any heeds
A stranger's worthy acts, or takes the pains   365
Them to record, but for reward and gains:
For which respect Consalvo so much renowned,
Besides the Spaniards that his praises sound,
Hath had the learned Giovio him to praise:
Who by the way, the more his worth to raise,   370

50 The River Garigliano meets the sea at Minturno (between Rome and Naples).
51 In 1502 at the Battle of Terranova (Terine) in Calabria, Aubigny defeated the Spanish forces
    commanded by Don Hugo de Cardona (a captain under Gonzalo of Córdoba who died at the
    Third Battle of Seminara (1503)): Stuart, *Traité*, p. xxvii; Rodríguez Villa (ed.), *Crónicas*, p.
    283.
52 Francesco Gonzaga, marquess of Mantua (1484–1519), had commanded the armies of the
    League of Venice fighting against Charles VIII's but by 1503 he was leading Louis XII's forces
    at Gaeta: Mallett and Shaw, *Italian Wars*, pp 30, 67–9.

In part the worth of d'Aubigny records,
As of his chief opponent: which affords
Occasion thus to paragon together
These two renowned warriors: whereof either
Did th'other's worth esteem and magnify,   375
Though different in this, that d'Aubigny
As best it with his master's pleasure stood,
Or most behoofull† was for public good,
Alone, or joined with others in the field
Did govern, or the place to others yield.   380
Whereas, such was the Spaniard's haughty heart,
As evermore he a commander's part
Did strive to act: for which he well compared
Was to a carrack† huge, built and prepared
Rigged, trimmed, and furnished with excessive charge,†   385
Which well may ride afloat, or sail at large
In the deep ocean, but cannot abide
A shallow haven, or near the shore to ride.
Whereas our British lord compared may be
To one of those ships royal, which we see   390
Near Chatham, fit to sail into the main
To serve her king, and to return again[53]
Into her haven, or, when a boisterous blast
At sea doth take her, near the shore to cast
Her anchor, riding there from storms secure.   395
So evermore did he himself inure
Both to his duty and his fortune still,
Though free from baseness to conform his will.
By all that hath been hitherto recorded
Of him, to him this praise may be afforded   400
Deservedly, that many did him give,
Who chanced in his company to live;
To wit, that among warriors none they knew,
That did in war more skill and valour show;
No councillor or governor in peace   405

---

53 The reference is a topical one. Despite the threat of pirates, very few ships had been built or
refitted in the previous decade. The earl of Buckingham turned this situation around and
became lord admiral in 1619 after a commission established the extent of fraud and malprac-
tice in the navy: David Loades, 'From the King's Ships to the Royal Navy, 1500-1642' in J.R.
Hill (ed.), *The Oxford Illustrated History of the Royal Navy* (Oxford: Oxford UP, 2002), pp 51–
2.

More wise; and in prosperity increase
None more humane and gently; as likewise
None in adversity that played his prize
More bravely against foes and Fortune's spite:
So as this praise doth justly me invite,   410
Together with his other merits rare,
With great Consalvo in worth him to compare.
    But that in matching them I may forbear
To be too tedious, after that they were
So graced by the kings of France and Spain,   415
Their fortune, like to Cynthia in her wane,[54]
Decreased, so as neither of them was
In warfare more employed: which came to pass,
Not for that they, as men with action cloyed,†
Were grown unwilling so to be employed,   420
But through their masters' great ingratitude,
Which them from such employment did exclude;
Were it for that so great were their deserts
And service, as their masters' narrow hearts
Did them, as too much owing to them, loathe,   425
Or that with them by whispering slanders wroth
They were become, or did their faith distrust.
But whatsoever was the cause, so thrust
They out of favour were. But the displeasure
Of Ferdinand not having end nor measure   430
Against Consalvo, Louis did soon relent,
And reconciled to d'Aubigny, he meant
Him in some famous action to employ.
But sickness did him so much annoy,
As he therefore was counselled to repair   435
To Scotland, that by his native air
He might his health recover: which advice,
And country's love did him thereto entice.
    He hitherward through England took his way:
Where Henry the Eight by name, that then did sway   440
The sceptre of this land, remembering well,
What furtherance he heard his father tell
This lord him gave, when he to the crown he came,
And having understood by public fame

---

54 'Cynthia' was an epithet of Elizabeth I.

Much of his worthy deeds, him to present   445
His duty to him come with great content
Did graciously receive and entertain,
Inviting him in England to remain
By bounteous offers: but with reverence
He thanking that great monarch, homeward hence   450
Departed: where with honour and applause
The king and all estates, not without cause
His worth esteeming much, did him receive.
There shortly after death did them bereave
Of him their rare and precious ornament.   455
For which their loss in him they did lament:
As did his friends in France, and everywhere,
Enamoured with his virtue, as it were
A loadstone, drawing to him many hearts:
So as in many ages for deserts   460
None was beloved and honoured more, than he
In sundry lands by men of each degree.
    Yea death, which doth the greatest, while they live
Enjoying love and honour, oft deprive
Of both, yet could not him bereave of either,   465
As well we may by one example gather.
Which is, that the commander of the host
Of Francis, France's monarch, in the coast
Of Piedmont, having taken by surprise
Colonna a chieftain other times so wise,[55]   470
That he like Fabius was his country's shield;[56]
As prisoner himself he would not yield
To La Palisse, or Bayard, though renowned[57]

---

55 Prospero Colonna (*c.*1460–1523) was a Roman *condottiero* who had been in the service of
Charles VIII in 1494. In the following year he served Ferrandino of Naples. He subsequently
joined the army of Gonzalo de Córdoba: Franca Petrucci, 'Colonna, Prospero' (1982).

56 The general Quintus Fabius Maximus Verrucosus (*c.*180–203BC) employed tactics of attrition
against Hannibal as he believed that the Carthaginian army could not be beaten in open battle:
OCD. He was called the shield of Rome by Plutarch in 'Fabius Maximus': Plutarch, *Lives*, iii,
p. 174 [19].

57 Jacques de Chabannes, marshal of La Palice (*c.*1470–1525), was close to both Charles VIII and
Louis XII. He encouraged their claims in Italy: M. Prévost & Roman d'Amat (eds),
Dictionnaire de biographie française (21 vols, Paris: Letouzey & Ané, 1959), viii, col. 101. Pierre
Terrail, lord of Bayard (*c.*1473–1524), fought in the Italian wars for Charles VIII, Louis XII
and Francis I and was renowned for his bravery as a captain and in single combat. He was
known as 'the good knight' and 'the fearless knight'.

Above the rest they were: but having found
That d'Aubigny was of the chiefest one, 475
He did his person yield to him alone,
As nephew to our famous d'Aubigny,
Whom he had in the wars of Italy
Well known, and highly for his worth esteemed,
So as his nephew for his sake he deemed 480
Most worthy thus by him to be affected,
And more than all the rest to be respected.
To Bernard such was his respect and love,
As death from him could not the same remove.
    His worth, that did allure this worthy knight 485
Thus him to love, and honour doth by right
Stir up my homely Muse thus to renew
His memory with praises to him due
Among our Britains: to whom he their own
Should be as well, as among strangers known, 490
Yea better, since to him they partly owe
Both the unions (whence their happiness doth flow)
Of both the roses, and the kingdoms twain,
With double thanks for this their double gain.
Whose virtuous deeds the rather I set forth, 495
That worthy minds may imitate his worth,
And worthily aspire to his renown:
Which length of time shall not in Lethe drown,
While of his worth and name, the memory
Shall be preserved by many a history 500
In Roman, Tuscan, French and Spanish scrolls,
As also kept in these my English rolls.

Of His Last Retiring to Corstorphine[58] [sig. Fv]

Linternum, though obscure, the place became
Of famous Scipio's last abode, [59] when Spain
And Carthage having conquered, with disdain
Ungrateful Rome he loathed, and left the same.
    Corstorphine as obscure in show or name 5

58 A village west of Edinburgh that is now a suburb of the city.
59 Despite having defeated Hannibal, Cornelius Scipio Africanus the elder (d. 183BC) ended his
days in exile in the Roman colony of Linternum near Cumae: *OCD*.

Did noble Bernard for her guest retain,
From thankless France when he came home again,
To Scipio like in fortune as in fame.
    Linternum, whilst her venerable guest
Did her inhabit, greater worth possessed,   10
Than great and wealthy Rome in all her treasure.
    Corstorphine also may be said as well,
While worthy Bernard deigned therein to dwell,
Of worth to have possessed, as great a measure.

Of His Burial in the Same Place [sig. Fv]

Brave Bernard of noble lineage born
In Scotland, whom such virtues did adorn,
As did him more ennoble, and in France
Deservedly to honour high advance;
Who England's parted roses, and with them   5
The Scottish thistle in their royal stem
Helped to unite; who of a ruler wise
And valiant warrior well deserved the prize
In Italy, chief theatre of his worth
And victories; whose fame from south to north   10
From east to west did through all Europe fly,
Interred doth in obscure Corstorphine lie.
But I mistake: his better part is passed
To heaven; on earth his fame shall ever last.

Of the Lords of Aubigny, Descended from the Most Noble House of Lennox [sig. F2r]

Among the fairest branches that have sprouted
From the illustrious stock of Lennox, three
Came in successive order lords to be
Of Aubigny, like Mars in arms redoubted.
    The first was John, whom for his service loyal,   5
And valiant deeds King Charles did so regard,
As he with princely gifts did him reward
And to his 'scutcheon add his lilies royal.[60]

60 Bernard Stuart's grandfather, Sir John Stewart of Darnley (c.1390–1429).

The next was Bernard who such honour gained
Both by his valiant acts and virtues rare,   10
As justly we may him with them compare,
That have by worth to honour's height attained.
    The third was Robert so for valour praised[61]
In many a fight, but chiefly in the field
Of Marignan, that sun and moon beheld,   15
As to be France's marshal he was raised.
    In calmer times their heirs occasion wanted,
Not valiant hearts, their worth in arms to show:
And now their worthy offspring doth renew
Their honour in Great Britain, there transplanted: 20
    Where they in happy manner grow and flourish,
But chiefly he, who shines in worth and place
Among her peers, and whom our sovereign's grace
Deservedly doth so advance and cherish.
    These goodly branches, whom their worth commendeth   25
From stem have sprouted of that royal tree
Which doth from storms with sheltering shadow free
Great Britain, and in height to heaven ascendedth.

A Short Collection of the Most Notable Places of Histories Quoted in This
Memorial [sig. F2v]

I have thought it meet, the better to show how this memorial agreeth with historical truth, to add thereunto the most notable places of histories quoted in the
margins, without altering the sense of the authors, yea, or their words, but only
in that they are translated, and in the abridgement of some narrations wherein
other men's actions are interlaced.[62] To the said passages I have added nothing
but the connection and some few brief observations. Which collection I have
rather made, for that the things contained in this memorial, that are of least
importance and doubtfulness, being drawn from records and relations of honourable and creditable persons, the contents thereof which are of greatest
importance, and may seem most doubtful, are testified and averred by these passages.

61 Bernard Stuart's cousin and son-in-law, Robert Stewart (c.1470–1544).
62 Apart from some slight errors, the text clearly distinguishes Quin's connecting passages from
    his sources by printing the former in italics. The side notes identifying Quin's sources have
    been reproduced here only where they add information to the main text. The references in
    these notes have been regularized.

The charge which he had of a company of men of arms is thus recorded by Malingre, a French historiographer: 'Charles the Seventh, who did first institute the ordinary companies of men of arms in France, erected the company of Scottish men of arms of the remnants of the Scottish men overthrown at Vernueil, which consisted of an hundred men of arms and two hundred archers, giving them the first place among the French bands of that kind.'[63] Of which company the said author saith, that Bernard Stuart, lord d'Aubigny, was the second captain.

Of his embassy to the king of Scotland, Lesley, bishop of Ross, maketh mention in this manner: 'Charles the eight sent into Scotland Bernard Stuart, lord d'Aubigny, and Doctor Mallart his ambassadors, to renew the ancient league between the two kings and nations.'[64]

Of his coming to England with King Henry the Seventh, the said Lesley writeth thus: 'He commanded those forces, that accompanied the earl of Richmond into England, and did him good service against the usurper, King Richard. So as the said earl being crowned king, did therefore ever after favour the Scottish nation.'[65]

The same is confirmed by the aforesaid Malingre, who affirmeth, 'that he was the king's lieutenant general of the army which was sent to England to assist Henry the Seventh against Richard the Third.'

Of his embassy to the pope, Guicciardini writeth thus: King Charles sent to the pope four ambassadors, to wit, 'Bernard d'Aubigny, a chieftain, being a Scottish man by nation, one of the treasurers of France, the president of the parliament of Provence, and Peron de Baschi.'[66]

Where it is to be noted, that among men of such dignity he had the first place. Yea, he was of such reputation, as Paolo Giovio doth name no other ambassador but him, writing of his embassy in this wise: 'To the pope was sent for ambassador Bernard d'Aubigny, a Scottish man of the royal family of the Stuarts, a renowned warrior, who had direction in his journey to Rome to treat with John Bentivoli, then lord of Bononia; Hercules d'Este, duke of Ferrara; Peter de Medici, chief commander of the Commonwealth of Florence; and Pandolfo Petrucci of Siena.[67] As also coming to those cities to learn what power

63 At the Battle of Verneuil (1424), during the Hundred Years War, the English army roundly defeated a Franco-Scottish one.
64 Side-note: Lesley, *Origins*, book viii: John Lesley, *De origine, moribus & rebus gestis Scotorum libri decem [...]* (Rome: In Aedibus Populi Romani [Paulus Manutius], 1675), p. 314.
65 Side-note: Lesley, *Origins*, book viii: Lesley, *De origine*, p. 333.
66 Side-note: Guicciardini, book i, ch. 1. Perron de Baschi was an Angevin diplomat who made visits to the major Italian courts in preparation for Charles VIII's Neapolitan campaign: Mallett and Shaw, *Italian Wars*, p. 13.
67 Giovanni Bentivoglio (1443–1508) was the ruler of Bologna. Ercole d'Este (1431–1505), the duke of Ferrara, sided with Charles VIII. Pietro de' Medici (1472–1503) had ruled Florence

they had, and how they were affected: and moreover to view and make well the passages of the Alps.'⁶⁸

The said Giovio saith that d'Aubigny in Rome accompanied with the ordinary ambassador in the consistory did gravely show upon what right was grounded the king's design of invading the kingdom of Naples, and seriously advised the pope and his cardinals that they would rather try the friendship, than the power of the French.⁶⁹

He relateth, and what forces he commanded in these words: 'D'Aubigny, with a powerful number of Helvetians† and his horsemen of Great Britain, and about three hundred Frenchmen of arms, went to Romagna, whither was come a little before the earl of Gayazzo, commander of the forces of Milan, which were six hundred men of arms, and about three thousand footmen, to join himself with him.'⁷⁰

Mariana, describing the success of this enterprise, saith, 'that the forces of France and Milan, d'Aubigny being their chief conductor, did oppose themselves to Ferdinand, duke of Calabria, in Romagna, and forced him to return homeward.'⁷¹

Serres writeth, 'that being sent to Calabria with some forces, he subdued the same wholly, except the town of Regium.'⁷²

Of his advancement at the king's departure from Naples, Giovio saith: 'The province of Calabria was committed to d'Aubigny's charge, whom the king made also great constable, which is the chief honour of warfare.'⁷³

And Philippe de Commines writeth, 'that the king left in Calabria the lord d'Aubigny, a Scottish man by nation, a good knight, wise and honourable, who was great constable of the kingdom. And the king gave him the earldom of Acri and the marquisate of Squillazzo.'⁷⁴

As for the manner of his government, Giovio testifieth, 'that he governed with great moderation and mildness this nation demi-Grecian.'⁷⁵

since the death of his father, Lorenzo. He ultimately sided with Charles VIII in the Italian wars. Pandolfo Petrucci (1452–1512) was ruler of Siena, a position to which he was restored in 1503 by Louis XII having been exiled by Cesare Borgia: *ODR*; ibid., pp 16–17.

68 Side-note: Giovio, *History*, book i, ch. 1.
69 Side-note: Ibid.
70 Side-note: Giovio, *History*, book i, ch. 1. Galeazzo Sanseverino (d. 1525), count of Caiazzo, was a commander of the Milanese forces and a son-in-law of Ludovico Sforza ('il Moro'). He subsequently entered the service of France and in 1501 accompanied Stuart in the Neapolitan campaign: Tatò (ed.), *Enciclopedie*; Stuart, *Traité*, p. xxi.
71 Side-note: Mariana, book xxvi, ch. 7.
72 Side-note: 'In the reign of King Charles.' Reggio di Calabria is a port on the Strait of Messina in the toe of Italy.
73 Side-note: Giovio, *History*, book i, ch. 1.
74 Side-note: Commines, book viii, ch. 1. Acri and Squillace are towns in Calabria.
75 Side-note: Giovio, *Consalvo*.

Whereunto Mariana addeth, 'that d'Aubigny, a Scottish man, and a valiant chieftain, did by his valour and wisdom uphold the French part in Calabria.'[76]

Of the duke of Montpensier, whose government is sometimes taxed in the precedent memorial, Philippe de Commines speaketh thus: 'For chief governor there remained the duke of Montpensier of the house of Bourbon, a good knight and valiant, but not very wise. He was wont to lie a bed till noon.'[77]

The lord d'Aubigny's victory in the battle fought against Ferdinand, king of Naples, is described at length by Paolo Giovio in the third book of his *History*, and by Du Haillan in the reign of Charles VIII.

Mariana thus maketh mention thereof: 'D'Aubigny knowing our men's design, went fiercely against the king, where he must needs have passed. Consalvo advised him not to fight, but the king, carried away with the heat of youth and neglecting his counsel, resolved to fight, and was overcome.'[78]

Of his sickness after the victory Guicciardini speaketh in these words: 'The prosperity of the Frenchmen began to decline, d'Aubigny being fallen into a long sickness which interrupted the course of his victories.'[79]

And Du Haillan making mention as well of his sickness as of the decay of the French faction, saith, 'that d'Aubigny afflicted with sickness was vexed with impatience to see that by the negligence of Gilbert of Montpensier the king's affairs grew weak, and worse and worse every day. But it was long since the soldiers had received their pay, the money which the kingdom yielded being already wholly consumed.'[80]

Which disorder and the like having been the cause of the Frenchmen's decay, yet Mariana, ascribing to the valour and diligence of Consalvo the good success which he had in Calabria during the sickness of Lord d'Aubigny, writeth of the one and the other in this manner: 'The day after the capitulation of Atella' (whereby the Frenchmen, after a great overthrow, the duke of Montpensier being their general, were bound to depart out of the kingdom of Naples),[81] 'Consalvo returneth into Calabria, the greatest part whereof was in his absence brought under the French yoke by d'Aubigny, a most valiant and stirring warrior, but a man of valour and wisdom more approved than fortunate, for that he had to deal with so strong an adversary, whose diligence pressing him every-

---

76 Side-note: Mariana, book xxvi, ch. 10.
77 Side-note: Commines, book viii, ch. 1. Gilbert de Bourbon (d. 1496), count of Montpensier, led the advance guard of King Charles' army and was subsequently made viceroy of Naples: Mallett and Shaw, *Italian Wars*, pp 20–1.
78 Side-note: Mariana, book xxvi, ch. 10.
79 Side-note: Guicciardini, book iii.
80 Side-note: 'Reign of King Charles VII.'
81 Montpensier surrendered Atella, a town in the province of Potenza and his last foothold in the Kingdom of Naples, in July 1496: Mallett and Shaw, *Italian Wars*, pp 33–4.

where, he was constrained to yield to the articles of agreement made with common consent by the Frenchmen, and, leaving Italy, to return into France.'[82]

Of the enterprize of Milan, Du Haillan hath these passages that follow: 'The king [Louis XII] has assembled an army of five and twenty thousand footmen, and of five thousand horsemen. He gave the conduct of them to Bernard Stuart, lord d'Aubigny; Lewis of Luxembourg, lord of Ligni; and John Giacomo Trivulcio, all men of great experience and sufficiency in the mystery of arms.[83] D'Aubigny, assaulting Nona with his troops, took it at the first assault. The city of Dertona was yielded immediately after to him.[84] And they of Pavia, fearing the misfortune of the Alexandrians, did not make longer resistance.'[85]

Paolo Giovio naming d'Aubigny the principal leader of this enterprize saith, 'that Sforza being astonished by the news which he had of the defeat of his army, and of the taking of Alexandria, was quite disheartened, and leaving Milan, fled to the Emperor Maximillian, and that soon after King Louis, having received the most pleasing news of this victory, came to Milan; and that all the towns of Sforza's dominion, with the city of Geneva, yielded to him.'[86]

Of the enterprize of Naples Du Haillan hath written that which followeth in sundry places: 'D'Aubigny departed from Milan with twenty thousand footmen and four thousand horsemen. He took the castles of the lords of the House of Colonna well-fortified, some by force and some by composition.'†[87]

'When he came to pass the River of Gariglian, the Frenchmen were molested by the enemy's army.[88] But the lord d'Aubigny loudly reproaching to the French horsemen their arrogant boasting a little before, that they alone,

82 Side-note: Mariana, book xxvi, ch. 12.
83 Louis de Luxembourg, count of Ligny, was the son of Louis de Luxembourg (d. 1475), constable of France, and a cousin of Charles VIII: Phillipe de Commynes, *Mémoires*, ed. Joël Blanchard (2 vols, Geneva: Droz, 2007), ii p. 1224. Gian Giacomo Trivulzio (1441–1518), 'one of the best Italian generals of his day', served in the Neapolitan army before going over to the service of Charles VIII. He was at the head of Louis XII's army when it invaded Milan in 1499: Christine Shaw, *The Politics of Exile in Renaissance Italy* (Cambridge: Cambridge UP, 2000), p. 23.
84 Having resisted the French army for four days, the Milanese garrison at Annona was extirpated. This prompted the city of Dertona (modern Tortona) to surrender without resistance: Mallett and Shaw, *Italian Wars*, p. 48.
85 Side-note: 'Reign of Louis XII.' Alessandria in Piedmont was besieged and partially sacked by Trivulzio.
86 Side-note: Giovio, *History*, book xvii.
87 Side-note: 'Reign of Louis XII.' Prospero (c.1460–1523) and his cousin Fabrizio Colonna (d. 1520) were Roman *condottieri* who had been in the service of Charles VIII in 1494. In the following year they were hired by Ferrandino of Naples and Fabrizio lost Capua to Aubigny. They subsequently joined the army of Gonzalo de Córdoba: Franca Petrucci, 'Colonna, Fabrizio' (1982); Petrucci, 'Colonna, Prospero'.
88 The River Garigliano meets the sea at Minturno (between Rome and Naples).

without the help of footmen, would overcome their enemies, they set on them so courageously as at the first encounter they put them to flight.

'Soon after, Naples yielded, and King Frederick did capitulate with the lord d'Aubigny, that the king should give him a certain yearly pension. He had leave also to carry away his movables and contented himself with the lord d'Aubigny's letters to the king, and without any other assurance, came into France to the king, who gratified him not only with the pension promised to him, but also gave him many good towns, houses, and fair gardens.

'The affairs of Naples being ended, the king was troubled with no other care but of settling the state thereof, which (as it happeneth in time of war) was very much shaken. To which end he commanded five civilians of honest life and good reputation to be admitted into the Senate. And some telling the lord d'Aubigny of the learning of Jovianus Pontanus, he fell into such a liking of him, as sending for him, the next day he bestowed on him great and rich presents, and offered him a place in the Senate with the five already chosen.'[89]

Hitherto, Du Haillan maketh no mention of the duke of Nemours, but ascribes to the lord d'Aubigny whatsoever was done, either in war or in the settling of the state. But he saith, 'that after, the king gave the chief authority to Louis of Armagnac, duke of Nemours.'[90]

As for the discord which fell between the Frenchman and the Spaniards, for the confines of that kingdom divided between both their kings, Mariana saith, 'that after the taking of Naples, there arose discord between both nations, as it must needs have come to pass, they being in condition, manners, and fashions extremely different.'[91]

Of the lord d'Aubigny's journey into Calabria, going to war against the Spaniards, Giovio writeth in this manner: 'D'Aubigny, who had next to the duke of Nemours the greatest authority in the army, went to Calabria with the third part thereof, being there much renowned, both for having in the time of King Charles with great moderation and mildness governed that nation demi-Grecian, and for that by his martial prowess he overcame King Ferdinand and Consalvo in a memorable battle, so as in all men's judgment he was preferred before all other French commanders. For which respects there were many beholding and well affected to him in particular, besides them which were of the Angevin faction. The principal of those were the princes of Bisignan and Salerno, and the earl of Mileto, who revolted from the Spaniards as soon as the

---

89 Giovanni Pontanus (1426/9–1503), a humanist scholar who, in 1495, negotiated the surrender of Naples to Charles VIII: ODR.

90 Louis d'Armagnac, duke of Nemours, was appointed viceroy of Naples in 1501. His military command ended with his death at the Battle of Ceringola in Apr. 1503 when the French were defeated by Gonzalo: Mallett and Shaw, *Italian Wars*, pp 64–5.

91 Side-note: Mariana, book xxvii, ch. 10.

two kings fell at variance.[92] The lord d'Aubigny's coming was much desired by them, desiring as much to help him in the war with their service and means, which were more than mean. They, together with others of the same part, invited him by letters and messages to hasten his coming and to show the banners of France to that people ready to follow them. Wherefore, satisfying their desire, as soon as he came he found himself not deceived in the expectation which he had of their affection and service. For both in Cosenza, their chief city, and in all the other towns of that province, the gates were opened to him and the Spanish garrisons and officers driven out of them so as with very little bloodshed he won all the country, even to the very straits of Messina.'

The Battle of Terine, and his victory is set forth by the said Giovio: 'Don Hugo de Cardona with an army which he had brought from Sicily, having much annoyed the French party in Calabria, the lord d'Aubigny went to encounter him, having in his army the princes of Bisignan and Salerno with their troops, Grigni with his light horsemen and Malherbe with his Gascon archers, and three companies of Helvetians.[93] But his principal strength consisted in his men of arms, among which was most eminent a wing of Scottish men, which were his familiars and faithful to him. The enemies, informed of his preparation, did not expect him till two days after they had notice thereof. But this excellent and vigilant captain beguiled their expectation, for with French expedition, marching night and day through ways little haunted, he showed himself to them the next morning and forthwith set on them. The Spaniards sustained courageously the assault, so as the combat was alike fierce and bloody on both sides. D'Aubigny seeing this, commanded Grigni with his wings to rush upon the Spanish and Sicilian infantry, which, he doing, disordered them. On the other side, the enemy's horsemen, by the encouragement and example of Cardona, sustained the assault of the Calabrians, with like slaughter on both parts. But d'Aubigny, advancing his troops, the Spanish and Sicilian cavalry not being able to resist the Scottish men of arms, was defeated, and therewithal the infantry was overthrown and cut to pieces. Grigni, a most valiant knight, was slain in the combat, and d'Aubigny himself, being in like danger, was rescued by means of John, duke of Albany, calling others to succour him', as Du Haillan testifieth.

As concerning the overthrow which he had not long after this victory, Du Haillan relateth it to this purpose: 'Don Hugo de Cardona, having repaired his

---

92 The references are to Bernardino Sanseverino, prince of Bisignano (in Naples); his brother, the count of Mileto, and their cousin, Antonello Sanseverino (d. 1499), prince of Salerno, all of whom welcomed the French army into Italy in 1494: Tatò (ed.), *Enciclopedie*.

93 In 1502 at the Battle of Terranova (Terine) in Calabria, Aubigny defeated the Spanish forces under the command of Don Hugo de Cardona (a captain of Gonzalo of Córdoba): Stuart, *Traité*, p. xxvii. Claude de Grignan, lord of Grigny, was killed in the battle.

army, increased the same with a new supply of five thousand, so that his army consisted of eight thousand men in arms. And albeit the lord d'Aubigny knew the advantage they had in number, nevertheless, being confident in his own sufficiency, and the tried valour of his soldiers, and weary of waiting for new supply from the king, he resolved to try the fortune of war. But his army was defeated, and he himself being in danger to be slain was rescued by a troupe of Scottishmen'[94] whose valour in this fight Giovio commendeth, as also he telleth how d'Aubigny was saved by them.[95]

In naming the general of the Spanish in the battle Mariana and Giovio differ from Du Haillan, for they call the general, Ferdinand Andrada.[96]

Guicciardini maketh mention of his defeats in these words: 'D'Aubigny was defeated and taken in the same place wherein some years before he had with so much glory overcome and discomfited King Ferdinand and Consalvo, so inconstant is the prosperity of Fortune. He was one of the most excellent captains that Charles brought into Italy, and of a free and noble disposition, and this his misfortune proceeded only from too earnest desire of victory.'[97]

This testimony of Guicciardini (who is held to be sparing, yea, niggardly in commending any man) especially being given in the time of his misfortune, maketh much for his honour. But the too great earnestness whereof he seemeth to tax him, is by Mariana (though otherwise as tart in censuring as he is), accounted warlike policy, howbeit wanting success. For he telleth, 'that by the death of Porto Carrerro, general of the Spanish army, chancing at that time, there arising a jealousy between the chief of the army about the succeeding to him, and the soldiers being discontented for want of pay, d'Aubigny, having intelligence thereof, and hoping thereby to win advantage, did then offer them battle, albeit he failed in the success.'[98]

It is likewise probable that he was rather moved to fight, seeing the decay of the Frenchmen, and the Spaniards prevailing, as also the king's slackness in sending thither supply of men and money, the said king being (as Du Haillan saith) 'so niggardly and pinching, that it is the common opinion, that fearing he should spend money in vain, he suffered the kingdom of Naples and the Duchy of Milan to be lost.'

Giovio saith, 'that after this overthrow, d'Aubigny withdrew himself into the Forest of Angitola, complaining of Fortune, which had so deceived him, having been till then invincible, and twelve times been victorious in battle, since he

94 Side-note: 'Reign of Louis XII.'
95 Side-note: Giovio, *Consalvo*, book ii.
96 Fernando de Andrade de las Mariñas (1477-1540), commander of Calabria, defeated the French at the Third Battle of Seminara (1503): Mallett and Shaw, *Italian Wars*, p. 64.
97 Side-note: Guicciardini, book v.
98 Side-note: Mariana, book xxvii, ch. 20.

began to be a warrior in France and Britain.'[99] Whence we may gather, that many of his military actions and victories are wrapped in oblivion.

That same Giovio telleth, 'that whiles he was besieged in the said forest, the duke of Nemours, having been slain, and his army defeated by the Spaniards at Cerignola,[100] and Consalvo's letters touching this victory, having been sent to the Spanish commanders that besieged him, and by them to him, he said that he perceived Fortune to be very opposite to the French part, and therefore judging it folly and wilfulness to withstand her, he promised that he would yield himself, if that were true which was written. Whereof being certified by messengers which he had purposely sent out to know the truth, he came out of the castle apparelled in cloth of tissue,† and with a cheerful and merry countenance yielded himself, upon condition that all those of his company should be set at liberty, and himself only kept in free custody. And it is said that he sharply reproved two young lords, his kinsmen (who were afterwards renowned warriors), for that more faintly than was fit for men, namely, for them being Scottish men, and of the blood royal, they did bewail the unfortunate success of the war, not remembering that valiant men should never be disheartened, but seek by a fresh endeavour of virtue revived and grown invincible, to recover Fortune's favour.'[101]

A witty conceit of his and Consalvo's return to him, whereof I have made mention, are contained in this relation of the same author: 'When the Frenchmen, after Gaeta was yielded,[102] were ready to depart from the kingdom of Naples, Consalvo, offering horses to many of them, d'Aubigny, their commander, said to him, smiling: "Sir, let us then have good and strong horses, that may serve us both for our journey into France, and our return hitherward", giving him to understand that they would come back to renew the war. Consalvo understood him, and required him with this return: "Come back as when it shall please you, for then you shall find me as liberal as I am now in giving you horses, apparel, and passport", hereby signifying that, if they came, his fortune and theirs should be such as it had been.'[103]

Of the honour done to these two worthy persona at Savona, Mariana writeth thus: 'At a feast in Savona made by the French king to the king of Spain, the two kings would have Consalvo to sit with them at their table.[104] During the banquet, the king of France showed much respect and courtesy to

---

99 Side-note: Giovio, *Consalvo*, book ii.
100 The Battle of Cerignola (1503) was a comprehensive defeat for the French who lost their commander, Nemours, along with their artillery and baggage. It was considered a major victory for Gonzalo: Mallett and Shaw, *Italian Wars*, pp 64–5.
101 Side-note: Giovio, *Consalvo*, book ii.
102 Gaeta is a fortified town in Lazio on the west coast of central Italy. The French surrendered it to Gonzalo in 1504: Mallett and Shaw, *Italian Wars*, p. 69.
103 Side-note: Giovio, *Consalvo*, book iii.
104 Savona is in Liguria in northern Italy.

him (notwithstanding he had been his adversary), extolling his virtue, his martial skill, his good fortune, and the notable monuments of his victories won in so many places. King Ferdinand entertained the lord d'Aubigny with like honour and favour.'[105]

The example cited by me of the honour done to his memory after his death is thus related by Giovio: 'Prospero Colonna, having been surprised at Villafranca in his lodging by the chief commanders by King Francis his army, and not being able to escape, he asked from a high window their names, and understanding that the lord d'Aubigny, nephew to the worthy Lord Bernard, was one of them, he yielded himself to him, as having had acquaintance with him at his giving over the town of Brescia (whereof he had been governor), and being well affected to him for the remembrance of his uncle.'[106]

This Prospero was then the chiefest and worthiest commander of Italy; and the chief commanders of the French army, besides the Lord d'Aubigny, as Giovio nameth them, were La Palisse, who was lord of Chabannes and marshal of France; Bayard, a famous commander; the lords of Imbercourt and Sancerre.[107]

These are the most notable places which I could gather concerning this most worthily renowned lord. Wherewith if something written of him in Guicciardini, de Serres, or any other do not wholly agree, as not ascribing to him so much as the relations of other histories, he cannot in reason be any whit disparaged thereby, seeing that they who have written most to his honour (as, namely, Giovio and Mariana, the one of them an Italian prelate, the other a Spaniard), were in no way partial to him, writing only by the way of him in that part of their histories wherein they do purposely extoll and magnify his adversaries being of their own nations, so as it may be justly thought that they have ascribed to him rather too little than too much.

---

105 Side-note: Mariana, book xxix, ch. 9.

106 Side-note: Giovio, *History*, book xv. Prospero Colonna (*c.*1460–1523) was a Roman *condottiero* who had been in the service of Charles VIII in 1494 and King Ferrandino of Naples. In 1515 he was captured in Villafranca in northern Spain by French troops: Petrucci, 'Colonna, Prospero'. Robert Stewart was Bernard's cousin and son-in-law.

107 Jacques de Chabannes, marshal of La Palice (*c.*1470–1525), was close to both Charles VIII and Louis XII. He encouraged their claims in Italy: M. Prévost and Roman d'Amat (eds), *Dictionnaire* (1959), 8, col. 101. Pierre Terrail, lord of Bayard (*c.*1473–1524), fought in the Italian wars for Charles VIII, Louis XII and Francis I and was renowned for his bravery as a captain and in single combat. He was known as 'the good knight' and 'the fearless knight'. Charles de Bueil, count of Sancerre, and Adrien de Brimeau, lord of Humbercourt, died at the Battle of Marignano (near Milan (1515)): *ODR*. Bernard Stuart had a low opinion of Humbercourt's abilities: Stuart, *Traité*, p. xxvii.

[Dedication to Prince Charles] [sig. G4v]

These wishes following, directed and presented to the prince's highness at his creation, I have put to the press rather now, than heretofore; for that I thought them, being contained in so few leaves, less fit to be published apart under the shelter of his princely name, than now, when they add somewhat to the precedent memorial dedicated to his Highness. And I have the rather at this time published them, how homely and unpolished soever they be, because I hope that the worthiness both of their honest subject, and princely object will make them not to seem at any time unseasonable.

To the Prince's Highness [sig. G4v]

Thee to instruct it is not here my drift,
Great prince: I only wish that such thou prove
As thee to be thy royal father's love
And wisdom teacheth in his royal gift.

Wishes Presented to the Prince's Highness at His Creation [sig. H1r]

Now that each loyal heart of kingdom's three
Doth joyfully congratulate with thee,
Most worthy prince, in this thy honour new,
Which by thy birthright doth to thee accrue,
All wishing thee all joy and happiness   5
Their inward joy all striving to express
With cheerful countenance and applauding words,
With bonfires, triumphs, musical accords;
And some with Muses' panegyric strains;
Though I come short of them, whose happy veins   10
Of poetry can make thy fame to flourish,
Yet sith† thy worth and favour to me nourish
My love to thee, and cherish my desire
To honour thee, as fuel doth the fire,
I must at this thy new advancement use   15
To show my joy, the chanting of my Muse.
     But sith† it is too homely to set forth
In any panegyric verse thy worth,
I leave the task of acting such a part

To them who can it act with better art,   20
And to the honour of this happy day,
In lieu of praises, wishes I do pay.
    And first I wish and pray to mighty Jove,
This day to thee may a commencement prove
Of happy days, months, years, and jubilees;   25
Wherein thy bliss may grow still by degrees;
That after that they great and royal sire
Long shall have reigned (as is thy due desire)
Instructions and examples thee to give,
An old and happy king long mayest thou live.   30
    But seeing that there is no other way,
Whereby a prince more than a subject may
Attain to solid honour, joy and bliss,
Save only virtue, which whoso doth miss,
The greater in degree and state he be,   35
The more reproach and woe incurreth he;
I wish and pray to God, that every kind
Of princely virtue may enrich thy mind:
    That in religion thou be neither thrall
To superstition, nor fanatical;[108]   40
But as thy lord and father fear and love
Almighty God, that blessed thou mayest prove.
    I wish thee to be wise, as needing more,
Then other men, to follow wisdom's lore;
That thou thereby mayest both preserve thy self,   45
And those whom thou shalt rule, from mischief's shelf:†
That prudence of thy virtues be the square;†
Without which, seeming virtues vices are:
And that thy prudence ruled by honesty,
Make thee detect all wicked policy: 50
That prudence thee induce those things to learn,
Which do thy weal and honour most concern:
That by experience so it daily grow,
As that thou mayest thy self and others know:
That by self-love thou be not so beguiled,   55
As on thine own conceit too much to build:
That thou a prey to flatterers never be,
In judgment being from self-flattery free:

---

108 Compare *Basilicon doron*'s insistence of a middle way between papistry and Puritanism: *Selected Writings*, pp 203–6.

That, loathing all their Siren songs, thou love
Such as with love and duty will reprove   60
What is amiss, and not those sores offend
With corrosives, that lenitives† may mend:
That wise men's counsel, and not theirs thou take,
Whom overweening thoughts presumptuous make;
Who judgment and experience want t'advise,   65
Or rather sly and witty are than wise:
That men thou use for what they are most fit,
And not too much to any one commit:
That thou both know and curb him, that pretends
Thy weal, but aimest at his own crooked ends: 70
That so thou do not men or things mistake,
As for the worst the better to forsake;
As most men do, whom fancy blind do move
More glittering shows, than solid worth to approve:
That none but good and worthy men thou favour,   75
To sweeten of thy worth and fame the savour:
That prudence teach thee so thyself to use,
As none may thee, and thou wilt none abuse:
That wise in speech, but more in deeds thou be;
Which is of wisdom a more high degree: 80
That secrecy and speech thou use in season;
And trust not, or distrust not without reason:
That both the substance of affairs thou know,
And circumstances; whence doth prudence grow:
That, when thou aught attemptest by reason moved,   85
By constancy thy wisdom be approved:
For prudence, and all virtues, that direction
Take from her, have by constancy perfection:
That God's assistance may thy wisdom bless,
In all that thou attemptest with good success.   90
     Then wish I thee this truth in mind to bear,
That kings for justice first appointed were:
That thou mayest justice do, and love it too,
Since tyrants for their ends oft justice do:
And that thy sword of justice do not spare   95
Such crimes, as heinous and malicious are:
That thou her balance equally do weight,
Not suffering spleen or favour it to sway:
That men accused may have this just refuge

That thou wilt hear both parties ere thou judge: 100
That in rewards as well as punishment,
Thy justice men's deserts to weight be bent:
That it may give to every man his own,
Nor favour more the courtier than the clown:
And that thou see they, as thyself, be just,   105
Whom to do justice, thou shalt put in trust:
That spiders' webs they make not laws betoken,
Which catching smaller flies, by wasps are broken:
That to their suitors' grievance and decay,
They may not frustrate justice by delay,   110
Nor by renewing suits, like Hydra's heads,[109]
To cram the crew, that writes, reports, and pleads:
That from pretence of conscience and law
Decrees against them both they may not draw:
That th'under-rulers of thy flocks might fear   115
To flay them, or unjustly them to shear:
That as the members do the head defend,
And as it to them doth health and safety send;
So may thy subjects thee, thou them protect,
And may thy justice none of them neglect: 120
That, when thou shalt thy royal sire succeed,
Thy justice may thee love and glory breed.
    But for that justice is a kind of rack,
If mercy make it not with measure slack,
I wish that thou do clemency embrace,   125
As best resembling God in such a case:
That men to love thee rather thou allure
By mercy, than by rigour awe procure:
That thou sometime thy clemency extend,
Where there is hope th'offender will amend;   130
And when as thence no public scandal grows,
Nor wrong to any private person flows;
Or when the fault concerns thee in such wise,
As thence to thee no danger may arise:
That rather in thine own, than others' wrong,   135
To true remorse thy mercy do belong:
That wilful malice with far greater terror

109 The Hydra may recall the reference to Hercules (who slew her as part of his second labour) in
   the history of Aubigny (p. 156), but given that Quin's book is in two parts this seems more
   likely to be a coincidence of popular imagery.

Thou punish, than weak frailty or blind error:
That thou, as above slander's reach, contemn
The slanderer, making himself condemn;   140
As Philip, Julius, August, Antonine,
Vespasian did; whose glory still doth shine:[110]
That thou delight men to relieve and spare;
But punish them with grief that guilty are;
Your temper so in country, court, and city   145
Thy mercy, as it prove not foolish pity:
That when thou shalt this virtue put in ure†
With honour, safety it may thee procure.
    Then with I, that, as justice thou shalt cherish,
And clemency her sister, so thou nourish   150
Faith in performing promises, the prop
Of justice, and of honour's height the top:
That for a certain truth thou understand
This virtue rare to be the surest band
Of friendship, commerce and society,   155
And truest badge of moral honesty;
That thou in word and practice it observe,
And never from it be induced to swerve:
And that not only for thy wished ends
Thou keep thy promise, or for love to friends,   160
But also to thy foes for virtue's sake;
Whereby of foes thy friends thou mayest them make:
That thou but for some urgent cause be loth
T'engage thyself by word, but more by oath:
But that, when thou shalt do it, no respect   165
Thy plighted faith induce thee to neglect;
So as thy promise just and lawful be,
Which ever to be such thou must foresee:
That thy respect of honesty and fame
May win thee of a faithful prince the name: 170
That such perfidious counsel thou detest,
As would remove this virtue from thy breast,
Since not the purchase of a diadem
Can countervail the loss of such a gem.
    And since no virtue to a prince or king   175

110 Philip, king of Macedon (d. 336BC), Julius Caesar, and the emperors Augustus, Antoninus
    Pius and Vespasian. Antoninus Pius' biography appears in *Corona virtutum*. *Basilicon doron* praises
    Caesar as an excellent emperor and military leader: *Selected Writings*, pp 243–4.

More love doth purchase then his bounty, spring
And fountain of his bountiful rewards,
And princely gifts; thy honour who regards,
Cannot but wish thee to be liberal,
And so do I: yet wish I therewithal,   180
That judgment may thy bounty so direct
As therein be no notable defect,
Nor great excess; both which extremities
Are vices that do blind men's inward eyes,[111]
And make them without measure spend or spare: 185
Wherefore I wish that with a heedful care
Thou to the golden mean thyself apply,
In being frugal, and not niggardly;
As also that thou spend with a due measure
And not exhaust by lavishing thy treasure: 190
That ordering so thy bounty by proportion,
Thou never need supply it with extortion:
That thrift thy bounty's treasurer thou make:
That men of merit may thereof partake;
To wit, such as for service done deserve   195
Or they who can thee and their country serve:
That thy rewards for service place may have
Before thy gifts, as equity doth crave:
Yet that thy bounty also thou extend
To men distressed, and for thy honour spend   200
In all occasions, that may it advance,
And namely in the princely maintenance
Of thine estate and court in every thing,
Which might neglected stain to honour bring:
And that too much thou do not give to any,   205
That thou thereby mayest give the more to many:
That imprudence and importunity
May not extort thy liberality:
But that thou freely most on them bestow,
Who best deserve, although in asking slow: 210
And that to such as by thy gifts would thrive,
Much rather, then to spendthrifts, thou do give:
That, where to impart thy bounty thou hast reason,
Thou do not long delay, but give in season:

111 Compare *Basilicon doron*: ibid., pp 245–6.

That as by others rather, than by thee,   215
That should be done which may distasteful be:
So merely from thy self thy bounty flow
That men may thanks to thee, not t'others owe:
That, as to many thou shalt liberal prove,
So God to thee be in his grace and love.   220
    Moreover, sith† a prince not only decked,†
Must be with virtues, that may him direct
To rule in peace, but must be armed likewise¹¹²
With fortitude against each enterprise
Of foes, or rebels, that would make a breach   225
Of peace in his estate, or yet impeach
His honour with insufferable wrongs,
This virtue as my wishes eke† belongs,
Most noble prince, since it belongs to thee,
Their worthy object, whom I wish to be   230
A second Magnus, or first Maximus,¹¹³
As thou are born to be first Carolus
Of kingdoms three: which that thou mayest defend,
And them repress, that would thy hurt intend,
I wish thou be as stout and valiant found,   235
As Charlemagne for valour most renowned:
Yet that as, war for dread thou do not shun,
So thou not to it through ambition run:
That war thou justly make, desiring peace,
And wrong not any for thy state's increase: 240
That thou in time of peace provide for war;
For good provision daring foes doth scare:
That, when thou shalt be forced war to wage,
Not thine, but th'enemy's state may be the stage:
That thou, whom it be housed by sea, and land   245
To be well armed, both warfares understand:
That when Bellona's blast shall sound the charge
To bloody battle, fraughting† Charon's barge,
Thy courage so may in thy deeds appear,
As that thy wisdom shine in them as clear: 250
That so thou happy made by good success

---

112 *Basilicon doron* passes over 'the forme of making warres' as the topic has been so extensively
   treated elsewhere: ibid., p. 230. Although brief, Quin's treatment of the topic is more practical and, although he counsels peace, his exempla include military leaders.
113 Charles will be a second Charles the Great (Charlemagne) or the first 'Charles the Greatest'.

Mayest all thy enemies vanquish and repress;
And fraught† with glory turning home again,
In peace a happy monarch long time reign.
    And though by many temperance be thought[114]   255
A guest to prince's courts not to be brought,
Yet I to thee with duty her present,
And wish that thou to cherish her be bent,
Much rather than intemperance her foe,
Which works to them, that entertain her, woe: 260
For in the mind, and body, goods and fame,
She breedeth sin, and fickleness, loss, and shame.
Wherefore I wish that her thou do reject,
And temperance for thy behoof† affect:
That she may make thee continent in mind;   265
In diet, to sobriety inclined;
And moderate in every kind of pleasure;
Whence with thy body's health there shall a measure
In thy expenses to thy profit flow;
For health and wealth by temperance doth grow: 270
That she in thee all kind of virtue nourish,
And, as she made the praise and fame to flourish
Of Cyrus, both the Scipios, Antonine,[115]
And other princes rare, so may she thine.
    Yet one remaineth of this sacred crew,   275
Whom fully to be thine by reason due
I wish, thou her already in good measure
Possessing, with the rest of virtue's treasure;
The name whereof is lowly modesty,[116]
Yet well becoming highest majesty.   280
I wish therefore thou modest be in mind,
Nor vain like a balloon blown up with wind;
Sith† this vainglorious vapour venteth forth,

---

114 *Basilicon doron* praises temperance as the queen of the cardinal virtues: *Selected Writings*, p. 240.

115 Cyrus the Great (d. 530BC), king of Persia; Scipio Africanus, the Roman general who defeated Hannibal in 202BC; Scipio Aemilianus Africanus, the Roman general who captured Carthage in 146BC, and the emperor Antoninus Pius. Cyrus' abstemiousness is noted in *Basilicon doron* and James commissioned a translation of Xenophon's *Cyropaedia* for Prince Henry: ibid., pp 247, 253. Scipio Africanus is paralleled with Bernard Stuart in 'Of His Last Retiring to Corstorphine' (p. 184) and is quoted in *Basilicon doron* (p. 201). The biography of Antoninus Pius appears in *Corona virtutum*, pp 137–42.

116 Compare the treatment of humility in *Basilicon doron*: *Selected Writings*, pp 244–5.

Bewrays in the inward emptiness of worth:
That greatness do not make thee swell with pride,   285
Since it must ebb without a turning tide:
And since it maketh many a man himself
To cast away upon ambition's shelf:†
That lewd nor vaunting thou be not in words,
Sith† modesty in speech great praise affords: 290
That, as in words, so modest in aspect
Thou be, to purchase love and due respect:
That in attire thy modestly may mend
Th'excesse, which Britain's wealth doth vainly spend:
And that, therein eschewing curious art,   295
With virtue thou adorn thy better part;
As did Augustus, Flavius, Trajan, Mark,[117]
Whoso glory shines free from oblivion dark:
That so with virtue and true honour decked,†
Thou make my wishes have their wished effect.   300

[Charles, qui fais honneur à ta principauté] [sig. I1v]

Charles, qui fais honneur à ta principauté,
Non moins qu'à t'honorer d'elle sert la puissance,
Maintenant qu'investi tu en es, par la naissance
Digne héritier étant d'une haute royauté.
   Pour tes faveurs et dons, amour et loyauté   5
Te débutant, ce beau jour, qui d'honneur accroissance
Te donne, je célèbre avec réjouissance,
Et te rends par ma Muse humble hommage et féauté.
   Ce que dignement fait en hymnes ou cantiques
Ne pouvant par ses vers, et chansons trop rustiques,   10
D'elle aidé je le fais par mes voeux et souhaits ;
   Priant, qu'après ton père en la Grande Bretagne
Tu règnes longuement en autre Charlemagne,
Grand en mérite, et gloire, et plein d'heur à jamais.

---

117 The emperors Augustus, Vespasian, Trajan and Marcus Aurelius were credited with having
   built up the social and economic fabric of Rome, thus they were not only successful generals.
   Marcus Aurelius' biography appears in *Corona virtutum*, pp 145–63. *Basilicon doron* praises the
   wisdom of Augustus: ibid., p. 209.

[Charles, You Do Honour to Your Princedom] [T]

Charles, you do honour to your princedom, no less than you used to honour the power in which you are invested there, by birth worthy to inherit, being of high royalty.

Your favours and gifts, love and loyalty – beginning on this fine day which gives you increasing honour – these I celebrate with rejoicing, and with my humble Muse give you homage and fealty.

These poems and all too rustic songs which I assist with my best wishes and desires cannot do that which is properly done in hymns and canticles;

Praying that after your father you reign for a long time in Great Britain; like another Charlemagne, great in merit and glory, and full of happiness for ever.

[Non tibi delato, princeps, tam laetor honore] [sig. I1v]

Non tibi delato, princeps, tam laetor honore,
    Quam magis excelsum quod mereare decus.
Nam generis qui iure tui, ceu more vetusto,
    Iam tibi contingit, sit lices amplus honos;
Maiori tamen esse parem te, quae indolis altae   5
    Virtutisque tuae das, documenta docent:
Quae precor augescant, possis ut semper honores
    Crescentes meritis antevenire tuis.

[I Do Not So Much Rejoice, Prince, in the Honour Bestowed on You] [T]

I do not so much rejoice, prince, in the honour bestowed on you, as I do in the more distinguished honour that you earn for yourself. Although by right of family, just as by ancient custom, the honour which falls to you is ample; nevertheless, the examples you give of your innate nobility and virtue show that you are equal to a greater honour. I pray that these increase, so that you can always anticipate increasing honours by your own merits.

In nomen illustrissimi principis, *Carolus princeps Walliae* anagramma: *clarus in pace, praelio, lusu.* Acrostichis utrumque continens [sig. I2v]

Carolus incedit tam re, quam nomine	Clarus,
Auctus honore novo, defert quem pectore	Laeto
Rex illi genitorque; unda urbs laetatur, et	Aula,
Omnis et triplicis gratatur et incola	Regni.

Laeto hinc applausu quisque, et modulamine	Vocis,	5
Vultu hilari, et cunctis animo quae gaudia	Sentit	
Significare modis gestit: sibi debita	Iure	
Princeps eximia quae sint facit indole	Noster.	
Regem spondet eum namque haec fore tempore	Pacis	
Institia, pietate, fide, tum Palladis	Arte,	10
Necnon magnanimo, sed miti, pectore	Clarum;	
Commoda curantem populorum, his ceu pater	Esset;	
Egregium belloque ducem, cui robore	Pectus	
Polleat invicto, gestarum encomia	Rerum	
Sint cui grande decus parituraque nomen in	Aevum,	15
Virtutis specimen cum classe per aequora	Late	
Victor praebuerit, terraque hostilibus	Instans	
Armatus cuneis hostes superaverit	Omnes.	
Laudem hanc ipse tuus praesagit, Carole,	Lusus:	
Ludis eques tu, sive pedes, tua vivida	Virtus	20
Inde futura patet: successu haec numina	Summa	
Aetheris esse meis dent omnia consona	Votis.	

On The Name of the Most Illustrious Prince, *Charles, Prince of Wales*, an Anagram: *Famous in Peace, War and Sport*. Both Contained in an Acrostic [T]

Charles appears brilliant both in fact and in name, augmented by a new honour which the king, his father, grants to him with happy heart; thus the city and the court rejoice, and every inhabitant of the threefold kingdom gives thanks. Therefore each person, with happy applause, with modulation of the voice, with cheerful expression and in all ways, desires to show the joys he feels in his mind. Our prince exhibits with outstanding character those things that are due to him by right: for he promises the king that in peacetime he will be renowned for his justice, piety, faith and the art of Pallas, as well as for a magnanimous and merciful heart, looking after the condition of the people, just as his father looked after them; and for an outstanding general in war, whose chest is powerful through its invincible strength, and for whom there may be encomia about the deeds he will have done which will bring him great honour and renown for ages to come, when, as victor he will have shown proof of his virtue with his fleet far and wide over the seas, and by attacking the opposition with his troops on land, he will have overcome all enemies. Even your sport presages this praise, Charles: you play the part of a knight or foot soldier, from which it is clear that your lively virtue will emerge. May the highest divine powers of heaven grant all things that are consonant with my pledges.

13
From John Stradling's *Beati pacifici* (1623)

Sir John Stradling (1563–1637) was born in Bristol and, having been adopted by a childless relative, in 1609 he inherited a large estate in Glamorgan. Stradling was educated at Brasenose College, Oxford, where he was associated with the Latin epigrammists of the circle around the recusants Lawrence, Edward and Thomas Michelbourne, a group that included Thomas Campion (1567–1620), who later provided masques and music for the court of James I. Stradling was one of the English adherents of Justus Lipsius and he published translations of some of the neo-Stoic's works. He served as an MP and at the time he wrote *Beati pacifici* he was a supporter of James I's pacific approach to European politics. An engraving of the king under his motto appears opposite the title page in the British Library copy of the work.[1]

'W.Q.' was one of six people who provided commendatory verses at the end of Stradling's book. The others who can be securely identified were the bishop of Llandaff, Theophilus Field (d. 1636) and three men of Glamorgan families.[2] It is unknown who the sixth poet, 'T.H.', was.[3] The ascription of the poems below to Quin cannot, therefore, be certain. In its favour are the absence of other known candidates for W.Q., the likelihood that Stradling could have known Quin from court and the latter's use of Lipsius in *Corona virtutum*, which may be an indication of common intellectual ground. On the other hand, in the absence of knowing the identity of T.H., Quin would be out of place since he has no Welsh connections. It may also be worth noting that Quin is absent from the list of over a hundred dedicatees in Stradling's collection of epigrams (1607).[4] The evidence of this volume is ambiguous however, as it is of a much earlier date and again there are common interests in it (such as the praise of the Gowrie Plot heroes) that might have drawn the two authors together.

1   Mihail Dafydd Evans, 'Stradling, Sir John, first baronet (1563–1637)', *ODNB*; L.V. Ryan, 'The Shorter Latin Poems in Tudor England', *Humanistica Lovaniensia: Journal of Neo-Latin Studies*, 26 (1977), 101–31.

2   See the notes to John Stradling, *Beati pacifici* (1623), ed. Glyn Pursglove, The Philological Museum, www.philological.bham.ac.uk/strad2 (Shakespeare Institute, University of Birmingham, 2003), accessed 21 Mar. 2014.

3   It is unlikely, but not impossible, that it was Thomas Herbert, for whose *Travels* Quin provided a verse.

4   John Stradling, *Epigrammata* (London: George Bishop & John Norton, 1607).

The main reason for attributing these poems to Quin is the absence of any other likely candidates for its authorship. None are to be found in *ODNB*, *ESTC*, *Elizabethan Poetry: A Bibliography*, the *Index of Dedications and Commendatory Verses* or the *Union First Line Index of English Verse, 13th–19th century*.[5] As Franklin B. Williams has observed: 'Now and then there is a signature that, to one working in the period, has the stamp of inevitability either from the rarity of the combination or the familiarity of the attributes' and 'W.Q.' is one of these.[6]

The contributions of W.Q. are the only ones in Latin. His 'In laudem authoris' is followed by a distich, signed 'W.Q.' Beneath this is a heading 'The same in English', which introduces a work the beginning of which is a translation of the Latin poems and which is signed 'T.H.' (the text of this poem can be found in the appendix below, p. 265). The contributions of the other authors are clearly and systematically delineated from one another by headings, names at the end of the poems and a dividing line. Their integrity is evident to the eye alone: the grammar of this layout suggests that W.Q.'s text ends with his initials and that the translation that follows is by T.H. who uses W.Q.'s work as the beginning of his own English poem or who, having provided his translation, begins an independent work that lost the marks of an autonomous text in the printing process. Of course once the layout is called into question it is possible that W.Q. translated his own work.

Copy-text

John Stradling, *BEATI PACIFICI:* | *A DIVINE POEM.* | *WRITTEN* | *TO THE KINGS* | *MOST EXCELLENT* | *MAIESTIE. By Sir IOHN STRADLING,* | *Knight and Baronet.* | *Perused by his Majesty, and printed* | *by Authority.* London: [Felix Kingston] for The Company of Stationers, 1623. 4°. ESTC S117913 (five copies). BL, General Reference Collection 11626.e.54.

A copy of this edition is available on *EEBO*.

---

5 Steven W. May & William A. Ringler Jr (eds), *Elizabethan Poetry: A Bibliography and First-line Index of English Verse, 1559–1603* (3 vols, London: Thommes Continuum, 2004); Franklin B. Williams, Jr., *Index of Dedications and Commendatory Verses in English Books before 1641* (London: Bibliographical Society, 1962), p. 152; Carolyn W. Nelson, *Union First Line Index of English Verse, 13th–19th Century* (Folger Shakespeare Library, 2013), http://firstlines.folger.edu, accessed 7 Apr. 2014). The *Union First Line Index* includes indexes of material from BL, the Bodleian, the Henry E. Huntington Library, the Beinecke Rare Book and Manuscript Library, the University of Leeds, the Houghton Library, the Folger Shakespeare Library and the Rosenbach Museum and Library.

6 Franklin B. Williams, Jr., 'An Initiation into Initials', *Studies in Bibliography*, 9 (1957), 163–78 at 172.

[Flos equitum] [sig. M3r]

Ni tua flos equitum mens coeli arderet amore,
  Nique edocta simul coelitus illa foret
Non sic flagrares tu pacis amore nec hymnus
  Sic bona tot pacis promeret iste tuus
Quo ceu rite Deo pacis sine thure litasti   5
  Pacifico regi sic quoque iure places.

[Flower of Knights] [T]

If, flower of knights, your mind did not burn with heavenly love, and if it were
not simultaneously divinely learned, you would not be burning so much with a
love of peace, nor would your hymn of peace thus promise so many good
things, by which, just as you have rightly propitiated the God of peace without
incense, you also rightly please the king of peace.

[Classica qui cantis praecones munere pacis] [sig. M3r]

Classica qui canitis praecones munere pacis.[7]
  Pacis eques praeco vos agit ecce reos.

[You Who Play the War Trumpets] [T]

You who play your war trumpets as heralds with the gift of peace: see, the
knight, a herald of peace, treats you as defendants.

---

7 The copy-text's 'cantis' has been emended to 'canitis.'

14

In nuptiis principum incomparabilium (1625)

Charles I married Henrietta Maria (1609–69) by proxy at Notre Dame on 1 May
1625. The queen was the sister of King Louis XIII and the daughter of Henry
IV and Quin wrote his *Recueil* for her, celebrating the talents of her renowned
father. Initially, the match between the 25-year-old king and his 16-year-old
bride was an unhappy one. In part this was due to personal differences, and in
part to the political and religious tensions that accompanied a match between the
royal houses of England and France.[1]

In the background of the marriage was the 'Spanish Match', the planned
marriage between Charles and the Infanta Maria Anna of Spain. As part of his
European strategy, King James thought to balance the marriage of his daughter
to the Protestant Frederick V, the Elector Palatinate and king of Bohemia, with
that of his son to a Catholic power. Negotiations with Spain, in the person of
the unpopular ambassador Gondomar, went on from 1613 to 1618 despite opposition from pulpit and parliament. In 1622 the English ambassador in Madrid was
urging the desirability of the union and the matter came to a head in March
1623 when Charles and Buckingham took the extraordinary decision to ride to
Spain incognito. There, the marriage plans were bogged down in Spanish wran-
gling and Charles returned to England and a hero's welcome.[2] When it became
apparent to Buckingham that the Infanta would never marry the prince, he proposed a French match instead, thus going against the wishes of the king who had
not abandoned his hopes of a Spanish alliance.[3] The acrimony that this created
culminated in the allegation of a Spanish envoy that Buckingham was going to
depose James in favour of his son.[4] When Charles did at last take a Catholic
bride, she was often regarded as the lesser of two evils: critics descried this union
with idolaters, while the more optimistic hoped for the queen's conversion.[5] It
is in this tumultuous context that Quin's poems must be read and this explains
the references to strife that might otherwise seem odd in epithalamia.
Furthermore, as Charles hoped that France would aid him against the Habsburgs
in restoring his brother-in-law to the Palatinate, the marriage was also a harbin-
ger of future war.[6]

---

1 For the details of the marriage, see Charles Carlton, *Charles I: The Personal Monarch* (2nd ed.;
   London: Routledge, 1995), pp 63–6.
2 Ibid., pp 34–9.   3 Ibid., p. 47.   4 Ibid., pp 50–1.
5 Thomas Cogswell, '1625' in Joad Raymond (ed.), *The Oxford History of Popular Print Culture:
   Vol. I, Cheap Print in Britain and Ireland to 1660* (Oxford: Oxford UP, 2011), pp 596–7.
6 Carlton, *Charles I*, p. 55.

Iuncta magis florent.

6 *In nuptiis principium*, sig. A1v (© The British Library Board, General
Reference Collection, C.28.g.8.(4)).

Copy-text

Walter Quin, *IN* | *NVPTIIS* | *PRINCIPVM* | *INCOMPARABILIVM,* | *CAROLI BRITANNICI* | *Imperii Monarchae potentissimi, et HEN-* | *RIETTAE MARIAE, HENRICI MAGNI,* | *Galliarum Regis Filiae, Gratulatio quadrilinguis* | *Gvalteri Qvinni.* London: George Purslow, 1625. 4°. *ESTC* S103172 (one copy). BL, General Reference Collection, C.28.g.8.(4).

This copy is available on *EEBO.*

[Haec, quae floruerant regum ornamenta seorsum] [sig. A1v]

Haec, quae floruerant regum ornamenta seorsum,
Juncta magis florent, auspice rite Deo.

[These Ornaments of the Kings] [T]

These ornaments of the kings which flowered separately flourish more when joined under the proper auspices of God.

[Symbola prisca rosae cum sint, et lilia stirpis] [sig. A1v]

Symbola prisca rosae cum sint, et lilia stirpis
   Principibus summis, quos modo junxit Hymen;
Vere bonis avibus, junctos hos cernis adulto;
   Lilia quo florent tempore juncta rosis.
Unde, rosae ut florent prae cunctis veris honore   5
   Floribus, et cultu lilia pulchra suo:
Sic, prae principibus toto florentibus orbe,
   Hos fore florentes spem pia vota fovent.

[The Ancient Symbols] [T]

Since the ancient symbols for the highest rulers of the stock that Hymen recently joined together are roses and lilies, you see these joined together with good auspices in the middle of spring, in which time lilies flourish when joined to roses. Therefore, in order that roses flourish more than other flowers in the honour of spring and the beautiful lilies in their cultivation, so may pious prayers nourish these two to flourish more than the foremost flowers of the whole world.

Epithalamium [p. 1]

Hoc erat in fatis dudum votisque Britannis
Gentibus, et Celtis, novus ut prius icta suorum
Nexus amicitiae firmaret foedera regum,
Gallica et Albionis taedis felicibus essent
Lilia iuncta rosis: quamvis ea fata morari   5
Et pia vota diu potuerunt, arte Pelasga
Qui superant Danaos, spondentes aurea mala
Hesperidum, dives Phryxaeum vellus, et auri
Montes, et quid non, pulchra cum coniuge dotem.
    At velut intutum scopulis qui navigat aequor,   10
Si vetet hos cerni caligo tetra, periclum
Grande adit imprudens, saxis ne lusus et undis
Mersus aquis fiat: sin claro lumine Phoebus
Hanc fuget, hinc fugiens cursum, qua tutior unda est,
Dirigit, optatas ut navem appellat ad oras: 15
    Sic modo qui occultae fraudis caligine lusi
Foedus, cui suberant metuenda pericla, fovebant,
Caelitus his nebulis diffuso lumine pulsis,
Suspectos fugiunt Hymenaeos: iamque secundis
Auspiciis renovant quae foedera debita Fatis   20
Sunt, et Celtarum votis, vestrisque Britanni.
Regius hinc iuvenis, qui sceptra Britannica gestat,
Et, magno decorat quae lilia digna parente,
Regia nympha Deo felices auspice amoris
Iunguntur stabili nexu, vincloque iugali.   25
Quam bene iuncta rosis sic lilia? foedere reges
Quam bene sic ambo coeunt, populique potentes?
Quo vel honorificum magis, aut magis utile nullum
Esse potest ipsis, nec non (sua si bona norint)
Regibus et populis aliis venerantibus unum   30
Mente Deum: namque hoc felix concordia nexu
Quae coalescit habet vim, prae quacunque medela,
Tot mala sanandi, fera quae discordia gignit
Christicolis inter sese certantibus armis,
(Certavit veluti quondam Cadmeia proles)   35
Mutuum in exitium: iunctorum foedere regum
Namque horum pacem, quae non sit iniqua, colentum
Exemplo, monitis, et maiestate verenda
Discordes inter poterit pax conciliari.

Aut, si turbet eam pacem quis raptor iniquus,   40
Praedae inhians Aquilae vel milvi more rapacis,
Et rapiens aliena, ferox sit quamlibet, armis
Amborum poterit facile et virtute domari;
Rapta simul cogi reddat, domitusque quiescat:
Nec vetet inter se concordi pace fruentes   45
Christicolas reliquos, felici et foedere iunctos,
Quo minus auspiciis superorum bella gerentes
Iusta feros Thracas Mahometis sacra colentes
Impia, qui, Christi pia sacra colentibus hostes
Infensi, tot iis regna eripuere, receptis   50
His postliminio, debellent fortiter ausi.
      Haec pia pax, haec arma simul pia iure vocanda
Foederis huius erunt firmati vinculo Hymenaei,
(Sic sperare iuvat) fructus heroe marito
Tanto, heroina tali ceu coniuge digni.   55
      In quos fortunae bona si collata benigne,
Quaeque favor superum effuse largitus utrique est,
Corporis atque animi spectes bona maxima; prorsus
Nulla ipso tam digna viro, tam coniuge dignus
Nullus et hac potuit toto orbe petique, legique.   60
      Natales decorant utriusque illustria regum
Stemmata magnorum, quibus aut splendore vetusto,
Imperio aut propriis opibus, proprioque potenti
Robore, nemo praeit regum, quos suspicit orbis,
Adde quod imperii longe lateque patentis   65
Sponsus sit merita ceu fausta forte monarcha,
Participemque facit coeli indulgentia sponsam
Fortunae omnigenum, fruitur quibus ille, bonorum.
      Sani agilis validi sponsum laus corporis ornat,
Dexteritasque, pedes seu sese exercet, equesve,   70
Et digna imperio species faciesque decora.
      Sponsa Venus forma, vultu Dictynna pudico,
Iuno et iure cluat nova maiestate verenda.
      Disparibusque annis aliquot, ceu sexus uterque
Fert, bene conveniens est flos utrique iuventae: 75
Unde magis constans amor est utriusque futurus,
Et magis hinc vegetam prolem sperare licebit.
      His etiam maiora animi bona largus in illos
Contulit haud parce superum favorque unde relucent
Virtutes animi tot in illo principe dignae.   80

Sexu et sponsa suo dignis, et sanguine, tanti
Heroisque toro virtutibus anteit annos.
    Tot tantisque bonis cum sit dotatus uterque,
Invicem et aptati sibi cum sint coelitus; illos
Auspiciis superum iunctos vinclo esse iugali   85
Quis neget? Aut orbi felix faustumque futurum
Coniugium hoc dubitet? Cum Celtis ergo Britanni
Unanimes merito celebrabunt hos Hymenaeos
Cantibus, et choreis, et plausibus, ingeminantes
Hymen, o Hymenaee, Hymen, Hymen, o Hymenaee.   90
    Coniugibus celsis et gratabuntur ovantes,
Hisque precabuntur pariter fausta omnia mecum,
Qui praecentor iis sic praecino voce canora.
    Sponse, ac sponsa, rosas et lilia condecorantes,
Quod nemo potuit vel praesentiscere dudum,   95
Vel sperare, toro vos ut quis iungeret auspex,
Auspiciis factum cum sit coelestibus illud;
Tam vestro superis, quam nostro nomine grati
Nunc agimus grates, et agemus rite perennes:
Et vobis merito laeti gratamur amore   100
Iam pariterque tori felici foedere iunctis.
    Inde Deum grata venerati mente precamur,
Ut, velut estis eo feliciter auspice iuncti,
Illius auspiciis vobis sic vivere detur
Nestoreos sanis usque et felicibus annos: 105
Huic et vester amor sit longo aequaevus ut aevo:
Ut numerosae etiam reddat vos ille parentes
Et pulchrae sobolis, variis quae regnet in oris:
Dumque superfuerit, qui pareat, usque supersit,
Imperet ex vestra clara qui stirpe Britannis: 110
Denique ut in terris vobis sit vestra superstes
Gloria, vosque illi coelestes incolae in aevum
Omne supersitis, superorum sorte beati.

Epithalamium [T]

It has long been in the fates and prayers of the British and Celtic peoples that a
new bond of friendship would firm up the treaties of their kings that had
recently been attacked, and that French lilies would be joined to English roses
by a happy marriage: although they who with Greek artifice conquer the
Trojans, promising the golden apples of the Hesperides, the rich fleece of

Phrygia,[7] and mountains of gold and quite everything, as dowry along with the beautiful wife, have been able to delay these fated events and pious prayers.

One who navigates the sea keeps an eye out for rocks (should black darkness stop these from being seen), so that he does not approach a great danger imprudently and be cheated and submerged by waves in the water. But if Phoebus drives this [darkness] away with his bright light, [the navigator] in his flight directs his course to where the waves are safer, so that he may guide his ship in to the desired shores.

Now that the clouds have been driven from them by light diffused from heaven, so too do those who supported the treaty, being deceived by the blackness of hidden treachery in which several fearsome dangers lurked, flee from the marriages they suspected, and now they renew with favourable auspices the treaties that were due to the Fates, to the prayers of the Celts, and to yours too, Britons. Therefore the royal youth, who bears the sceptres of Britain, and a royal nymph who ornaments the lilies worthy of a great parent, are joined together prosperously by a stable union under the auspices of love and the conjugal bond. How well are the lilies thus joined with roses? How well do both of these kings and powerful peoples come together by means of this treaty? Nothing can be more honourable or more useful to them and, if they know their goods, to the kings and other people who venerate the one God in their mind, because this blessed concord, which is joined by this bond more so than any other remedy, has the power to heal so many ills which engender fierce discord amongst Christians who fight against one another with weapons – just like the race of Cadmus once fought[8] – to their mutual destruction: for by the example, advice and venerable majesty of these kings joined together in concord as they cultivate just peace, peace can be negotiated amidst discord. Or, should any hostile plunderer – however fierce he be – disturb that peace, gaping after his prey like a rapacious eagle or kite and snatching others' property, he will be subdued easily by the arms and virtue of both of them. Let that which is caught be forced to obey, and let that which has been tamed grow quiet: and may he not forbid the

7 These apples were from the orchard of the goddess Hera and were closely guarded. There may be a suggestion of deception as Hippomenes used the apples to distract Atalanta, thereby beating her in a race and winning her hand. The union of the couple led to a desecration and they were turned into lions. Francis Bacon used the apples as symbols of distraction from scholarship in *De sapienta veterum* (1609): Eva Dewes, 'Atalanta', *Brill's New Pauly Supplements I, vol. 4: The Reception of Myth and Mythology*, ed. Maria Moog-Grünewald (Brill Online, 2011), http://referenceworks.brillonline.com/entries/brill-s-new-pauly-supplements-i-4/atalanta-e205130, accessed 28 Jan. 2014. Phrygia refers to Asia Minor.

8 Cadmus was the founding king of Thebes. Although there was dissent in his family, the reference is more likely to be to the race of men he created by sowing the teeth of a dragon he had slain. The teeth produced armed men who, after Cadmus threw a rock among them, fought one another to the death until only five of them remained: *OCD*.

remaining Christians, who enjoy harmonious peace with one another and are joined by a happy treaty, from waging just wars under the auspices of the gods against the wild Thracians who worship the impious rites of Mohammed, and who, as hostile enemies of those who worship the pious rites of Christ, have stolen so many kingdoms from them [Christians]. Having recovered these again, [the Christians] would dare to defeat [the Muslims] bravely.

This may rightly be called pious peace, and these pious arms, and they will be the bonds of this treaty of marriage that has now been confirmed (so we like to hope), enjoying so great a hero as the husband, one worthy of such a heroine.

If the goods of fortune have been kindly bestowed upon them, and the favour of the gods has been liberally poured upon each of them, you may see the greatest qualities of body and mind; no woman so worthy of this very man, and no man so worthy of this bride could be found and chosen in the whole world.

Both of their illustrious family trees of great kings adorn their lineage, whom no king that the world looks upon surpasses in ancient splendour, power, their own resources, or their own powerful strength; add the fact that the spouse is the monarch – by either their deserved or favourable fortune – of an empire that stretches far and wide, and the indulgence of heaven makes his spouse a partner in fortune of all the kinds of goods that he enjoys.

Praise for his healthy, agile and strong body adorns the spouse, and his skill exercises his feet, himself and his horses.[9] Moreover, his becoming appearance and countenance are worthy of rule.

The bride may rightly be called a Venus in beauty, a Dictynna in her chaste expression, and a new Juno in her venerable majesty.[10]

Differing somewhat in their years, which is fitting for their sexes, the flower of youth well becomes each of them and thus the love of both of them is destined to be more constant, and one may hope from them for more healthy offspring.

The generous favour of the gods has unstintingly brought to them greater qualities than these, and therefore very many virtues of the mind shine forth in such a prince.

The bride surpasses her years with virtues worthy of her sex, her family and the marriage bed of so great a hero.

Since each has been endowed with so many and so great gifts, the heavenly powers have made each of them in turn suited to one another. Who would deny that they have been joined under the auspices of the gods by a conjugal

9 Charles had been born with rickets and as a child had often been ill, physical problems that he overcame. He was a skilled horseman and on his ride to Madrid had covered six hundred miles in twelve days: Carlton, *Charles I*, pp 2, 16, 39. Quin's reference to Charles' 'strong body' is, therefore, more than conventional.

10 In escaping from the sexual attentions of Minos, Dictynna went as far as to jump into the sea. She is also associated with (or conflated with) Diana: *OCD*.

bond? Who would doubt that this is to be a happy and prosperous marriage for the world? Therefore, the Britons along with the Celts will rightly and unanimously celebrate these marriages with songs, dances and praises, repeating 'Hymen, o Hymenaeus, Hymen, Hymen, o Hymenaeus.'[11]

In their joy they will rejoice in such lofty spouses and will pray, in equal measure with me that everything will be prosperous for them, and I will sing before them, just as I sing now with sonorous voice.

Husband and wife adorned with roses and lilies, something which only a little while ago, no one could have seen or hoped for; so that some guide may unite you in the marriage bed, since that was done with heavenly omens. We now give thanks to the gods both in your name and in ours; and, with good reason, we will do this for an eternity. Moreover, in our happiness we will rejoice in your well-deserved love, now you have been in equality joined by the blissful bond of the marriage bed.

Therefore, as we venerate God with grateful minds, we pray that you will be happily joined by such an auspice that you may be allowed to live thus under it, being healthy and happy for a lifespan like Nestor's;[12] that your love be as lengthy as a long age; that it makes you the parents of numerous and beautiful offspring who will reign in various lands; that it will endure for as long as anyone survives to obey; that one who is from your celebrated family will rule the Britons, so that your glory will survive in your lands; and that you will survive as heavenly inhabitants for all time, blessed by the destiny of the gods.

A Nuptial Song, of the Union of the Roses and Lilies in This Royal Couple
[p. 5]

No garden fair, or ground that men enclose,
So fair and sweet a flower yields, as the rose:
No open field, that standeth low or hilly,
Brings forth a fairer flower, than is the lily:
Faire Albion, as by Neptune being walled   5
May, not unfitly, be a garden called:[13]
And as an open field is France, that stands
Not severed by the sea from sundry lands.
Of Albion's garden fair the flowers most rare;

11 Similar refrains can be found in the epithalamia of Catullus (for example, nos 61–2): *Catullus. Tibullus. Pervigilium Veneris*, trans. Francis Ware Cornish et al., ed. G.P. Goold (2nd corr. ed.; Cambridge, MA: Harvard UP, 2005), pp 69–90.
12 Homer's King Nestor was famous for his longevity.
13 Compare 'our sea-wallèd garden' in *Richard II*, iii.4.44: *The Oxford Shakespeare: The Complete Works*, eds Stanley Wells & Gary Taylor (2nd ed.; Oxford: Clarendon Press, 2005).

Most fair and fragrant, both her roses are: 10
Of France's fields above all flowers commended
The royal lilies are, from heaven descended.
Great Britain's royal roses, fading never,
In beauty and in honour flourish ever:
And France's lilies royal still do flourish,   15
Heav'n, whence they came, so doth them always cherish.
Of buds from England's roses springing forth,
None ever passed our royal Charles in worth:
And from French lilies never flower did spring,
More faire and meet, then Mary, for a king: 20
Of this faire lily's flower so worthy none
Is, as that goodly royal rose alone:
And none so worthy, as that flower of France,
Of this our British rose's alliance.
By blood he is, and in his fortune fair,   25
To both th'united roses royal heir:
By blood she is, and in her fortune high,
The lilies, and great Henry's progeny.
Of roses and of lilies in his face
A mixture shines, yet joined with manly grace: 30
As in like sort, of lilies and of roses
A mixture in her cheeks itself discloses.
His royal virtues do resemble well
The roses' beauty, and their fragrant smell:
The lily's colour white, and free from stain   35
Is of her virtuous mind an emblem plain.
No wonder then that these respects do move
Him, honour of the roses, her to love;
And her, the lily's ornament, incite
His love with mutual love for to requite;   40
That by this happy means his roses may,
Matched with her lilies, more their worth display:
And eke† her lily in Great Brittanie
Joined with his roses, flourish gloriously.
So may they live and love long flourishing,   45
That many a goodly bud from them may spring:
And lilies may with roses still agree,
As fitly coupled in my verse they be.

A Nuptial Ditty, of Love and Hymen Joining These Royal Mates [p. 7]

Now that each true heart rejoices
At this great solemnity,
Let us with the melody
Both of instruments and voices,
Blithely dancing in a ring,   5
Love and Hymen's praises sing.
    Duty doth us bind together
Both to praise, since both have brought
So much good to us, as ought.
Thus to make us, slighting neither,   10
Jointly them with heart and tongue,
Thank and praise in this our song:
    And first love such combining,
As should be combined by right,
Both for worth and beauty bright,   15
Like two happy planets shining:
Whose conjunction and aspect
Doth our happiness effect.
    But the knot which love had tied,
Might have been untied again,   20
Had not Hymen tied them twain,
When as time their love had tried,
With a knot, which nothing shall
Loose, but death, that looseth all.
    Love, which them to love incited   25
By the fame of their deserts,
By his wondrous power their hearts
Sundered far in place united:
But their bodies, and their minds
Hymen with this union binds.   30
    Him of roses sweet in favour,
Her of lilies without spot
Honour chief, love with his knot
Tied, them matching with due favour:
But now Hymen in his bands: 35
Binds their hearts with their own hands.
    Let us then, our song addressing
To them both, thus both them greet:
Gentle love and Hymen sweet,

Blest be ye; who, thus us blessing 40
By this couple blest, us make
Of their blessings to partake.

Ode nuptial [p. 9]

Toujours l'audace, et la malice humaine
Contre le ciel, et ses arrêts est vaine :
Ainsi jadis de ces géants hautains,
Qui follement entreprirent la guerre,
Contre le ciel, les efforts furent vains : 5
Gisants iceux morts foudroyés en terre.
    On l'a pu voir, ans y a neuf et trois,
  tre l'arrêt du ciel propice aux rois,
Et nations de Grande Bretagne, et France,
Que par le noeud d'amour, et les saints liens 10
D'Hymen se fit entre eux une alliance,
Qui leur devait produire des grands biens.
    Lequel grand heur par la fraude et malice
Des envieux avec grand artifice
Jusqu'à cette heure a été retardé ; 15
Faisant ceux par la faux semblance
D'un plus grand bien, qu'on se soit hasardé
De préférer au vrai bien l'apparence.
    Mais maintenant du ciel la grande faveur
A dépêtré des lacs de ce malheur : 20
Ceux, qui devant embarrasser y furent,
En leur faisant ces trompeurs délaisser,
Et ceux, desquels la foi ils reconnurent,
Pour alliés et amis embrasser.
    Et par le noeud d'un amour conjugal 25
Entre la rose, et fleur de lys royale,
Cette alliance étreint tellement ;
Que nul effort de malice ou d'envie
L'ébranler puisse, ou faire aucunement,
Que par discord icelle se délie. 30
    Le ciel peut-être, a si longtemps permis
Aux envieux, sous le masque d'amis
De traverser cette alliance heureuse
Par les appas d'une autre ; afin qu'on vit,
Qu'elle est bien moins que la leur dangereuse, 35

Et que tant plus elle nous réjouit.
    Aussi afin que ce grand prince attende,
Et pour compagne au lit et trône prendre
Dû cette belle et très aimable fleur,
Semblable en nom au feu grand roi son père,   40
Comme en bon sens et magnanime coeur,
Et tout de même à sa royale mère.
    Jamais ne fut autre conjonction
Plus désirable, et d'une affection,
Vive et ardente et en la Grande Bretagne,   45
Et en la France, et en maints autres endroits,
Que maints grands fleuves, en[14] bras de Thétis bagne,
Plus souhaitée et prince a bon droit.
    D'autant qu'à tous cet heureux mariage
En tous ces lieux sert d'assurance et gage   50
De leur sûreté, et de leur affranchissement
De tous les maux, qui ores les assaillent,
Et de leur gain et de leur enrichissement
Par tous les biens, qui ores leur défaillent.
    Les peuples donc de France et d'Albion,   55
Et ceux, auxquels la monstre ambition
Fait tort ou peur, ont de quoi faire fête,
Pour être autant munis, que réjouis,
Du don que fait de la belle Henriette
À Charles, seul digne d'elle, Louis.   60
    Louis grand roi, fils d'Henri le grand digne
Pour sa justice et sa valeur insigne :
Qui assisté d'un champion si preux,
Et puissant roi, son très bon et beau frère,
Rembarrera l'ambition de ceux,   65
Qui troublent tant l'un et l'autre hémisphère.
    Mais vous, deux fleurs, des roses et des lys :
La gloire et l'heur, soient toujours bénis
Les liens d'amour, et d'Hymen, qui ensemble
Heureusement vous ont joints et liés,   70
Et qu'en vous deux tout l'heur et bien s'assemblent,
Qu'ont du ciel tous les mieux mariés.

---

14 The copy-text has 'et'.

Nuptial Ode [T]

Audacity and human malice are always vain in the face of heaven and its judgments. Thus the efforts of the haughty giants who once foolishly undertook war against heaven were vain: struck down, they lie dead in the earth.[15]

One can see this when, nine and three years ago, heaven's favour to the kings and nations of Great Britain and France ceased.[16] Only by the bond of love, and the holy ties of Hymen could an alliance be made between them that would give rise to abundant good things.

This great moment was delayed until now by the fraud and malice of the envious and by their considerable trickery; making by false pretence a greater more preferable good which was to be ventured instead of the real presence of a true good.

Now, the great favour of heaven has released the snares of this misfortune: those who, formerly, were there to hinder them with these deceptions are abandoned; and those whose faith they acknowledged are embraced as allies and friends.

Moreover, by the knot of a conjugal love between the rose and the royal lily, this alliance is so well accepted that no effort of malice or envy can shake it, nor can it in any way be untied by discord.

Heaven, perhaps, has for such a long a time permitted the envious ones – in the guise of friends – to thwart this happy alliance by means of the charms of another, until it comes to be seen that this happy alliance is much less dangerous than theirs, and that it affords us all the greater pleasure.

In addition, so that this great prince attains his end, for a companion in bed and on the throne he had to take this beautiful and lovable flower, similar in name to the great king, her father, just as in good sense and magnanimity of heart she is wholly the same as her royal mother.

Never has there been a more desirable union, and a lively and ardent affection felt both in Great Britain and in France, and in many another place, nor was there a prince with just right more wished for than the longing of many a great river to bathe itself in the arms of Thetis.[17]

To such an extent this happy marriage serves for all people and in all these places as an assurance and token of their safety and as a liberation from all the evils which at present beset them, and also of their benefit and enrichment with all good things which at present are wanting.

---

15 The Gigantomachy, the war between the giants and the gods, was a much-retold myth.

16 A reference to the death of Prince Henry.

17 'Arms of Thetis' is a personification of the ocean. Thetis was a sea-nymph and the mother of Achilles. Although she was depicted as being very desirable, and Ovid's *Metamorphoses* (xi, 221–65) recounts the strategies her husband had to employ to wed her, she is an unfortunate choice in this context as she eventually abandoned her marriage: *OCD*.

Therefore, the peoples of France, Albion and people in any place the monster of ambition causes harm or fear, have something to celebrate, being so well supplied that they rejoice in the gift that Louis made of the beautiful Henrietta to Charles, the only man worthy of her.

Great King Louis, son of Henry of great worth, distinguished for his justice and his valour: he who aids a champion of such a brave and powerful king, your fine brother-in-law, will rebuff the ambition of those who disturb either hemisphere.

But you two flowers, roses and lilies, may you be always blessed with glory and happiness, the bonds of marriage and of Hymen, both of which fortunately link and tie you, and in you two may every happiness and good gather themselves, who from heaven are married for the best.

[Avec douce mélodie] [p. 11][18]

Avec douce mélodie
Chantons nous réjouissants,
Puis qu'en ce plaisant printemps,
Au royal Charles Marie
Est uni par amour,   5
Et par Hymen ce beau jour.
    Jour, dont la belle lumière
Nos yeux et coeurs réjouit ;
Jour, dont l'heur nous assouvit,
Et tout malheur chasse arrière ;   10
Jour, dont la fin, qui le suit,
Est sa très heureuse nuit.
    Nuit joyeuse claire et belle,
Ne cédant aux jours plus beaux :
Car feux de joie, et flambeaux   15
La feront luire, et en elle
De plaisir rassasiés
Seront les deux mariés.
    Mariés de tout heur dignes,
Non pareils, comme en leur sang,   20
Et en royal lustre et rang,
Et perfections insignes,
Tant au dedans, qu'au dehors,
De leurs âmes, et leurs corps.

18 The poem employs concatenation: the last word of a stanza is the first word of the following
    stanza.

Corps si beaux, que la Nature   25
Les a pour chefs-d'oeuvre exquis
Moulés et au monde mis.
Ce qu'en d'autres créatures
De beau se trouve est en eux,
Joint à esprits vertueux.   30
    Vertueux il est, et sage,
Preux en armes, et adroit ;
Et en elle vertu croît
Par-dessus son sexe et âge :
Dont bien agrée à nos coeurs   35
L'union de ces deux fleurs.
    Fleurs d'élite, et les plus belles
Tant des roses, que des lys,
Qui vinrent du ciel jadis :
Dont la faveur les rend telles,   40
    Qu'heureuse est leur union
À la France, et à l'Albion.
    L'Albion avec la France
Des ejouir sujets ont
(Comme de fait elles font)   45
De cette heureuse alliance :
Dont les innombrables fruits
Bien raconter je ne puis.
Je ne puis donc plus, ni ose
Chanter d'Hymen les beaux liens,   50
Qui apportent tant des biens,
La fleur des lys à la rose
Unissant, mais finirai,
Et sans fin les bénirai.

[With Soft Music] [T]

With soft music we sing our delights in this pleasant spring. To royal Charles Henrietta Maria is united by love and by Hymen on this fine day.

Day, whose beautiful light delights our eyes and hearts; day whose happiness satisfies us and drives back every misfortune; day whose ending is followed by a very happy night.

Night, joyous, bright and beautiful, not yielding the advantage to more beautiful days, because the celebratory fires and torches will make it sparkle, and in her wholly satisfying pleasure will the pair be married.

Married with all happy dignities, unmatched in their blood, in their royal lustre and rank and in the distinguished perfections – as much interior as exterior – of their souls and of bodies.

Bodies so beautiful that Nature moulded them and placed them in the world as exquisite masterpieces. Any beauty to be found in another creature is also to be found in them where it is joined to minds that are virtuous.

Virtuous he is and wise, valiant and skilled in arms; and in her is bred virtue beyond her sex and age. Our hearts are well pleased by the union of these two flowers.

Flowers of the best and most beautiful, the roses as much as the lilies, which came from heaven once, whose favour makes them as happy in their union as are France and Albion.

Albion and France both have reason to rejoice (as in fact they do) in this happy alliance whose innumerable fruits I cannot adequately relate.

I cannot do more, nor dare to sing to Hymen of the beautiful ties which bring so much good: the lily is joined to the rose, but I will finish, albeit without finishing blessing them.

[Felice nodo e vincula d'amore] [p. 14]

Felice nodo e vincolo d'amore,
E d'Hymeneo, giungendo alle rose
I gigli, unisce in nozze gloriose
Coppia di quelle, e questi eccelso onore:
    L'un, ch'a niun' marito in gran valore   5
Cede, ne l'altra alle più degne spose.
Dunque le stelle loro avventurose
Gli fan' d'unirli debito favore.
    Onde gioiscon' Francia e Gran Bretagna
Liete e felici: e con felice effetto   10
Gioia ne nasce in altre spiaggie ancora,
    Ch'il Rheno, l'Albi, e il Baltico mar', bagna,
Il Po, la Brenta, il golfo, ove han ricetto,
E'l mar', ch'all' Hespero vien' dall' Aurora.

[The Fortunate Knot and Bond of Love] [T]

The fortunate knot and bond of love, and Hymen, joining to the roses the lilies, unites in a glorious wedding, a pair of these and those, highest of honours:

The one, who yields to no bridegroom in great valour, the other to no worthier bride. Thus their propitious stars makes of their union a proper favour.

At which France and Great Britan rejoice, delighted and happy: and with happy effect joy springs on yet other shores

Bathed by the Rhine, the Elbe and the Baltic Sea, the Po, the Brenta, the gulf which shelters them, and the sea that reaches to Hesperus from the dawn.

15

Recueil des reparties, rencontres et autres dits mémorables du roi Henri le grand (1625)

Although undated, this work was most likely produced for Queen Henrietta Maria shortly after her marriage in 1625 (see below). *A Collection of Retorts, Bon Mots and Other Memorable Sayings of King Henry the Great* was calculated to appeal to the queen, not only because of its flattering portrayal of her father, but also because of its having been written in French (the queen was still learning English in the 1630s and was corresponding with some of her English subjects in French during the 1640s).[1] As its name suggests, the work is not a systematic biography of Henry but, of course, its court audience did not require any background information to read it. English works on Henry had appeared in print since 1585, and, for example, Quin's colleague Sylvester had translated a poem by Du Bartas celebrating Henry's victory over the League in *A Canticle of the Victorie Obteined by the French King, Henrie the Fourth, at Yvry* in 1590. Although it might be expected that Quin would have been only one of many authors adapting themselves to the times with an account of so eventful a life, *ESTC* lists no printed work about Henry in the 1620s. It may not be an accident, therefore, that Quin's text remained in manuscript and in French (while his other historical work, *Bernard Stuart*, was eventually translated and printed by him).

Henry IV, king of France and Navarre (1589–1610), was born in 1553 to Antoine de Bourbon, duke of Vendôme, and Jeanne d'Albret, queen of Navarre. Although baptized a Catholic, under the influence of his mother he was raised as a Calvinist and fought for the Huguenots in the French Wars of Religion (1562–98). In 1572 Queen Catherine de Médicis, mother and regent of Charles IX, arranged Henry's marriage to her daughter, Marguerite of Valois, in an effort to reconcile Catholics and Protestants, but these plans ended in the Saint Bartholomew's Day massacre of Huguenots arranged by the Catholic house of Guise. Henry escaped death only because he abjured his faith, but he was nevertheless confined under house arrest from which he eventually escaped in 1576 to rejoin military service in the Huguenot cause.

On the death of Charles IX in 1574, his brother Henry III assumed the crown. As the new king's marriage was childless and female claims to the French throne were blocked by the Salic law, when the king's remaining brother died,

---

1 R. Malcom Smuts, *Court Culture and the Origins of a Royalist Tradition in Early Stuart England* (Philadelphia: University of Pennsylvania Press, 1987), p. 186.

Henry of Navarre became heir to the throne. This prospect horrified many French Catholics, and the Catholic League (which had existed during an earlier phase of the Wars of Religion) was reformed under the leadership of Henry de Guise. The League put forward Henry III's uncle, Cardinal Charles de Bourbon, as the legitimate heir and it enjoyed international and local successes. Recognized by Philip II of Spain and buoyed up by Sixtus V's excommunication of Navarre, the League captured Paris from Henry III in 1588. In retaliation, the king had Henry de Guise and his brother assassinated and he joined forces with Navarre to besiege Paris, where, in 1589, he himself was assassinated and Navarre acceded to the throne of France as Henry IV.

As king, Henry still faced League resistance and the hostility of Spain (the support of James VI and I did not translate into practical assistance).[2] Although he won famous military victories, denied access to an unyielding Paris, he publicly converted to Catholicism in 1593 and received an absolution from Clement VIII two years later. Having been crowned at Chartres in 1594, he finally took possession of his capital city. In 1598 he was reconciled both to his Huguenot and to his Spanish opponents with the signing, respectively, of the Edict of Nantes and the Peace of Vervins. Shortly afterwards his first marriage was annulled and he married Marie de Médicis with whom he had two sons as well as three daughters (including Henrietta Maria). Henry's relationships with various mistresses was well known and, for example, the births of his children with Gabrielle d'Estrée in the 1590s were, to the shock of many, marked with his public approval.[3] In his last years he made himself ridiculous in the pursuit of the 15-year-old Charlotte-Marguerite de Montmorency, whom he married to Henry II de Condé, a prince of the blood, to keep the girl at court. However, the Condés fled France and removed themselves to Habsburg dominions. Plots involving kidnapping and papal annulment having failed, Henry opposed what he regarded as excessive Habsburg influence in the question of the succession to the Duchies of Jülich-Cleves (an issue in which he tried to interest a sympathetic James I).[4] It was while in 1610 he was making the military plans to oppose the Habsburgs that he was stabbed to death in Paris by a Catholic zealot concerned with his heresy rather than his political or amorous designs.

Copy-text
Walter Quin, *Recueil des reparties, rencontres & autres | dits memorable du Roy | Henry le grand.* BL, Royal MS 16 E XLI, fos 22–46. Written in a single, formal italic hand with corrections in a more rapid hand. Brown/black ink on paper,

2   See *The Trew Law of Free Monarchies* in *Selected Writings*, p. 278.
3   Vincent J. Pitts, *Henry IV of France: His Reign and Age* (Baltimore, MD: Johns Hopkins UP, 2009), pp 216–18.
4   Ibid., pp 306–16.

200x145mm. Its current binding dates to 1969.[5] This manuscript was part of the collection gifted to the nation by George II in 1757.

Quin's texts are bound with one other work, a manuscript copy of *Au roi de la Grande Bretaigne: ode*, by Marc de Maillet (or Mailliet, d. 1628), who had been a member of the circle of poets around Marguerite de Valois and who had spent twenty months visiting England. Maillet's text was addressed to King James and Prince Charles and the poems for the king were printed by Purslowe (who also published Quin) in London in 1617.[6]

The manuscript is not dated. It seems likely that it was prepared to mark the marriage of Charles and Henrietta Maria. Although it could have been written after this, there is some circumstantial evidence against a later date. Firstly, it would have been unusual for Quin to have made only passing reference to François de Bassompierre (1579–1646),[7] who, in 1626, was sent by Louis XIII as an ambassador to England charged with smoothing over the then rocky relationship of the royal couple, and securing rights of Catholic observance for the queen. Henrietta Maria had known Bassompierre since she was a child and although Charles' reception of the ambassador was initially cold, the Frenchman eventually won the king around and his embassy ended in a fortnight of elaborate entertainments including a masque in which the French royal family were depicted as bringing peace to Europe.[8] It is true that in the end the resultant treaty was rejected by King Louis, but that was due to manoeuvring by Cardinal Richelieu. Whether or not Bassompierre was blamed for this as well, Quin's references to him seem too neutral in respect of someone that had played such an important part in the private and public lives of the royal family.

Bassompierre's mission prompts another argument. As the marriage at first proved to be a frosty one, it is unlikely that Quin would have produced such a conspicuous gift for the difficult wife of King Charles. It is much more plausible that it was produced in anticipation of the queen's becoming an integrated part of the royal household.

---

5   I owe this information to the Manuscripts & Maps Reference Service of the British Library.

6   Patrick Dandrey (ed.), *Dictionnaire des lettres françaises: le xviie siècle* (2nd ed.; Paris: Fayard, 1996), pp 789–90; Marc de Maillet, *A la louange du serenissime roy, de la Grande Bretaigne: ode par le sieur de Mailliet gentilhomme françois* (London: George Purslow, 1617). For his English visit, see ibid., sig. A1v.

7   A soldier and courtier, Bassompierre ultimately became marshal of France. He was born in Lorraine but abandoned his German name (Betstein) to be integrated into his new country. He was a close companion of Henry IV: François Bluche (ed.), *Dictionnaire du grand siècle* (Paris: Fayard, 1990), p. 168 (see below, p. 258).

8   Katie Whitaker, *A Royal Passion: The Turbulent Marriage of Charles I and Henrietta Maria* (London: Weidenfeld & Nicholson, 2010), pp 86–8.

À la Sérénissime Reine de la Grande Bretagne [fo. 23r]

Madame,

Le respect et l'honneur qui est due à Votre Majesté et le peu de suffisance en esprit, savoir et langage, dont je me sens être fourni, m'eussent bien engardé de prendre la hardiesse, de vous offrir ce petit recueil, si le sujet d'icelui ne m'eût convié, et mêmement par le devoir de bienséance obligé à se faire. Car puisque c'est un recueil des dits mémorables de ce grand roi votre père d'heureuse mémoire, à qui le devrai-je présenter sinon à vous sa très digne fille qui lui ressemblez non seulement aux traits de visage, mais aussi, en tant que votre sexe et âge le permettent, en ses rares vertus et perfections. À quoi se peut ajouter, pour rendre cette mienne hardiesse d'autant plus excusable, qu'étant serviteur ancien de votre royal mari, et lui ayant une fois ou l'autre offert et dédié quelques mien écrits qu'il lui ont plu favorablement accepter, je ne pense point faire chose impertinente en offrant à vous, sa très chère consorte, quelques fruits de mon labeur, mêmement le sujet en étant tel qu'il est. Que si ce que j'y ai contribué du mien est de si bas aloi et si peu de valeur, qu'il ne mérite pas que vous en fassiez tant soit peu d'estime. J'espère toutefois, qu'attendu qu'étant conjoint aux mots dorés de votre royal père, il leur sert comme de lustre, pour faire mieux paraître leur bon aloi et haut prix. Vous ne dédaignerez pas de l'accepter bénignement, et ensemble les prières affectueuses que je fais à Dieu pour l'accroissance et durée perpétuelle de votre heur et prospérité. Comme étant de Votre Majesté le très humble et très dévot sujet et serviteur,

Gualtier Quinne

To the Most Serene Queen of Great Britain [T]

Madam,

The respect and the honour which is due to Your Majesty and the little sufficiency in spirit, knowledge and language with which I feel myself to be furnished, would almost have prevented me from being so bold as to lay before you this humble collection if its subject had not urged me and in the same manner the duty of propriety obliged me to undertake it. Since it is a collection of the memorable saying of the Great King, your father of happy memory, to whom could I present it if not to you, his very worthy daughter, who resembles him not merely in complexion, but also, as far as your sex and age allow, in his rare virtues and perfections? To this can be added (to render this audacity of mine more excusable), that being an ancient servant of your royal husband, and having at times offered and dedicated some of my writings to him which it pleased him to accept favourably, I do not think it at all impertinent to offer you, his very dear consort, some fruits of my labour, even with the subject being what it is.

16 E XLI. p. 290.

A la Sereniſſime Royne
de la Grande Bretagne.

Madame,

Le reſpect & l'honneur qui eſt deu à Voſtre
Majeſté, & le peu de ſuffiſance en eſprit, ſçavoir &
langage, dont je me ſens eſtre fourni, m'euſſent bien
engardé de prendre la hardieſſe, de vous offrir ce petit
recueil, ſi le ſubject d'iceluy ne m'euſt convié, & meſmement
par le debvoir de bien-ſeance obligé a ce faire. Car
puiſque c'eſt vn recueil des dicts memorables de ce
grand Roy voſtre pere d'heureuſe memoire, a qui
le devroy-je preſenter ſinon à Vous ſa treſdigne fille,
qui luy reſſemblez non ſeulement aux traicts de viſage,
mais auſſi (en tant que voſtre ſexe & aage le permet)

7 The beginning of *Recueil* (BL Royal MS 16 E XLI, fo. 25r © The British
Library Board).

[232]

That which I have contributed of my own is of such low value and of such small worth that it does not deserve even a modicum of esteem. However, I hope that because it is joined with the golden words of your royal father, it will set them in relief, the better to show their great worth and high value. You will not distain to benignly accept this and with it the affectionate prayers that I make to God for the increase and everlasting duration of your happiness and prosperity.

Your Majesty's very humble and very devout subject and servant,
Walter Quin.

Recueil des reparties, rencontres, et autres dits mémorables du roi Henri le grand [fo. 25r]

Le sage philosophe Plutarque dit que la nature et les moeurs de grands personnages apparaissent mieux en leurs dits, qu'en leurs faits : d'autant qu'en la plupart de leurs faits la Fortune y est ordinairement mêlée. Là où en leurs dits, elle n'y ayant nulle part, on aperçoit plus clairement et plus nettement, comme dans des miroirs, leurs coeurs et pensées. Ce fut pour ce regard que le même Plutarque fit un recueil des dits notables de quelques anciens rois, princes, et grands capitaines, par lui dédiés à l'empereur Trajan : et qu'après lui Antoine de Palerme composa un livre entier aussi bien des dits que des faits d'Alphonse roi de Naples et Aragon ; et qu'Aneas Silvius (qui après devient pape et fut nommé Pie Second) fit aussi un recueil tant des dits mémorables du dit roi Alphonse, que de ceux de quelques empereurs et autres princes.

Mais à mon jugement entre tous ceux-là il n'y en eut aucun, de qui les dits mémorables fussent plus dignes d'être recueillis, que ceux du roi Henri le grand : lesquels à quelques hommes ingénieux et curieux eussent peu fourni de quoi faire un bon manuel. Et toutefois jusqu'à maintenant je n'ai pas vu aucun recueil. Ce qui m'a donné occasion d'en faire ce petit recueil, tiré tant des histoires de son règne et de sa louange, que du rapport de personnages dignes de crédit, qui l'ont servi, ou hanté sa cour. Et d'autant que parmi les reparties, rencontres et autres dits mémorables de ce grand roi, que ce recueil contient, il y en a quelques-uns, dont on ne peut pas bien comprendre le sens et l'efficacité, sans faire préalablement mention de ses faits héroïques qui en ont donné le sujet, j'ai trouvé bon de les conjoindre ensemble, où l'occasion s'en présentera, le plus brièvement que faire se pourra.

Mais avant que d'entrer au récit de ses dits mémorables, je veux raconter un de ses faits et propos bien semblable[9] en apparence à ceux que j'ai entrepris de vous réciter, provenant toutefois de mêmes esprit et prudence.

---

9 The manuscript has *dissemblables*.

Après les noces funestes de la Saint-Barthélemy, il fut détenu en court contre son gré, et néanmoins entretenu avec les appâts de toutes sortes de plaisirs et délices, et avec promesse, qu'il serait fait lieutenant général du roi. Mais lui ressemblant à un oiseau enserré dans une cage dorée, en ce qu'il préférait sa liberté à ces délices et promesses de telle charge (qu'il savait être feintes et frauduleuses, comme n'étant pas ignorant, qu'en même temps où entretenait monsieur frère du roi avec la même espérance) donna ordre à aucun sien serviteur et confident de se trouver prêt en un jour et lieu assigné, avec chevaux et toute autre équipage nécessaire pour sa délivrance. Cependant dissimulant son dessein, et faisant semblant de se contenter de son traitement, et de croire ce qu'on lui disait de son avancement à la charge de lieutenant du roi, un jour avant qu'il fut prêt à déloger ; il alla trouver monsieur de Guise dans sa chambre, où ledit prince (selon sa coutume) le saluant par le nom de son maître, et lui demandant comment il se portait. Il lui répondit : mieux que jamais, puisque le roi lui faisait tant d'honneur ; que de le vouloir faire son lieutenant ; à quoi il ajouta les merveilles qu'il ferait ayant cette charge. Monsieur de Guise, qui montrait par un sourire qu'il prenait plaisir en ses devis, aussitôt qu'il fut parti, alla trouver le roi : auquel riant à gorge déployée il raconta la vanité et les vanteries (ainsi en parlait-il) du roi de Navarre. Mais le matin suivant tous deux furent bien étonnés, lorsqu'ils savaient qu'il s'était échappé et qu'il était parti en poste la nuit auparavant, par une dissimulation prudente, non seulement excusable mais aussi louable (attendu qu'il s'en était aidé pour se sauver du danger ; auquel il se trouvait, et non pour nuire à personne), ayant vérifié ce vers d'un ancien poète, « stultitiam simulare loco prudentia summa est » (en temps et lieu pouvoir le fou bien contrefaire, doit être réputé prudence singulière). Par telle prudence étant encore jeune il échappa des filets auquel il avait être pris par l'amorce des noces malencontreuses pour lui, mais bien plus pour le public, Dieu l'ayant ainsi préservé et réservé à un autre plus heureux mariage.

Or pour commencer désormais à vous raconter ses dits mémorables, quelques temps après son partir de la cour. Il se retira à La Rochelle, vers où la reine mère, le voulant derechef tirer à la cour, fit un voyage accompagné du duc de Nevers italien de nation, comme elle-même était. Ladite reine lui ayant envoyé un gentilhomme pour lui dire, qu'elle était venue pour conférer avec lui ; il l'alla trouver dans un lieu où elle était bien près de La Rochelle. Où elle ayant employé en vain tous ses artifices pour le tirer à sa cordelle, le duc de Nevers la secondant ; entre autres propos lui dit, que ce lui serait bien plus d'honneur de faire la cour au roi, que non pas au maire de La Rochelle, en laquelle il n'avait pas la puissance d'imposer un sol, lorsqu'en quelque occasion il aurait besoin d'argent ni d'y faire en autre chose ce qu'il voudrait. À quoi il repartit en ces paroles : « Il n'y a point d'Italiennes en La Rochelle qui me puissent apprendre l'artifice et le moyen d'y pouvoir faire quelque imposte, et en autres choses j'y fais ce que je veux, d'autant que je ne veux que ce que je dois ».

Cette repartie aux premiers mots pointe et pique tellement que je crois, que ce prince italien eut bien voulu, qu'il n'en eut donné l'occasion, et aux derniers mots, elle montre la grande modération, prudence et probité de ce grand roi.

En la bataille de Coutras, où il se montrait non moins vaillant gendarme que grand capitaine, il assaillit un gentilhomme de l'armée des ennemis, qui était de taille plus que moyenne, en lui disant comme par gausserie et manière de sobriquet : « rends-toi Philistin » par où il montra son hardi courage, et la grande assurance qu'il avait de la victoire (puisqu'en telle saison il pouvait ainsi railler) et ensemble le désir qu'il eut de sauver la vie au dit gentilhomme. Ce qui appert en ce qu'ayant gagné la journée, il regretta la mort de ses ennemis mêmes, et fit penser et traiter avec grand soin le sieur de Saint-Sauveur, frère du duc de Joyeuse leur chef occis en la bataille, à qui il eut volontiers sauvé la vie, s'il eut pu. Comme aussi il usa de grands bonté et clémence envers tous les prisonniers, en les renvoyant libres et sans rançon. Aussi en cette occasion ne fut pas moins admirable sa modération, que sa valeur et clémence. Car plusieurs qui eussent bien voulu qu'il eut tiré de cette victoire tous les avantages qu'il eut pu, pour lui-même et son parti, lui demandant, quelles conditions il demanderait ayant si heureusement vaincu ses ennemis. Il leur répondit : « Les mêmes que je demanderais si j'eusse perdu la bataille. » Ce qu'il dit ; d'autant qu'il préférait la paix et la faveur du roi de France, qu'il en espérait, à tous autres avantages.

Ledit roi, après qu'il eut fait mourir le duc de Guise et le cardinal son frère, s'étant retiré pour sa sûreté à la ville de Tours, et l'armée de la Ligue l'ayant jusque-là poursuivi, le roi de Navarre y vint pour le recouvrir avec une belle compagnie de noblesse et autres gens de guerre, et lui rehaussa tellement l'espérance et le courage fort ravalé auparavant, qu'il montrait avoir envie de présenter la bataille aux ligueurs. Mais ce roi, qui n'était pas moins sage que vaillant, lui dit qu'il serait bien de temporiser, d'autant que le délai viendrait à augmenter ses forces, et à diminuer celles des rebelles. Toutefois l'autre roi voyant qu'ils venaient jusqu'aux faubourgs de ladite ville pour le braver et l'irriter, lui dit, qu'il endurait mal volontiers leurs bravades. À quoi il répondit : « Sire ne hasardons point un double Henri contre un Carlos. » Par laquelle rencontre de noms aussi ingénieuse et pertinente, qu'il y en eut jamais aucune de cette sorte, il lui donna à entendre, qu'il y avait autant de différences entre eux deux, qui s'appelaient par le nom d'Henri, et le duc de Mayenne, chef de la Ligue, qui se nommait Carolus en Latin ; qu'entre un double Henri d'or et un Carolus, espèce de petite monnaie. Certes il est malaisé de juger laquelle de deux choses se doit plus admirer, où son bon sens en modérant son propre courage, et en donnant par cette rencontre si bon conseil à l'autre roi, où la vivacité de son esprit en rencontrant si bien à propos.

Son armée en la bataille d'Arques étant bien petite aux prises avec la grande armée des Ligueurs, il fut contraint de se servir de tous les avantages dont il se pouvait aviser. Or étant le champ de bataille parmi des collines, où il ne se pouvait pas si bien aider de sa cavalerie qu'en une campagne rasée, il voyait qu'il lui était nécessaire de se servir de ses gens de pied le mieux qu'il pouvait. Desquels les Suisses étant ceux en la prouesse et formeté desquels il se fiait le plus, il les alla trouver, comme la bataille fut preste à se donner, et dit à haute voix à leur colonel : « Courage, compère Galatie, je viens pour gagner de l'honneur ou mourir avec vous », paroles suffisantes pour donner courage auxdits Suisses, s'ils n'en eussent point eu auparavant.

Lorsque la bataille d'Ivry fut prête à commencer, un de ses vieux capitaines lui demanda en la présence de plusieurs seigneurs et gentilshommes de son armée, où a tout événement (les armes étant journalières) serait son lieu de retraite : auquel il répondit avec une brièveté laconique, « ici ou là », montrant au doigt lorsqu'il disait « ici » le champ de bataille, lorsqu'il disait « là » le camp des ennemis. On peut bien juger que par ces mots il a voulu ôter aux siens toute autre espérance que de vaincre ou mourir, et leur montrer aussi, que lui-même était résolu ou de mourir au champ de bataille, ou de passer au camp des ennemis comme victorieux.

Laquelle sienne résolution il montra bien aussi en ces mots de la courte harangue qu'il leur fit : « Si vous perdez vos guidons, ralliez-vous à cette panache blanche que je porte : vous la trouverez au chemin de la victoire et de l'honneur. »[10]

Ces dernières paroles, qui se trouvent en l'histoire du sieur d'Aubigné, sont autrement racontées par Matthieu, Cayet, et quelques autres historiens en cette façon : « Si elle vous montre que je tourne le dos et m'enfuie, je vous permets d'en faire autant. » Or en quelque manière de ces deux qu'il ait parlé, il n'eut su par une longue et curieuse harangue avec plus d'efficacité encourager les siens.

À Fontaine-Française, où il ne combattit point, comme il avait fait aux autres batailles, pour de défendre, ou pour gagner un royaume, qui par droit lui appartenait, mais poussé d'une valeur héroïque attaqua l'armée espagnole, commandée par le grand constable de Castille, et les restes de la Ligue, dont le duc de Mayenne était chef. Le maréchal de Biron étant allé pour charger les ennemis fut par le grand nombre de leur cavalerie tellement accablé, qu'il fut blessé et en très grand danger d'être ou pris ou tué. Mais le roi suivant avec deux ou trois compagnes de sa cavalerie seulement, le délivra, et mit en route la grande armée des ennemis. Or après le combat étant allé visiter ledit maréchal entre autres paroles il lui dit : « Ne vous vantez plus, Maréchal, des services que m'avez fait en la guerre, puis qu'à ce coup je vous ai payé en même monnaie. » Ce qu'il lui dit pour faire qu'il se deportat de ses vanteries accustumées, qui lui etait devenues trop ennuyeuses.

---

10 There are two deletions in this paragraph: after 'guidons', the words 'ou enseignes' have been crossed out, and after 'je porte', 'vous servira de guidon. Suivez la' has been crossed out.

Le duc de Savoye au commencement des remuements de la Ligue et des guerres civiles, durant le règne d'Henri Troisième, s'était emparé par surprise du marquisat de Saluces, qui appartenait à la couronne de France. Mais entendant que ce grand roi le voulait ravoir ou de gré ou par force, il le vint trouver bien fourni d'or et de joyaux, pour gagner la bonne grâce de ceux qu'il pensait avoir le plus de crédit auprès de lui ; et d'artifices et compliments pour induire le roi même, s'il pouvait, à quitter le droit et prétention qu'il avait au dit marquisat. Or comme en un jour solennel il allait à la chapelle, ledit duc qui l'accompagnait s'ébahissant de voir, que les seigneurs et gentilshommes, qui le convoyaient, sans lui porter en apparence si grand respect et révérence, que ses Piémontais et Savoyards portaient à lui-même, l'environnaient de tous les côtés et de bien près. Le roi s'en aperçut et lui dit : « Mon cousin, vous seriez bien plus étonné de voir comme ceux-ci en un jour de bataille m'enserrent de plus près. » On peut bien croire que ledit duc fut étonné à bon escient se sentant menacé couvertement par ces mots provenant d'un esprit vif et éveillé.

Plusieurs courtisans gagnés par les dons et courtoisies de ce même duc, pour induire le roi à lui être favorable en ce qu'il désirait obtenir de lui, disaient plusieurs choses à sa louange. Mais le roi leur répondit : « Louez-le tant que vous voudrez ; je trouverai à redire en lui, qu'il me retient mon marquisat. »

Une autre fois comme il se faisait détacher les aiguilletés pour jouer à la paume, ledit duc se trouvant auprès de lui, fut aussi prêt qu'un autre à les détacher. Ce que lui étant sorti du jeu de paume, quelques courtisans lui ramentevoient pour marque du respect et de l'honneur que ce duc lui portait. Auxquels il répondit : « Au lieu qu'il m'a voulu détacher, je le dépouillerai, s'il ne me rend mon marquisat. » Et de fait peu s'en fallut qu'il ne le dépouillât tout à fait quelques temps après comme il eut pu faire, si sa bonté n'eut surmonté son juste ressentiment et courage.

La première fois que Don Pedro de Toledo, envoyé d'Espagne pour ambassadeur extraordinaire eut audience de lui, il se promena avec lui dedans les galeries du Louvre si longtemps, que ledit Don Pedro s'en retourna à sa maison si las et débile, qu'il fut contraint de se mettre au lit. Ce qu'étant rapporté au roi, qui un peu auparavant avait été travaillé des gouttes, il dit : « J'ai fait cela tout exprès, afin que l'espagnol sache, que je n'ai pas tant les gouttes, que s'il me voudra faire la guerre, je n'ai plutôt le cul en la selle, qu'il n'aura mis le pied dedans l'étrier. »

Ayant été averti que la trahison du maréchal de Biron contre lui était fomentée non seulement par le duc de Savoie, mais aussi par le roi d'Espagne, il dit à son Ambassadeur, qui l'excusait le mieux qu'il pouvait : « Votre maître me fait la guerre en renard ; mais je la lui veux faire en lion. »

Ayant ouï raconté quelques traits frauduleux et malicieux d'un grand prince trop accoutumé à manquer à sa foi et promesse, il montra bien que tels traits lui déplaisent, en disant ces paroles : « La tromperie est partout odieuse, mais surtout en un prince de qui la parole doit être inviolable. »

Quelques gentilshommes de la religion, après qu'il se fut déclaré catholique romain, venant à parler avec lui de quelques affaires, mais avec plus de doute et méfiance qu'ils n'avaient fait par le passé. Il s'en aperçut, et leur dit : « Mes amis ne vous défiez pas ainsi de moi, car nul de mes sujets ne s'est jamais tant fié en moi, que je ne me sois encore plus fié en lui. »

Ceux de la même religion lui envoyèrent des députés, qui lui demandèrent quelques villes et places outre celles qu'ils avaient déjà, pour leur assurance. Auxquels il dit : « Ne puis-je pas servir d'assurance à mes sujets ? » Toutefois poursuivant leur demande, ils lui disent, que le roi son prédécesseur leur avait donné les places qu'ils tenaient, et qu'ils espéraient que sa majesté ne ferait pas moins pour eux. À quoi il répondit : « Ventre Saint Grégory, le plus roi vous craignait et ne vous aimait pas, mais moi je vous aime et ne vous crains pas ! »

Monsieur de Villeroy lui faisant le rapport de quelques affaires d'État et de guerre, qui se traitaient en son conseil, pour en savoir sa résolution, il lui dit : « Pour ces affaires d'État je m'en rapporte au jugement de vous autres, qui sont de mon conseil ; mais pour les affaires de guerre, je crois que le meilleur conseiller que le roi de France ait, c'est le roi de Navarre. » Et certes il pouvait bien dire cela sans vanité ni vanterie, ne s'attribuant rien en ce disant, que ce que tout le monde lui attribuait.

Ces trois ou quatre dits qui suivent ne sont pas si notables pour la pointe d'esprit, qui se montre en eux moins qu'aux autres, que pour la clémence et bonté de ce brave roi, qu'on y voit reluire et notamment ès deux premiers. Ce qui fait que j'en raconte le sujet et l'occasion un peu plus au long.

Un gentilhomme nommé de Bourg qui avait été du parti de la Ligue, après qu'il se fut soumis à son obéissance lui donna telles preuves de sa valeur et suffisance, qu'il lui bailla commission de lever un régiment. Mais un des anciens serviteurs de sa majesté qui portait envie et maltalent au dit gentilhomme, pour lui faire ôter, s'il pouvait, non seulement cette commission, mais aussi l'honneur et la vie même, mis sous la serviette du roi, un peu avant qu'il se mit à table, un billet auquel était contenue une accusation dudit de Bourge comme traître et déloyal envers sa majesté. Le roi l'ayant lu, après y avoir un peu pensé dessus, regarda ceux qui étaient auprès de la table, entre lesquels se trouva ce gentilhomme. À qui lui ayant mandé qu'il s'approchât, il donna en main ledit billet. De Bourg l'ayant lu, sans montrer en sa contenance aucun signe de frayeur, se voulut purger envers sa majesté qui lui dit : « Je m'aperçois bien que ces quelques hommes envieux et malins, qui ont forgé cette calomnie contre vous, mais je vous tiens pour homme de bien. Allez, levez vos gens et continuez à bien faire. Ainsi accroîtrez-vous ma faveur envers vous et ferez crever vos ennemis de dépit. » Or si ce gentilhomme eut eu affaire à quelques princes ombrageux et pusillanimes, il eut été en danger de vie, ou pour le moins de sa disgrâce. Mais il eut affaire à un roi magnanime, et qui tant s'en fallait que par soupçon il fit aucun déplaisir ou mal aux innocents, qu'au contraire envers ceux qui l'avaient grièvement offensé, il usa de douceur et clémence admirable, comme il appert par ce sien fait et dit notable qui s'ensuit.

Un homme lettré mais malin et médisant, ayant publié quelques libelles diffamatoires remplies de calomnies horribles contre l'honneur de sa majesté, aussitôt qu'il vit, que, comme un autre Hercule, il avait vaincu et abattu l'hydre de la Ligue à plusieurs testes, il s'enfuit à Bruxelles. Où ayant vécu quelques temps en pauvre et misérable état, il fit prier le roi par quelques courtisans, qu'il lui pardonnas ses crimes, et ensemble lui permit de s'en retourner en France. Ce que sa majesté lui octroya. Mais plusieurs s'en ébahissant, et lui demandant, comment il pouvait faire cette grâce à un qui l'avait si outrageusement offensé. Il leur répondit : « Si en allant par les rues quelque forcené vous rencontrant venait à vous dire forces injures, et à vous ruer de pierres, vous ne voudriez pas (ce crois-je) vous venger de lui, mais plutôt en auriez compassion. Aussi ne me veux-je pas venger de ce pauvre chétif, lequel la freinasse, dont il était alors possédé, avait poussé à médire de moi. » Ce fait et ces propos dignes de sa clémence et générosité lui rapportèrent de la plume de ce même médisant un remerciement, autant ou plus plein de ses louanges, et de regrets de l'avoir offensé que ses autres écrits n'avait été farcis d'opprobres et calomnies.

Quelque déloyal et perfide que le maréchal de Biron s'était montré en son endroit, toutefois il était délibéré de lui sauver la vie, s'il eut voulu confesser sa trahison. Mais lui étant obstiné en la niant, quoiqu'il lui eut fait entendre par plusieurs indices, qu'il en avait été bien averti, de là il juge, qu'il était aussi obstiné en sa malice contre lui et ses enfants. Dont il fut contraint de le mettre entre les mains de la justice, quoiqu'à son grand regret, comme il montra bien en disant : « Je voudrais qu'il m'eut coûté cent mille écus et que le maréchal de Biron m'eut donné le moyen de lui pardonner. »

Lorsque le malheureux Chastel écolier des Jésuites induit par leurs enseignements pernicieux, s'étant efforcé de le massacrer, lui eut donné d'un couteau dedans la bouche ; avec une patience et modération admirables (eu égard à l'a-trocité du crime de ceux qui avaient été auteurs de ce détestable attentat), il dit : « Fallait-il que les Jésuites fussent convaincus par ma bouche ? » Desquels mots, quoi que proférait en un si grand danger de sa vie, l'on peut remarquer la pointe et vivacité accoutumées de son esprit : puisque par eux il montrait que c'était par les bouches de témoins et de juges que les Jésuites dussent être convaincus, et non par la sentence, et beaucoup moins par la blessure de sa bouche.

Étant sa majesté une fois en la foire de Saint-Germain, ceux de sa suite s'e-cartants çà et là par la foire le laissèrent appuyé sur un étal de mercier avec peu de gens. Ce qui fut cause qu'un gentilhomme passant auprès de lui par mégarde lui foula le bout du pied. De quoi se fâchant, et levant une baguette qu'il avait en sa main pour lui en donner, le regardant attentivement, il s'apperçut que c'é-tait un gentilhomme, qui lui avait rendu bon service en la guerre, pourquoi soudainement arrêtant sa main il dit : « Il ne faut pas que je me venge de ce gentilhomme pour m'avoir un peu foulé le bout du pied puisqu'il m'a talonné souvent en la guerre pour me faire service. »

Lorsqu'il s'en allait au siège d'Amiens, ayant mandé à un prince de sang, comme il avait fait aux autres princes et seigneurs du royaume, qu'il eut a le venir trouver pour lui assister avec son bon conseil et ses armes en cette entreprise ; ledit prince priait le gentilhomme qui lui fut envoyé, de dire à sa majesté qu'il désirait bien de lui rendre très humble service en cette occasion et en toutes autres ; mais qu'il était tellement dépourvu des moyens de pouvoir venir avec la compagnie et l'équipage sortable à son sang et rang de prince et pair de France, qu'il suppliât sa majesté de se contenter pour cette fois, que demeurant en sa maison il pria Dieu pour sa prospérité. Ledit gentilhomme étant de retour en cour rapporta au roi sa réponse et mêmement comme il avait dit, qu'il prierait Dieu pour lui. À quoi il repartit : « Il faut donc, puisque les meilleures prières sont celles qui se font à jeun, qu'il jeûne de sa pension de 5.000 écus. »

Au même prince étant entré en quelque pique et querelle avec le duc de Sully, et l'ayant appelé en duel, il dit : « Mon cousin, pourvoyez vous d'un bon second, car je veux servir de second au duc de Sully. »

Au siège de Paris quelques-uns des principaux de son armée lui dirent, qu'il pourrait prendre ladite ville par une brèche ou escalade. Mais lui ne la voulant forcer en telle sorte, de peur qu'elle ne fut pillée et saccagée, leur dit : « J'aime bien mieux avoir l'oiseau avec ses plumes que déplumé. »

Ceux de la dicte ville ayant été réduits en grande extrémité, envoyèrent quelques députés pour implorer sa miséricorde, et demander un délai de quelques jours pour la reddition d'icelle. Mais lui sachant bien qu'ils demandaient ce délai pour l'espérance qu'ils avaient d'être secourus, leur dit : « Si d'ici a trois jours vous ne vous rendez de la miséricorde que vous me demandez vous n'avez que la corde. »

Étant averti qu'un gentilhomme, qui lui était bien connu, pour l'avoir suivi et servi en la guerre, avait fait changement de sa profession mal à propos, et celui qui l'en avertit lui disant, qu'il avait fait le sault, il repartit : « Il a fait le sot vraiment. »

Un gentilhomme à qui une bonne somme d'argent était due pour ses gages et quelques dépens, qu'il fit pour le service de sa majesté ne pouvant être payé sans son mandement au trésorier ; s'adressa à lui plusieurs fois pour l'obtenir. Mais le roi se tournait toujours d'un autre côté, lorsque ce gentilhomme lui voulait parler. Enfin le rencontrant en un passage si étroit, qu'il ne se pouvait bonnement détourner de lui, il lui dit : « Sire, je n'ai que trois mots à vous dire, argent ou congé. » À quoi le roi repartit : « Et en aussi peu de mots je vous réponds : ni l'un, ni l'autre. » On peut bien croire pourtant, qu'il lui fit payer son argent ; puis qu'il avait si bonne opinion de lui qu'il ne lui voulait point donner son congé, et qu'il lui fit cette réponse comme en se jouant, et pour lui montrer, qu'à ses trois mots prémédités il savait répondre à propos et à l'improviste en aussi peu de mots et syllabes.

Son tailleur à peine sachant écrire ou lire, mais ayant un valet, qui avait été aux écoles, il se servit de lui pour coucher par écrit quelques règlements pour la reformation d'habits et quelques autres choses, qu'il fit relier en forme d'un livre, qu'il présenta à sa majesté. Le roi lui demandant qui était l'auteur. Il lui répondit que c'était lui-même. « Comment, dit le roi, se peut-il faire, que vous qui à peine savez lire, et beaucoup moins écrire, ayez fait un livre. » Il répondit, qu'il l'avait dicté, et qu'un sien valet l'avait écrit. Lors le roi en ayant vu le titre, et lu quelques passages, dit à un de ses valets de chambre : « Allez-me quérir mon chancelier afin qu'il me fasse un habillement ; puisque mon tailleur fait des règlements. »

Après que par la faveur de Dieu et par sa valeur et prudence, il eut régné et réuni presque toutes les provinces et villes de la France sous son obéissance ; monsieur de Roquelaure, maître de sa garde-robe lui demandant, ores qu'il était devenu grand roi et paisible ; quel ordre il plairait à sa majesté de lui donner concernant ses habillements. Il lui répondit en ces mots : « Pourvu que j'aie bottes qui l'eau ne perce point, souliers que ne me blessent point, et que je sois vêtu chaudement en hiver ; légèrement en été, me voila bien habillé. » Ici est remarquable la frugalité de ce sage roi, qui voulait que ses habits lui servissent pour leurs vrais usages et commodités, et non pour parade excessive en dépense ou curiosité.

Maintenant vous veux-je rencontrer deux de ses dits ou plutôt billets facétieux en rime. Le sujet d'un d'iceux était une mésaventure du duc de Mercure, gouverneur de Bretagne pour la Ligue, qui toutefois à quelques temps de la donna plus à faire au roi qu'aucun autre chef de la Ligue, et après qu'il se fut soumis à sa majesté fait lieutenant général de l'empereur en Hongrie, fit de si beaux exploits, et rapporta de si grandes victoires des Turcs, qu'il fut le plus renommé capitaine qui leur ait fait la guerre depuis le temps de Scanderbeg et Hunniades.

Or la disgrâce de ce duc était, que lui ayant assiégé Fontenay-le-Comte, et étant logé en un faubourg de ladite ville nommé Loges, le roi qui en fut averti vint avec quelques compagnies de cavalerie pour le surprendre, cependant qu'il se faisait faire la barbe : de sorte qu'il fut contraint de s'enfuir sa barbe n'étant faite qu'à demie. Bientôt après le roi alla visiter un de ses serviteurs, gentilhomme de ce pays là, qui était malade de la fièvre quarte ; avec lequel ayant parlé de cette disgrâce dudit duc non sans quelque risée, et après être entré en quelque propos touchant sa maladie, il lui dit qu'il avait appris un charme lequel le pourrait guérir, ou pour le moins lui donner quelque soulagement. Ce qu'ayant dit il demanda du papier et de l'encre, qui lui fut apporté. Il alla de là donc vers une table où il écrivit quelques paroles en un billet, qu'il fit attacher à un cordon et pendre au col dudit gentilhomme, en lui disant, qu'il le devait tenir ainsi pendu quelques heures sans lire ce qu'il y était contenu. Mais le roi étant parti un peu après, il prit envie au dit gentilhomme de voir ce billet : Alors il le détacha et y lu ce que s'ensuit :

Fièvre quarte je te conjure
Par la barbe de Mercure
Que de ce corps tu te déloges
Ainsi que lui fit de Loges.

L'ayant lu il s'en prit à rire si fort, que comme le roi lui avait prédit, il se sentit pour le moins bien soulagé de sa fièvre.

Le sujet de l'autre rime facétieuse fut tel : il y avait une grande dame en la cour sa proche parente, qui entretenait (a ce qu'on disait) pour son serviteur un gentilhomme, lequel pour quelque occasion fut contraint de se partir de la cour, pour n'y retourner pas si tôt qu'il eut bien désiré. Par quoi devant son partement ; y ayant un lut en la chambre de ladicte dame, duquel il soulait jouer, il y colla en un papier ce qui s'ensuit :

Mon âme sera bien dolente
Longe de votre divinité.

Mais le roi entrant en ladite chambre, et maniant ledit lut, vit ces paroles, et en voulant faire une rime accomplie, y attacha en un papier ce couplet :

Ne dites pas cela de ma tante,
Elle aime trop l'humanité.

À quelques-uns qui parlaient douteusement de la valeur du feu Archiduc Albert, il répondit en ces paroles : « Combien que l'archiduc ait fait paraître son courage en plusieurs occasions, et que le roi de la Grande Bretagne par ses faits et ses écrits mêmes ait donné preuve suffisante de sa religion, et que par ma profession et mes actions je l'aie aussi donné de la mienne. Si est ce qu'il y en a qui[11] ne veulent pas croire l'archiduc être vaillant, ni le susdit roi vrai protestant ; ni moi bon catholique. »

Se trouvant une fois au Jardin des Tuileries, et y voyant en même temps la reine sa femme et sa maîtresse, monsieur de Sully et un autre seigneur qui ne s'accordait pas bien avec lui, le père Cotton Jésuite et un ministre mais tous séparés en divers lieux dudit jardin, il en prit occasion de se donner quelque passe-temps. Il alla donc premièrement trouver sa maîtresse et la menant avec lui à la reine, se mit à les entretenir toutes deux de quelques propos gracieux et plaisants : mais lorsqu'il les eut fait parler l'une à l'autre, il prit congé d'elles, les priant de deviser ensemble jusqu'à ce qu'il les revint trouver. De là il s'en alla vers le duc de Sully, et le mena où se trouvait l'autre seigneur qui était en discord avec lui, et ayant commencé à les mettre en quelque propos ensemble, il

---

11 In the manuscript 'qu'il y en a qui' replaces the deleted phrase 'que plusieurs'.

les laissa, pour aller trouver le père Cotton, qu'il mena vers le ministre, avec lequel il le fit entrer en quelque dispute, qui était pour les arrêter quelques temps ensemble. Ce qu'ayant fait il s'adressa aux princes et seigneurs qui étaient là, et leur montrant ces trois paires discordantes si étrangement accouplées. Il leur dit : « Vous semble-t-il pas que je vous fais voir jouer une belle farce ? »

L'ambassadeur d'Espagne étant auprès de lui une fois lorsqu'on portait le sacrement quelque part, accompagné de peu de personnes, et lui disant, qu'aux bonnes ville d'Espagne ledit sacrement pour l'honneur de qui s'y trouvait présent ; était porté avec grande solennité et accompagné de plusieurs et mêmes de gens armez. Il lui repartit : « Il n'a pas besoin d'être accompagné en France de gens armés car il y est entre ses amis. »

Comme on louait en sa présence la bonté de quelques fruits et vins et autres choses d'Espagne, il répondit, 'Je vous accorde bien que tout ce qui ne parle point en Espagne est bon.'

Ayant lu en la chapelle de la maison de monsieur de Bassompierre ce vers d'un psaume peint en grandes lettres : « Quid retribuam Domino pro omnibus quae tribuit mihi ? » Il dit, qu'il y pouvait répondre par le vers en suivant : « Calicem salutaris accipiam, etc. » Ce qu'il dit en se jouant d'autant qu'il était presque allemand par naissance et non qu'il prit la coupe pour s'enivrer à l'allemande.

Le naturel de ce prince était si libre et plein d'ingénuité, qu'il ne se jouait pas seulement avec les autres, mais aussi parfois se gaudissait de lui même, comme il faisait, lorsque n'étant que roi de Navarre il disait qu'il était marié sans femme, roi sans royaume, et faisait la guerre sans argent.

Aussi ne s'offensait-il pas de la liberté que d'autres prenaient de se railler et gaudir de lui, comme on peut voir par ces deux où trois exemples qui suivront.

Une fois entre les autres, monsieur de Bassompierre et quelques autres seigneurs jouant avec lui, à la première, les cartes lui furent si favorables, qu'un de ses valets de chambre qui lui servait en cette occasion emplit son chapeau de leurs restes qu'il avait gagnés. Ce que voyant il quitta le jeu, de quoi monsieur de Bassompierre se plaignait, comme d'un tort que le roi leur faisait, en leur ôtant le moyen de pouvoir regagner ce qu'ils avaient perdu. Mais le roi lui disant, que ce leur était un honneur de perdre en jouant avec lui. Il a repartit : « Sire si vous joueriez de cette sorte, il n'y a que l'empereur, le roi d'Espagne et autres grands rois vos compagnons, qui devraient avoir l'honneur de jouer avec vous. »

Se levant de grand matin une fois il courut le cerf si longtemps en une de ses fôrets, que l'heure de midi étant passée, la faim et la soif qu'il avait le contraignent de s'en aller à une hostellerie près de la fôret, où comme inconnu il se mit à table avec quelques paysans et passagers : entre lesquels il y avait un a qui se moquant des courtisans. Il demanda quelle opinion il avait du roi même. Le paysan lui répondit, que le roi était brave et vaillant, mais que sa poche sentait le hareng saur. Sa majesté sans se piquer de cela ne fit qu'en rire, quoique ce paysan le voulant taxer, usa de ce mot de hareng saur, comme approchant aucunement en lettres et son du mot d'hérésie.

Voyant en la foire de Saint-Germain la femme d'un mercier, qui avait été autrefois assez belle, mais alors commençait a avoirs la face ridée et les joues avalées, il lui dit en une manière de langage, qui montre le changement que l'âge fait aux femmes, « Depuis que je vous ai vu il a bien plu sur vos merceries » : à quoi elle repartit : « Et en même temps, sire, il a neigé sur vos cheveux. »

Pour revenir maintenant auxdits notables de sa majesté. Comme il donnait une fois ses ordres à quelques seigneurs et gentilshommes de qualité, parmi eux se trouvait un gentilhomme officier principal de la maison du duc de Nevers, qui n'était pas ni pour sa qualité ni pour ses propres mérites si dignes de cet honneur que les autres. Celui-ci se mettant à genoux, comme eux avaient fait, et lui disant : « Domine, non sum dignus. » Sa majesté repartit : « Je le sais bien ; mais ce que je sais est d'autant que mon cousin le duc de Nevers m'en a prié. »

En la conférence où dispute qui se fit à Fontainebleau en la présence de sa majesté entre cardinal du Perron, lors évêque d'Evreaux, et le sieur de Plessis-Mornay, un ministre, qui était en la presse du grand nombre d'auditeurs qu'il y avait, ne se pouvant contenir de dire à haute voix son opinion touchant quelque point de la dispute, et en ayant après honte, se tira en arrière pour n'être pas connu et remarqué. Et comme ceux qui était près de sa majesté regardaient çà et là, et s'enquerraient qui était cet étourdi, le roi leur dit « C'est un carabin, qui a tiré son coup de pistole, et puis s'en est allé. »

La Provence étant entièrement réduite sous son obéissance, ceux de ladite province lui envoyèrent quelques députés pour lui offrir leurs services et féauté ; desquels celui qui avait la charge de porter la parole, jaçoit qu'il fut tenu pour homme savant et bien disant ; au commencement même de sa harangue fut tellement étonné qu'il ne su plus dire mot. De quoi le roi s'apercevant lui dit : « Ne vous troublez pas mon ami, car je sais bien que ce que vous voudriez dire est que la Provence est à moi et non au duc de Savoie. »

Comme il faisait son entrée environ l'heure de midi en une bonne ville, le maire et les bourgeois principaux d'icelle lui étant allés au devant, il y en eut un qui commençait a lui faire une harangue dont les premiers mots étaient « Alexandre le Grand et Jules César Empereur. » Mais le roi qui se doutait qu'il la ferait bien longue, ne le voulant plus écouter lui dit : « Alexandre et César qui n'ont plus faim comme moi, ne me doivent pas retarder que je n'aille dîner. »

Un recteur de l'université de Paris, qui était docteur en médecine, selon la coutume des autres recteurs lui faisant une harangue, et en un passage d'icelle lui disant : « Votre fille l'université de Paris est maintenant bien malads je le crois bien (dit-il) puisqu'elle est sous le régime d'un médecin. »

Quelques ambassadeurs des Suisses étaient venus à Paris pour renouveler leur ancienne ligue avec lui, il donna charge au Prévost et bourgeois principaux de ladite ville de les loger et traiter à leur dépens. Mais eux lui disant que le trésor de l'hôtel de la ville était tellement épuisé, qu'ils ne pouvaient bonnement fournir à cette dépense, si sa majesté ne leur octroyait quelque chose, dont ils pussent tirer de l'argent. Le roi leur dit, qu'il en était content, pourvu qu'ils trouvassent quelque bon moyen par lequel cela se pourrait faire. Lors ayant pris congé de lui, après qu'ils eussent consulté de cette affaire, ils revenaient le lende-main, et lui disent, que le moyen dont ils s'étaient avisé était, qu'il leur permit de prendre pour un temps limité quelque petite pièce de monnaie à chaque fois que ceux qui viendront à tirer de l'eau des fontaines publiques de la ville. À quoi il repartit : « Messieurs, trouvez quelque autre expédient : car il n'appartient qu'à Jésus Christ de changer l'eau en vin. »

Or quoique cette réponse ne semble pas être plus d'une rencontre de bonne grâce, sur ce que le changement d'eau en vin était demandé par des Messieurs, pour fournir à la beuverie des Suisses, comme sa majesté facétieusement le don-nait à entendre : si est-ce que si on prend garde à la raison qui le mût à leur dire, qu'ils trouvassent quelque autre expédient, on peut bien remarquer que ce fut d'autant qu'il voulait, que ce traitement se fît par les plus riches, et non aux dépens des pauvres, qui étaient ceux qui dévaient tirer le plus d'eau des fontaines publiques. En quoi il montra sa justice et le soin qu'il avait de ses plus pauvres sujets.

A Collection of Retorts, Bon Mots and Other Memorable Sayings of King Henry the Great [T]

The wise philosopher Plutarch said that the nature and the way of life of great people appears more clearly in their sayings than in their deeds since Fortune is mixed up in the greater part of the latter.[12] In their sayings, where she has no part, one sees more clearly and more distinctly as in mirrors, their hearts and thoughts. It is because of this that the same Plutarch made a collection of the notable sayings of some ancient kings, princes and generals, which he dedicated to the emperor Trajan, and that after him Antonio of Palermo composed a whole book, which was as much about the sayings as the deeds of Alfonso, king of Naples and Aragon,[13] and also that Aeneas Silvius (who subsequently became

12 This well-known reference is to the opening of Plutarch's biography of Alexander in his *Parallel Lives*: 'For it is not Histories that I am writing, but Lives; and in the most illustrious deeds there is not always a manifestation of virtue or vice, nay, a slight thing like a phrase or a jest often makes a greater revelation of character than battles when thousands fall, or the great-est armaments, or sieges of cities': Plutarch, *Plutarch's Lives*, trans. Bernadotte Perrin (11 vols, London: Heinemann, 1914–26), vii, p. 225.

13 Antonio Beccadelli, 'Il Panormita' (1394–1471), wrote a laudatory biography of King Alfonso V, *De dictus et de factis Alfonsi regis* (*The Sayings and the Deeds of King Alphonsus*, 1455): ODR.

pope and was called Pius II) also made a collection of the memorable words of the aforesaid King Alfonso, as well as of many of those of some emperors and other princes.[14]

However, to my mind there is not one from amongst all these whose memorable sayings were more worthy to be collected than those of King Henry the Great. From them, some clever and curious men had little to supply to have the wherewithal to make a good book of instruction; however, to this day I have not seen such a compilation. This gave me the opportunity to produce this small collection as much drawn from accounts of his reign and in his praise as from the report of credible persons who served him, or who lived at his court. Moreover, insofar as amongst these retorts, bon mots and other memorable sayings of this great king there are some of which their sense and import cannot be properly understood without prior mention of the heroic deeds which gave rise to the subject, I thought it useful to combine these together in the briefest manner possible when the occasion arose.

Nevertheless, before entering into an account of his memorable sayings, I want to relate one of his deeds and sentiments similar in appearance to those which I undertook to recount to you (coming as they always do from the same spirit and prudence).

After the fateful wedding-celebrations of Saint Bartholomew he was kept at court against his will, and yet he was maintained with the lures of all sorts of pleasures and delights and with the promise that he would be made lieutenant general to the king. But like a bird trapped in a gilded cage, he preferred his freedom to the price of these delights and promises (that he knew to be false and fraudulent, not being ignorant that at the same time the king's brother was maintained with the same hope), and he ordered certain of his own servants and confidants to be ready at a day and at an assigned place with horses and any other equipment necessary for freeing him. Nevertheless, concealing his purpose, and feigning to be content with his treatment and to believe that which had been said to him about his promotion to the post of the king's lieutenant, a day before he was ready to leave he went to find Lord de Guise in his room, where the said prince (according to his custom) greeting him in the name of his master, asked him how he was faring. He replied to him that he was better than ever, since the king did him so much honour that he would make him his lieutenant; to which he added the marvels that he would do having been given this responsibility. Lord de Guise, who showed with a smile that he took pleasure in these fables, went to find the king as soon as he was gone: laughing heartily he recounted the vanity and the boasts (thus he called them) of the king of Navarre. But the fol-

14 Enea Silvio Piccolomini (1405–64), later Pius II, included Alfonso V in *De viris illustribus* (*On Illustrious Men*, c.1450).

lowing morning both of them were astonished when they learnt that he was escaped and had left post haste the previous night by means of a sensible dissimulation which was not merely excusable, but praiseworthy (considering that he was helping to save himself from the danger in which he found himself, and not so that he could harm anyone), confirming the truth of this verse of an ancient poet, 'stultitiam simulare loco prudentia summa est' (in the right time and place the ability to feign foolishness must be deemed singular prudence).[15] With such prudence, while he was still young he escaped the nets in which he had been captured by the bait of the marriage which was unfortunate for him, and, even better for the commonweal, God thus preserved him and kept him for another, happier marriage.

Now, to commence to tell you about his memorable sayings. Sometime after he left the court he withdrew himself to La Rochelle whither the queen mother went, accompanied by the duke of Nevers (an Italian like herself), wishing to take him back to the court again.[16] The aforementioned queen had sent him a gentleman to inform him that she had come to speak with him; Henry would find the place where she was quite near La Rochelle. Having vainly employed all her artifices to draw him to her faction, and, seconded by the duke of Nevers, amongst other suggestions she said to him that he would have much more honour at the royal court than at the town hall of La Rochelle, where he did not have the power to command a penny if on some occasions the need arose or if he had something that he wanted there. To this Henry replied with these words: 'There are no Italians in La Rochelle who could make me learn trickery and the ways to be able to carry off some impostures, and in other things I do as I please, inasmuch as I do not want anything other than what I should.'

The opening words of this reply stung and provoked to such a degree that I believe that this Italian prince wished that he had not provided the occasion for

---

15 'Insipiens esto, cum tempus postulat ipsum: | Stultitia simulare ioco, cum tempore laus est (To fit th' occasion laughable appear; | 'T is sometimes wisdom folly's mask to wear': Cato, *The Distichs of Cato: A Famous Medieval Textbook*, ed. Wayland Johnson Chase (Madison: University of Wisconsin Press, 1922), pp 26–7 [ii, 18]. Several English printers produced editions of this well-known text, which had been revivified in the Renaissance with Erasmus' annotations. Henrietta Maria may have required the translation, as 'Although she had a tutor, she does not seem to have progressed much beyond reading and writing': Caroline M. Hibbard, 'Henrietta Maria (1609–1669)', *ODNB*.

16 Queen Catherine de Médicis and Ludovico (Louis) Gonzaga, duke of Nevers (1539–95). The latter was the fourth son of the duke of Mantua. In 1549 he went to Paris to claim the inheritance of his grandmother Anna d'Alençon. He was close to Henry III and his political influence was matched by his wealth. A fervent Catholic, he supported the Jesuits in their work in France. He made his support of Henri IV conditional on the king's conversion to Catholicism and fought against the League. Satisfied about his monarch's Catholicism, he went on a failed mission to Rome to seek a papal pardon for Henry's previous misdeeds: Arlette Jouanna et al. (eds), *Histoire et dictionnaire des guerres de religion* (Paris: Robert Laffont, 1998), pp 1149–52.

it in the first place, and its finishing words showed the great moderation, prudence and probity of this great king.

In the Battle of Coutras,[17] where he showed himself no less a valiant soldier than a great captain, he attacked a gentleman of the enemy's army who was taller than usual, and he said to him as if by mockery and a kind of nickname: 'surrender, Philistine!',[18] by which he showed his stout courage and the great certainty he had of victory (when, at such a moment he could joke like this) and, in addition, the desire that he had to spare the life of this gentleman. When it was apparent to him that he had won the day, he even regretted the death of his enemies and he thought of and treated with great care the lord of Saint-Sauveur[19] (the brother of the duke of Joyeuse, their chief foe in the battle), and wished to save his life if he could. In the same manner, he treated his prisoners with great generosity and clemency, releasing them without any ransom; consequently, he was on this occasion no less admirable in his lack of greed than in valour and clemency. Because many greatly wished that he would take all the advantages that he could from this battle, both for himself and for his side, they asked him what terms he would look for if he were to be so lucky as to defeat his enemies. He replied to them: 'The same that I would look for if I lost the battle.' That is to say, he preferred peace and the favour of the king of France [Henry III], in which he hoped, as much as any other advantages.

The said king, after he had brought about the death of the duke of Guise and of his brother, the cardinal,[20] retired himself to the safety of the town of Tours, and the army of the League having pursued him there, the king of Navarre came there to rescue the king with a goodly company of nobles and other men of war, and Navarre refreshed Henry III's hope and courage (greatly reduced before), to such a degree that Henry III showed that he wished to give battle to the Leaguers. But Navarre, who was no less wise than valiant, said to him that it would be better to play for time, seeing that delay increased his forces and diminished those of the rebels. However, the king of France seeing that the enemy had come as far as the outskirts of the aforesaid town to defy and irritate

---

17 In 1587 Henry's army met with the forces of Henry III's commander Anne d'Arques, duke of Joyeuse (c.1560–87), at Coutras in the Gironde. Joyeuse's cavalry lines broke, allowing Henry's followers to slay him and hundreds of his noble companions with comparatively few losses. After the battle, Henry's magnanimity was shown in the honour he afforded the enemy dead and in his release of prisoners without ransom: David Buisseret, *Henry IV* (London: George Allen & Unwin, 1984), pp 21–5; Pitts, *Henry IV*, pp 126–9.

18 Goliath was a Philistine (1 Sam. 17). Quin found the incident in Agrippa d'Aubigné's, *Histoire*, vii: Pitts, *Henry IV*, p. 128.

19 Claude de Joyeuse, baron of Saint-Sauveur (1569–87), was the younger brother of the duke of Joyeuse. He died at Coutras.

20 In 1588 Henry III had arranged for the assassination of Henry de Guise and his brother Louis, cardinal of Guise.

him, said to Navarre that he found it difficult to endure their bravadoes. To this Navarre replied: 'Sire, there is no need to risk a double Henry for one Charles.' By which pun (so ingenious and so apt that he never made the like again), he gave it to be understood that there was as much difference between those two who were called by the name Henry, and the leader of the League, the duke of Mayenne (who was called *Carolus* in Latin) as there was between a double Henry of gold and a *Carolus*, a coin of small worth.[21] Truly, it is difficult to judge which of these two things should be admired more, his good sense in reigning in his natural bravery (and in giving by happy expression such good advice to the other king), or the liveliness of his mind in striking on such fitting words.

At the Battle of Arques, his army being small in comparison to the great army of the Leaguers, the king contrived to use all the advantages he could think of.[22] Now the field of battle being between hills where he could not assist with his cavalry which required level countryside, he saw that it would be necessary for him to make use of his infantry in the best way possible. The Swiss being those of whose prowess and order he had the most confidence, he went to find them as he was about to give battle and he said in a loud voice to their colonel, 'Courage, Commander Galatie, I have come to win honour or to die with you', words which were sufficient to give courage to the Swiss, if they did not possess any hithertofore.

When the Battle of Ivry was about to commence, one of his old captains asked him in the presence of several lords and gentlemen of his army, where their place of retreat would be should the need arise (wars being capricious), to which the king replied with laconic brevity, 'here or there' indicating the battlefield with a finger as he said 'here', and the enemy camp as he said 'there'.[23] One can easily tell that by these words he wished to remove from the man any hopes other than to win or to die, and also to show that he himself was resolved either to die on the field of battle, or to arrive at the enemy camp as a victor.

Such resolution of his was well demonstrated in these words of a short speech that he made to them: 'If you lose your bearings, rally to this white panache that I carry: there you will find the way to victory and honour.'

21 Charles of Lorraine, duke of Mayenne (1554–1611), the second son of François, duke of Guise, and a brother of Henry de Guise and Cardinal Charles de Guise, became head of the Catholic League in 1588. Having (with Spanish aid) fought against Henry IV, he made his peace with the king in 1596 and was appointed governor of Île de France: ODR.

22 In Sept. 1589 Henry was defending Dieppe against the duke of Mayenne, who sought to come at the city, via a fortified crossing at Arques, with an army that was more than four times the size of his. In part because of the resolution of Henry's Swiss infantry, Mayenne was beaten back: Buisseret, *Henry IV*, pp 29–31.

23 At the Battle of Ivry in Normandy (14 Mar. 1590), Henry IV defeated the numerically superior forces of the Catholic League, led by the duke of Mayenne, and Phillip II of Spain: ibid., pp 32–4.

These latter words, which can be found in Aubigny's history, are also recounted by Matthieu, Cayet, and some other historians in this way: 'If the panache shows you that I turn my back and flee, I give you permission to do so as well.'[24] Regardless of which of these two things he said, he could not have better encouraged his men with a long and careful speech.

At Fountain-Française, he did not as he had in other battles, fight to defend himself or to win the kingdom that was his by right; but driven by heroic bravery, he attacked the Spanish army commanded by the great constable of Castile, and the rest of the League (of which the duke of Mayenne was the leader).[25] Marshal de Biron, who had gone to charge the enemy, had been so overwhelmed by their great numbers that he had been injured and in danger of being taken or killed. However, the king, followed only by two or three companies of his cavalry, saved him and sent the great army of his enemies on its way. Then, after the combat, having gone to visit the said marshal, amongst other things he said to him, 'Never again boast, marshal, of the services you have done for me in war, since by this stroke I have repaid you in the same coin.' He said this to him to make him leave off his habitual boasts which had made him become extremely tedious.

At the beginning of the stirring of the League and of the civil wars during the reign of Henry III, the duke of Savoy unexpectedly came into possession of the marquisate of Saluces which appertained to the crown of France.[26] But hearing

24 Théodore-Agrippa d'Aubigné (1552–1630) was a historian, soldier and poet who was both a companion to and sometimes critical adviser of Henry IV. He remained loyal to the king's memory despite being opposed to Henry's abandonment of his Huguenot faith. His *Histoire universelle* appeared between 1616 and 1620: Jouanna et al. (eds), *Histoire*, pp 681–3. Pierre Matthieu (1563–1621) was a militant supporter of the Catholic League who was made a royal historiographer by Henry IV (a post he retained in Louis XIII's reign). He wrote extensively on Henry IV: see, for example, *Histoire des derniers troubles de France* (Lyon, 1594–5); *Histoire de France et des choses memorables […] du règne de Henry IIII* (Paris, 1605); *Histoire véritable des guerres des deux maisons de France et l'Espagne* (n.p., 1603); *Histoire de la mort de Henri IV* (Paris, 1611). Michel Simonin (ed.), *Dictionnaire des lettres françaises: le xvie siècle* (2nd ed.; Paris: Fayard, 2001), pp 817–18. Fr Pierre Palma-Cayet (1525–1610) was a Catholic convert and well-known historian who published *Chronologie septénaire* (1607) and *Chronologie novénaire* (1608), accounts of the periods 1598–1604 and 1589–97 respectively: Jouanna et al. (eds), *Histoire*, p. 1178.
25 Fontaine-Française, about twenty miles from Dijon, was in 1595 the site of one of Henry's celebrated victories. That year the king moved against Spanish forces in Burgundy. A small force led by Maréchal Armand de Biron encountered the joint armies of the duke of Mayenne and Fernando de Velasco, constable of Castile. Falling back to his rendezvous point with Henry at Fontaine-Française, Biron discovered that the king's forces were unprepared. Without time to don his armour, but nevertheless undeterred, Henry engaged his enemy and his victory drove a wedge between Mayenne and the Spanish that allowed him to secure Burgundy: Pitts, *Henry IV*, pp 194–5.
26 In 1588 the marquisate of Saluzzo (Saluces) in Piedmont was captured by Charles Emmanuel, the duke of Savoy. The question of its ownership was subsequently a matter that involved

that this great king wished to remove him from it willingly or unwillingly, the duke came to him well furnished with gold and gems to win the goodwill of those he thought had the most influence with the king; and he had stratagems and compliments to induce, if he could, the king himself, to give up the right and pretension he had to the marquisate. At this time, on a holy day, the king went to chapel and the aforesaid duke who was with him was astonished to see that the lords and gentlemen escorted the king, pressing around him without making any more show of respect and reverence than his Piedmontese or Savoyards showed to him. The king noticed this and said to the duke: 'Cousin, you would be more surprised to see how on a day of battle they encircle me even more tightly.' One can well believe that the aforementioned duke was astonished, reasonably feeling himself threatened by these words sprung from a lively and bright mind.

Several courtiers, having been purchased by the gifts and courtesies of this duke, to induce the king to be well-disposed to him regarding what the duke desired to have from him, said various things in the duke's praise. But the king replied to them: 'Praise him as much as you like; I too would find it in me to repeat these things about him if he returned my marquisate to me.'

On another occasion, when he was having his aiguillette untied to play real tennis, the said duke finding himself with the king, asked him to untie his.[27] Having come out of the tennis game, some courtiers reminded the king of the respect and the honour which this duke had for him, to which he replied: 'Instead of that which he wished me to untie, I will strip him, if does not return my marquisate'. Moreover, he had in fact been able to do this some time later, if his generosity had not overcome his just resentment and courage.

The first time that Don Pedro de Toledo (sent from Spain as ambassador extraordinary), had an audience with the king, the king walked with him in the galleries of the Louvre for such a long time that the said Don Pedro returned to his house so weary and feeble that he was obliged to go to bed.[28] Having been told this, the king, who shortly beforehand had been suffering from gout said: 'I did all that deliberately, in order that the Spaniard knows that I do not have so much gout that if I wished to wage war I would not have my rump in the saddle sooner than he could put a foot in the stirrup.'

both the pope and the patriarch of Constantinople as mediators. When these negotiations failed, Henry waged a war on Savoy that concluded with the Treaty of Lyon (1601) in which France ceded Saluzzo in exchange for other territories: Buisseret, *Henry IV*, pp 79–81, 83–6.

27 Real – or royal – tennis is played on indoor courts.

28 Don Pedro was at court between 1608 and 1609 to explore the possibility of a marriage between the royal houses of France and Spain. He attended many court events and was magnificently treated but left with his mission having failed: Buisseret, *Henry IV*, p. 148.

Having been informed of the treason of Marshal de Biron who had been incited not only by the duke of Savoy, but also the king of Spain, the king said to his representative who excused him as well as he could, 'Your master wages war on me like a fox, but I want to make it like a lion.'

Having heard recounted some false and malicious traits of a great prince who was too used to go back on his word and his promises, he clearly showed that such characteristics displeased him by saying these words: 'Falseness is everywhere hateful, but especially in a prince, the word of whom should be inviolable.'

After he announced himself a Roman Catholic, some Protestant religious gentlemen came to talk with him about various things, but with more doubt and distrust than they had had in the past. He noticed this and said to them: 'My friends, do not challenge me like this, because none of my subjects has ever been so sure of me that I have not had more confidence in him.'

Those of that religion sent him deputies who asked him for some towns and other places which he had previously promised to them for their security. He said to them: 'I cannot not give security to my subjects.' However, persisting in their suit, they said to him that his royal predecessor gave them the places that they held and that they hoped that His Majesty would do no less for them. To this he replied, 'By the stomach of St Gregory! You feared the former king who did not like you, but, you do not fear me who does like you!'[29]

To Monsieur de Villeroy, delivering a report of various matters of state and military affairs which he had dealt with in his council so that he would learn the king's decision, he said: 'For these affairs of state I yield myself to the judgement of you others of my council, but for matters of war, I believe that the best counsellor that the king of France has is the king of Navarre.'[30] Truly he could well state this without vanity or boasting, attributing nothing to himself in saying it that all the world did not attribute to him.

These three or four sayings that follow are not so notable from the point of view of wit, of which they show less than the others do, but are instead notable for the clemency and generosity of this brave king which shine particularly in the first two (this means that I will tell a little more about their substance and circumstances).

A gentleman named de Bourg who had been on the League's side, after he had submitted, gave the king such proofs of his valour and satisfactoriness that the

---

29 Pope St Gregory the Great was known for his stomach problems, brought on by the strict religious regime he followed: Jacobus de Voragine, *The Golden Legend*, trans. William Granger Ryan (2 vols, Princeton, NJ: Princeton UP, 1993), ii, p. 172. Henry's audience is unlikely to have been reassured by this exclamation.

30 Nicolas de Neufville de Villeroy (1543–1617) served as secretary of state for Charles IX, Henry III, Henry IV and Louis XIII. His position allowed him privileged insight into the diplomatic and domestic affairs of France. Some of these are recorded in his *Mémoires d'État* (Sedan, 1622): Jouanna et al. (eds), *Histoire*, pp 1367–71.

king gave him a commission to raise a regiment. However one of the old servants of His Majesty who was envious of and badly disposed towards this gentleman, to deprive him, if possible, not only of this commission but also of honour and even of life, put a note under the king's napkin which contained an accusation that de Bourg was a traitor and disloyal to His Majesty. The king having read it, after he had thought about it a little, looked at those near him at the table, amongst whom he found this gentleman, de Bourg, to whom, having asked that he would approach, the king gave the aforementioned note. Having read it, de Bourg, without betraying any fear in his countenance, wished to prostrate himself before His Majesty, who said to him: 'I know well that it is some envious and malicious person who has forged this calumny against you, but I believe you to be a worthy man. Go, levy your soldiers and continue to do well. In this manner you will increase my goodwill towards you and make your enemies die of pique.' Now, if this gentleman had had to deal with a prince who was touchy and nervous he would have been in danger of his life, or at least of his disgrace. However, he had a magnanimous king to deal with, one who hated suspicion and the injury of the innocent to such a degree that towards those that had been injured in this manner he showed an admirable mildness and clemency, as is apparent by the notable deed and expression that follows.

An educated man, but one who was malevolent and spoke badly of others, having published some defamatory libels full of horrible calumnies against the honour of His Majesty; as soon as he realized that, like another Hercules, the king had defeated and destroyed the hydra of the League in several trials, he fled to Brussels. There, having lived for some time in a poor and miserable state, he had a courtier beg the king to pardon his crimes and at the same time to allow him to return to France. His Majesty granted him this. However, several people were astonished about this and they asked the king how he could be so gracious to one who had so outrageously offended him. He replied, 'If while on the road you meet a maniac who has come to do you harm, and throws stones at you, you would not (I think) take vengeance on him, but instead you would have compassion for him. In the same way, I do not want to revenge myself on this poor frenzied wretch who, while he was possessed, was driven to speak badly of me.' This deed and these worthy words brought from the pen of this same vilifier a thanks, all the fuller of the king's praises, and his regret for having offended in his other writings which were only stuffed with condemnations and calumnies.

When someone disloyal and perfidious such as the marshal de Biron appeared before him, the king always decided to spare his life if he confessed his treason. However, the marshal was obstinate in his denial, a fact the king knew from many indications by which he was well warned and by which he judged that the marshal was still obstinate in his malice against him and his children. In consequence, the king was constrained to pass him over into the hands of the law, at which he showed his great regret by saying: 'I would prefer pay one hundred thousand *écus* and that the marshal de Biron gave me the way to pardon him.'

At the time that the unfortunate Jesuit student Châtel, led by the Jesuits' pernicious teachings, tried to slaughter him, giving him a knife wound in the mouth, he said (with an admirable patience and moderation, bearing in mind the atrocity of the crime of those who had been the authors of this despicable attack): 'Must it be that the Jesuits are convicted by my mouth?'[31] From these words, which he uttered when his life was in such great danger, one can see the usual sharpness and vivacity of his mind, since by them he showed that it was by the mouths of witnesses and judges that the Jesuits would have to be convicted, and not by his sentence, let alone by the injury to his mouth.

Once, His Majesty being at the fair of Saint-Germain, those of his retinue spread here and there in the fair leaving him leaning on a merchant's stall with few people around. This was the cause of a gentleman passing near him accidentally treading on his foot. This angered him, and raising a stick he had in his hand to strike him with it, regarding him attentively he saw that it was a gentleman who had given him good service in the war, because of which suddenly stopping his hand he said: 'I must not revenge myself on this gentleman for slightly treading on me with his foot since he has so often served me in battle by following at my heel.'

At the time he went to the siege of Amiens, having ordered a prince of the blood – just as he had done with other princes and lords of the realm – that he come and seek him to aid him in this enterprise with his good counsel and his arms, the said prince requested the gentleman who had been sent by the king to say to His Majesty that he well-desired to give him most humble service on this occasion and on all others, but that he was so unprovided with the means to be able to come with the soldiers and equipment fitted to his blood and rank as a prince and peer of France that he begged His Majesty to be content this time if he remained in his dwelling and prayed to God for the king's prosperity. The aforesaid gentleman, having returned to the court carrying the prince's response to the king and in the same fashion, as he had said, [the information] that he prayed to God for the king. To which the king replied: 'Therefore, because the best prayers are those which are made when fasting, it must be the case that he will fast from his pension of five thousand *écus*.'

31 In 1594 the 19-year-old Jean Châtel, a student at the Jesuit school in Paris, tried to stab Henry but his blow went amiss and he merely cut his lip. Châtel was drawn and quartered, one of his teachers was tortured and another executed. The Jesuit's protestations of innocence were not heeded and the order was expelled from France until it was recalled by Henry in 1603: Pitts, *Henry IV*, p. 192.

The same prince having entered into a quarrel and argument with the duke of Sully, and having called him out for a duel, the king said: 'My cousin, provide yourself with a good second, because I would like to serve as the second of the duke of Sully.'[32]

At the siege of Paris, some of the principal men of his army said to him that he could take the said city with a breach or with ladders. However, he did not wish to use force of this sort out of fear that the city would be pillaged and sacked, so he said to them: 'I much prefer to have birds with their feathers than to have them plucked.'

Those of the aforementioned city having been reduced to great extremity sent some deputies to beg for the king's mercy; but he, knowing well that they requested a delay in the hope that in the meantime they would receive aid, said to them: 'If three days from now you do not give the mercy that you ask of me, you will get nothing but the rope.'

Having learnt that a gentleman that he knew well for having followed and served him in the war had unluckily changed his profession, and he who informed him of this having said that he had made the move, he replied, 'Truly, he has jumped like a jackass'.

A gentleman to whom a good sum of money was owed for his debts and some expenses, who by the service of His Majesty could not be paid without the king's order to the treasurer, approached him several times to obtain this. However, the king always went in another direction when the gentleman wished to speak with him. Finally meeting him in a passage that was so narrow that he could not well turn away from him, the gentleman said to him, 'Sire, I only have three words to say to you, money or authorization.' To which the king replied, 'I answer you in as few words: no and no.' Nevertheless, one can well believe that he paid the gentleman his money; he had then such a good opinion of the man that he did not intend to refuse to give him his authorization, and that he made this reply to him in jest, and to demonstrate that he knew how to reply to these three premeditated words while improvising in equally few words and syllables.

His tailor, barely knowing how to read or write, but having an educated valet, had him write down some rules for the reformation of dress and some other matters, which the tailor had bound in the form of a book which he presented to His Majesty. The king asked him who the author was. The man replied that it was he himself. 'How', asked the king, 'could it happen when you can hardly read, much less write, that you have produced a book?' The tailor

---

32 Maximilien de Béthune, baron of Rosny and duke of Sully (1560–1641), was a committed Huguenot who survived the St Bartholomew's Day massacre and fought for Henry IV in the Wars of Religion. He acted variously as superintendent of finances, artillery commander and ambassador to England: ODR.

responded that he had dictated it and that one of his valets had written it. Then the king, having seen its title and read a few passages, said to one of the grooms of his chamber, 'Go and find my chancellor so that he can make me an outfit since my tailor is now making laws.'

After, by the favour of God and by his own valour and prudence, he had ruled and reunited almost all of the provinces and towns of France under his obedience, Monsieur de Roquelaure, his master of robes, asked him since he had now become a great king and was no longer at war, what orders His Majesty would like to give him concerning his attire.[33] The king replied in these words: 'As long as I have boots that keep out water, shoes that do not hurt me at all, and that I am warmly clothed in winter and lightly clad in summer, I will be well dressed.' The frugality of this wise king can be remarked here; he wished his clothes to be functional and practical, and not for excessive show of expense or for elaborateness.

Now I wish to recount two of his sayings, or rather his facetious notes in verse. The subject of one of these was a misadventure of the duke of Mercure, the League's governor of Brittany, who, although he at times gave more trouble to the king than any other leader of the League, after he submitted to His Majesty and was made lieutenant-general to the emperor of Hungary, carried out great exploits and won such great victories against the Turks, that he was the most famous captain that had waged war against them since the time of Skanderbeg or Hunyad.[34]

Now the disgrace of this duke was that when he was laying siege to Fontenay-le-Comte, residing in Loges, a suburb of the aforementioned town, the king who was informed of this came with some companies of cavalry to sur-

33 Antoine de Roquelaure (1543–1625) was Henry IV's *maitre de la garderobe* and part of an inner circle in which the king spent some of his leisure time: Buisseret, *Henry IV*, pp 94, 105.

34 Philippe Emmanuel, duke of Mercoeur (1558–1602), was the brother-in-law of Henry III and a military leader of the Catholic League. In 1598 the near-bankrupt Mercoeur surrendered his holdings in Brittany and his daughter married the king's illegitimate son, César. Mercoeur's capitulation – witnessed by Robert Cecil, Elizabeth I's envoy – marked the end of organized Catholic resistance to Henry's kingship: Pitts, *Henry IV*, pp 207–8. Skanderbeg (Iskander Bey, 1405–68) led the Albanian war against the Ottomans. He accepted the suzerainty of Alfonso of Naples (whom Quin mentions above p. 246) in 1450. Successive popes gave him the dignities of 'Champion of Christendom', captain-general of the Holy See and 'Athleta Christi'. His fame ensured that he was the subject of several Renaissance works, including one by Paolo Giovio (Quin's source for some of his material on Berault Stuart, see p. 149): Margherita Sarocchi, *Scanderbeide: The Heroic Deeds of George Scanderberg, King of Epirus*, ed. Rinaldina Russell (Chicago: University of Chicago Press, 2006), pp 22–4. János Hunyadi (Johannes de Hunyad, c.1408–56) was a Hungarian nobleman and military hero who fought against the Ottomans. He captured Sofia and raised Mehmet II's siege of Belgrade: Joseph R. Strayer (ed.), *Dictionary of the Middle Ages* (13 vols, New York: Charles Scribner's Sons, 1982–9), xi, pp 363–4.

prise him, which happened while he was shaving.[35] In this way he was obliged to flee having only half-shaved. Shortly afterwards the king went to visit one of his servitors, a gentleman of that region who was ill with *fièvre quarte* (a recurring fever); having spoken with him of the disgrace of the aforementioned duke (not without some mockery) and afterwards asking some questions about the man's malady, he said to him that he had learnt a charm with which he could cure him, or at least give him some relief. Having said this he asked for paper and ink which was brought to him. He then went to a table where he wrote some words in a note which he attached by a string to the collar of the said gentleman, saying to him that he had to keep it tied there for a few hours without reading what it contained. However, the king having left shortly afterwards, the said gentleman desired to see this note. He therefore detached it and read in it the following:

> *Fièvre quarte* you I conjure
> By the beard of Mercure
> From this body to dislodge
> As long as he's at Loges.

Having read this he took such a strong fit of laughing that, as the king predicted, he at the very least felt relieved of his fever.

The subject of the other facetious poem he made was this: there was a great lady in the court, his close relative, who maintained 'in her service' (as it was said) a gentleman, who, for a time was obliged to leave the court to which he was not to return as soon as he wished. For this reason, before his departure, having left a sealed paper note in the bedroom of the previously mentioned lady whom he was wont to strum. On it was that which follows:

> My soul is greatly sorrowed
> While separated from your divinity.

However, the king, entering the said bedroom, and happening on this note, saw these words, and wishing to make it into an accomplished verse, appended to this paper this couplet:

> Say not this of my aunt,
> She loves humanity too much.

---

35 Henry IV was at Les Loges, a suburb of Fontenay-le-Comte in the Vendée, at the beginning of June 1587 as part of a campaign capturing small towns around La Rochelle: Buisseret, *Henry IV*, p. 22.

To some people who spoke doubtingly of the bravery of the late Archduke Albert he responded in these words: 'The archduke had made his courage evident on many occasions, and by his own deeds and writings the king of Great Britain had given sufficient proof of his religion, and by my profession and my deeds I have also given mine.[36] If there is one here who does not wish to believe that the archduke is valiant, then the said king is not a good Protestant nor am I a good Catholic.'

Finding himself once in the Tuileries garden and seeing there simultaneously the queen his wife in addition to his mistress; Monsieur de Sully and another lord with whom he was not on good terms; the Jesuit Fr Cotton and a Protestant minister, but all of them separated in different parts of the said garden, he took the opportunity to give himself some amusement.[37] He thus went first to find his mistress and brought her with him to the queen, manoeuvring them with some graceful and pleasant words into conversation together; however, while he put them talking together, he took leave of them, praying them to find something to do together until he returned. From there he went to the duke of Sully, and brought him to where the other lord who was in disagreement with him was to be found, and having begun to put them talking together, he left them to find Fr Cotton whom he brought to the minister with whom Fr Cotton had entered into a quarrel, to make them spend some time together. Having done this he addressed the princes and lords that were there, pointing out these three opposed couples so unusually paired. He said to them: 'Does it not seem to you that I have let you see the playing out of a good farce?'

The ambassador of Spain, being with him once at mass somewhere when he was accompanied by few retainers, said to him that in the good towns of Spain the said sacrament in honour of those who were present, was carried with great solemnity and accompanied by many people, even soldiers. The king replied that 'It was unnecessary to be accompanied by armed men in France because there he is amongst friends.' When, in his presence, the ambassador praised the excellence of certain fruits or wines or other Spanish things, the king responded, 'I wholly agree with you that anything Spanish that we do not discuss further is good.'

In the chapel of the house of Monsieur de Bassompierre, having read the following words of the psalm painted in large letters: 'Quid retribuam Domino pro

36 Albrecht von Habsburg (1559–1621), the son of Emperor Maximillian II, had been a cardinal before marrying Isabella, daughter of Philip II of Spain and becoming co-ruler with her of the Spanish Netherlands. In this role he was, in 1609, party to a peace treaty that Henry had partly orchestrated. Quin either is unaware of, or glosses over, differences between England and France at the time: Pitts, *Henry IV*, pp 298–301.
37 Pierre Coton SJ (1564–1626) was Henry's confessor and was regarded as having had a good deal of influence over the king: Buisseret, *Henry IV*, p. 122.

omnibus quae tribuit mihi?'[38] He said that Bassompierre could respond with the following verse: 'Calicem salutaris accipiam, etc.'[39] He said this making play of the fact that Bassompierre was almost German by birth but did not take the cup to get drunk in the German fashion.

The disposition of this prince was so open and full of ingenuousness that he not only made fun of others, but sometimes he mocked himself, as he did while he was no more than the king of Navarre when he said that he was married without a wife, a king without a kingdom and that he waged war without money.

Additionally, he was not offended by the liberties that others took to tease and mock him, as one can see by the two or three examples that follow.

One of the times he was playing cards with Monsieur de Bassompierre and some other lords the cards were so favourable to him at the outset that one of the grooms of the chamber who was waiting on him on the occasion, filled his hat with the surplus of what he had won. Seeing that he was leaving the game, this Mr Bassompierre complained of the wrong that the king did to them in taking away their opportunity to regain that which they had lost. However, the king said to them that it was an honour to lose playing with him. Bassompierre answered back: 'Sire, if you will play in this fashion, no-one but the emperor, the king of Spain and your peers, other great kings, ought to have the honour of playing with you.'

Once, getting up at the crack of dawn, he hunted the stag in one of his forests for such a long time that, noon having passed, hunger and thirst drove him to go to a hostelry near the forest where, unknown, he placed himself at the table with some farmers and travellers, amongst whom there was one who mocked the courtiers. The king asked him what opinion he held of the monarch himself. The farmer replied to him that the king was brave and valiant, but that his pocket stank of smoked herring. His Majesty, without being piqued by this, did nothing but laugh even though this farmer, using the phrase 'smoked herring', wished to call him a heretic (without in any way employing the actual word in sense or sound).

At the fair of Saint-Germain, seeing the wife of a merchant who had been quite beautiful in former days, but who was now beginning to become wrinkled in the face and hollow of cheek, he said to her in a manner that showed the change that age makes to women: 'Since I saw you it has truly rained on your goods'; to which she replied, 'And at the same time, sire, it has snowed on your hair.'

---

38 Psalm 115:12: 'What shall I render to the Lord, for all the things that he hath rendered to me?' For François de Bassompierre, see the headnote.

39 Psalm 115:13. The full quotation is: 'Calicem salutaris accipiam, et nomen Domini invocabo', 'I will take the chalice of salvation, and I will call upon the Name of the Lord.' These verses were used in the Catholic Canon of the Mass: *Missale Romanum ex decreto sacrosancti concilii Tridentini [...]* (Ratisbon: Friderici Pustet, 1862), p. 264.

Now, to return to the memorable sayings of His Majesty. Once, handing out decorations to some lords and gentlemen of quality, amongst whom was to be found a gentleman who was the main officer of the house of the duke of Nevers, and who was neither for his quality nor for his own merits so worthy of this honour as the others were, this man, kneeling as the others had, said to the king, 'Domine, non sum dignus.' His Majesty replied: 'I know it well, but what I know just as well is that my cousin, the duke of Nevers has requested this of me.'

At the conference or debate that took place at Fontainebleau in the presence of His Majesty, between the cardinal of Perron (then bishop of Evreux), and the lord de Plessis-Mornay, a minister who was in the press of the great number of listeners that there were could not suppress delivering in a loud voice his opinion of some point of the dispute, and being ashamed afterwards, kept himself back so that he would not be recognized or remarked.[40] When those near His Majesty saw this and enquired who this thoughtless one was, the king said to them: 'It is a soldier who has shot off his pistol and then quit the field.'

Provence having been entirely reduced to his obedience, those of the aforesaid province sent some deputies to him to offer their fealty and service. Amongst these was one who had the responsibility to carry the pledge and although he was held to be a knowledgeable and well-spoken man, at the very beginning of his speech he was so stunned that he could not say a word. Seeing this the king said to him: 'Do not be troubled my friend, because I know well that you would wish to say that Provence belongs to me and not to the duke of Savoy'.

One time, as he made his entrance into a good town around noon, its mayor and its principal citizens coming before him first, one of them began to make an oration for him of which the first words were: 'Alexander the Great and the

40 Philippe du Plessis-Mornay (1549–1623) escaped the massacre of Saint Bartholomew's Day and took refuge in England, where he became a friend of Sir Philip Sidney. On returning to France, he served the Protestant cause as a soldier and as a diplomat for Henry, whose conversion to Catholicism appalled him. He published several works on religion including *De l'institution, usage et doctrine du saint sacrement de l'Eucharistie en l'Église ancienne* (*The Institution, Custom and Doctrine of the Holy Sacrament of the Eucharist in the Ancient Church*, 1598). This book was criticized by Jacques Davy du Perron (1556–1618), the bishop of Evreux (and subsequently cardinal archbishop of Sens), who accused du Plessis-Mornay of misquoting patristic sources. This resulted in a public debate between the antagonists, which was held before Henry IV and which du Plessis-Mornay was judged to have lost: *ODR*. Du Perron's name was familiar at the Stuart court as he was an intellectual foe of James I who believed that du Perron's political philosophy supported regicide and had been an encouragement to the Gunpowder Plot. James objected to the cardinal's work in his own writing, via his ambassador in France, and through enlisting writers such as Isaac Casaubon to refute du Perron in print. The cardinal's *Réplique à la réponse du [...] roi de la Grande Bretagne* (*Reply to the Response of the King of Great Britain*) was posthumously published in 1620: W.B. Patterson, *King James VI and I and the Reunion of Christendom* (Cambridge: Cambridge UP, 1997), pp 185–9.

emperor Julius Caesar.' However, the king, doubting not but that it would be very long, did not wish to listen further and he said to him: 'Alexander and Caesar were not hungrier that I am so do not delay me while I go to eat.'

A rector of the University of Paris who was a doctor of medicine delivered a speech to him in the manner of the other rectors, and during a passage of it the king said to him: 'I well believe now that your daughter, the University of Paris, is really ill since she is under the care of a doctor.'

Some Swiss ambassadors having come to Paris to renew their former pact with him, he charged the provost and principal citizens of the aforementioned city to house and feed them at the citizens' expense. However, they said to him that the treasury of the town hall was so exhausted that they could not well furnish this cost if His Majesty did not grant them something so that they could draw some money. The king said to them that he was happy with this once they found a good way by which he could do it. Then, having asked to be excused, after they had discussed the matter they returned the following day and said to him that the manner which they advised was that he allow them for a specific period to levy a small charge every time people wished to draw water from the city fountains. To this the king replied, 'Sirs, find another way, because the ability to change water into wine was given to Jesus Christ only.'

Now, even though this reply may seem no more than a joking one to the request made by the burghers that water be changed into wine in order to provide for the drinking sessions of the Swiss, as His Majesty facetiously framed it; nevertheless, if one notes the reason which moved him to say to them that they should find some other expedient, one can clearly see that it was his wish that this initiative be undertaken by the most wealthy, and not be at the expense of the poor, who were the ones who would be bound to draw the most water from the public fountains. In this he showed his justice and the care he had for his least well-off subjects.

16

From Thomas Herbert's *Some Years' Travels* (1638)

Thomas Herbert (1606–82) was born into a prominent mercantile family of York and was educated at Oxford, Cambridge and the Inns of Court (but without taking a degree). Benefitting from a distant family relationship to William Herbert, the third earl of Pembroke, he was attached to a diplomatic mission that set off for Persia in 1627, which furnished him with some of the material for his *Travels*. Having, in 1632, married the daughter of Sir Walter Alexander (a relative of William Alexander, see p. 110) who was a gentleman usher to Charles I, and having attracted the patronage of the fourth earl of Pembroke, the king made Thomas an esquire of the body; however, in the civil wars he joined the parliamentarian cause where eventually he was chosen to wait on the captive monarch. He served in the parliamentary armies in England and Ireland and so was knighted by Henry Cromwell and was created a baronet at the Restoration for his services to the dead king.[1]

Quin provided a short Latin poem for Herbert (signed 'Walt. O-Quin Armig.').[2] Other verses were supplied by Herbert's cousin, Christopher Herbert, Thomas, lord Fairfax, Arthur Johnston MD (who also wrote a poem on the death of Anne Quin, see below, p. 267), and Mark Belwood MD. The book was dedicated to a distant relative, Philip Herbert, the fourth earl of Pembroke, then lord chamberlain.

Copy-text

Thomas Herbert, SOME YEARES | TRAVELS | Into | AFRICA & ASIA | the Great. | Especially Describing the | Famous Empires of | PERSIA and INDUS-TANT. | As also | Divers other Kingdomes in the | Orientall INDIES, and I'les Adjacent. | By Tho[mas] Herbert Esq.[3] 2nd ed. London: by R[ichard] B[ishop] for

1 Ronald H. Fritze, 'Herbert, Sir Thomas, first baronet (1606–1682)', *ODNB*; Charles Rogers (ed.), *Memorials of the Earl of Stirling and of the House of Alexander* (2 vols, Edinburgh: William Paterson, 1877), i, pp 259–67.

2 'Armig.' is the equivalent of 'gentleman' and does not imply that Quin had a coat of arms. See the Introduction, p. 30.

3 Following this engraved title page is another that reads: 'SOME YEARES | TRAVELS | INTO DIVERS PARTS OF | Asia and Afrique. | Describing especially the two famous Empires, | the Persian, and great Mogull: weaved with | the History of these later Times | As also, many rich and spatious Kingdomes in | the Orientall India, and other parts of Asia; | Together with the adjacent Iles. | Severally relating the Religion, Language, Qualities, | Customes, Habit, Descent, Fashions, and other | Observations touching them. | With a revivall of the first Discoverer of America | Revised and

Jacob Blome and Richard Bishop, 1638. 2°. *ESTC* S119691 (forty-eight copies). BL, General Reference Collection C.55.g.8.

Herbert's work first appeared in London in 1634 (in two imprint variants), but Quin's poem is absent from these. However, it was retained in the third and fourth editions (London, 1664, 1665 and 1677). These editions are available on *EEBO*.

Amico suo nobilissimo Thomae Herberto armigero [sig. A5r]

Urbes quod varias solers vidisset Ulisses
    Et mores hominium, clarus honore fuit.
Sola inter Phrygiam licet errans Hesperiamque
    Littora lustrasset per duo lustra maris.
Tu spatia ut saperes immensa emensus es orbis   5
    Herberte inque salo graviter inque solo.
Comperta unde tibi nova multa et mira Britannis
    Candidus impertis veridicusque tuis.
Fallacem hoc Ithacum superasque peritia rerum
    Quod tua candori sit fideique comes.   10

To his Friend, the Most Noble Thomas Herbert, Knight [T]

Because skilful Ulysses[4] had beheld various cities and the manners of men, he was famous for his dignity. When wandering alone in Phrygia[5] or the west, he ranged over the shores of the sea for ten years. In the same way, you have solemnly measured out the immense regions of the world, so that, Herbert, you could learn on land and sea. You impart frankly and truthfully to your fellow Britons the many new and astonishing things that you have discovered, thus you surpass this treacherous Ithacan, because your experience of things is a companion to your candour and fidelity.

   Enlarged by the Author.'
4   Ulysses is the Roman name for Odysseus, the king of Ithaca who appears in *The Iliad* and *The Odyssey*. In the latter, he is depicted as deceitful and cunning, in the course of his ten-year journey home after the Trojan War.
5   Hecuba, the wife of Priam, king of Troy, was from Phrygia in Asia Minor and here 'Phrygia' may mean Troy or its vicinity: *OCD*.

Appendix: Writings to and about Quin

The works listed in this appendix appear in the alphabetical order of the their author's surname.[1]

Sir William Alexander

For Sir William Alexander and his relationship to Quin, see p. 110.

To his Worthy Friend Master Walter Quin[2]

I must commend the clearness of thy mind,
Which (still ingenuous) bent true worth to raise
Though in the grave an object fit will find,
Not flattering living men with questioned praise.
Brave Bernard's valour noble Naples sounds:⁣   5
Which scarce his country ventures to proclaim.
But since his sword prevailed in foreign bounds,
Their pens should pay a tribute to his fame.
Lest natives vaunt, let strangers then deal thus:
For I confess they prove too oft ingrate.⁣   10
What deeds have smothered been, or robbed from us
By Frenchmen first, by Flemings now of late?
    Where, had all met with such a Muse as thine,
    Their lightning glory through each age might shine.

John Dunbar

Dunbar (*c.*1585–1626) was born in Wigtown, Dumfries and Galloway, and educated at the University of Edinburgh. He may have visited the Huguenot community at La Rochelle and he was strongly Presbyterian. He married the daughter of an English clergyman in 1614 and settled in the West Country. He wrote epigrams to a number of writers including Ben Jonson and William Camden, but what is most striking is the number he dedicates to Scottish authors.[3]

---

1   I am grateful to Jamie Reid Baxter for directing me to the poems by Arthur Johnston and Thomas Murray.
2   Quin, *Bernard Stuart*, sig. A4r.
3   See the introduction to Jamie Reid Baxter and Dana Sutton, *Introduction* (2013). The poem is listed in Sidney Lee, 'Quin, Walter (*c.*1575–1641)', *ODNB Archive*.

Ad Gwalterum Guyneum[4]

Seu regum historias, rerum seu tempora nostri:
Sive anagrammata facis, sive epigramma facis;
Sic ipsum aequiparas Phaebum, ut Grynaeus Apollo
Sit dubium, an dici Guyneus ille velit.

To Walter Quin [T]

Whether you write about the histories of kings or the affairs of our times, whether you compose anagrams or epigrams, you equal Phoebus himself, to the extent that Apollo Grynaeus[5] is uncertain if he would not prefer to be called 'Quinaeus'.

T.H.
This poem is in part a translation of Quin's contribution to John Stradling's *Beati pacifici*. For an explanation of the difficulties of determining its relationship to Quin's work see p. 208.

[Except Thy Mind, with Flames of Heavenly Love] [sig. M3r]

Except thy mind, with flames of heavenly love
Did burn, most worthy knight, and from above
Enlightened, thou could'st not be so inflamed
With love of peace, nor yet could'st thou have framed
A poem, so divinely setting forth,   5
Of blessed peace, the plenteous fruits, and worth:
Whereby much do'st thou please the God of peace,
(Who thee to bless therefore will never cease:)
And a peace-making, wise, and pious king;
From whom, through peace, our earthly bliss doth spring.   10

Lo! how a marital knight, who peace proclaims,
And at all Christians' good, so doing aims,
Convinceth you, that of peace being preachers
By function, are the strife and discord teachers.

---

4   John Dunbar, *Epigrammaton Ioannis Dunbari Megalo-Britanni centuriae sex, decades totidem* (London: Thomas Purfoot, 1616), p. 22.
5   Grynium was the site of an Aeolian sanctuary dedicated to Apollo (see *Aeneid*, 4.345).

Sweet is the name of peace, sweeter the thing;   15
Blessed be our halcyon days, our peaceful king:
From England's peace, as from a fountain pure,
May Christendom draw peace that may endure.

Let swords de turned to scythes, the blood that's spilt,
Is too much; too heinous is the guilt.   20
Repentance fits both sides; both sides had fits;
God send these calmer times more temperate wits.

Were worthy Stradling's spirit, in heart or brain
Of arming Germany, or armed Spain,
Or France, that swelters in her own dear blood,   25
Whilst Jesuits laugh, and sing, and cry 'Good! Good!'

Then might our baronets, bannerettes of alliance,
Joyfully hold, not banners of defiance:
And English trumpets, sound to nations far,
Music for peace, not onsets for the war.   30

William Hart
The poem is signed 'Gulielmus Hartus, Scoto-Britannus'. Quin's advice to
Prince Charles is contrasted with the falsity of flatterers.

In *Coronam virtutum* clarissimi viri domini Gualteri Quinni[6]

Ullus adulator regi dat verba, potentes
    Aurum cum gemmis munera plena dolis:
Melle sed haec mero, et medicato rore perennis
    Diffluit aethereo lecta corona jugo.
Regum sublimes animos dum hoc nectare Quinne   5
    Imbius, et summo munere sceptra beas,
Atque una regum populos, aulaeque clientes,
    Debentur meritis praemia tuis?

On the *Corona Virtutum* of the Most Illustrious Master Walter Quin [T]

Any flatterer gives a king words, while the powerful give power and gold along
with gems, gifts full of treachery. However, this *corona*, eternal with pure honey

6   Quin, *Corona virtutum* (3rd ed.), sig. *8v.

[266]

and magical dew, flows from a heavenly mountain. Quin, as long as you imbue the sublime minds of kings with this nectar, and you bless their sceptres with the greatest gift, and you bless the kings' people and the courtiers, are rewards due for your merits?

Arthur Johnston

Arthur Johnston (*c*.1579–1641) was born in Aberdeenshire. Educated at the University of Aberdeen and at Padua (where he received his doctorate in medicine), he taught at Heidelberg and at the Huguenot Academy of Sedan, before returning to Aberdeen where he became rector of King's College.[7] James I appointed him a royal physician. His poem to Anne Quin first appears in his *Epigrammata* (1632). Along with Quin, he contributed a dedicatory verse to Thomas Herbert's *Some Years' Travels* (see p. 262). He is best known for being one of the compilers of *Delitiae poetarum Scotorum* (1637) in which this work is reprinted.[8] For the relationship of Anne Quin and Walter Quin, see the Introduction, p. 30.

In obitum Annae Quiniae ae puerperae[9]

Hic, sexus regina sui, Quiniaea sepultus est,
    Qua tegitur, veneres mille teguntur humo.
Haec veneres, mors haec charites simul abstulit omnes,
    Et reliquum terris quod pietatis erat.
Horruit ipsa nefas Lachesis, sed nescia flecti   5
    Lex agit, et retro volvere fila vetat.
Hoc tantum extorsit pietas, Quiniaea renasci
    Ut possit moriens funere facta parens.
Sic volucrum regina, animam dum exspirat in ignes,
    Se reparat phoenix, unica semper avis.   10
Plus tamen hoc meruit pietas et candida virtus;
    Phoenicis senio debuit ante frui.

7   Nichola Royan, 'Johnston, Arthur (*c*.1579–1641)', *ODNB*. Steven J. Reid, '"Quasi Sibyllae folia dispersa": The Anatomy of the *Delitiae poetarum Scotorum* (1637)' in Janet Hadley Williams & J. Derrick McClure (eds), *Fresche Fontanis: Studies in the Culture of Medieval and Early Modern Scotland* (Newcastle upon Tyne: Cambridge Scholars Publishing, 2013), p. 398.

8   John Scot of Scotstarvit & Arthur Johnston (eds), *Delitiae poetarum Scotorum hujus aevi illustrium* (2 vols, Amsterdam: Johannes Blaeu, 1637), i, p. 616.

9   Arthur Johnston, *Epigrammata A. Jonstoni Scoti, medici regii* (Aberdeen: Edward Raban, 1632), p. 16.

On the Death of Anne Quin in Childbirth [T]

Here is interred Quin, a queen of her sex. Where she is buried a thousand charms are buried in the earth. Her death took away all these charms at once, all these graces, as well as what piety remained on earth. Lachesis[10] herself shuddered at this outrage, but her law cannot be bent, and it forbids the threads to be rolled back. Only this did Anne's piety extort, that Quin could be reborn when dying, having been made a parent through death. Thus the queen of fowl, the phoenix, while it breathes out its spirit into the fires, renews itself and is always the same bird. Her piety and candid virtue deserved more than this, however: she should have enjoyed beforehand the old age of the phoenix.

Thomas Murray

Thomas Murray (1564–1623) was attached to the court of James VI and was a tutor of Prince Charles, a role that may account for his awareness of Quin's work. In 1622 he became provost of Eton. Some of his poems appeared in *Delitiae poetarum Scotorum* (1637).[11]

In regii nominis anagrammata quaedam, ex quibus regi Anglicum regnum deberi anno 1600 eruebatur[12]

Omina nominibus quid certa subesse retextis?
  Quid certam et certis esse sub ominibus
Rem dubitas? Probat ominibus rex esse sub ipsis
  Rem; certa et versis omina nominibus.
Quisnam igitur dubitet? Spero tandem fore, tota   5
  Anglia, si dubites, Anglia tota, probes.

On Some Anagrams of the King's Name, From Which It Was Discovered That the Kingdom of England Was Due to the King in the Year 1600 [T]

Why do you doubt that certain omens underlie the names woven into them and why do you doubt that particular things exist in particular names? The king proves that this fact underlies these very omens, and that there are particular omens in particular names. Who, therefore, would doubt this? Oh all England,

10 One of the three Fates, Lachesis decided the length of the thread of a person's life.
11 R. Malcom Smuts, 'Murray, Thomas (1564–1623)', *ODNB*.
12 Thomas Murray, *Naupactiados, sive Lepantiados Iacobi magni, Britanniarum, Franciae, & Hiberniae regis, fidei vere Christianae vindicis, & assertoris vere Christianissimi metaphrasis poetica* (London: John Norton, 1604), p. 40.

I hope that this will eventually happen, and that if, all England, you doubt it, you will then esteem it true.

In roseum quoddam *Sertum poeticum* regi eodem anno oblatum

Quod roseum tibi, iam sertum datur, ominor illud
  Cui rosa iam signum est, rex, fore, magne, tuum.
Hoc durum: in duris rosa spinis nascitur, ex his
  Quaeritur, at spinis absque, vides, geritur.

On *Sertum Poeticum*, a Poetic Garland of Roses Presented to the King in the Same Year [T]

I predict that the garland of roses that is now given to you, for which the rose is now the seal, will be yours, great king. This is harsh: a rose is born from harsh thorns, and from these is it sought; but it is worn, as you see, without thorns.

Robert Turner

This letter of 1591 was published in in a posthumous collection of works by Robert Turner (1547–99, see p. 41): *Roberti Turneri Devonii oratoris et philosophi in academia Ingolstadiensi epistolae* (*The Letters of Robert Turner of Devon, Lecturer and Philosopher of the Academy of Ingolstadt*, 1595). His writing is described as 'pompous, pretentious and affectedly classical' in the *Allgemeine Deutsche Biographie*.[13]

Epistolae CL[14]

Robertus Turnerus doctori Gualtero Gwinno, salutem plurimam dicit.
   Io triumphe, vivit Gwinnus: io, io, vivit et non contemnit Turnerum. Sic oportuit esse. Nam ego amo. Huic tu amori si reposuisses contemptionem aut odium, iure exclamassem, vae capiti infausto, quod semper frustra amat. Sed vae, vale: subi, subi, io. Non amat solum Gwinnus, sed elicit etiam in campum literarum? Egone detrectem hunc campum? Campum amoris? Campum ingenii? Campum gloriae? Si vis ioco, ego ex Aristippo? Si serio congredi, petam ex Aristotele arma. Quanquam frustra mihi Aristippus frustra Aristoteles in hoc

13 Alois Knöpfler, 'Turner, Robert', *Allgemeine Deutsche Biographie* (Bayerischen Staatsbibliothek, 1895), www.deutsche-biographie.de/pnd128565101.html, accessed 28 Nov. 2013.

14 Letter no. 150 of the postumous series in Robert Turner, *Roberti Turneri Devonii oratoris et philosophi in academia Ingolstadiensi epistolae, quae reperiri potuere, additis centuriis duabus posthumis [...]* (Cologne: Johann Kinckius, 1595), pp 354–6. Note that in this volume, page 354 is incorrectly numbered 545.

stadio erit. Amor, amor suppeditabit huc omnia, quibus tecum certem, sed certem tantum. Nam vincere, vinci, voces sunt honoris non amoris. Honor locum sibi si prenset in amore, non solum superbus, sed impius etiam sit. Amor et honor certant diversa certamina: hic, ut sit superior, ille, ut aequalis. Quam suave certamen amoris? Congredere, mi Gwinne. Theseus invenisti tuum Patroclum. Satis deliciarum. Serio iam laetor, placere te Domino, Dominum tibi. Fac, ut semper placeas, virtute, officio. Te tamen habes post alios? Cogita, cogita finem tuum, literas, et Deum per literas. Aula, via est: hic haeres? Tibi via non iam est, sed scopulus. Bonum factum, quod Domini tui filium imbuis politiori litteratura religionis, hic velim potiores tibi partes haberi.

Innuisti de Bervitio. Tene te. Novi illum bonum. Tu ponis mihi vestigium in aula? Infelix vestigium. Exibis, nisi sis miraculum hominis, alio vitae morumque colore. Non te tango, sed omnes; heus, omnes tamen, propter te. Cave, cave tibi picem, et qui reprehendis alios, ne fias alius. De Bervitio, plane statuo illum mihi amicum, amicum meum offendis? Uno verbo, non pecasse videtur de Hungaricis illis. Misit, expectat, ut remittantur. Hactenus expecta tu: neque te misce turbis, rixis. Piscem te volo in aula. Nosti naturam piscis. Nec inficit, nec inficitur scabie. Dedi etiam literas tibi ad Haberstockium. Quis hic homo? Integellus? An adfrictu aulae, tanquam picis, alius?

Southbeum hunc si non nosti, nosce ame, bonum virum, et mihi probatum, usu aliquot septimanarum. Hominis causa, si quid possis, facies id libenter, et quod sic soles, et quod ille mihi probatus. Non utar hic multis. Tantum fac, homo intelligat me a te amari, et illum in me.

Stanhurstus ad me rescripsit. Quid vero? Mel merum. Amat, laudat, offert se, offert sua, nihil non agit, ut suae suavitatis mihi explicet divitias. Etiam communicavit aliquot Campiani epistolas. Hic te volo mihi virum. Si quid Campiani scriptum possis emere, expilare, dono accipere, orationes, dialogos, poemata, horum tu mihi copiam. Si redimas pecunia sive scripta illius, sive laborem scribentium, illa tibi repraesentabitur a me, bona fide. Librorum Anglicorum nihil? Vide impudenter mendicum, sed apud Gwinnum tantum. Saluta mihi tuum Dominum, quam potes officiosissime. Eystadii, 18 Maii, Anno 1591.

Letters, No. 150 [T]

Robert Turner sends warm greetings to the teacher Walter Quin.[15]

Hurrah, a triumph! Quin lives! Hurrah, hurrah! He lives and does not despise Turner. So it should have been. For I love him. If you had repaid this love with

---

15 'Doctor' cannot here refer to Quin's possession of a doctoral degree as he is not listed as having one in the records of Ingolstadt or St Andrews.

contempt or hatred, I would have justly exclaimed, 'Woe to the unlucky man that always loves in vain!' But farewell woe: submit, submit! Hurrah! Does Quin not only love me but also draw me out into the field of letters? Am I to spurn this field? The field of love? The field of intellect? The field of glory? If you want me to enter the field only in play, am I to seek my weapons from Aristippus?[16] If you want me to be in earnest, I will seek them from Aristotle. Although Aristippus will be useless to me in this arena, and Aristotle useless too, love, love will supply all the things for this with which I can contend with you, but I will only contend, for to conquer and to be conquered are the words of public honour, not of love. If honour acquires a place for itself in love, it may not only be proud but also impious. Love and honour fight different contests: honour, in order to be the superior; love, in order to be an equal. How sweet is the contest of love? Enter into it, my Quin. Theseus, you have found your Patroclus.[17] Enough of merriment. I now rejoice in earnest that you please the Lord and that the Lord pleases you. Ensure that you always please him through your virtue and duty. Yet do you deem yourself inferior to others? Think! Think of your goal: literature, and God through literature! The court is a path: do you delay here? Now there is not a path for you, but an obstacle. It is a good thing that you initiate the son of your lord with the more refined literature of religion: I would wish that here you would have the more powerful role.

You gave your approval about Bervitius.[18] Restrain yourself. I know that he is good. Do you leave a track for me in the court? It is an unhappy track. You will come out, unless you are a miracle of a man, with a different colour of life and manners. I do not refer to you but to all men: nevertheless, listen, it is all on account of you. Look out, look out for pitch, and, as one who censures others, do not become changed. As regards Bervitius, I state openly that he is a friend of mine: do you offend my friend? In a word, he does not seem to have sinned in the case of those Hungarians. He sent a message, he is waiting for them to be sent back. You should be waiting to the same degree: do not involve yourself in discord or quarrels. I want you to be a fish in court. You know the nature of a fish: he infects others with an itch but is not infected himself. I also gave you the letters to Haberstock.[19] Who is this man? Is he safe enough? Or is he another touched by the pitch that is the infection of the court?

16 Aristippus of Cyrene was a contemporary of Socrates who both advocated and lived a life of hedonism: *OCD*.

17 The legendary Athenian king Theseus had a close bond with the Lapith king Pirithous. Patroclus was a comrade of Achilles. The two pairs were epitomes of friendship and it unlikely that Turner would have confused them by accident.

18 Johann Bervitius was a Bavarian ambassador at the Imperial court. Turner published letter number 21 that he sent to him at Cologne, and letters numbers 110–11 (sent to him at Prague) were published posthumously: Turner, *Epistolae*, pp 41–2, 274–6.

19 Ludwig Haberstock was in the employ of Duke William V of Bavaria. One of Turner's letters

If you do not know this Southbey, take it from me that he is a good man and has been tested by me, through the experience of several weeks. If you can do anything for his sake, do it willingly, both because that is your usual practice and because he has been tested by me. I will not expend many words on this. Only ensure that the man knows that I am loved by you, as he is in me.

Stanihurst[20] writes back to me. What of it? Pure honey. He loves, he praises, he offers himself, he offers his possessions, he does everything to make clear the wealth of his sweetness towards me. He has also shared some of Campion's letters.[21] Here I want you to be a servant for me. If you can purchase, steal or receive as a gift any collection of writing by Campion get them for me. If you spend any money either on his writings or on the labour of scribes, it will be repaid to you by me with good faith. Is there nothing of English books?

Behold someone who is shamefully indigent, but only in the company of Quin! Greet your Lord for me, as officiously as you can. At Eichstätt, 18 May 1591.

(no. 115 in the posthumous series), addressed to him at Prague, can be found in ibid., pp 282–3.

20 The Dublin scholar, Richard Stanihurst (1547–1618), had been a friend of Edmund Campion. Turner's Letter no. 139 is addressed to him: ibid.

21 Edmund Campion, Jesuit martyr (1540–81). Turner had been taught by Campion and was dedicated to disseminating his works: Peter E.B. Harris, 'Turner, Robert (d.1599)', ODNB.

Glossary

Glossed words are marked with an obelisk† in the main text. This glossary is based on the *Oxford English Dictionary*. Where necessary, nouns and verbs have been disambiguated. Where a word appears in Quin's writing in only one form it is used below, otherwise the basic form of the word is given.

behoof	benefit (n)
behove	benefit (v)
carrack	large ship
charge	load (n)
cloyed	overfed
composition	treaty
decked	adorned
ditties	lyrics
earst	first
eftsoones	again
eke	in addition
fraught	load (v)
gan	began
glistering	sparkle
hap	good fortune
Helvetians	Swiss
hie	haste, speed
hight	is called
indite	inspire a form of words
juggler	deceiver
lenitive	soothing medication
let	impede, impediment
North-Britains	Scots
overthwart	oppose, confound
range	cause to submit
scan	examine
seeing	considering
shelf	a dangerous sandbank or rock

sith	since
square	guiding principle
story	historical account
tissue	a rich cloth
turn	consider
ure	practice (n)
valiancy	valour
wight	person
wote	know
ywis	certainly

Bibliography

MANUSCRIPTS AND SPECIAL COLLECTIONS

British Library (BL)
Additional MS 69915: Coke Papers (series ii), vol. 48.
Royal MS 16 E XLI, fos 22–46: *Recueil.*

John Rylands Library, Manchester
William Camden, *Annales rerum Anglicarum, et Hibernicarum, regnante Elizabetha [...]* (London, 1615–27). Unitarian College Printed Collection, Q. Q1914: autographed gift to Quin from Camden.

London Metropolitan Archives
St Mary the Virgin, Twickenham, DRO/174/A/01, item 002: parish registers.
St Mary the Virgin, Twickenham, DRO/174/A/01, item 003: burial register.

National Archives, Kew
PROB 6/17: Administration Act Book of the Prerogative Court of Canterbury.
State papers (including SP 52/57, doc. no. 79: *Anagrammata*).

National Library of Scotland (NLS)
Advocates MS 33.2.31: annotated copy of *Elogium.*
Hawthornden MS 2065, fos 44–7: *Alexander and Erskine.*

University of St Andrews Library
Acta rectorum 4 (UYUY305/3): university matriculation records.

PRINTED SOURCES

'An Account of James Quin.' *The European Magazine and London Review*, 21:1 (1792), 323–5.
Acts of the Privy Council of England, 1621–1623, (ed.) J.V. Lyle. London: HMSO, 1932.
Adams, Geoff W., *Marcus Aurelius in the Historia Augusta and Beyond*. Lanham, MD: Lexington Books, 2012.
Adams, Sharon, 'Ruthven, William, fourth Lord Ruthven and first earl of Gowrie (*c.*1543–1584)', *ODNB*. Oxford UP, 2006, www.oxforddnb.com, accessed 24 Mar. 2014.
Alexander, William, *The Tragedie of Darius*. Edinburgh: Robert Waldegrave, 1603.
—, *The Monarchick Tragedies*. London: V[alentine Simmes] [and G. Elde] for Edward Blount, 1604.
—, *The Monarchick Tragedies*. London: Valentine Simmes for Edward Blount, 1607.
—, *The Monarchick Tragedies*. London: William Stansby, 1616.
—, *Recreations with the Muses: By William Earle of Sterline*. London: Thomas Harper, 1637.
—, *The Poetical Works of Sir William Alexander, Earl of Stirling*, (eds) L.E. Kastner & H.B. Charlton. 2 vols. Edinburgh: Scottish Texts Society, 1921–29.

Allan, David, *Philosophy and Politics in Later Stuart Scotland: Neo-Stoicism, Culture and Ideology in an Age of Crisis, 1540–1690*. East Linton: Tuckwell Press, 2000.

Asch, Ronald G., 'Elizabeth, Princess (1596–1662)', *ODNB*. Oxford UP, 2008, www.oxforddnb.com, accessed 1 Mar. 2014.

Ashbee, Andrew (ed.), *Records of English Court Music*. 8 vols. Snodland: Ashbee, 1986–96.

—, 'Quin, Walter. Teacher of Music, 1611–1632' in Andrew Ashbee & David Lasocki (eds), *A Biographical Dictionary of English Court Musicians, 1485–1714*. 2 vols. Aldershot: Ashgate, 1998, ii, pp 936–7.

—, 'Ferrabosco, Alfonso (*c*.1575–1628)', *ODNB*. Oxford UP, 2008, www.oxforddnb.com, accessed 1 Mar. 2014.

Aughterson, Kate, 'Livingstone, Helen, countess of Linlithgow (d.1627)', *ODNB*. Oxford UP, 2004, www.oxforddnb.com, accessed 1 Mar. 2014.

Aylmer, G.E., *The King's Servants: The Civil Service of Charles I, 1625-1642*. 2nd ed. London: Routledge & Kegan Paul, 1974.

Bakos, Adrianna E., 'Commynes, Philippe de' in Paul F. Grendler (ed.), *Encyclopedia of the Renaissance*. 6 vols. New York: Charles Scribner's Sons, 1999, ii, p. 58.

Barbour, Reid, *English Epicures and Stoics: Ancient Legacies in Early Stuart Culture*. Amherst: University of Massachusetts Press, 1998.

Barrow, G.W.S., 'Robert I (1274–1329)', *ODNB*. Oxford UP, 2008, www.oxforddnb.com, accessed 1 Mar. 2014.

Binns, J.W., *Intellectual Culture in Elizabethan and Jacobean England: The Latin Writings of the Age*. Classical and Medieval Texts, Papers and Monographs 24. Leeds: Francis Cairns, 1990.

Bliss, Alan, 'The English Language in Early Modern Ireland' in T.W. Moody, et al. (eds), *A New History of Ireland, Vol. III: Early Modern Ireland 1534–1691*. Oxford: Oxford UP, 1991, pp 546–60.

Bluche, François (ed.), *Dictionnaire du grand siècle*. Paris: Fayard, 1990.

Boulton, Jeremy, 'Wage Labour in Seventeenth-Century London.' *The Economic History Review*, 49:2 (1996), 268–90.

Boyd, Percival, 'Boyd's Marriage Index', *SoG Data Online*. Society of Geneaologists, 2011, www.sog.org.uk/search-records/search-sog-data-online, accessed 13 Apr. 2014.

Braun, Harald Ernst, *Juan de Mariana and Early Modern Spanish Political Thought*. Catholic Christendom, 1300–1700. Aldershot: Ashgate, 2007.

Buchanan, George, *Rerum Scoticarum historia*. Edinburgh: Alexander Arbuthnot, 1582.

Buisseret, David, *Henry IV*. London: George Allen & Unwin, 1984.

Burrows, Montagu (ed.), *The Register of the Visitors of the University of Oxford, from A.D. 1647 to A.D. 1658*. Camden Society, New Series 29. Westminster: J.B. Nichols and Sons, 1881.

Calendar of Inquisitions Formerly in the Office of the Chief Remembrancer of the Exchequer Prepared from the MSS of the Irish Record Commission, (ed.) Margaret C. Griffith. Dublin: Stationery Office, 1991.

Calendar of Patent and Close Rolls of the Chancery in Ireland, of the Reign of Charles the First […], (ed.) James Morrin. Dublin: HMSO, 1863.

Calendar of State Papers, Domestic Series, of the Reign of Charles I, (eds) John Bruce & William Douglas Hamilton. 22 vols. London: Longmans, Green and Co., 1858–93.

Calendar of State Papers, Domestic Series, of the Reign of Charles II, (eds) Mary Anne Everett Green, et al. 28 vols. London: Longman, Green, Reader and Dyer and HMSO, 1860–1939.

Calendar of the State Papers Relating to Scotland and Mary, Queen of Scots, 1547–1603, (eds) Joseph Bain, et al. 13 vols. Edinburgh: HMSO, 1898–1969.

Camden, William, *Remaines of a Greater Work, Concerning Britaine […]*. London: by G[eorge] E[ld] for Simon Waterson, 1605.

Campbell, Gordon (ed.), *The Oxford Dictionary of the Renaissance*. Oxford: Oxford UP, 2003.

Carlton, Charles, *Charles I: The Personal Monarch*. 2nd ed. London: Routledge, 1995.

Carpenter, Andrew (ed.), *Verse in English from Tudor and Stuart Ireland*. Cork: Cork UP, 2003.

Casaubon, Isaac, *In Aelius Spartianum, Julium Capitolinum, Aelium Lampridium, Vulcatium Gallicanum, Trebellium Pollionem, & Flavium Vopiscum: emendationes ac notae*. Paris: Ambrose and Hieronymus Drouart, 1603.

Cato, *The Distichs of Cato: A Famous Medieval Textbook*, (ed.) Wayland Johnson Chase. University of Wisconsin Studies 7. Madison: University of Wisconsin Press, 1922.

Catullus & Tibullus, *Catullus. Tibullus. Pervigilium Veneris*, trans. Francis Ware Cornish, et al., (ed.) G.P. Goold. Loeb Classical Library 6. 2nd corr. ed. Cambridge, MA: Harvard UP, 2005.

Chamberlaine, Bartholomew, *The Passion of Christ, and the Benefites Thereby*. London: George Purslow, 1615.

Cheney, C.R. & Michael Jones (eds), *A Handbook of Dates for Students of British History*. Royal Historical Society Guides and Handbooks 4. New ed. Cambridge: Cambridge UP, 2000.

Clavin, Terry, 'Wadding, Ambrose' in James McGuire & James Quinn (eds) *Dictionary of Irish Biography*. Cambridge UP, 2013, http://dib.cambridge.org, accessed 1 Mar. 2014.

Cockshoot, John V. & Christopher D.S. Field, 'Ferrabosco: (5) Alfonso Ferrabosco (ii)', *Grove Music Online. Oxford Music Online*. Oxford UP, 2013, www.oxfordmusiconline.com/subscriber/article/grove/music/09507pg5, accessed 1 Mar. 2014.

Cogswell, Thomas, '1625' in Joad Raymond (ed.), *The Oxford History of Popular Print Culture: Vol. I, Cheap Print in Britain and Ireland to 1660*. Oxford: Oxford UP, 2011, pp 589–98.

Commynes, Phillipe de, *Mémoires*, (ed.) Joël Blanchard. Textes Littéraires Français. 2 vols. Geneva: Droz, 2007.

Commynes, Phillippe de, *The Historie of Philip de Commines Knight, Lord of Argenton*, trans. Thomas Danett. London: Ar. Hatfield for I. Norton, 1596.

Contamine, Philippe, 'Stuart, Bérault (1452/3–1508)', *ODNB*. Oxford UP, 2004, www.oxforddnb.com, accessed 1 Mar. 2014.

Cooper, Thompson & Sarah Bakewell, 'Hollings, Edmund (c.1556–1612)', *ODNB*. Oxford UP, 2004, www.oxforddnb.com, accessed 1 Mar. 2014.

Coryate, Thomas, *Coryats Crudities Hastily Gobled Up in Five Moneths Trauells in France, Savoy, Italy, Rhetia [...]*. [London]: W[illiam] S[tansby], 1611.

Craik, Katharine A., 'Reading *Coryats Crudities* (1611).' *Studies in English Literature 1500–1900*, 44:1 (2004), 77–96.

Croce, Benedetto, *Uomini e cose della vecchia Italia*. Scritti di storia letteraria e politica 21. 2 vols. Bari: G. Laterza, 1927.

Croeselius, Johannes, *Parentalia anniuersaria reverendissimo et illvstrissimo principi ac domino, dn. Ioanni Egolpho à Knoeringen*. 2nd ed. Ingolstadt: David Sartorius, 1591.

Cust, Richard, *Charles I: A Political Life*. Harlow: Pearson Education, 2007.

D'Alton, John, *Illustrations, Historical and Genealogical, of King James's Irish Army List, 1689*. Dublin: For the Subscribers, 1855.

Dandrey, Patrick (ed.), *Dictionnaire des lettres françaises: le xviie siècle*. Encyclopedies d'aujourd'hui. 2nd ed. Paris: Fayard, 1996.

Dewes, Eva, 'Atalanta' in Maria Moog-Grünewald (ed.), *Brill's New Pauly Supplements I, Vol. 4: The Reception of Myth and Mythology*. Brill Online, 2011, http://referenceworksbrillonline.com/entries/brill-s-new-pauly-supplements-i-4/atalanta-e205130, accessed 28 Jan. 2014.

Donaldson, Ian, *Ben Jonson: A Life*. Oxford: Oxford UP, 2011.

Donne, John, *The Complete Poems of John Donne*, (ed.) Robin Robbins. Longman Annotated English Poets. 2nd ed. Harlow: Pearson Education, 2010.

Dunbar, John, *Epigrammaton Ioannis Dunbari Megalo-Britanni centuriae sex, decades totidem.* London: Thomas Purfoot, 1616.

Dunbar, William, *The Poems of William Dunbar,* (ed.) Priscilla Bawcutt. 2 vols. Glasgow: Association for Scottish Literary Studies, 1998.

Eerde, Katherine S. Van, 'Robert Waldegrave: The Printer as Agent and Link Between Sixteenth-Century England and Scotland.' *Renaissance Quarterly,* 34:1 (1981), 40–78.

'England Marriages, 1538–1973', *FamilySearch.* Church of Jesus Christ of the Latter-day Saints, 2014, https://familysearch.org, accessed 17 Jan. 2014.

Enright, Michael J., 'King James and His Island: An Archaic Kingship Belief?' *Scottish Historical Review,* 55:159 (1976), 29–40.

Epithalamia Oxoniensia in auspicatissimum, potentissimi monarchae Caroli [...] cum Henr[i]etta Maria, aeternae memoriae Henrici magni Gallorum regis filia, connubium. Oxford: John Lichfield & William Turner, 1625.

Eucharistica Oxoniensia: in exoptatissimum & auspicatissimvm Caroli [...] serenissimi & clementissimi regis nostri e Scotia reditum gratulatoria. Oxford: Leonard Lichfield, 1641.

Evans, Mihail Dafydd, 'Stradling, Sir John, first baronet (1563–1637)', *ODNB.* Oxford UP, 2004, www.oxforddnb.com, accessed 1 Mar. 2014.

Ferrabosco, Alfonso, *Lessons for 1. 2. and 3. Viols.* London: Thomas Snodham for John Browne, 1609.

Finegan, Francis, 'Members of the "Third Mission" of the Society of Jesus in Ireland, 1598–1773'. (2013), http://www.jesuitarchives.ie/research/digital-material/, accessed 2 Feb. 2014.

Flood, John, 'Walter Quin: Virtue in a Life of Change' in David J. Parkinson (ed.), *James VI and I, Literature and Scotland,* pp 251–66.

Flood, John L., *Poets Laureate in the Holy Roman Empire: A Bio-bibliographical Handbook* 4 vols. Berlin: Walter de Gruyter, 2006.

Foster, Joseph, *Alumni Oxonienses: The Members of the University of Oxford, 1500–1714.* 2nd ed. 2 vols. Oxford: Parker and Co., 1891–92.

Fowler, William, *The Works of William Fowler, Secretary to Queen Anne, Wife of James VI,* (eds) Henry W. Meikle, et al. Scottish Texts Society, Third Series 13. 3 vols. Edinburgh: Blackwood, 1940.

France, Peter (ed.), *The Oxford Guide to Literature in English Translation.* Oxford: Oxford UP, 2000.

Fraser, Antonia, *Cromwell: The Lord Protector.* New York: Grove Press, 1973.

Fritze, Ronald H., 'Herbert, Sir Thomas, first baronet (1606–1682)', *ODNB.* Oxford UP, 2004, www.oxforddnb.com, accessed 1 Mar. 2014.

Gaskell, Philip, *From Writer to Reader: Studies in Editorial Method.* Oxford: Clarendon Press, 1978.

Gillespie, Raymond, *Reading Ireland: Print, Reading and Social Change in Early Modern Ireland.* Manchester: Manchester UP, 2012.

Goldberg, Jonathan, *James I and the Politics of Literature: Jonson, Shakespeare, Donne, and Their Contemporaries.* Stanford: Stanford UP, 1989.

Goodare, Julian, 'Erskine, John, eighteenth or second earl of Mar (c.1562–1634)', *ODNB.* Oxford UP, 2006, www.oxforddnb.com, accessed 1 Mar. 2014.

—, 'The Scottish Presbyterian Movement in 1596.' *Canadian Journal of History,* 45 (2010), 21–48.

Gowreis Conspiracie: A Discourse of the Unnatural and Vyle Conspiracie Attempted Against the Kings Majesties Person at Sanct-Johnstoun upon Twysday the 5. of August 1600. Edinburgh: Robert Charteris, 1600.

Grafton, Anthony, et al. (eds), *The Classical Tradition.* Cambridge, MA: Belknap Press, 2010.

Gray, Douglas, 'A Scottish "Flower of Chivalry" and his Book.' *Words*, 4 (1974), 22–34.

Grenham, John, 'Dublin City Library and Archive, Ancient Freemen of Dublin', Dublin City Library & Archive, 2011, http://dublinheritage.ie/freemen/index.php, accessed 1 Mar. 2014.

Guicciardini, Francesco, *The Historie of Guicciardin Containing the Warres of Italie and Other Partes [...]*, trans. Geoffrey Fenton. London: Richard Field, 1599.

Gwynn, Aubery & R. Neville Hadcock, *Medieval Religious Houses: Ireland*. London: Longman, 1970.

Hadfield, Andrew, *Shakespeare, Spenser and the Matter of Britain*. Early Modern Literature in History. Basingstoke: Palgrave Macmillan, 2004.

Harris, Peter E.B., 'Turner, Robert (d.1599)', *ODNB*. Oxford UP, 2004, www.oxforddnb.com, accessed 1 Mar. 2014.

Haynes, Alan, *Invisible Power: The Elizabethan Secret Services, 1570–1603*. Stroud: Alan Sutton, 1992.

Heninger, S.K., Jr, 'Sidney and Serranus' Plato' in Alfred F. Kinney (ed.), *Sidney in Retrospect: Selections From English Literary Renaissance*. Amherst: University of Massachusetts Press, 1988, pp 27–44.

Herodian of Antioch, *History of the Roman Empire*, trans. Edward C. Echols. Berkeley: University of California Press, 1961.

Hibbard, Caroline M., 'Henrietta Maria (1609–1669)', *ODNB*. Oxford UP, 2008, www.oxforddnb.com, accessed 1 Mar. 2014.

Higham, N.J., *King Arthur: Myth-Making and History*. New York: Routledge, 2002.

Horace, *Horace: Satires, Epistles and Ars poetica*, ed. and trans. H. Rushton Fairclough. Loeb Classical Library 194. Cambridge, MA: Harvard UP, 1929.

—, *Horace: Odes and Epodes*, ed. and trans. Niall Rudd. Loeb Classical Library 33. Corr. ed. Cambridge, MA: Harvard UP, 2012.

Hornblower, Simon & Antony Spawforth (eds), *The Oxford Classical Dictionary*. 3rd rev. ed. Oxford: Oxford UP, 2003.

Hunter, Michael, *Editing Early Modern Texts: An Introduction to Principles and Practice*. Houndmills: Palgrave Macmillan, 2009.

James VI and I, *The Poems of James VI of Scotland*, (ed.) James Craigie. Scottish Text Society. 2 vols. Edinburgh: William Blackwood & Sons, 1955, 1958.

—, *Letters of King James VI & I*, (ed.) G.P.V. Akrigg. Berkeley: University of California Press, 1984.

—, *King James VI and I: Selected Writings*, (eds) Neil Rhodes, et al. Aldershot: Ashgate, 2003.

Johnston, Arthur, *Epigrammata A. Jonstoni Scoti, medici regii*. Aberdeen: Edward Raban, 1632.

Jonson, Ben, *The Complete Masques*, (ed.) Stephen Orgel. The Yale Ben Jonson. New Haven, CT: Yale UP, 1969.

Jouanna, Arlette, et al. (eds), *Histoire et dictionnaire des guerres de religion*. Paris: Robert Laffont, 1998.

Juhala, Amy L., 'The Household and Court of King James VI of Scotland, 1567-1603.' Unpublished PhD thesis. University of Edinburgh, 1999.

—, 'Ruthven, Alexander, master of Ruthven (1580?–1600)', *ODNB*. Oxford UP, 2004, www.oxforddnb.com, accessed 1 Mar. 2014.

—, 'Ruthven, John, third earl of Gowrie (1577/8–1600)', *ODNB*. Oxford UP, 2004, www.oxforddnb.com, accessed 1 Mar. 2014.

King, Adam, *Ad Iacobum sextum Scotorum regem a nefaria fratrum Ruvenorum coniuratione divinitus servatum soteria (1601)*, (ed.) Jamie Reid Baxter. The Philological Museum, 2008, www.philological.bham.ac.uk/king, accessed 11 Apr. 2014.

Kirk, James, 'Melville, Andrew (1545–1622)', *ODNB*. Oxford UP, 2004, www.odnb.com, accessed 1 Mar. 2014.

Knöpfler, Alois, 'Turner, Robert', *Allgemeine Deutsche Biographie*. Bayerischen Staatsbibliothek, 1895, www.deutsche-biographie.de/pnd128565101.html, accessed 28 Nov. 2013.

Kraye, Jill, 'Marcus Aurelius and Neostoicism in Early Modern Philosophy' in M. van Ackeren (ed.), *A Companion to Marcus Aurelius*. Malden, MA: Wiley-Blackwell, 2012, pp 515–31.

Kurelac, Iva, 'Robertus Bonaventura Britanus (Robert Turner) and the Lost Manuscript of Dinko Zavorovi's De rebus Dalmaticis.' *Journal of Croatian Studies*, 48 (2007), 98–113.

Laing, David, 'A Brief Account of the Hawthornden Manuscripts in the Possession of the Society of Antiquaries of Scotland: With Extracts, Containing Several Unpublished Letters and Poems of William Drummond of Hawthornden.' *Archaeologia Scotica*, 4 (1857), 56–116, 225–40.

Langbaine, Gerard, *An Account of the English Dramatick Poets [...]*. Oxford: George West and Henry Clements, 1691.

Larocca, Donald J., 'A Neapolitan Patron of Armor and Tapestry Identified.' *Metropolitan Museum Journal*, 28 (1993), 85–102.

Lee, Maurice, Jr, 'The Gowrie Conspiracy Revisited' in Maurice Lee, Jr (ed.), *The 'Inevitable Union' and Other Essays on Early Modern Scotland*. East Linton: Tuckwell Press, 2003, pp 99–115.

—, 'King James's Popish Chancellor' in Maurice Lee, Jr (ed.), *The 'Inevitable Union' and Other Essays on Early Modern Scotland*. East Linton: Tuckwell Press, 2003, pp 145–57.

Lee, Sidney, 'Quin, Walter (c.1575–1641)', *ODNB Archive*. Oxford UP, 1896, www.oxforddnb.com, accessed 1 Mar. 2014.

Lee, Sidney & J.K. McGinley, 'Quin, Walter (c.1575–1641)', *ODNB*. Oxford UP, 2004, www.oxforddnb.com, accessed 1 Mar. 2014.

Lennon, Colm, *Richard Stanihurst the Dubliner 1547–1618: A Biography With a Stanihurst Text On Ireland's Past*. Dublin: Irish Academic Press, 1981.

—, 'Stanihurst, Richard (1547–1618)', *ODNB*. Oxford UP, 2008, www.oxforddnb.com, accessed 1 Mar. 2014.

—, 'White, Stephen (b.c.1574, d. in or after 1646)', *ODNB*. Oxford UP, 2009, www.oxforddnb.com, accessed 1 Mar. 2014.

Lesley, John, *De origine, moribus & rebus gestis Scotorum libri decem [...]*. Rome: In Aedibus Populi Romani [Paulus Manutius], 1675.

Leslie, John, *The Historie of Scotland*, trans. James Dalrymple, (ed.) E.G. Cody. The Scottish Text Society 5. 2 vols. Edinburgh: William Blackwood & Sons, 1888, 1895.

Lipsius, Justus, *Politica: Six Books of Politics or Political Instruction*, ed. and trans. Jan Waszink. Bibliotheca Latinitatis Novae. Assen: Royal Van Gorcum, 2004.

Loades, David, 'From the King's Ships to the Royal Navy, 1500-1642' in J.R. Hill (ed.), *The Oxford Illustrated History of the Royal Navy*. Oxford: Oxford UP, 2002, pp 24–55.

—, *The Cecils: Privilege and Power Behind the Throne*. Kew: National Archives, 2007.

MacDonald, Alan R., 'Ramsay, John, earl of Holdernesse (c.1580–1626)', *ODNB*. Oxford UP, 2008, www.oxforddnb.com, accessed 1 Mar. 2014.

Macdonald, Alastair J., 'Stewart, Sir John, of Darnley (c.1380–1429)', *ODNB*. Oxford UP, 2006, www.oxforddnb.com, accessed 1 Mar. 2014.

MacDonald, R.H. (ed.), *The Library of Drummond of Hawthornden*. Edinburgh: Edinburgh UP, 1971.

MacIntosh, Gillian H., et al. (eds), *The Records of the Parliaments of Scotland to 1707*. University of St Andrews, 2014, http://www.rps.ac.uk, accessed 1 Mar. 2014.

MacLeod, Catharine, et al. (eds), *The Lost Prince: The Life and Death of Henry Stuart.* London: National Portrait Gallery, 2013.

Macpherson, Rob, 'Stuart, Ludovick, second duke of Lennox and duke of Richmond (1574–1624)', *ODNB.* Oxford UP, 2006, www.oxforddnb.com, accessed 1 Mar. 2014.

—, 'Colville, John (1542?–1605)', *ODNB.* Oxford UP, 2009, www.oxforddnb.com, accessed 1 Mar. 2014.

Magie, David (ed.), *The Scriptores Historiae Augustae.* Loeb Classical Library 139. 3 vols. Cambridge, MA: Harvard UP, 1991.

Maillet, Marc de, *A la louange du serenissime roy, de la Grande Bretaigne: ode par le sieur de Mailliet gentilhomme françois.* London: George Purslow, 1617.

Malingre, Claude, *Histoire chronologique de plusieurs grand capitaines, princes, seigneurs, magistrats, officiers de la couronne, et autres hommes illustres [...].* Paris: Adrian Tiffaine, 1617.

Mallett, Michael & Christine Shaw, *The Italian Wars, 1494–1559: War, State and Society in Early Modern Europe.* Modern Wars in Perspective. Harlow: Pearson, 2012.

Maltby, William S., 'Mariana, Juan de' in Hans J. Hillerbrand (ed.), *The Oxford Encyclopedia of the Reformation.* 4 vols. Oxford: Oxford UP, 1996, iii, pp 7–8.

Marshall, Rosalind K., 'Lesley, John (1527–1596)', *ODNB.* Oxford UP, 2007, www.oxforddnb.com, accessed 1 Mar. 2014.

May, Steven W. & William A. Ringler Jr (eds), *Elizabethan Poetry: A Bibliography and First-line Index of English Verse, 1559–1603.* 3 vols. London: Thommes Continuum, 2004.

McCabe, Richard A., 'The Masks of Duessa: Spenser, Mary Queen of Scots, and James VI.' *English Literary Renaissance,* 17:2 (1987), 224–42.

McCoog, Thomas M., *The Society of Jesus in Ireland, Scotland, and England 1541–1588: 'Our Way of Proceeding?'.* Studies in Medieval and Reformation Thought 60. Leiden: Brill, 1996.

McGladdery, C.A., 'Bowes, Robert (d.1597)', *ODNB.* Oxford UP, 2004, www.oxforddnb.com, accessed 1 Mar. 2014.

McShane, Angela, 'Ballads and Broadsides' in Joad Raymond (ed.), *The Oxford History of Popular Print Culture: Vol. I, Cheap Print in Britain and Ireland to 1660.* Oxford: Oxford UP, 2011, pp 589–98.

Melles, Etienne de, et al., *Steph. de Melles [...] Ethica particularis seu institutiones privaae, oeconomiae, et politiae [...] annexa ejusdem opera et studio duo opuscula: I. Celsi [...] princeps ex. C. Tacito; Q. Quinni de virtutibus principis [...].* Paris: Dionysius Thierry, 1670.

Melville, James, *The Autobiography and Diary of Mr James Melvill [...] with a Continuation of the Diary,* (ed.) Robert Pitcairn. Edinburgh: The Wodrow Society, 1842.

Missale Romanum ex decreto sacrosancti concilii Tridentini [...]. Ratisbon: Friderici Pustet, 1862.

Müller, Rainer A., *Universität und Adel: Eine Soziostrukturelle Studie zur Geschichte der bayerischen Landesuniversität Ingolstadt, 1472-1648.* Ludovico Maximilianea, Universität Ingolstadt-Landshut-München: Forschungen 7. Berlin: Duncker & Humblot, 1974.

Murray, Thomas, *Naupactiados, sive Lepantiados Iacobi magni, Britanniarum, Franciae, & Hiberniae regis, fidei vere Christianae vindicis, & assertoris vere Christianissimi metaphrasis poetica.* London: John Norton, 1604.

Nelson, Carolyn W., *Union First Line Index of English Verse, 13th–19th Century.* Folger Shakespeare Library, 2013, http://firstlines.folger.edu, accessed 7 Apr. 2014.

Norbrook, David & H.R. Woudhuysen (eds), *The Penguin Book of Renaissance Verse.* Penguin Classics. 2nd ed. London: Penguin, 1993.

Nugent, Richard, *Cynthia,* (ed.) Angelina Lynch. The Literature of Early Modern Ireland. Dublin: Four Courts Press, 2010.

The Odcombian Banquet: Dished Foorth by Thomas the Coriat, and Serued in by a Number of Noble Wits in Prayse of his Crudities and Crambe Too. [London]: [by George Eld] for Thomas Thorp, 1611.

Ohlmeyer, Jane & Éamonn Ó Ciardha (eds), *The Irish Statute Staple Books, 1596–1687*. Dublin: Four Courts Press, 1999.

Parkinson, David J. (ed.), *James VI and I, Literature and Scotland: Tides of Change, 1567–1625*. Groningen Studies in Cultural Change 47. Leuven: Peeters, 2013.

Parsons, Leila, 'Prince Henry (1594–1612) as a Patron of Literature.' *Modern Language Review*, 47:4 (1952), 503–7.

Patterson, W.B., *King James VI and I and the Reunion of Christendom*. Cambridge Studies in Early Modern British History. Cambridge: Cambridge UP, 1997.

Petrucci, Franca, 'Colonna, Fabrizio', *Dizionario biografico degli italiani*. Istituto della enciclopedia italiana, 1982, www.treccani.it/biografie/, accessed 2 Mar. 2014.

—, 'Colonna, Prospero', *Dizionario biografico degli italiani*. Istituto della enciclopedia italiana, 1982, www.treccani.it/biografie/, accessed 2 Mar. 2014.

Pettegree, Andrew (ed.), *Universal Short Title Catalogue*. University of St Andrews, 2013, http://ustc.ac.uk/, accessed 5 Dec. 2013.

Pittock, Murray G.H., *Poetry and Jacobite Politics in Eighteenth-Century Britain and Ireland*. Cambridge Studies in Eighteenth-Century English Literature and Thought. Cambridge: Cambridge UP, 1994.

Pitts, Vincent J., *Henry IV of France: His Reign and Age*. Baltimore, MD: Johns Hopkins UP, 2009.

Plutarch, *Plutarch's Lives*, ed. and trans. Bernadotte Perrin. Loeb Classical Library 46–7, 65, 80, 87, 98–103. 11 vols. London: Heinemann, 1914–26.

Pollard, A.W., et al. (eds), *A Short-Title Catalogue of Books Printed in England, Scotland, & Ireland and of English Books Printed Abroad 1475–1640*. 2nd ed. 3 vols. London: The Bibliographical Society, 1976–1991.

Porter, Stephen, 'University and Society' in Nicholas Tyacke (ed.), *The History of the University of Oxford, Vol. IV: Seventeenth-Century Oxford*. Oxford: Clarendon Press, 1997, pp 25–104.

Prévost, M. & Roman d'Amat (eds), *Dictionnaire de biographie française*. 21 vols. Paris: Letouzey & Ané, 1959.

Quin, Walter, *Sertum poeticum, in honorem Iacobi sexti serenissimi, ac potentissimi Scotorum regis*. Edinburgh: Robert Waldegrave, 1600.

—, *Corona virtutum principe dignarum [...]*. London: John Bill, 1613.

—, *Corona virtutum principe dignarum [...]*. 2nd ed. London: John Bill, 1615.

—, *Corona virtutum principe dignarum [...]*. 2nd ed. London: John Bill, 1617.

—, *The Memorie of the Most Worthie and Renowmed [sic] Bernard Stuart, Lord D'Aubigni Renewed [...]*. London: George Purslow, 1619.

—, *In nuptiis principum incomparabilium, Caroli, Britannici Imperi monarchae potentissimi, et Henriettae Mariae*. London: George Purslow, 1625.

—, *Corona virtutum principe dignarum [...]*. 3rd ed. Leiden: Elsevier, 1634.

—, *Corona virtutum principe dignarum [...]*. 4th ed. Hanover and Frankfurt: Johann Henry Duncken for Thomas Henry Havenstein, 1678.

—, *Elogium serenissimi regis, carmine acrostico, cuius singuli versus quinque vocabulis constant, totidem columnis nomen eiusdem complectente*. [London]: [George Purslow], [1616].

Real, Heinz Jürgen & Arno Seifert, *Die privaten Stipendienstiftungen der Universität Ingolstadt im ersten Jahrhundert ihres Bestehens*. Ludovico Maximilianea, Universität Ingolstadt-Landshut-München: Forschungen 4. Berlin: Duncker & Humblot, 1972.

Reid Baxter, Jamie & Dana Sutton (eds), *Epigrammaton Ioannis Dunbari Megalo-Britanni centuriae sex, decades totidem*. Philological Museum. Shakespeare Institute, University of Birmingham, 2013, www.philological.bham.ac.uk/dunbar, accessed 4 Mar. 2014.

Reid, David, 'Alexander, William, first'earl of Stirling (1577–1640)', *ODNB*. Oxford UP, 2006, www.oxforddnb.com, accessed 1 Mar. 2014.

Reid, Stephen J., *Humanism and Calvinism: Andrew Melville and the Universities of Scotland, 1560-1625*. St Andrews Studies in Reformation History. Aldershot: Ashgate, 2011.

Reid, Steven J., '"Quasi Sibyllae folia dispersa": The Anatomy of the *Delitiae poetarum Scotorum* (1637)' in Janet Hadley Williams & J. Derrick McClure (eds), *Fresche Fontanis: Studies in the Culture of Medieval and Early Modern Scotland*. Newcastle upon Tyne: Cambridge Scholars Publishing, 2013, pp 395–412.

Reiter, Ernst, 'Martin von Schaumberg', *Neue Deutsche Biographie*. Bayerischen Staatsbibliothek, 1990, www.deutsche-biographie.de/sfz58605.html, accessed 28 Nov. 2013.

Rickard, Jane, 'The Cultural Politics of Translation: King James VI and I, Du Bartas and Josuah Sylvester' in David J. Parkinson (ed.), *James VI and I, Literature and Scotland*, pp 100–17.

Riezler, Sigmund Ritter von, 'Wilhelm V., der Fromme, Herzog von Baiern', *Allgemeine Deutsche Biographie*. Bayerischen Staatsbibliothek, 1897, www.deutsche-biographie.de/pnd118771841.html, accessed 12 Feb. 2013.

Rodríguez Villa, Antonio (ed.), *Crónicas del Gran Capitán*. Neuva Biblioteca de Autores Españoles 10. Madrid: De Bailly, 1908.

Rogers, Charles (ed.), *Memorials of the Earl of Stirling and of the House of Alexander*. 2 vols. Edinburgh: William Paterson, 1877.

Roth, Friedrich, 'Johann Egolf von Knöringen', *Allgemeine Deutsche Biographie*. Bayerischen Staatsbibliothek, 1905, www.deutsche-biographie.de/pnd100118747.html, accessed 1 Mar. 2014.

Royan, Nichola, 'Johnston, Arthur (*c*.1579–1641)', *ODNB*. Oxford UP, 2004, www.oxforddnb.com, accessed 1 Mar. 2014.

Ryan, L.V., 'The Shorter Latin Poems in Tudor England.' *Humanistica Lovaniensia: Journal of Neo-Latin Studies*, 26 (1977), 101–31.

Salmon, J.H.M., *Essays in the Intellectual and Social History of Early Modern France*. Cambridge: Cambridge UP, 1987.

—, 'Seneca and Tacitus in Jacobean England' in Linda Levy Peck (ed.), *The Mental World of the Jacobean Court*. Cambridge: Cambridge UP, 1991, pp 169–88.

Sarocchi, Margherita, *Scanderbeide: The Heroic Deeds of George Scanderberg, King of Epirus*, (ed.) Rinaldina Russell. The Other Voice in Early Modern Europe. Chicago: University of Chicago Press, 2006.

Sayce, R.A., 'Compositorial Practices and the Localization of Printed Books 1530–1800.' *The Library*, 21 (1966), 1–45.

Scot of Scotstarvit, John & Arthur Johnston (eds), *Delitiae poetarum Scotorum hujus aevi illustrium*. 2 vols. Amsterdam: Johannes Blaeu, 1637.

Scott, Hew (ed.), *Fasti Ecclesiae Scoticanae: The Succession of Ministers in the Church of Scotland from the Reformation*. Vol. 4. New ed. Edinburgh: Oliver and Boyd, 1923.

Seneca, *Seneca: Moral Essays*, ed. and trans. John W. Basore. Loeb Classical Library 310. 3 vols. London: Heinemann, 1964.

Serres, Jean de, *A General Inventorie of the History of France from the Beginning of that Monarchie, unto the Treatie of Vervins, in the Year 1598 [...]*, trans. Edward Grimeson. London: George Elde, 1607.

Shakespeare, William, *The Oxford Shakespeare: The Complete Works*, (eds) Stanley Wells & Gary Taylor. 2nd ed. Oxford: Clarendon Press, 2005.

Shaw, Christine, *The Politics of Exile in Renaissance Italy*. Cambridge: Cambridge UP, 2000.

Shipley, Graham, et al. (eds), *The Cambridge Dictionary of Classical Civilization*. Cambridge: Cambridge UP, 2008.

Shire, Helena Mennie, *Song, Dance & Poetry of the Court of Scotland Under King James VI*. Cambridge: Cambridge UP, 1969.

Simonin, Michel (ed.), *Dictionnaire des lettres françaises: le xvie siècle*. Encyclopedies d'aujourd'hui. 2nd ed. Paris: Fayard, 2001.

Smuts, Malcolm, 'Prince Henry and His World' in Catharine MacLeod (ed.), *The Lost Prince*, pp 19–31.

Smuts, R. Malcom, *Court Culture and the Origins of a Royalist Tradition in Early Stuart England*. Philadelphia: University of Pennsylvania Press, 1987.

—, 'Murray, Thomas (1564–1623)', *ODNB*. Oxford UP, 2004, www.oxforddnb.com, accessed 1 Mar. 2014.

Snyder, Susan, 'Du Bartas, Guillaume de Salluste' in A.C. Hamilton (ed.), *The Spenser Encyclopedia*. Rev. ed. Toronto: University of Toronto Press, 1997, p. 80.

State Papers Online, (eds) Stephen Alford & John Miller. Gale Cengage Learning, 2014, http://gale.cengage.co.uk/state-papers-online-15091714/part-i.aspx, accessed 5 Apr. 2014.

Stevenson, David, 'Erskine, Thomas, first earl of Kellie (1566–1639)', *ODNB*. Oxford UP, 2006, www.oxforddnb.com, accessed 1 Mar. 2014.

Stewart-Brown, R., 'The Exchequer of Chester.' *The English Historical Review*, 57:227 (1942), 289–97.

Stewart, Alan, *The Cradle King: A Life of James VI & I*. London: Chatto & Windus, 2003.

Stilma, Astrid, 'William Alexander, King James and Neo-Stoic Advice to Princes in *The Monarchik Tragedies*' in David J. Parkinson (ed.), *James VI and I, Literature and Scotland*, pp 233–49.

Strachan, Michael, 'Coryate, Thomas (1577?–1617)', *ODNB*. Oxford UP, 2006, www.oxforddnb.com, accessed 1 Mar. 2014.

Stradling, John, *Ioannis Stradlingi epigrammatum libri quatuor*. London: George Bishop & John Norton, 1607.

—, *Beati Pacifici: A Diuine Poem. Written To The Kings Most Excellent Maiestie*. London: Company of Stationers, 1623.

—, *Beati pacifici (1623)*, (ed.) Glyn Pursglove. The Philological Museum. Shakespeare Institute, University of Birmingham, 2003, www.philological.bham.ac.uk/strad2, accessed 21 Mar. 2014.

Strayer, Joseph R. (ed.), *Dictionary of the Middle Ages*. 13 vols. New York: Charles Scribner's Sons, 1982–9.

Stuart, Berault, *Traité sur l'art de la guerre*, (ed.) Elie de Comminges. Archives internationales d'histoire des idées 85. La Haye: Martin Nijhoff, 1976.

Suetonius, *The Twelve Caesars*, trans. Robert Graves. Penguin Classics. Harmondsworth: Penguin, 1970.

Sylvester, Josuah, *Lachrimae Lachrimarum or the Distillation of Teares Shede for the Untymely Death of the Incomparable Prince Panaretus*. London: Humfrey Lownes, 1612.

Tallon, Geraldine (ed.), *Court of Claims: Submissions and Evidence, 1663*. Dublin: Irish Manuscripts Commission, 2006.

Tatò, Francesco (ed.), *Enciclopedie on line*. Istituto della enciclopedia italiana, 2014, www.treccani.it, accessed 1 Mar. 2014.

Taylor, John, *Laugh, and be Fat: or, A Commentary upon the Odcombyan Blanket*. [London?]: [W. Hall?], 1612.

Turner, Robert, *Roberti Turneri Devonii oratoris et philosophi in academia Ingolstadiensi epistolae, quae reperiri potuere, additis centuriis duabus posthumis [...]*. Cologne: Johann Kinckius, 1595.

— (ed.), *Roberti Turneri Devonii oratio et epistola de vita et morte reverendissimi et illustrissimi dn. Martini a Schaumberg [...]*. Ingolstadt: Wolfgang Ederus, [1590].

Unger, Emma Va. & William A. Jackson (eds), *The Carl H. Pforzheimer Library: English Literature 1475-1700*. Rev. ed. 3 vols. New Castle, DE: Oak Knoll Press, 1997.

Voragine, Jacobus de, *The Golden Legend*, trans. William Granger Ryan. 2 vols. Princeton, NJ: Princeton UP, 1993.

Welch, Joseph (ed.), *The List of the Queen's Scholars of St. Peter's College, Westminster*. 2nd ed. London: G. W. Ginger, 1852.

Wells, Stanley, *Re-editing Shakespeare for the Modern Reader*. Oxford: Clarendon Press, 1984.

Westermayer, Georg, 'Engerd, Johannes', *Allgemeine Deutsche Biographie*. Bayerischen Staatsbibliothek, 1877, www.deutsche-biographie.de/pnd116503610.html, accessed 28 Nov. 2013.

—, 'Rotmar, Valentin', *Allgemeine Deutsche Biographie*. Bayerischen Staatsbibliothek, 1889, www.deutsche-biographie.de/pnd119810731X.html, accessed 28 Nov. 2013.

Whitaker, Katie, *A Royal Passion: The Turbulent Marriage of Charles I and Henrietta Maria*. London: Weidenfeld & Nicholson, 2010.

Wilks, Timothy, 'Introduction' in Catharine MacLeod (ed.), *The Lost Prince*, pp 11–17.

Williams, Franklin B., Jr., 'An Initiation into Initials.' *Studies in Bibliography*, 9 (1957), 163–78.

—, *Index of Dedications and Commendatory Verses in English Books before 1641*. London: Bibliographical Society, 1962.

Williamson, J.W., *The Myth of the Conqueror. Prince Henry Stuart: A Study of 17th Century Personation*. New York: AMS Press, 1978.

Wolff, George (ed.), *Die Matrikel der Ludwig-Maximilians-Universitat: Ingolstadt-Landshut-Munchen, Teil 1*. Munich: J. Lindauersche, 1937.

Wolff, Helmut, *Geschichte der Ingolstäder Juristenfakultät, 1472-1625*. Ludovico Maximilianea, Universität Ingolstadt-Landshut-München: Forschungen 5. Berlin: Duncker & Humblot, 1973.

Wood, Anthony, *Athenae Oxonienses*, (ed.) Philip Bliss. 3rd ed. 4 vols. London: F.C. and J. Rivington, 1813–20.

Yellowlees, Michael J., *'So Strange a Monster as a Jesuiste': The Society of Jesus in Sixteenth-Century Scotland*. Colonsay: House of Lochar, 2003.

Zimmermann, T.C. Price, *Paolo Giovio: The Historian and the Crisis of Sixteenth-Century Italy*. Princeton, NJ: Princeton UP, 1995.

Zotter, Hans, 'Bibliotheca Craesseliana: Johannes Krösel aus Vilseck.' (1983), http://sosa2.uni-graz.at/sosa/druckschriften/druckschriften/g-craesseliana.php, accessed 25 Jan. 2014.

Index of titles

Translations are marked with a [T].

WORKS BY QUIN

Abominable Crimes [T], 102

A Collection of Retorts, Bon Mots and Other Memorable Sayings of King Henry the Great [T], 245

A Congratulatory Poem Recited in the Presence of the Most Serene King in St Salvator's College in St Andrews [T], 87

Á la sérénissime reine de la Grande Bretagne, 231

A Nuptial Ditty, of Love and Hymen Joining These Royal Mates, 220

A Nuptial Song, of the Union of the Roses and Lilies in This Royal Couple, 218

A Peerless Pearl and Prince Claims Arthur's Seat, 74

A Prayer of the Same Kind in an Acrostic Poem That Repeats the Name of the Most Illustrious Prince [T], 144

A Scottish Rose Twice Over [T], 71

A Short Collection of the Most Notable Places of Histories Quoted in This Memorial, 186

A Treacherous Plotter Promised You Gold [T], 93

A Worthy Peerless Prince Claims Arthur's Seat, 51

Ad clarissimum equitem, Hugonem Herrisium, serenissimi regis medicum, 104

Ad Deum optimum maximum ob serenissimum regem e variis periculis, praesertim vero ex insidiis perthi nuper vitae illius structis feliciter ereptum, 89

Ad illustras equitem, Thomam Areskinum, 103

Ad lectorem [Corona virtutum], 137

Ad nobilem equitem Iohannem Ramisaeum, 105

Ad regem comites aditu perrumpere, 96

Ad revenderum Turnerum, 43

Amico suo nobilissimo Thomae Herberto armigero, 263

An Anagram on the Name of the Author, William Alexander [T], 116

An Elogium of the Most Serene King, in an Acrostic Poem, Each of Whose Verses Consists of Five Words, Containing His Name in As Many Columns [T], 143

Arthuri in sede futurus crescis, 76

Aurum pollicitus tibi perfidus insidiator, 93

Aux chevaliers, qui ont aidé à sauver la vie de sa majesté, 109

Avec douce mélodie, 224

Bis rosa Scotus, 70

Carmen gratulatoriam coram serenissime rege in gymnasio S. Salvatoris Andraeapoli recitatum, 84

Cease Lets Arthur I Am, of Britain King, 51

Charles, qui fais honneur a ta principauté, 204

Charles, You Do Honour to Your Princedom [T], 205

Clarus scuto abavis ortus, 71

Classica qui cantis praecones munere pacis, 209

Coelicolis, vitam dum corpore tectus agebat, 43

Credulus es nimium visus, 93

Cum superis reges communi iure fruuntur, 48

De illustrimo principe primum ex arce Sterlinensi in publicum, 81

De tumultibus aliquot regis serenissime virtute, eloquentia, et prudentia sedatis, 83

Dear to His People and Destined to Rule Courageously [T], 78

Discours sur la même anagramme, en forme de dialogue enter un zélateur du bien public et une dame, laquelle représente le royaume d'Angleterre, 53

Discourse on the Same Anagram, in the Form of a Dialogue between a Partisan of the Public Good and a Lady Who Represents the Kingdom of England [T], 58

Dum gravidae matri intentarunt, 101

Dum venare feras, 92

Elogium serenissimi regis, carmine acrostico, cuius singuli versus quinque vocabulis constant, totidem columnis nomen eiusdem complectente, 142

En salvus, carus iam stas, rex inclyte, victor, 103

Epigram of Walter Quin, Irish Student of Law, in Praise of the Aforementioned Most Reverend Bishop Von Knöringen [T], 46

Epithalamium, 213

Epithalamium [T], 215

Epithalamium by Walter Quin for the Marriage of William Alexander and Janet Erskine, 111

Exceptum hospitio patriae patremque, 94

Felice nodo e vincula d'amore, 226

Fierce, Hardy, Earnest, True, Thou Named Art, 78

Floribus et variis, en, haec tibi texta corolla est, 137

Flower of Knights [T], 209

For Reverend Turner [T], 43

For the Illustrious Knight, Thomas Ereskine [T], 104

Fruit hérité rendras, prince sorti d'un père, 79

Gourius et vulgo fuit, et se iudice, magnus, 99

Gowrie Was Adjudged Great by Common Consent and by Himself [T], 99

Gualteri Guinni Hyberni I.U. studiosi epigramma, in ejusdem reverendissime episcopi Knoeringeri laudem, 45

Haec, quae floruerant regum ornamenta seorsum, 212

He Believed That Mars Would Always Be Favourable to Him [T], 97

He Perished Before His Time [T], 127

How Great a Man Has Fallen by the Fatal Spear of Death? [T], 42

I Do Not So Much Rejoice, Prince, in the Honour Bestowed On You [T], 205

I Who Owe More to You Alone Than to Anyone Else [T], 67

If God and the Peridies Who Favour You [T], 101

Il fior' de principi nel fior' de gl'anni, 131

Illustrious in Coat of Arms and Ancestors, 72

Illustrissimo principi, 135

Impietas Ruthveni concita diris, 96

Impiety Was Stirred up by the Furies of Ruthven [T], 97

In 19 Iunii, 81

In lode dell'arte e dell'autore, 117

In nomen authoris Guilelmus Alexander,

anagramma, 115

In nomen illustrissimi principis, Carolus princeps Walliae anagramma: clarus in pace, praelio, lusu. acrostichis utrumque continens, 205

In Praise of the Art and the Author [T], 118

In Wedlock's Yoke Now Love and Hymen Tie, 113

Kings Enjoy a Law Shared with the Gods [T], 49

L'accorto, giusto re ama, o Inghilterra, 50

L'accorto, giusto re ama, o nobil regno, 75

La cornamusa di Gualtero Quin, 120

Let No One Be Amazed [T], 95

Look, Unharmed Victor [T], 103

Look, This Garland Has Been Woven for You from Various Flowers [T], 137

Love the Wise, Just King O England [T], 50

Love the Wise, Just King O Noble Kingdom [T], 76

Maiden of Scotland [T], 80

Most Illustrious Prince [T], 81

Most Worthy Couple, Happy Is Your Lot, 113

Non stupeat, 95

Non tibi delato, princeps, tam laetor honore, 205

Nuptial Ode [T], 223

Nympha Caledoniae, 80

Occidit ante diem iuvenum flos

Ode Nuptial, 221

Of His Burial in the Same Place, 185

Of His Last Retiring to Corstorphine, 184

Of the Danger Wherein His Majesty Was Lately at Saint Johnstone, and of His Happy Delivery, 106

Of the Lords of Aubigny, Descended From the Most Noble House of Lennox, 185

On 19 June [T], 82

On Some Disturbances Quelled by the Virtue, Eloquence and Prudence of the Most Serene King [T], 84

On the Most Illustrious Prince's First Entry into Public from Stirling Castle [T], 81

On the Name of the Most Illustrious Prince, Charles, Prince of Wales, an Anagram: Famous in Peace, War and Sport. Both Contained in an Acrostic, 206

Orta salus ubi tu coruscas, 72

Praefatio [Sertum poeticum], 67

Preface [Bernard Stuart], 152

Preface [*Sertum poeticum*] [T], 69
Proditor atrox, 94
Propitium martem sibi credidit usque futurum, 97
Prosperity Arises Where You Gleam [T], 73

Qui est là? Arthus sacré, roi de la Grande Bretagne, 74
Qui est là? César, Arthus, princes de grands honneurs, 52
Qui tibi plus uni, quam cunctis, optime regum, 65
Quos scenae tragicae insignes spectare cothurnos, 100

Recueil des reparties, rencontres, et autres dits mémorables du roi Henri le grand, 233
Regibus esse ratus perthum fatale, 97
Rex, tua cum virtus, 98

Savage Traitor [T], 94
Semotos comites, 95
Separated Attendants [T], 95
Si Deus, o heros, tibi pieridesque faventes, 100
Suis charus fidenter recturus, 77
Symbola prisca rosae cum sint, et lilia stirpis, 212

Tant plus qu'un bien est grand, et rare en excellence, 127
Ter tua Ruthvenae infando, 102
The Ancient Symbols [T], 212
The Bagpipe of Walter Quin [T], 122
The Father of the Fatherland Received with Hospitality [T], 94
The Flower of Princes in the Flower of His Age [T], 131
The Fortunate Knot and Bond of Love [T], 226
The Memory of the Most Worthy and Renowned Bernard Stuart, Lord d'Aubigny, Renewed, 153
The More That a Good Person Is Great and Rare in Excellence [T], 129
The Prince's Epitaph, Written by His Highness' Servant, Walter Quin, 125
These Ornaments of the Kings [T], 212
Thinking That Perth Was Fatal to the King [T], 98
Those Whom It Delights to Watch the Tall Boots of the Tragic Stage [T], 100
To Almighty God on Account of the Most Serene King's Being Fortunately Saved From Various Dangers, Especially From the Ambush That Was Recently Set Upon His Life at Perth [T], 91

To His Friend, the Most Noble Thomas Herbert, Knight [T], 263
To Sir Hugh Herries, Knight, and Physician to His Majesty, 108
To Sir John Ramsay, Knight, 108
To the Knights Who Helped Save His Majesty's Life [T], 109
To the Most Famous Knight, Hugh Herries, Physician to the Most Serene King [T], 105
To the Most Honourable Lord, the Duke of Lennox, 106
To the Most Serene Queen of Great Britain [T], 231
To the Noble Knight John Ramsay [T], 105
To the Noble Knight Sir Thomas Erskine, 107
To the Prince My Most Gracious Master, 152
To the Prince's Highness, 196
To the Reader [*Corona virtutum*] [T], 138
To the Right Honourable the Earl of Mar, 107
Triumphant Victor [T], 49
Tu victor salvus, carus stabis, 73

Unharmed Victor, You Remain Beloved [T], 74

Victor ovans, collis domitis virtute superbis, 49
Vir quantus cecidit fatali cuspide mortis?, 42
Votum eiusdem generis carmine acrostico illustrissimi principis nomen iterante, 143

When As the Macedonian Conqueror Came, 115
When They Threatened a Pregnant Mother [T], 101
While Attendants Strive to Break Through to the King [T], 96
While He Lived His Life [T], 43
While You Hunted Wild Beasts [T], 93
Who Is There? Caesar and Arthur, Princes of Great Honour [T], 52
Who Is There? Sacred Arthur, King of Great Britain [T], 75
Wishes Presented to the Prince's Highness at His Creation, 196
With Soft Music [T], 225

You Grow Up Destined for the Throne of Arthur [T], 77
You Seem to Be Too Credulous [T], 93
You Who Play the War Trumpets [T], 209
You Will Yield Inherited Fruit [T], 79
Your Virtue, O King [T], 99

WORKS BY OTHER AUTHORS

Alexander, William, 'To His Worthy Friend
Master Walter Quin', 264

Dunbar, John, 'Ad Gwalterum Guyneum', 265

Dunbar, John, 'To Walter Quin', [T], 265

Hart, William, 'In *Coronam virtutum* clarissimi viri
domini Gualteri Quinni', 266

Hart, William, 'On the *Corona Virtutum* of the
Most Illustrious Master Walter Quin', [T], 266

H., T., Except Thy Mind, with Flames of
Heavenly Love', 265

Johnston, Arthur, 'In obitum Annae Quiniae ae
puerperae', 267

Johnston, Arthur, 'On the Death of Anne Quin
in Childbirth', [T], 268

Murray, Thomas, 'In regii nominis anagrammata
quaedam, ex quibus regi anglicum regnum
deberi anno 1600 eruebatur', 268

Murray, Thomas, 'In roseum quoddam *Sertum
poeticum* regi eodem anno oblatum', 269

Murray, Thomas, 'On *Sertum Poeticum*, a Poetic
Garland of Roses Presented to the King in the
Same Year', [T], 269

Murray, Thomas, 'On Some Anagrams of the
King's Name, From Which It Was Discovered
That the Kingdom of England Was Due to the
King in the Year 1600', 268

Turner, Robert, *Epistolae*, CL, 269

Turner, Robert, *Letters*, no. 150, [T], 270

General index

Achilles, 114, 115, 143, 223n, 271n,
acrostic, 139–45
Albion, 74, 160, 213, 218, 219, 222, 224, 225–6
Alexander of Macedon, 114, 115, 245, 260–1
Alexander, William, 26, 110–3, 114–6, 152, 262, 264
Allen, William, 41
Alfonso V of Aragon, 246
Armagnac, Louis d', 148, 171n, 191
Arques, Anne d', 248n
anagram, 27, 34–5, 47–62, 63, 67–82, 103, 115–6, 205–6, 265, 268–9
Anne of Denmark, 21
Antoninus Pius, 133, 136, 200n, 203n
Apollo, 84, 87, 89n, 108, 160, 265
Arthurian legend, 27, 47, 51–62, 63, 68, 70, 74–5, 76–7,
Aubigné, Théodore-Agrippa d', 248n, 250n
Augustus Caesar, 200n, 204
Aversa, 169n

Baschi, Peron de, 187
Bassompierre, François de, 230, 243, 258–9
Bellona, 142, 143, 162, 177, 202
Bentivoli, John, 187
Béthune, Maximilien de, duke of Sully, 240, 242–3, 255, 258
Bill, John, 134
Biron, Armand de, 236, 237, 239, 250, 252, 253–4
Bosworth, Battle of, 146, 159n
Bourbon, Charles de, 229
Bourbon, Gilbert de, count of Montpensier, 147, 163, 189
Bowes, Robert, 22, 23, 25, 47
Brimeau, Adrien de, lord of Humbercourt, 195
Bueil, Charles de, count of Sancerre, 195

Camden, William, 47, 264
Campion, Edmund, 20, 272
Campion, Thomas, 207
Cardona, Hugo de, 172, 180n, 192
Casaubon, Isaac, 133, 260n
Cassius Dio, 133, 134

Catholic League, 228, 229, 235–6, 237, 239, 241, 247n, 248–9, 250, 253, 256
Cecil, Robert, 24, 25, 47, 48, 256n
Cecil, William, 47, 54, 59, 61
Cerignola, Battle of, 194
Chabannes, Jacques de, marshal of La Palice, 183, 195
Charlemagne, 160, 202, 204, 205
Charles I of England, 27–30, 31, 81–2, 117, 132, 135–7, 139, 143–5, 196–206, 210–27, 230, 268
Charles II of England, 31
Charles VIII of France, 146–7, 158, 161, 162, 169, 185, 187, 193,
Charles IX of France, 69, 228
Charles of Lorraine, duke of Mayenne, 249
Colonna, Fabrizio, 190
Colonna, Prospero, 183, 190, 195
Colville, John, 23
Commines, Philippe de, 149, 188, 189
Consalvo (see Gonzalo Fernández)
Corstorphine, 184–5
Coryate, Thomas, 26, 119
Coton, Pierre, 258
Croesselius, Johannes (see Johann Krösel)
Cromwell, Oliver, 32
Cyrus the Great, 203

Davy Du Perron, Jacques, 244, 260
Doleman, Robert, 23
Donne, John, 119, 125
Drummond, William, 110, 125
Du Bartas, Guillaume de Salluste, 27, 73n, 97n, 124, 228
Du Haillan, Bernard de Girard, 149, 189–93
Dunbar, John, 264–5
Dunbar, William, 151
Du Plessis-Mornay, Philippe, 244, 260

Elizabeth I, 16, 23, 25, 63, 64, 70, 81, 143, 182
epithalamium, 110–3, 210–27
Erskine, Janet, 110–3
Erskine, John, earl of Mar, 25, 64, 107
Erskine, Thomas, 65, 104, 107
Este, Ercole d', 187

Ferdinand II (Ferrandino) of Naples, 147, 165
Ferdinand of Aragon, 146, 147–8, 149, 171, 182
Fernández, Gonzalo (Consalvo), 147–8, 149,
    171n, 182n, 189, 191, 192n, 193–4, 164, 165–6,
    171, 175, 177–80, 182
Ferrabosco, Alfonso, II, 26, 117–8
Fitzgerald, Gerard, 15
Fontaine-Française, 236, 250

Garigliano, River, 168, 180, 190
Giovio, Paolo, 149, 180, 187–95
Gonzaga, Francesco, 180
Gonzaga, Louis, duke of Nevers, 234, 244, 247,
    260
Gowrie conspiracy, 63–5, 89–109, 114, 207
Great Britain, 26, 51–2, 52–3, 70, 74–5, 76–7, 79–
    80, 100, 127, 142–3, 152, 159, 160, 178, 180,
    184, 186, 188, 204–5, 216, 219, 223, 258
Grignan (Grigny), Claude de, 173, 192
Guicciardini, Francesco, 149–50, 187, 189, 193,
    195
Gunpowder Plot, 151, 260n

Habsburg, Albrecht von, 242, 258
Hart, William, 266–7
Henrietta Maria, 210–27, 228–33, 247n
Henry I, duke of Guise, 229, 234–5, 246–7, 248n
Henry III of France, 228–9, 235, 248
Henry IV of France, 133, 151, 228–9, 233–61
Henry VII of England, 26, 47n, 63, 68, 69, 79,
    146
Henry VIII of England, 68, 69–70
Herbert, Thomas, 30, 207n, 262–3
Hercules, 84, 156, 199n, 253
Herodian of Syria, 133–4
Herries, Hugh, 65, 104–5, 108–9
Historia Augusta, 132, 133
Holland, Hugh, 119, 125
Horace, 46n, 132, 152, 153
Huguenots, 228–9, 264, 267 (see also Henry IV of
    France)
Hymen, 111–3, 212, 213–8, 220, 221–7

Ingolstadt, University of, 16, 17–20, 41, 44–5
Italian Wars (see Bernard Stuart)
Ireland, 28–30
    Dublin, 16–17, 146
    literature, 16–17, 29–30, 146

James VI and I of Scotland and England, 21–6,
    47–62, 63–76, 81–103, 139–44, 207, 210, 229,
    260n
    succession to English throne, 21, 22–6, 63, 64
    (see also Elizabeth I)

Basilicon doron, 133, 136, 155n, 197n, 200n,
    201n, 202n, 203n, 204n
Trew Law, 23, 48n, 229n
Jesuits, 17–20, 21, 41, 44, 64, 239, 242, 247n, 254,
    258, 266, 272
Johnston, Arthur, 262, 267–8
Jonson, Ben, 27, 47, 117, 119, 264
Jove, 67, 93, 94, 197
Julius Caesar, 52–62, 121–2, 163, 200, 260–1
Justus Lipsius, 132–3, 137–8, 207

Knöringen, Johann Egolf von, 44–6
Krösel, Johann, 18, 44

Lesley, John, 41, 148, 150, 152, 153, 187
Linternum, 184–5
Louis XII of France, 147–8, 190–5
Luxembourg, Louis de, 190

MacCartney, James, 22–3, 47
Maillet, Marc de, 230
Malingre, Claude, 150, 153, 187
Marcus Aurelius, 132n, 133, 135, 136, 204
Marguerite of Valois, 228, 230
Mariana, Juan de, 150–1, 188–95
Marignano, Battle of, 148, 195n
Matthieu, Pierre, 236, 250
Médicis, Catherine de, 228, 247
Medici, Pietro de', 187
Melville, Andrew, 20–1, 24–5
Murray, Thomas, 268–9
music, 24, 26, 32, 112, 117–8, 196, 224–6, 266

navy, 181
neo-Stoicism, 30, 114, 132–8, 207
Nicolson, George, 22, 24–5

Odcombian Banquet, The, 119
Oxford, University of, 16n, 31–2, 207, 262

Petrucci, Pandolfo, 187
Philip II of Spain, 23, 229, 258n
Philip of Macedon, 200n
Philippe Emmanuel, 256
Pius II, 246
Plutarch, 114, 122n, 132, 147n, 149, 163n, 174n,
    183n, 233, 245
Purslow, George, 139, 151, 212, 230

Quin, Ann, wife of John, 31
Quin, Anne, wife of Walter, 27, 30
Quin, James, actor, 17n
Quin, James, son of Walter, 30, 31
Quin, John, 31,

Quin, Lucy, 30
Quin, Mark, 17n
Quin, Mary, 30
Quin, Peter, 16, 17, 29–30
Quin, Walter
   attribution problems, 21, 142, 207,
   biography, 15–30, 41, 44, 47–8, 117, 119, 132–
      3, 135–6, 196, 231–3, 269–72
   Irish income, 28–30
   (see neo-Stoicism)
Quin, Walter, Jr, 30

Ramsay, John, earl of Holderness, 65, 96, 105–6,
   108
Robert I, 174
Roquelaure, Antoine de, 241, 256
roses of Lancaster and York, 63, 66–7, 68–71, 71–
   2, 74, 159, 184, 185, 211, 212, 213–26
Ruthven family (see Gowrie conspiracy)

Saint Andrews, University of, 20–1, 22, 84–9, 134
Saint Bartholomew's Day massacre, 228, 234, 246
Sanseverino, Galeazzo, 172, 188
Sanseverino, Antonello, 172, 192
Sanseverino, Bernardino, 172, 192
Schaumberg, Martin von, 18, 41
Scipio Aemilianus Africanus, 184–5, 203
Scotland, 20–6, 62, 68, 70, 71–2, 148, 155, 158,
   159, 165, 173, 176, 182, 185
Seminara, First Battle of, 147, 165
Seminara, Second Battle of, 148
Seminara, Third Battle of, 148, 193n
Seneca, 132, 135n,
Serres, Jean de, 151, 188, 195
Spenser, Edmund, 24
Stanihurst, Richard, 15, 16, 20, 23, 270, 272,

Stewart, John, first lord of Aubigny,
Stewart, John, of Darnley, 146, 158, 185
Stewart, Robert, fourth lord of Aubigny, 148,
   186, 195
Stradling, John, 207–9, 265–6
Stuart, Bernard, third lord of Aubigny, 146–95
Stuart, Elizabeth, queen of Bohemia, 80–1, 161,
   210
Stuart, Henry Frederick, prince of Wales,
Stuart, John, second lord of Aubigny,
Stuart, Ludovick, second duke of Lennox, 64, 65,
   96, 106
Stuart, Mary, queen of Scotland, 24, 64, 150
Sylvester, Josuah, 27–8, 124, 228

Terine, Battle of (see Battle of Terranova)
Terrail, Pierre, lord of Bayard, 183, 195
Terranova, Battle of, 148, 180, 192
Timoleon, 174
Toledo, Pedro de, 237, 251
Trajan, 204, 233, 246
Trivulzio, Gian Giacomo, 190
Turner, Robert, 18, 20, 21, 41, 43, 44, 150, 269–
   72

Verneuil, Battle of, 187n
Vespasian, 200, 204
Virgil, 132, 155

Wadding, Ambrose, 17
Waldegrave, Robert, 24–5, 65, 114
Wars of Religion, French (see Henry IV)
Wars of the Roses (see roses of Lancaster and
   York)
White, Stephen, 17